अभिज्ञानशाकुन्तलम्

ABHIJÑĀNA ŚĀKUNTALAM

(A Sanskrit Drama By Kālidāsa)

ABHIJÑĀNA ŚĀKUNTALAM

(A Sanskrit Drama By Kālidāsa)

The Devanāgarī Recension of the Text with English Translation, Critical and Explanatory Notes

By

Monier Williams

Edited and Revised

By

Dr N.C. Panda

V.V.B.I.S. & I.S.

Panjab University, Hoshiarpur

Punjab

BKP

BHARTIYA KALA PRAKASHAN

Delhi : : (India)

Published by :
BHARATIYA KALA PRAKASHAN
(Indological Publisher & Distributor)
3421-A, IInd Floor, Narang Colony
Tri Nagar, Delhi-110035 Ph : 32967505, Telefax : 27393083
E-mail : bkp3421@yahoo.co.in, website : www.bkpbooks.com

First Edition : 1867

Revised Edition : 2010

ISBN : 978-81-8090-243-7

Printed by :

G.S. Offset Process, Delhi-52

DEDICATION

Dedicated With Profound Regards

To

PROFESSOR DR. HAREKRISHNA SATAPATHY

A Great Acharya

An Ideal Teacher, a Renowned Poet
&
An Eminent Scholar of Sanskrit & Indology

And

Honourable Vice-Chancellor
of

RASHTRIYA SANSKRIT VIDYAPEETHA

(Deemed University)

Tirupati

Contents

Foreword	ix
Preface	xi
List of Transliteration	xiii
List of Abbreviation	xv
Introduction	xvii
Prologue (Prastāvanā)	1-8
Act - I	9-58
Act - II	59-93
Act - III	98-131
Act - IV	140-179
Act - V	180-212
Act - VI	223-265
Act - VII	266-310
APPENDICES	
Appendix I (Selected Fragments)	311-313
Appendex II (Verse Fragments)	314-315
Appendix III (Verse Index)	316-319
Appendix IV (General Index)	320-324

शुभाशंसनम्
Foreword

विश्वविश्रुतस्य कविकुलगुरुकालिदासेन विरचितस्य अभिज्ञानशाकुन्तलमित्याख्यस्य नाटकस्य नैकासु देशीयविदेशीयभाषासु अनुवादः सञ्जातः। लौकिके संस्कृत–साहित्ये केवलम् अभिज्ञानशाकुन्तलस्यैवेदं वर्चस्वमस्ति, यदनेनैव नाटकेन सर्वप्रथमं पाश्चात्यविदुषां हृदयाकर्षणं कृतम्। सर्वप्रथमतया 1789 ईस्वीये वर्षे सरविलियम जोन्स महोदयेन अस्य नाटकस्य आङ्ग्लभाषायामनुवादं विधाय जर्मनविदुषः गेटे महोदयस्य हस्तयोरर्पितम्। अस्यैवाङ्ग्लानुवादस्य वर्षद्वयानन्तरम् ईस्वीये 1791 तमे वर्षे जार्ज फोस्टर महोदयेन जर्मन्भाषायामपि अनुवादो विहितः। अनुवादमेनं पठित्वा गेटे महादयैर्या अभिज्ञानशाकुन्तलस्य प्रशंसा कृता तस्याः संस्कृतेऽनुवादोऽत्र प्रस्तूयतेः–

वासन्तं कुसुमं फलं च युगपद् ग्रीष्मस्य सर्वं च यत्
यच्चान्यन्मनसो रसायनमतः सन्तर्पणं मोहनम्।
एकीभूतमभूतपूर्वमथवा स्वर्लोकभूलोकयो
रैश्वर्यं यदि वाञ्छसि प्रिय सखे शाकुन्तलं सेव्यताम्।।

उपर्युक्तम् आङ्गलानुवादं पठित्वा पाश्चात्या विद्वांसो न केवलम् अभिज्ञानशाकुन्तलं प्रति प्रत्युत समस्तसंस्कृत–साहित्यं प्रति तथा च तत्र निहितां भारतीयां संस्कृतिं प्रति समाकृष्य श्रद्धावान्तश्चाऽभुवन्।

अस्यैव अभिज्ञानशाकुन्तलम् नाटकस्य पाश्चात्य विदुषा मोनियर विलियमेनाऽपि आङ्गलानुवादः कृतः। अस्य प्रथमसंस्करण 1867 तमे ईस्वीये वर्षे प्रकाशितम्। भारतीयसंस्करणं चाऽस्य ईस्वीये 1961 तमे वर्षे प्रकाशितम्। तदनन्तरं न कोऽपि सवर्द्धितं सशोधितञ्च संस्करणं अद्यावधि प्रकाशितम्। **अस्य वर्तमान नवीनसंशोधित संवर्द्धितसंस्करणास्य सटिप्पणं सम्पादनाय डॉ. नरसिंह चरण पण्डा महोदयैरथकप्रयासः कृतः**। एतदर्थ मेते प्रशंसार्हाः सर्वथाऽभिनन्दनीयाश्चेति। अथ च–

पण्डानृसिंहचरणेति विख्यातो विद्वानयम्।
सततं संस्कृत-सेवा-कार्ये लग्नो दिवानिशम्।।
विद्वद्भिः सभाजितोऽयमुत्साहश्चाऽस्य वर्द्धितः।
एतस्यैव फलं जातं ग्रन्थस्याऽस्य प्रकाशनम्।।
अस्मत्पक्षतः सततं क्रियते शुभकामना।
यद्ग्रन्थोऽयं समुदाये विदुषामादरं लभेत्।।

गणेश चतुर्थी
23.8.2009

कन्हैयालालः पाराशरः
आचार्यचरः
पंजाब विश्वविद्यालयः
तथा च
पूर्व संस्कृत-प्रोफेसरः,
आयुर्वेदिक महाविद्यालयः
होशियारपुरम्।

Preface

This is a valuable edition of Abhijñānaśākuntalam. The English translation and Notes have been throughly revised in this edition. Therefore, it is hoped that this new revised critical edition will be found more helpful by those for whom it is intended. Specially the English knowing students must be benefitted by this authentic revised edition.

I extend my sincere thanks to all those learned editors whose works I have duly consulted in preparation of this revised edition. Dr. K.L. Parashar has written the foreword to this book in Sanskrit. So, I am very much thankful to him for this great job.

I feel it a honour in dedicating this book to Prof. H.K. Satapathy a great Sanskrit scholar, a poet, a researcher and a man of inspiring attitude.

I have no words to express my sincere feelings of gratefulness to Prof. Raghbir Singh, Chairman, V.V.B.I.S. & I.S., P.U., Hoshiarpur, for his affectionate attitude and constant encouragement.

I also owe sincere thanks and gratitude to Prof. Indra Dutt Uniyal, Prof. B.B. Chaubey, Prof. Shuk Dev Sharma, Prof. Vikram Kumar, Prof. Surendra Mohan Mishra, Prof. Gopabandhu Mishra, Prof. Rajinder Kumar Sharma, Prof. Prem Lal Sharma and Prof. Krishna Murari Sharma for their invaluable suggestions and over all help and support, whenever I needed. I am extending my special thanks to my wife Mrs. Sharadhanjali Panda for her utmost co-operation and constant encouragement.

I am thankful to Mr. C.P. Gautam of Bharatiya Kala Prakashan, Delhi, for having undertaken the publication of the work.

Dated : 17th Oct. 2009

Dr. N. C. Panda
Associate Professor
V.V.B.I.S. & I.S.
Panjab University
Hoshiarpur, Punjab

List of Transliterations

अ	:	a	ख्	:	kh	ध्	:	dh
आ	:	ā	ग्	:	g	न्	:	n
इ	:	i	घ्	:	gh	प्	:	p
ई	:	ī	ङ्	:	ṅ	फ्	:	ph
उ	:	u	च्	:	c	ब्	:	b
ऊ	:	ū	छ्	:	ch	भ्	:	bh
ऋ	:	ṛ	ज्	:	j	म्	:	m
ॠ	:	ṝ	झ्	:	jh	य्	:	y
ऌ	:	lṛ	ञ्	:	ñ	र्	:	r
ॡ	:	lṝ	ट्	:	ṭ	ल्	:	l
ए	:	e	ठ्	:	ṭh	व्	:	v
ऐ	:	ai	ड्	:	ḍ	श्	:	ś
ओ	:	o	ढ्	:	ḍh	ष्	:	ṣ
औ	:	au	ण्	:	ṇ	स्	:	s
•	:	ṃ/ṁ	त्	:	t	ह्	:	h
:	:	ḥ	थ्	:	th	ळ्	:	ḷ
क्	:	k	द्	:	d			

List of Abbreviations

Amara-k	: Amara-kosha.
B. and R.	: Boehtlingk and Roth.
Beng.	: Bengālī (MSS.) or Bengālī recension
Bhartri-h	: Bhartri-hari (Bohlen's ed.) Bhaṭṭi-k, Bhaṭṭi-kāvya.
C	: the commentator Candra-śekhara.
chap.	: chapter.
cl.	: class of verbs.
Deva-n.	: Deva-nāgarī (MSS.) or Devanāgarī recension.
Dict.	: Sanskṛit-English Dictionary.
Draupadī-h	: Draupadī-haraṇa in Johnson's Selection from the Mahābhārata.
ed.	: edition.
Gīta-g.	: Gīta govinda (Lasen's ed.)
Gram.	: Sanskṛit Grammar, 4th ed.
Hari-v.	: Hari-vanśa, the last Book of the Mahābhārata.
Hitop.	: Hitopadeśa (Johnson's Ist ed.)
I.O.	: India Office.
K.	: the commentator Kāṭavema.
Kumāra-s	: Kumāra-sambhava.
l.	: line.

Laghu-k	: Laghu-kaumudī
Mahā-bh. Sel.	: Johnson's Selections from the Mahābhārata
Mālatī-m	: Mālatī-mādhava (the Calcutta ed. 1820)
Mālavik.	: Mālavikāgnimitra (Tullberg's ed.)
Megha-d.	: Megha-dūta
Mṛicch. or Mricchak	: Mricchakaṭika (Calcutta ed.)
Mudrā-r.	: Mudrā-rākshasa (Calcutta ed. 1831)
Nalod	: Nalodaya.
Pāṇ.	: Pāṇini (Boehtlingk's ed.)
Prāk.	: Prākrit.
Raghu-v.	: Raghu-vaṇśa
Rāmāy.	: Rāmāyaṇa (Calcutta ed. 1832)
rt.	: root.
Ś.	: the commentator Śaṅkara.
Sāhit-d.	: Sāhitya-darpaṇa (Calcutta ed. 1828)
Sk.	: Sanskrit
Vikram.	: Vikramorvarśīyam
Vishṇu-p.	: Vishṇupurāṇa (Wilson's translation, large ed.)

Introduction

Kālidāsa is unamimously recognised as an eminent Sanskrit poet and dramatist of India. There is scarcely any Indian lierature in which we do not find adoptations of stories of Kālidāsa's works. So, in India scholars from all parts from Kashmir in the North to Chennai in the South and from Gujarat in the West to Bengal in the East have tried to solve the different problems presented by his date, life and works. Though several scholars have written on the great poet, the problems of his date, place, life and works are still unsolved. Various conflicting views have been expressed by scholars of India and Abroad about his life and works.

Regarding the date and place of Kālidāsa Monier Williams writes : "This work is by the illustrious Kālidāsa, who is supposed by some native authorities (though on insufficient grounds) to have lived in Ujjayinī, the capital of king Vikramāditya, whose reign in the starting point of Hindu era called Saṁvat, beginning 57 years B.C. Kālidāsa is described as one of the *'nine gems'* of that monarch's splendid court. It seems, however more probable that Kālidāsa flourished in the third century of the christian era". Prof. A.B. Keith, an eminent scholar writes : "Kālidāsa was later than Aśvaghoṣa and than the dramatist Bhāsa; he know Greek terms as his use of Jāmitra proves; the Prākrit of his dramas is decidedly later than Aśvaghoṣa's and Bhāsa's and he cannot be put before the Gupta age.....We must remember that Chandragupta II had the style of Viramāditya with whose name tradition consistently connects Kālidāsa." (Hist.

of Skt. 1920, p. 80). Sir William Jones places Kālidāsa in the first century B.C. Dr. Peterson says : "Kālidāsa stands near the beginning of the christian era, if indeed, he does not overtop it."

Kālidāsa's native place is also uncertain. He travelled widely in India and seems to have been familiar with the geography of the country from the Himālayas to Kanyākumārī. From his writings it is clear that he was a devotee of Śiva. The internal evidence furnished by his writings, though meagre, may well warrant the inference that his birth place was Malwa, very probably Ujjayini. The keen interest and admiration with which the poet describes the Lord Mahākāla (Śiva), the river Siprā and other beauties of Ujjayini, unmistakably point to be the conclusion that he must have been a native of that holy city.

Kālidāsa is admittedly the greatest classical poet of India. The Indian poets and writers have praised him like a gem in the history of Sanskrit Literature. Ānandavardhana, the celebrated author of Dhvanyāloka, a standrad work on poeties, says that though this world presents on endless succession of diverse poets, yet only two or three or at the most five or six, deserve to be ranked with Kālidāsa as great.

"अस्मिन्नतिविचित्रकविपरम्परावाहिनि संसारे कालिदासप्रभृतयोद्वित्राः पञ्चषा वा महाकवय इति गण्यन्ते।"

–ध्वन्यालोक, II.

Likewise, Jayadeva, the famous author of the Gītagovinda, extols Kālidāsa as the brightest star in the Galaxy of Sanskrit poets. (**कविकुलगुरुः कालिदासो विलासः**)

A famous Subhāṣita rightly says by praising him in the following verse :

पुरा कवीनां गणनाप्रसङ्गे कनिष्ठिकाधिष्ठितकालिदासा।
अद्यापि तत्तुल्य कवेरभावादनामिका सार्थवती बभूव।।

On the occasion of couting the number of poets, the little

finger happend to be bent first with the mention of Kālidāsa name as number one. Thereafter, as none else was found to equal him in merit, the next finger ramained unbent for want of a suitable name and thus, though arbitrarily called nameless, *i.e. anāmikā* in Sanskrit, it has significantly become so now in point of fact.

There is no wonder that the western scholars also have paised Kālidāsa and called him *'the Shakespeare of India'*. However, they have, with one accord, included his name among the world's greatest poets.

Regarding the works of Kālidāsa it is not clear so far that how many works attributed to him. Poet Kālidāsa speaks very little of himself and about his writings too. There is however, general agreement about Kālidāsa's authorship of the following famous works :

1. Raghuvaṁsa : An epic poem of Nineteen cantos describing the lives of the kings of the solar race (*sūrya=vaṁśa*). This great epic describes the lives and achievements of twenty-eight kings of the solar dynasty. Among them king Raghu stood pre-eminent both in powers of arms and in openness of hand. Indeed, his valour was irresistible and his liberality poverbial, and since it is his descendants that are described in this epic, it is appropriately named the race of Raghu.

2. Kumārasambhava : The text that we have today has only seventeen cantos, of which only the first eight are said to have been written by Kālidāsa and the rest were composed by someone else to complete the work. The theme of Kumārasambhava is the birth of Kumāra, the son of Lord Śiva and Devī Pārvatī and the destroyer of Tārakāsura, the demon Tārakāasura who had become a terror to the denizens of heaven by virtue of the born of invincibility confered upon him by Brahmā, the Lord of creation. Finally, the demon was killed by Kumāra, born of the union of Śiva and Pārvatī the daughter of Himālaya.

3. Meghadūta : A lyric of about 111 verses describing the message of a Yakṣa to his wife, to be conveyed through a cloud. This lyric is devided into two parts, *viz*. Pūrva-Megha and Uttara-Megha. A certain young Yakṣa a semi-divine being forcebly separated from his wife by the curse of his master Kubera (god of riches), loosing his mental balance, in his helpless and bewildered condition importunes a passing cloud to play the part of his messenger and deliver his love message to his sorrowing wife in the city of Alakā. Thereafter, he moved southward and took up his abode on one of the hermitages on mount Rāmagiri, which abounded in trees yielding thick shade and waters sanctified by Devī Sītā's ablutions. Having passed some how the eight months (out of one year) of his total exile, he became almost crazy with pangs of separation from his wife at the starting of the rainy season, and thinking that she, too, must be lamenting his absense from home, he sincerely prayed a passing cloud to bear his beloved the news (*sandeśa*) of his welfare and the assurance of his anything attachment. So, this way the Yakṣa emotionally tries his best to send his welfare message to his dear wife through the cloud. Here, clould (*Megha*) is designated as a messanger (*dūta*) by the poet Kālidāsa.

4. Ṛtusaṁhāra : This poetic composition of Kālidāsa consists of about 158 verses. The verses are classified seasonwise and arranged systematically into six cantos. These six cantos describe the six seasons of the Indian traditional year in order, *viz*. Grīṣma, Varṣā, Śarad, Hemanta, Śiśira and Vasanta. In describing these seasons the poet tells us how each season, as it glides in, changes the look of Nature in general, how it attens the form an colour of trees and creepers, how it affects the behaviour of birds and animals, and how it pays upon the moods of young men and women, husbands and wives.

However, among the works of Kālidāsa, the Ṛtusaṁhāra is considered a work of inferior merit. So, a number of scholars had doubted Kālidāsa's authorship of it. But, this work also contains so many striking similarities of fancy and phrace with the recognized works of Kālidāsa, that there should exist no doubt regarding the real authorship of Ṛtusaṁhāra.

5. Vikramorvaśīya : A drama of five acts dealing with the love and marriage of Purūravas and Ūrvaśī. The word *Ūrvaśī* (*Ūrū+as* or *vas*) means vast or pervading and is the dawn. Purūravas means endowed with light (*rava* means colour) and is the sun God. Actually, Purūravas was a king and Ūrvaśī was a celestial damsel (Apsarā). In the *Ṛgveda* the raferences of Purūravas and Ūrvaśī are found. So, the main theme of this story is available in the *Ṛgveda.* However, this Vedic legend as expanded and elucidated in the Śatapatha Brāhmaṇa, occurs in the Viṣṇu and Bhāgavata Purāṇa with some alternations.

The language of the play is more polished and expressive than that of Mālavikāgnimitra.

6. Mālavikāgnimitra : A drama in five Acts dealing with the love of Mālavikā and Agnimitra. The hero of this play is Agnimitra, the son of Puṣpamitra, who ruled Malwa with Vidiśā as its capital between 200 and 150 B.C. Agnimitra himself is not a well-known entity and had it not been for Kālidāsa making him the hero of one of his dramatic works, his name perhaps would have ramainded almost unknown to future generations. This drama appears to be and is generally considered the first literacy production of its kind of the poet, who very probably till then was a person unknown to fame. The works of older poets like Bhāsa, Saumillaka and Kaviputra were popular at the time.

The language of the play is, on the whole, simple and elegent. No where does the author overload the sense with figures of speech. At times alliteration creeps in spontaneously, and being spontaneous, it adds to the beauty of the sense which it echoes by its sound. Most of the verses are smooth running, rhythmical and characterized by a high level of peotical craftmanship.

7. Abhijñānaśākuntalam : Is an unparalleled work of the great poet and dramatist Kālidāsa. By praising this play V.V. Mirashi writes : "It is universally acclaimed as the best of Kālidāsa's works, representing the perfection of his art, upon which his fame as a dramatist mainly rests. From ancient times men of fine taste and critical accumen in India have been so taken up with its skillful plot-construction, vivid characterisation, effective delineatin of sentiment, and elegance of language that they have with one accord called it the crest-jewel of Sanskrit dramatic literature. Its fame has not ramained confined to India only, but has travelled to the West through translations." (Kālidāsa, ch. VI., p. 248). The great german poet Goethe is known to the Sanskrit world for his poetic appreciation of the Abhijñānaśākuntalam of Kālidāsa. He praises this play as :

"Wouldst thou the young year's blossoms
and the fruits of its decline,
And all by which the soul is charmed,
enraptured, feasted and fed,
Wouldst thou the earth, and heaven itself
in one sale name combine?
I name thee, Oh Śakuntalā!
and all at once is said."

(English Translation by E.B. Eastwick)

Prof. Monier Williams, an eminent scholar of Sanskrit and the translator of this work has rightly says : "The Sakuntalā is acknowledged on all hands to be the masterpiece of the great Indian poet. Indeed, no composition of Kālidāsa displays more the richness and fertility of his poetical genius, the exuberance of his imagination, the warmth and play of his fancy, his profound knowledge of the human heart, his delicate appreciation of its most refined and tender imotions, his familiarity with the workings and counter workings of its conflecting feelings,—in short, more entitles him to rank as the *'Shakespeare of India'*. On the continent such men as Goethe, Schlegel and Humboldt have all expressed their admiration of the Hindu poet's greatest work." (Śakuntalā, preface, 1876 edn.) The Abhijñānaśākuntalam is being praised by our Indian traditional scholars / puṇḍits as :

काव्येषु नाटकं रम्यं तत्र रम्यं शकुन्तला।
तत्रापि च चतुर्थोऽङ्कस्तत्र श्लोकचतुष्टयम्।।

The sense of the above verse is clear to all. It says : among the kāvyas the play (*Nāṭaka*) is ths most charming. Among the *Nāṭakas* the Abhijñānaśākuntalam is the most lovable and even most charming. The last two *pādas* specify that the fourth act is the best in this play, and in that act only four verses are most lovable and beautiful. Hence, from the above verse the importance of Abhijñānaśākuntalam is clearly understand.

So, the best known and most popular of Kālidāsa's plays is Abhijñānaśākuntalam, a *Nāṭaka* in seven acts dealing with the love and marriage of king Duṣyanta and Āśrama girl Śakuntalā.

The play begins with a salutation to Lord Śiva who is said to manifest in eight visible forms in this world, *viz.* the five elements, the sun, the moon and the sacrificer. The first Act of the play begins with the scene of the royal hunt. King Duṣyanta, the hero of the play, makes his introductory appearance before the audience in the pursuit of a dear, flying at a great speed to escape imminent death at his well-aimed arrow. The second Act starts with a very vivid and realistic description of the king's hunting expedition by his brahmin friend Vidūṣaka. The hunting however was suddenly brought to an end by the love lord condition of the king which disinclined him for the arduous life of a huntsman. The king therefore orders his associates to stop all hunting activities and prevent the army from causing trouble to the obcetics. Thereafter while the king was engaged in a confidential talk with Vidūṣaka regarding the growing attachment between himself and Śakuntalā. Then due to the request of the inmates of the Kaṇvāśrama the king used to stay in that Āśrama to protect the sacrifices and seers from the ravages of the demons. The content of the third Act is very interesting. As the king Duṣyanta was now residing in the very heart of the hermitage unencumbered by the presence of Vidūṣaka his love affair makes rapid head way under favourable environments and the smooth sailing courtship culminates in the consummation of a happy union which is described by the poet with a commendable delicacy and restraint. The Act four is the apex and very cream of the great play. The heroine of the play Śakuntalā departs for her husband's residence. On the eve of her departure from the holy Āśrama which long associations have endeared to her, bewildering grief at the separation from her lovable father sage Kaṇva and her dear friends, from the fondly cherished animals of the hermitage and even the plants and trees who she loves as her near relations invests in this Act with a deep pathos and moves the hearts of the readers almost to the verge of tears. The entire *āśrama* surrounding seems deeply affected by the pangs of separtion. This fourth Act also contains Maharshi Kaṇvas well-known advice to Śakuntalā on the duties of a wife and a daughter in law, as :

शुश्रूषस्व गुरून्कुरु प्रियसखीवृत्तिं सपत्नीजने
भर्तृविप्रकृतापि रोषणतया मा स्म प्रतीपं गमः।
भूयिष्ठं भव दक्षिणा परिजने भाग्येष्वनुत्सेकिनी
यान्त्येवं गृहिणीपदं युवतयो वामाः कुलस्याधयः।।

The above verse is a true advice for the newly married daughters. It rightly says : serve your eldered and act the part of a dear friend to your co-wives. Even though wronged by your husband, do not, out of anger, be of refractory spirit; be over courteous to your dependents and do not become elated with pride in prosperity. Thus, do young ladies attain the status of a housewife; those of an opposite character are banes of their family.

Through this type of advice and moral courage of a young

married lady was boosted. It is the duty of the adorable persons to show the real path to their children in such an auspicious occasion.

In the fifth Act, due to the curse of sage Durvāsā, along with the incident of the lost ring, king Duṣyanta failed to recognise Śākuntalā in his royal palace. Due to his forgetfulness of the king, Śākuntalā suffered the worst that could happen to a devoted wife. She is disowned by her husband and disgraced. Her mind became vacant and she stands their lonely, filled with terror, anguish and despair. The poet described her endurance of desertion, her fortitude in suffering, her later disciplined life till he is restored to her husband. Love is not a mere affair of senses; it is a kingship of spirit. Both Duṣyanta and Śākuntalā suffered, were disciplined by sorrow, and obtained the reward of a spiritual harmony. The youthful flush subsides; the gust of passion dies out. Love is won at a higher level and the brief glow of pleasure is turned into a steady life of bliss. Passion is linked with the sanctities of life. Nature and grace blend in harmony.

The main characters of Abhijñānaśākuntalam are : king Duṣyanta–the hero; Śākuntalā–the heroine; Maharshi Kaṇva–the foster father of Śākuntalā; Vidūṣaka; Anasuyā and Priyamvadā.

The design of the play is very significant and exhaustive in nature. Regarding this design M.R. Kale writes : "A closer observation will however, prove that the design of the play is very carefully planned, and the structural scheme is artistically commendable. The seven Acts of the play form a symmetrical design. The union, the separation, and reunion of Duṣyanta and Śākuntalā are the three main parts of the play. The fourth Act, which follows the union and leads to the repudiation occupies the central position, and links up the first three and the last three Acts." (Abhi. Śākun., Introduction, p. 73)

Now, I will add a few passages from the original preface

of Monier Williams, which he had written in 1876 to his revised edition of this text. Regarding the various edition of Abhijñānaśākuntalam Monier Williams writes as : "It was reserved for Dr. Boehtlingk to first edit the Devanāgarī recension of this play at Born in the year 1842. No other edition of the text of this recension was published until my first edition in 1853. An edition of the same recension was published at Bombay in 1861, and one at Breslace in 1872 by Dr. Burkhard, Professor in the University of Bonn, to which is added a glossary." The translations which have been published since that of Sir W. Jones and the German version of his translation by Forster, in 1971, are first, the French of M. Chézy; subsequently the German of Hirzal, Rückert, and Boehtlingk; a Dainsh translation by Hammerich; and more recently another German translation in prose and verse by Meier; not to speak of Danish and Italian versions of Sir W. Jones in English; and my own English translation, the forth edition of which was published (by W.H. Allen and Co. 13, Waterloo Place, London) in 1872."

Besides, Monier William also writes : "I am bound to acknowledge that I made free use of Dr. Boethlingk's edition of the text of the Śākuntalā in preparing the first edition for the press. The merit of his work can hardly be overrated, but I may, without presumption, say that I discovered many better readings, corrected a few errows, and introduced much original matter in the shape of annotations. In regard to the text of the present volume, if I have succeeded in producing a move correct edition of the Devanāgarī recension, than those of Dr. Boehtlingk and Dr. Burkhard, the merit is due to the more ample materials which have been place at my command. In preparing the first edition, I took care to avail myself of Dr. Boehtlingk's corrections of himself and his after thoughts at the end of his work, as well as of such critical remarks as concided with my won views."

At the time of critical edition of this text M. William had consulted a number of manuscripts and commentaries of

Abhijñānaśākuntalam. He further adds : "The Mss. which I principally used, were—

1. A Ms. from the colebrooke collection, and therefore from the eastern side of India, numbered 1718.

2. A Ms. from the Mackenzie collection, and therefore from Southern India, numbered 2696.

3. A Ms. from the Taylor collection, and therefore from Western India, numbered 1858, dated Śaka 1734.

All these belong to the India office library, and represent the Indian Presidencies respectively.

4. A Copy of a very good MS. at Bombay, presented to me by Mr. Shaw of Bombay Civil Service.

5. An Old Bengālī Ms. belonging to the India Office library numbered 1060.

6. A very old Bengālī Ms. from the Wilson collection in the Bodleian."

"I consulted other Bengālī MSS., but rarely admited readings from them, unless supported by some one of the Devanāgarī. Thus, the verses which I inserted at the beginning of the third Act are supported throughout by my own and the Taylor Ms. and partially by that of the Mackenzie collection." (Abhijñānaśākuntalam, preface, 1876 edn.)

In addition to these above MSS. M. William had used the following three commentaries while editing this text :

1. Kāṭavema, whose commentary, from the Mackenzie collection at the India office, is the only one in the Nāgarī character.

2. Śaṅkara, whose commentary, from the Wilson collection in the Bodleean Library, is on the Bengālī recension, and written in the Bengālī character.

3. Candraśekhara, whose commentary, belonging to the India office, is also on the Bengālī recension, and generally only repeats the words of Śaṅkara.

Dr. N.C. Panda

ABHIJÑĀNA ŚĀKUNTALAM

।। प्रस्तावना ।।

या सृष्टिः स्रष्टुर् आद्या वहति विधिहुतं या हविर् या च होत्री
ये द्वे कालं विधत्तः श्रुतिविषयगुणा या स्थिता व्याप्य विश्वम्।
याम् आहुः सर्वभूतप्रकृतिरिति यया प्राणिनः प्राणवन्तः
प्रत्यक्षाभिः प्रपन्नस् तनुभिर् अवतु वस् ताभिर् अष्टाभिर् ईशः[1] ।। 1 ।।

1. (That visible form) which (was) the first creation of the Creator [*i.e.,* water]; (that) which bears the oblation offered-according-to-scriptural-rule [*i.e.,* fire]; and (that) which (is) the offerer [*i.e.,* the officiating priest who offers the oblation]; (those) two (visible form) wich define the time [*i.e.,* the Sun and Moon which cause day and night]; (that) which perpetually pervades all space, having [conveying] the quality (sound) perceptible by the ear [*i.e.,* earth]; (that) which they call the birth-place [womb, proximate cause] of all created-things [*i.e.,* the earth]; (that) by which living beings are furnished with breath [*i.e.,* the air]; endowed with [manifested in, known by] these eight visible forms, may Īśa [the Supreme Lord] preserve you!' The play begins and ends with a prayer to Śiva : see the last note in this book. After every relative pronoun some case of *pratyakṣā tanuḥ* must be supplied. *Sṛṣṭir ādyā* : see Manu i., 8-10, *apa eva sasarja ādau,* '(the creator) first created the waters.' *Vidhi-hutaṁ, i.e., veda-vidhānena agnau kṣiptam* : Ch. *Hotrī, i.e., dīkṣita-mayī tanuḥ* : K. *yajamāna-rūpā tanuḥ* : Ch. 'the Brāhmaṇa who is qualified by initiation to offer the oblation.' *Kālam vidhattaḥ=samayaṁ kurutaḥ* : Ch., *=sṛjataḥ* : Ś. Hence the Sun is called *divākaṛa,* 'maker of the day;' and the moon, *niśākara,* 'maker of the night.' *Śruti,* etc. : the Hindu's reckon five elements, *viz.,* water, fire, ether, earth, and air. Ether [*ākāśa*] is held to be the vehicle of sound, or of that quality which is the object of perception to the

---

Verse 1. The metre is *Sragdharā* (variety of *Prakṛti*), in which there are twenty-one syllables to the half-line; each half-line being alike.

— — — — ◡ — — | ◡ ◡ ◡ ◡ ◡ ◡ — | — ◡ — — ◡ — — ||

नान्द्यन्ते[1]

ear : see Manu, i, 75, *Akāśasya śabdam guṇaṁ viduḥ. Vyāpya sthitā, i.e.*, 'keeps pervading.' Compare *vyāpya sthitaṁ rodasī* : Vikram. *Sthā* is joined with an indecl. part to express continuity of action. *Viśvam* = *prapañcam* : K. *Sarva-bhūta-prakṛtiḥ* : So reads Kāṭavema followed by my own MS., and supported by Manu, ix. 37,

Iyaṁ bhūmirhi bhūtānāṁ śaśvatī yonir ucyate, 'this earth is called the primeval womb [*yonih=kāraṇam* : Kul.] of all created things' [such as trees, etc. : Kul.]. The other MSS. have *sarva-vīja-prakṛtir. Prakṛtiḥ=upādāna-kāraṇam* : K. = *utpatti-sthānam* : Ch. = *nidānam* : Ś. *Prapannaḥ* = *upetaḥ* : K. The Beṅgālī MSS. have *prasannas.* The worshippers of Śiva, who were pantheists in the sense of believing that Śiva was himself all that exists as well as the cause of all that is, held that there were eight different manifestations of their god, called Rudras [or Rudra, Bhava, Sarva, Īśāna, Paśupati, Bhīma, Ugra, Mahādeva] and that these had their types or representatives in the eight visible forms enumerated here. So, the Viṣṇu-Purāṇa as quoted by Śaṅkara [p. 58, Wilson]—'Brahmā assigned to them their respective stations : water, the sun, earth, fire, air, ether, the officiating Brāhmaṇa [*dīkṣito brāhmaṇaḥ*], and the moon; these are termed their visible forms [*tanavaḥ*].' In the opening of Mālavik., Śiva is said to uphold the universe by means of these forms, *aṣṭābhir tanubhir bibhrataḥ kṛtsnaṁ jagadapi. See* also Kumāras., iv, 76. Śaṅkara, with far-fetched subtilty, points out how each of these types of Śiva is intended by the poet to typify events and circumstances in the life of Śakuntalā. Thus, *ya sṛṣṭiḥ*, etc. is compared with the sentiment in verse 43; and *ye dve*, etc., is supposed to be significant of her two female friends.

1. The opening benediction is called Nāndī because it is supposed to rejoice the hearts of gods and men. *Deva-dvija-nṛpādīnām āśīrvāda-parāyaṇā nandanty asyāṁ surā yasmāt tena nāndī prakīrtitā* : Ś. The Sūtradhāra was the manager [=*sthāpaka* : Ś.] who held and regulated the thread of the drama, or who developed the thread of the plot. *Yena nartanīya-kathā-sūtraṁ prathamaṁ sūcyate; nanu sūtra-paṭhanīyā nāndī sūtradhārasya ca pāṭhāvasaraḥ praveśānantaram* : Ś. He is otherwise, especially when not a Brāhmaṇa, called the Sthāpaka, 'he who fixes or directs the action of the play;' *kāvyārtha-sthāpanāt* : Ch. *Sthāpakaḥ sūtradhāra-sadṛśa-*

सूत्रधारः : (नेपथ्याभिमुखम् अवलोक्य[1]) आर्ये। यदि नेपथ्यविधानम् अवसितम्। तर्हीतस् तावद् आगम्यताम्।

नटी : (प्रविश्य) अज्ज। इअम्हि। आणबेदु अज्जो। को एओओ-

नटी : (प्रविश्य) आर्य। इयम् अस्मि। आज्ञापयतु आर्यः। को नियोगो-

अणुचिट्ठीअदुत्ति।

ऽनुष्ठीयतामिति।[2]

सूत्रधारः : आर्ये। अभिरूपभूयिष्ठा[3] परिषद् इयं। अद्य खलु कालिदासग्रथित-

gunākāraḥ : Sāh.-darp., p. 137, 1. 6. *Sūtra-dhāra-padena atra sthāpako-'bhimataḥ sūtradhāra-samānākāratvāt* : Ś. As to *nāndyante,* see the note in page 7 of this book.

1. 'Looking towards the tiring-room,' which was behind the stage, 'looking behind the scenes.' *Nepathyam = ryatiriktaṁ yavani-kāntaritaṁ varṇikāgrahaṇadi-yogyaṁ naṭa-varga-sthānam* : K. = *bhūṣaṇa-sthānaṁ raṅgād vahih-stham;* Ch., Ś. In a Hindū theatre, a curtain [*apaṭī paṭa yavanīkā*] suspended across the stage, answered all the purposes of scenes. Behind it there was the space or room called *nepathya,* where the decorations were kept, and where the actors attired themselves and remained in readiness before entering the stage; whither also they withdrew on leaving it. When an actor was to come on hurriedly, the stage-direction is *paṭākṣepeṇa* or *apaṭīkṣepeṇa,* 'with a hurried toss of the curtain.' When he was to say something whilst hidden from the audience in this space behind the curtain, the direction is *nepathye* '(a voice) in the postscenium.' As to *nepathya-vidhānam* [=*prasādhana-kriyā* : Ś.], it may be translated, 'the act of decoration,' 'making the toilet,' or perhaps, 'the arrangements of the tiring-room.' *Nepathye yad vidhīyate tan nepathya-vidhānam.* Kāṭavema has *naipathya. Nepathyam vidhā = nepathyaṁ rach or nepathyaṁ kṛ* : Compare Ratn., p. 2, 1.16.

2. The interrogative pronoun and *iti* show that the 'directa oratio' is here substituted for the *'obliqua.' Iti* may be omitted, but is generally the sign of the direct form. In the *'obliqua oratio,'* which the Hindūs more rarely use, the relative pronouns and particles would be used without *iti,* thus *ājñāpayatu yo niyogo anuṣṭhīyatām.*

3. 'For the most part (composed of) learned [educated] men.'

वस्तुना नवेनाभिज्ञानशकुन्तलाख्येन[1] नाटकेनोपस्थातव्यम् अस्माभिः। तत् प्रतिपात्रम् आधीयतां यत्नः।[2]

नटी : सुविहिदप्पओअदाए अज्जस्स ण किम्पि परिहास्ससदि।

नटी : सुविहितप्रयोगतया आर्यस्य न किमपि परिहास्यते।[3]

सूत्रधारः : (आर्ये) कथयामि ते भूतार्थं।[4]

The audience consisted chiefly of good judges, *cognoscenti.* [*abhirūpa=vidvas, paṇḍita :* K., Ch.] So *rāṣṭram śūdra-bhūyiṣṭham :* Manu, viii., 22.

1. 'With the new drama called "Token-Śakuntalā," or "Ring-(recognised) Śakuntalā."' *Abhijñāna-śakuntalā* is an anomalous Tatpuruṣa compound [Lagh.-kaum., 994]; not one in which the terms are inverted, but one in which there is *uttara-pada-lopa* or *madhyama-pada-lopa,* 'elision of the second member.' On the authority of Candraśekhara, the second member to be supplied is *smṛtā,* 'recognized;' and *abhijñāna* is 'the token of recognition—the ring.' The compound will thus be equivalent to *abhijñāna-smṛtā śakuntalā,* 'Śakuntalā recognized by the token.' So *śāka-pārthiva,* 'the king of the era,' is equivalent to *śāka-priya-pārthiva,* 'the king beloved by the era.'

2. 'Therefore, let care be applied by each to is own part or character,' 'let pains be taken by all in their several parts.' *Pratipātram=pātre pātre* : K. *Tat=tasmāt* : K. So *sveṣu sthāneṣu avahitair bhavitavyam* : Vikram., Act 1.

3. 'By reason of your honour's good assignment of (the parts of) the play (to the several actors), nothing will be wanting;' *i.e.,* 'by reason of your skill in casting the characters, nothing is likely to go amiss in the casting the characters, nothing is likely to go amiss in the acting;' or, 'by reason of (our) good acting nothing will be wanting to your honour;' or, 'by reason of your honour's (skill in the) management of the play,' etc. Such are the various interpretations of Kāṭavema, Candra-śekhara, and Śaṅkara : the first seems preferable. So *yah prayogo bhavatīṣu nibaddhaḥ :* Vikram., Act 2. [*prayogaṁ nibandh = prayogaṁ virac* : Schol.]

4. *Bhūtārtham=satyam* : Ś.=*satyārtham;* K., 'the real truth,' 'the true state of the case.'

आपरितोषाद् विदुषां न साधु मन्ये प्रयोगविज्ञानम्।
बलवदपि शिक्षितानाम् आत्मन्यप्रत्ययं चेतः[1] ।। 2 ।।

नटी : (सविनयं) एव्वं णेदं। अणन्तरकरणिज्जं दाव अज्जो आणबेदु।

नटी : (सविनयं) एवं न्विदं। अनन्तरकरणीयं तावद् आर्य आज्ञापयतु।

सूत्रधारः : किम् अन्यद् अस्याः परिषदः श्रुतिप्रसादनतः।[2]

नटी : अध कदमं उण उदुं अधिकरिअ गाइस्सं।

नटी : अथ कतमं पुनर् ऋतुम् अधिकृत्य[3] गास्यामि।

सूत्रधारः : नन्विमम् एव तावद् अचिरप्रवृत्तम् उपभोगक्षमं ग्रीष्मसमयम् अधिकृत्य गीयताम्। सम्प्रति हि :

सुभगसलिलावगाहाः पाटलसंसर्गसुरभिवनवाताः।
प्रच्छायसुलभनिद्रा दिवसाः परिणामरमणीयाः[4] ।। 3 ।।

1. 'I do not consider skill-in-the-representation-of-plays to be good [perfect] until (it cause) the satisfaction of the learned (audience); the mind of those even who are very well instructed has no confidence in itself.' *Balavad=suṣṭhu.*

2. Equal to *śravaṇendriya-tarpaṇāt;* K. Some MSS. insert *saṅgītāt karaṇīyam.*

3. *Lit.*, 'having placed over,' 'having made the prominent subject.' Hence, *adhikṛtya=kṛte,* 'about,' 'concerning,' 'with reference to :' Pāṇ., iv, 3, 87. So, in the next sentence : 'Assuredly let a song be sung concerning this very summer season, (so) suited to enjoyment, that has not long set in., As to *nanu*, see Pāṇ., viii., 1, 43.

4. 'For now (are) the days, on-which-there-are-grateful-bathings-in-the-water (and) on-which-sylvan-breezes-are-fragrant-

---

Verse 2. *Aryā* or *Gāthā,* in which there are thirty instants (a short syllable containing one, and a long, two) in the first line, and twenty-seven in the second. Each foot must contain four instants, except the sixth of the second line, which contains one; and the line must be divided by a pause at the end of the third foot.

— ◡ ◡ | — — | ◡ ◡ — || ◡ — ◡ | — — | ◡ — ◡ | — — | —
◡ ◡ ◡ ◡ | ◡ — ◡ | — — || — — | — — | ◡ | — — | —

Verse 3. *Āryā* or *Gāthā. See* Verse 2.

◡ ◡ ◡ ◡ | ◡ — ◡ | — — || — ◡ ◡ | — — | ◡ ◡ ◡ ◡ | ◡ ◡ — | —
— — | ◡ ◡ ◡ ◡ | — — || ◡ ◡ — | ◡ ◡ — | ◡ | ◡ ◡ — | —

नटी : तह (इति गायति)।

नटी : तथा (इति गायति)।

इसीसिचुम्बिआदं भमरेहिं सुउमारकेसरसिहाइं।

ईषदीषच्चुम्बितानि भ्रमरैः सुकुमारकेशरशिखानि।[1]

ओदंसअन्ति दअमाणा पमदाओ सिरीसकुसुमाइं।।

अवतंसयन्ति दयमानाः प्रमदाः शिरीषकुसुमानि।। 4।।

सूत्रधारः : आर्ये। साधु गीतं। अहो रागबद्धचित्तवृत्तिर् आलिखित इव सर्वतो [2]रङ्गः। तद् इदानीं कतमत् प्रकरणम् आश्रित्यैनम् आराधयामः।

from-contact-with-the-trumpet-flower : (now are the days) on-which-sleep-is-easily-induced-in-very-shady-spots (and) which-are-delightful-at-their-close.' *Prachāya,* etc.' *prakṛṣṭa-chāyā yatra tat sthānam prachāyaṁ tasmin sulabhā nidrā yeṣu te tathoktāḥ* : K. : *see* p. 37, note 1 of this book. A short vowel is the substitute for the crude of a fem. noun, when compounded with such prepositions as *pra, ati,* etc.; thus *pragrīva* from *grīvā; atimāla* from *mālā.* See lagh.-kaum., 1003. *Pariṇāma=virāma=sāyaṅkāla,* 'the evening :' K.

1. 'Loving [amorous] fair-ones make ear-rings of the Śirīṣa-blossoms that-are-very-gently-kissed by bees (and) the points-of-whose-filaments-are-very-delicate.' According to Śaṅkara, *keśara= kiñjalka,* and the whole compound is a Bahuvrīhi, agreeing with *śirīṣa-kusumāni.* There is an allusion to the blossoms of the Śirīṣa being thus used in Meghadūta, 67, *cārukarṇe śirīṣam;* and Raghu-vaṁśa, xvi, 48, 61. Compare also *karṇa-śirīṣa-rodhi,* at the end of Act 1. of this play; and Ṛtu-s., ii., 18, *kṛtāvataṁsaiḥ kusumaiḥ,* etc.

2. 'On every side, the audience, having all the feelings of its soul fixed on the melody, is as if formed into a picture;' *i.e.,* motionless or riveted with attention. *Ālikhita=nīścala* : K.; *raṅga* applies to the audience as well as to the stage.

Verse 4. A variety of *Āryā* called *Udgāthā* or *Gīti,* used in *Prākṛt.* It consists properly of four half-lines, containing eighteen instants in the fourth half-line as well as in the second (*see* Verse 69). But in this example the line is divided irregularly.

⏑ — ⏑ | ⏑ ⏑ — | — ⏑ — | — — || ⏑ ⏑ — | ⏑ — ⏑ | ⏑ ⏑ — | —

— — | ⏑ — ⏑ | ⏑ ⏑ — | — ⏑ ⏑ | — — || ⏑ — ⏑ | ⏑ ⏑ — | —

The first syllable of the second foot [cumbiā] is short by a license peculiar to Prākṛt prosody. [*See Colebrooke's Essays,* vol: ii, p. 71, note.]

नटी : णं अज्जमिस्सेहिं पढमं एव्व आणत्तं अहिस्णाणसउन्दलं णाम
नटी : ननु [1]आर्यमिश्रैः प्रथमम् एव आज्ञप्तम् अभिज्ञानशाकुन्तलं नाम
अपुव्वं णाडअं पओएण अधिकरीअदुत्ति।
अपूर्वं नाटकं प्रयोगेण अधिक्रियातामिति।[2]

सूत्रधारः : आर्ये। सम्यग् अनुबोधितोऽस्मि। अस्मिन् क्षणे विस्मृतं खलु मया। कुतः।

तवास्मि गीतरागेण हारिणा प्रसभं हृतः।
एष राजेव दुष्यन्तः सारङ्गेणातिरंहसा[3] ।। 5 ।।

।। इति निष्क्रान्तौ ।।

1. 'By your reverence;' *ārya-mīśraiḥ* is here an epithet of the manager; the respectful plural being used. In the Vikramorvaśīya, *ārya-vidagdha-mīśrāḥ,* 'respectable and intelligent persons,' occurs as an epithet of the audience. *Mīśra,* 'mixed,' in a compound of this kind has the force of 'gentleman.'

2. *Adhikṛyatām=prakaṭī-kriyatām*: K., *i.e.*, 'let it be made the subject of exhibition,' 'let it be brought prominently forward:' *see* p. 5, note 2. Some read *prayoge* : compare in Ratnāvalī, p. 2, 1. 15, *nāṭikā prayogeṇa nāṭayitavyā.*

3. In the Hindū drama every piece commences with a prologue, which is preceded by the Nāndī, invoking the favour of some deity. Bharata says, *Sūtradhāraḥ paṭhen nāndīm madhyamam* [*prathamam* : Ch.] *svaram āśritaḥ,* 'the Sūtradhāra may recite the Nāndī in a tone neither high nor low.' The stage-manager was generally a Brāhma, and therefore qualified to recite the Nāndī in his own person. He did so, however, as a Brāhmaṇa, and not in his character of Sūtradhāra, or manager, which he did not assume till he had concluded the Nāndī. *Nāndyante sūtradhāraḥ* is therefore equivalent to *nāndīṁ paṭhitvā sūtradhāro vadati.* So, Candra-śekhara, *Nāndī, etadante sūtradhāro vadati, nāndīm paṭhitvā anyad vadati ityarthaḥ.* Hence, the word *pravīśya,* 'entering,' is not required; the reciter of

---

Verse 5. *Śloka* or *Anuṣṭubh*, consisting of four half-lines of eight syllables.

⏓ ⏒ ⏓ ⏒ | ⏑ – – ⏓ || ⏒ ⏓ ⏒ ⏓ | ⏑ – ⏑ ⏒

⏒ ⏓ ⏒ ⏒ | ⏑ – – ⏒ || ⏒ ⏒ ⏒ ⏒ | – – ⏑ ⏒

The first four syllables and the last of each half-line may be either long or short.

the Nāndī remaining on the stage in the character of manager. [*Iti nayena nāndyante sūtradhāra-praveśo'pāstaḥ* : Ch.] If, however, the manager happened not to be a Brāhmaṇa, he seems to have had no right to the title Sūtradhāra, nor to have been qualified to recite the Nāndī, but in that case some Brāhmaṇa pronounced the blessing, and the Sthāpaka then entered as Sūtradhāra. Such, at least, seems to be the meaning of Bharata's aphorism [*raṅga-pūjām vidhāya ādau sūtradhāre vinirgate sthāpakaḥ pravīśet paścāt sūtradhāra-guṇākṛtiḥ*] though all the extant plays make the Sūtradhāra first recite the benediction, and then carry on the dialogue. The Sāh.-darp., p. 137, has the following : *Idānīm pūrva-raṅgasya samyak-prayogābhāvād eka eva sūtradhāraḥ sarvaṁ proyojayati iti vyavahāraḥ sa sthāpakaḥ*. The blessing is usually followed by some mention of the author of the piece, an appeal to the favour of the audience, and a short dialogue between the manager and one of the actors [*pāripārśvika*]. In the present play, the actress signs a song for the amusement of the audience; and in every case, the conclusion of the prelude prepares them for the entrance of one of the dramatis-personae. Hence, the manager exclaims, 'I was forcibly carried away by the ravishing melody of thy song, like king Duṣyanta here by the very fleet antelope.'

ACT - I

।। अथ प्रथमोऽङ्कः ।।

[ततः प्रविशति मृगानुसारी सशरचापहस्तो **राजा** रथेन सूतश्च]

सूत : [राजानं मृगं चावलोक्य] आयुष्मन्।[1]

कृष्णसारे ददच् चक्षुस् त्वयि चाधिज्यकार्मुके।
मृगानुसारिणं साक्षात् पश्यामीव पिनाकिनम्[2] ।। 6 ।।

राजा : सूत दूरम् अमुना सारङ्गेण वयम् आकृष्याः। अयं पुनर् इदानीमपि-

1. 'O long-lived one!' a respectful mode of addressing kings. Chandraśekhara quotes a verse of Bharata, *Vaded rājñīṁ ca ceṭīṁ ca bhavatīti vidūṣakaḥ, āyuṣhman rathinaṁ sūto vṛddhaṁ tāteti cetaraḥ.*

2. 'Casting (my) eye on the black-antelope and on thee with-thy-strung-bow I behold, as it were, Śiva visibly present chasing the deer.' *Adhi-jya,* 'having the string [*jyā*] up;' at the end of the chase the bow would be *sithila-jya* : seee verse 40. *Sa-jya* is used like *adhi-jya. Pinākin* is Śiva, armed with his bow or trident called *Pināka.* [So the bow of Viṣṇu has a name *Sārṅga,* and that of Arjuna, *Gāṇḍīva* : Megh., 48, 50.] In illustration, Kāṭavema refers to Raghu-v., xi, 44, *Dhanuḥ, yena vṛṣa-dvajo vāṇaṁ asṛjad vidruta-kratu-mṛgānusāriṇam.* Śiva, not being invited to Dakṣa's celebrated horse-sacrifice, was so indignant, that with his wife he suddenly presented himself, confounded the sacrifice, dispersed and mutilated the gods, and chasing *Yajña,* 'the lord of sacrifice,' who fled in the form of a fleet deer, overtook and decapitated him. The Vāyu-Purāṇa makes Śiva create a manifestation of himself as a monstrous being named Vīrabhadra, who pursues *Yajña* in the form of a deer : see Viṣṇu-Purāṇa, p. 65.

Verse 6. *Śloka* or *Anuṣṭubh. See* Verse 5.

ग्रीवाभङ्गाभिरामं मुहुर् अनुपतति स्यन्दने दत्तदृष्टिः
पश्चार्द्धेन प्रविष्टः शरपतनभयाद् भूयसा पूर्वकायम्।
दर्भैर् अर्द्धावलीढैः श्रमविवृतमुखभ्रंशिभिः कीर्णवर्त्मा-
पश्योदग्रप्लुतत्वाद् वियति बहुतरं स्तोकम् उर्व्यां प्रयाति[1] ।।7।।

[सविस्मयं] कथम् अनुपतत एव मे प्रयत्नप्रेक्षणीयः संवृत्तोऽयं मृगः[2]

सूत : आयुष्मन्। उत्खातिनी[3] भूमिरिति मया रश्मिसंयमनाद् रथस्य मन्दीकृतो वेगः। तेन मृग एष विप्रकृष्टान्तरः[4] संवृत्तः। सम्प्रति हि समदेशवर्तिनस् ते न दुरासदो भविष्यति।

राजा : तेन हि मुच्यन्ताम् अमीनषवः।

सूत : यथाज्ञापयत्यायुष्मान् [रथवेगं निरूप्य[5]] आयुष्मन्। पश्य पश्य।

1. 'There he is now, gracefully by the bending of his neck casting a glance ever and anon at the chariot which pursues him, by (the contraction of) the hinder half (of his body) repeatedly drawing himself into the fore (part of his) body through fear of the descent of the arrow; strewing the road with grass half-chewed which drops from his mouth kept open from exhaustion. See! by reason of his lofty boundings he goes chiefly in the air, and little on the ground.' *Praviṣṭaḥ pūrva-kāyam* is equivalent to *praviṣṭa-pūrva-kāyaḥ, lit.*, 'entering the fore part of his body,' a *Bahuvrīhi* compound analogous to *datta-dṛṣṭiḥ* and *kīrṇa-vartmā*. In regard to the *darbha* or *kuśa* grass, *see* the note to verse 15.

2. '[With surprize.] How now! the deer has become visible with difficulty [*lit.*, with effort] to me pursuing (him).'

3. *Utkhātinī, lit.*, 'full of trenches, excavations, or hoelows;' *i.e.*, 'hilly,' 'undulating.' The deer when running in the hollow would be visible with difficulty.

4. 'Separated by a longer interval' or 'distance.'

5. The expressions *nirūpya* and *nāṭayitvā*, which occur so frequently in the stage-directions, are undoubtedly synonymous. They may both be translated by 'acting,' 'gesticulating,' 'exhibiting by gesticulation.' The properties and paraphernalia of the Hindū stage were as limited as the scenery; and though seats, thrones,

---

Verse 7. *Sragdharā*. (*See* Verse 1.)

— — — — ⏑ — — | ⏑ ⏑ ⏑ ⏑ ⏑ ⏑ — | — ⏑ — — ⏑ — —

मुक्तेषु रश्मिषु निरायतपूर्वकाया
निष्कम्पचामरशिखा निभृतोर्ध्वकर्णाः।
आत्मोद्धतैरपि रजोभिर् अलङ्घनीया
धावन्त्यमी मृगजवाक्षमयेव रथ्याः[1] ।। 8 ।।

weapons, and cars were certainly introduced, yet much had to be supplied by the imaginations of the spectators, assisted by the gesticulations of the actors. Thus, though the car of Duṣyanta might have been represented on the stage, the horses would be left to the imagination, and the speed of the chariot would only be indicated by the gesticulations of the charioteer. In a subsequent part of this Act, Śakuntalā is pursued by a bee, which, by her gestures, she tries to beat off; but we are not to suppose that an artificial bee, suspended by an invisible wire, was brought upon the stage, as might be attempted in a modern theatre.

1. 'The reins being loosed, these chariot-horses run along as if with impatience of the speed of the deer [*i.e.*, impatient or emulous of its speed], having the fore-part of their bodies well stretched out, having the chowrie which forms their crests motionless, having the upper [part of their] ears depressed [or bent backwards], not to be overtaken even by the dust raised by themselves.'—The *cāmarī* or chowrie was formed of the white bushy tail of the Yak or Bos grunniens, and was used for whisking off flies; also as an emblem of princely rank. It was placed as an ornament between the ears of horses, like the plume of the war-horse of chivalry. The velocity of the chariot caused it to lose its play and appear fixed in one direction, like a flag borne rapidly against the wind. A similar idea occurs in the commencement of the Vikramorvaśīya, *citrārambha-viniścalaṁ hayasirasi cāmaram.* There is some difficulty in *nibhṛtorddhva-karṇāḥ*. The commentators explain *nibhṛta* by *niścala,* 'motionless.' This meaning is not supported by the dictionary, nor by any passage with which I am acquainted. The most usual sense of *nibhṛta* is 'secret,' 'modest,' 'humble,' 'low' [Git. Gov. ii, 11; ii, 21. Hitop. *passim.*] Hence, may easily flow the acceptation 'depressed,' 'bent down.' The ears of a horse while running at full speed are not

---

Verse 8. *Vasantatilakā* (a variety of the *Śakkarī* or *Śarkarī*) containing fourteen syllables to the half-line, each half-line being alike.

— — ⏑ — ⏑ ⏑ ⏑ — ⏑ ⏑ — ⏑ — — ||

राजा :(सहर्षं) सत्यम् अतीत्य हरितो हरींश्च वर्तन्ते वाजिनः।[1] तथा हि

> **यद् आलोके सूक्ष्मं व्रजति सहसा तद् विपुलतां**
> **यद् अर्द्धे विच्छिन्नं भवति कृतसन्धानमिव तत्।**
> **प्रकृत्या यद् वक्रं तदपि समरेखं नयनयोर्**
> **न मे दूरे किञ्चित् क्षणमपि न पार्श्वे रथजवात्[2] ।। ९।।**

exactly erect, but rather bent backwards so as to present the least resistance to the wind. This interpretation is confirmed by the reading of the Bengālī MSS., *cyuta-karṇa-bhaṅga,* 'having the flaccid part of the ear lowered;' but if the sense *niścala* be insisted on, translate—'having the ears immovably erect.'

1. 'Truly, the horses are [or appear as if] outstripping the horses of the Sun, and the horses of Indra,' *i.e.,* the speed of the chariot seems like that of the Wind and the Sun; for Indra, as god of the firmament presides over the forty-nine *martus* or winds. Such seems to be the sense of the passage. *Hariot* is taken by to be the genitive case of *harit,* 'the sun,' and *harīn* as the acc. case plural of *hari,* 'a horse.' But the *ca* after *harīn* indicates that both *harito* and *harīn* are acc. cases after *atītya.* The interpretation I have given rests on the authority of the Ṛgveda, where we find *harī'* in the dual, and *harayaḥ* and *haribhiḥ* in the plural [I. 16, 1; 101, 10; 16, 4; 52, 8] for 'the horses of Indra;' and *haritaḥ* in the plural for 'the seven horses of Sūrya or the Sun' [I. 50, 8; 115, 4]. In the Nirukta [i. 15] the different vehicles of the gods are given, and among them *harī Indrasya, haritaḥ ādityasya.* Hence, Indra is called *hari-haya* or *hari-vāhana* [Vikramorvaśī, Act 3], or in the Ṛgveda, *hari-yojana;* and the Sun is called *haridnaśva.* One of the name of the Sun is *saptāśva* 'having seven horses.' The Bengālī MSS. read *katham atītya hariṇaṁ harayo,* etc., but the *harito harīnśca* is supported by all the Devanāgarī MSS., and by a parallel passage in the beginning of the Vikramorvaśīya, *anena ratha-vegena vainateyam api āsādayeyam.*

2. 'That which in my sight (appeared) minute suddenly attains magnitude; that which was divided in half becomes as if united; that also which is by nature [really] crooked (appears) eve-lined

---

Verse 9. *Śikhariṇī* (a variety of the *Atyaṣṭi*) containing seventeen syllables to the half-line, each half-line being alike.

◡ — — — — — | ◡ ◡ ◡ ◡ ◡ — — ◡ ◡ ◡ — ||

सूत :। पश्यैनं व्यापाद्यमानं (इति शरसन्धानं नाट्यति)

नेपथ्ये। भो भो राजन्। आश्रममृगोऽयं न हन्तव्यो न हन्तव्यः।

सूत : [आकर्ण्यावलोक्य च] आयुष्मन्। अस्य खलु ते वाणपथवर्तिनः कृष्णसारस्यान्तरे तपस्विन उपस्थिताः।

राजा : (ससम्भ्रमं) तेन हि प्रगृह्यन्तां वाजिनः।

सूत : तथा (इति रथं स्थापयति)

[ततः प्रविशत्यात्मनातृतीयो[1] वैखानसः]

वैखानसः : (हस्तम् उद्यम्य) राजन्। आश्रममृगोऽयं न हन्तव्यो न हन्तव्यः।

[straight] to my eyes. Nothing (seems) at a distance from me nor at my side even for a moment, by reason of the velocity of the chariot.' This is a method of describing great velocity of motion, which may be well appreciated by any one, in these days, who may have taken notice of the effect produced upon adjacent objects by an express railway speed of a mile a minute. A building which as seen in the distance has several divisions, seems to combine into one solid whole when we are suddenly brought to look at it from another point of view, it separate parts being hidden behind each other. Again, an object which has in reality a crooked or irregular outline when close to one's side, will assume more evenness and regularity of shape we have left it at a distance.

1. 'With himself as the third,' or 'with himself making the third,' *i.e.*, himself and two others. This is a remarkable compound not unusual in Sanskrit. Compare *Pāṇḍavā mātṛ-ṣaṣṭāḥ*, 'the Pāṇḍavas with their mother as the sixth,' *i.e.*, five persons, or six counting their mother. [Hid. i. 1, Bopp.] Again, *chāyā-dvitīyo Nala,*'Nala made two by his shadow,' 'umbra-geminatus' [Nala, Bopp, ch. v, 26.] Also, *adhīte caturo vedān ākhyāna-pañcamān*, 'he reads the four Vedas with the *ākhyānas* as a fifth' [Nala, vi., 9]. A very similar idiom prevails in Greek, αντοδ being used after ordinal numbers to show that one person in conjunction with some others, whose number is less by one than the number mentioned, has done something : thus, πεμπτοδ αντοδ, 'himself with four ohers.' [Thucydides, I. xlvi] The τριτον ηριτον ημτāλαϖτον 'two talents and a half,' and ἑβΔομιτάλαντοϖ 'six talents and a half' of Herodotus [I. 15, 50] afford a further illustration of this idiom.

न खलु न खलु वाणः सन्निपात्योऽयम् अस्मिन्
मृदुनि मृगशरीरे पुष्पराशाव् इवाग्निः ।
क्व वत हरिणकानां जीवितं चातिलोलं
क्व च निशितनिपाताः वज्रसाराः शरास् ते[1] ।। 10 ।।

1. 'Not indeed, not indeed must this arrow (of thine) be allowed to descend upon this tender body of the deer, like fire upon a heap of flowers. Where, forsooth, on the one hand [*ca*], is the very frail existence of fawns? and where, on the other, are thy sharp-falling adamantine shafts?' *i.e.*, Where is the suitability or congruity between the one and the other? What has one got to do with the other? How great a contrast or difference is there between the one and the other! Let not your shafts waste their strength upon an object so frail and tender, but let them be directed towards a mark more fitted to prove their adamantine qualities. This repetition of *kva* to express great contrast or unsuitability between two things is very remarkable. It is used by Kālidāsa again at the end of the second Act of this play *kva vayam*, etc.; also in the fifth verse of the Meghadūta, thus,—'Where is a cloud which is a collection of vapour, fire, water, and wind? and where the meaning of messages to be received by intelligent mortals?' *i.e.*, Why deliver a message intended for intelligent human beings to a cloud? What possible connection can there be between objects whose nature is so different?—A very good example of this use of *kva* also occurs in the second line of the Raghuvaṁśa, 'Where is the race sprung from the sun? and where my scanty powers of mind? (In attempting the history of this race) I am foolishly about to cross the trackless ocean in a small boat.' This idiom is imitated in Telugu [see Morris' Selections, Story 39]: 'Where is the lake Mānasa? and where art thou?' *i.e.*, What hast thou to do with the lake Mānasa? What connection can there possibly be between you?—The majority of MSS. read *puṣpa-rāśau:* I cannot agree in preferring *tūla-rāśau*, for the very reason that cotton is more susceptible of fire than flowers, and there would be less of incongruity in throwing fire upon the former than upon the latter.

Verse 10. *Mālinī* or *Māninī* (a variety of Ati-*Śakkarī* or *Ati-Śarkarī*) containing fifteen syllables to the half-line, each half-line being alike.

◡◡◡◡◡◡——|—◡——◡——||

तत् साधु कृतसन्धानं प्रतिसंहर सायकं।
आर्त्तत्राणाय वः शस्त्रं न प्रहर्तुम् अनागसि[1] ।। 11 ।।

राजा : एष प्रतिसंहृतः (इति यथोक्तं करोति)

वैखानसः : सदृशम् एतत् पुरुवंशप्रदीपस्य भवतः।[2]

1. 'Therefore, replace (in the quiver) your well-aimed (*lit.*, well fitted to the bow], arrow. Your weapon is for the deliverance of the distressed, not to inflict a wound on the innocent.' *Sandhā* is properly 'to unite or fix an arrow to a bow,' hence 'to take aim' [Draup. Har., 149]; and *sandhānam*, 'the act of takng aim.' *Prahartum* is here used where *praharaṇaya* might be expected, but the infinitive is interchangeable with the dative, and generally has the force of that case.

2. 'This is worthy of your honour, who art the light of the race of Puru,' *i.e.*, an illustrious descendant of Puru. Compare in the beginning of the Vikramorvaśī, *sadṛśam idaṁ soma-vaṁśa-saṁbhavasya.* In English we have the same idiom, 'this is just like [*i.e.*, worthy of] one born in the Lunar race.' The two great lines or dynasties of kings according to Hindū mythology were the Solar and the Lunar. The Solar begins with Ikṣvāku the son of Vaivasvata, the son of Vivasvata, or the Sun, and is carried on through Kakutstha, Dilīpa, Raghu, Aja, and Daśaratha, to his son the great Rāma-candra, hero of the Rāmāyaṇa. Under the Lunar come Puru and Duṣyanta, and some of the most celebrated heroes and demi-gods, as—1. Soma; 2. his son, Buddha; 3. his son, Purūravas; 4. his son, Āyus; 5. his son, Nahuṣa; 6. his son, Yayāti; 7. his sons, Puru and Yadu. From Puru were edescended Taṁsu, Anila, Duṣyanta and Bharata. From his brother Yadu came Satvata, Śura, Vasudeva, and his sons Balarāma and Kṛṣṇa. From Bharata the son of Duṣyanta and descendant of Puru, came after a time Ajamiḍha, Saṁvaraṇa, Kuru, Śāntanu, Bhīṣhma, and Kṛṣṇadvaipāyana or Vyāsa. The latter was the father of Dhṛtarāṣtra and Pāṇḍu. The quarrels of the hundred sons of Dhṛtarāṣṭra with their cousins the five sons of Pāṇḍu (all of them being thus descended from Kuru and Puru) form the subject of the Mahābhārata, the great poem said to have been written by the father of Pāṇḍu and recited to his great-great-grandson Janamejaya. These two separate lines were, however,

Verse 11. *Śloka* or *Anuṣṭubh*. (*See* Verse 5.)

जन्म यस्य पुरोर् वंशे युक्तरूपम् इदं तव।
पुत्रम् एवं गुणोपेतं चक्रवर्तिनम्[1] आप्नुहि।। 12।।

इतरौ : (बाहू उद्यम्य) सर्वथा चक्रवर्तिनं पुत्रम् आप्नुहि।

राजा : (सप्रणामं) प्रतिगृहीतं।[2]

वैखानसः : राजन्। समिदाहरणाय[3] प्रस्थिता वयं। एष खलु कण्वस्य महर्षेर् उपमालिनीतीरम् आश्रमो दृश्यते। न चेद् अन्तकार्यातिपातस्[4] तत् प्रविश्य प्रतिगृह्यताम् आतिथेयः सत्कारः। अपि च–

रम्यास् तपोधनानां प्रतिहतविघ्नाः क्रियाः समवलोक्य।
ज्ञास्यसि कियद् भुजो मे रक्षति मौर्वीकिणाङ्क इति[5] ।। 13।।

occasionally intermixed by marriage, and a cross occurs at the very beginning, by the marriage of Ilā, daughter of Vaivasvata, with Budha. Paraśurāma, as a Brāhmaṇa, belonged to neither dynasty, but was connected with the Solar on his mother's side : he is said to have destroyed the whole Kṣatriya race (*see* the note to verse 22).

1. A *cakravartī*, an universal emperor, a monarch reigning over a *cakra*, or country reaching from sea to sea. According to the Viṣṇu-Purāṇa, a *cakravartī* is one in whose hand the *cakra*, or discus of Viṣṇu, is delineated. There have been twelve of these emperors, commencing with Bharata, the son of Duṣyanta.

2. This is the usual exclamation which serves to ratify any auspicious prayer or prophecy uttered by a Brāhmaṇa. *Brāhmaṇa. Brāhmaṇa-vacas* may be supplied; 'the word of a Brāhmaṇa is accepted.' *See* the same phrase in the Vikramorvaśī, Act 2.

3. Compare Raghuvaṁśa, xiv, 70; i. 49.

4. 'If it be not (the cause of) the neglect of any other duty,' or 'if it does not interfere with the discharge of any other duty.'

5. 'Beholding the pleasing rites of the hermits, all the hindrances to which are warded off (by you), you will think to yourself, how much this arm of mine, marked with the scar of the bow-string,

---

Verse 12. *Śloka* or *Anuṣṭubh*. (*See* Verse 5.)
Verse 13. *Āryā* or *Gāthā*. (*See* Verse 2.)
—— |◡—◡|——‖◡◡◡◡|——|◡—◡|◡◡—|—
—◡◡|◡—◡|——‖ —◡◡ |——| ◡ |—◡◡|◡

राजा : अपि सन्निहितोऽत्र कुलपतिः।

वैखानसः : इदानीम् एव दुहितरं शकुन्तलाम् अतिथिसत्काराय नियुज्य दैवम् अस्याः प्रतिकूलं शमयितुं सोमतीर्थं[1] गतः।

राजा : भवतु। तां द्रक्ष्यामि। सा खलु विदितभक्तिं मां महर्षेः करिष्यति।

वैखानसः : साधयामस् तावत् (इति सशिष्यो निष्क्रान्तः)।

राजा : सूत। चोदयाश्वान्। पुण्याश्रमदर्शनेन तावद् आत्मानं पुनीमहे।

सूत : यद् आज्ञापयत्यायुष्मान्। (इति भूयो रथवेगं निरूपयति)

राजा : (समन्ताद् अवलोक्य) सूत। अकथितोऽपि ज्ञायत एव यथायस् आभोगम्[2] तपोवनस्येति।

defends!' *Tapo-dhana* 'a devotee,' or one rich in devotion. A parallel passage occurs in Raghuvaṁśa, xviii, 47, 'the earth was preserved by his arm, though without the mark of the scar formed by the bow-string' (*abaddha-maurvī-kiṇa-lāñcūanena*). The ancient Hindu's extracted from the leaves of the Mūrvā plant (Aletris) very tough, elastic threads, with which they made their bow-strings [*maurvī*], and which for that reason, were ordained by Manu to form the girdle or zone of the military or Kṣatriya class. Manu, II., 42.

1. *Soma-tīrtha* is a place of pilgrimage in the West of India, on the coast of Gujarat, near the temple of Somanātha. It is also called Prabhāsa. The fable is that Soma, or the Moon, was here cured of the consumption brought upon him by the imprecation of Dakṣa, his father-in-law [Mahābhārata, vol. iii., p. 249; Viṣṇu Purāṇa, p. 561.] A *tīrtha* is a place of pilgrimage, generally fixed on the bank of some sacred stream, especially the Ganges; or in the vicinity of some holy spring. The word is derived from *tṛ*, 'to cross,' or 'pass over,' implying that the stream has to be passed through, either for the washing away of sin, or for extrication from some difficulty or adverse destiny. Thousands of devotees still flock to the most celebrated *tīrthas*, Varanasi, Haridvāra, *etc.*

2. The sense of *ābhoga* which is required here, has not been fixed in the dictionary. The commentators explain it by *vistāra*, 'extension,' 'breadth, 'amplitude.' One of them [Kāṭavema] gives an additional synonym, *paripūrṇatā*, 'fulness,' 'completion,' 'satiety.' Śaṅkara, in explaining the word *pariṇāha* in the sense of 'circumference,' gives *ābhoga* as a synonym. *Ābhoga* occurs in the Meghadūta [verse 90] in

सूत : कथमिव।

राजा : किं न पश्यति भवान्। इह[1] हि–

नीवाराः शुकगर्भकोटरमुखभ्रष्टास् तरूणाम् अधः
प्रस्निग्धाः क्वचिद् इङ्गुदीफलभिदः सूच्यन्त एवोपलाः।
विश्वासोपगमाद् अभिन्नगतयः शब्दं सहन्ते मृगास्
तोयाधारपथाश्च वल्कलशिखानिष्यन्दरेखाङ्किताः।। 14।।

the compound *gaṇḍābhoga* which is explained by *kapola-maṇḍalam*, 'the orb or circumference of the cheek;' and by *gaṇḍa-sthalam*, 'the region or neighbourhood of the cheek'. In Wilson's Dictionary *stanābhoga* occurs, and is said to mean 'a man with a round or full breast.' In Śaṅkara's commentary this very compound is used for 'fulness or roundness of breast.' Doubtless, the first meaning of *ābhoga* is 'enjoyment,' or (*adhikaraṇe*) 'the place or seat of enjoyment;' thence it passes into the sense 'fulness;' thence into 'roundness,' circumference;' and thence into 'circuit,' 'surrounding district,' 'region,' etc. Hence, it is clear that *ābhoga* must here mean 'the land stretching out in the neighbourhood of the sacred grove,' 'the district, grounds, or region surrounding it,' 'the domain or demesne.' Translate, 'Even without being told, it may be known indeed that this is the circuit [domain] of the sacred grove;' of 'that here (begins) the expanse [area] of the sacred grove;' or 'that these are the grounds of the sacred grove.'

1. 'For here are the (grains of) wild-rice beneath the trees, fallen from the mouths [openings] of the hollow-trunks [*koṭara*] filled with parrots; in other places the polished stones (used) for bruising the fruit of the *Iṅgudī* are plainly observed; the fawns too with undeviating step [*i.e.*, not starting aside] from having acquired confidence, bear the sound (of the voice); and the paths of the reservoirs are marked with lines by the drippings from the ends of the bark-clothes.' *Mukha* may be used for the mouth or opening of anything, as the hollow of a tree. *Garbha*, as the last member of a compound, often denotes 'filled with,' as *cūrṇa-garbhā nāḍiḥ*, 'a tube filled with powder.' The *Iṅgudī*, commonly called *Iṅgua* or *Jiyaputa*,

Verse 14. *Śārdūlavikrīḍita* (variety of Atidhṛti) containing nineteen syllables to the half-line, each half-line being alike.

— — — ◡ ◡ — ◡ — ◡ ◡ ◡ — | — — ◡ — — ◡ — ||

अपिच।

> कुल्याम्भोभिः पवनचपलैः शाखिनो धौतमूला
> भिन्नो रागः किसलयरुचाम् आज्यधूमोद्गमेन।
> एते चार्वाग् उपवनभुवि च्छिन्नदर्भाङ्कुरायां
> नष्टाशङ्का हरिणशिशवो मन्दमन्दं चरन्ति[1] ।। 15 ।।

is a tree from the fruit of which necklaces were made of a supposed prolific efficacy; whence the botanical name *Nagelia putran-jīva* or *jīva-putraka* [Rox.] In the Raghu-vaṁśa (xiv., 81) there is an allusion to the fruit being used by hermits to supply oil for lamps, and in Act 2 to its furnishing them with ointment. The synonym for the tree in the Amarakoṣa is *tāpasa-taru*, 'the anchorite's tree.' Śaṅkara calls it *muni-pādapa. Abhinna-gati* may also be translated 'not running away,' literally, 'not going apart or in a different direction.' Kāṭavema explains it by *avihata-gati*, 'not interrupted in their walk.' This meaning at least is suggested by *abhinna-svarı*, 'one who does not hesitate in speaking.' The sense of the last line is settled by a passage at the end of this act, where the dust is described as falling 'on the bark dresses, moist with water, hung up (to dry) on the branches of trees [*viṭapa-viṣakta-jalārdra-valkaleṣu*]. In carrying these dresses from the reservoir to the trees, a line would be formed by the drippings from the corners. [*śikhā=añchala* Schol.]

1. 'The trees have their roots washed by the waters of canals, tremulous in the wind; the tint of (those trees which are) bright with fresh-sprouts is diversified [partially obscured] by the rising of the smoke of the clarified butter (burnt in oblations); and in front, these young fawns, free from timidity, leisurely graze on the lawn of the garden, where the stalks of *darbha*-grass have been mown.' The Commentators explain *bhinna*, by *anyathā-bhūta*, 'altered,' 'made different;' but it may also mean 'broken,' 'interrupted,' 'partially obscured.' *Arvāk=agratas* 'in front,' 'near.' *Darbha* is another name for *kuśa* or sacrificial grass (*Poa cynosuroides*). This was the sacred plant or holy grass among the Hindūs, as was verbena among the Romans. In preparing the ground for a sacrifice

---

Verse 15. *Mandākrāntā* (variety of *Atyaṣṭi*) containing seventeen syllables to the half-line, each half-line being alike. This is the metre of the Meghadūta.

— — — — | ⏑ ⏑ ⏑ ⏑ ⏑ ⏑ — | — ⏑ — — ⏑ — ⏓ ||

सूत : सर्वम् उपपन्नम्।

राजा : (स्तोकम् अन्तरं गत्वा) तपोवनवासिनाम् उपरोधो मा भूत्। अत्रैव तावद् रथं स्थापय। यावद् अवतरामि।

सूत : धृताः प्रग्रहाः। अवतरत्वायुष्मान्।

राजा : (अवतीर्य) सूत। विनीतवेषेण[1] प्रवेष्टव्यानि तपोवनानि नाम। इदं तावद् गृह्यतां।। इति सूतस्याभरणानि धनुश्चोपनीय अर्पयति।। सूत। यावद् अहम् आश्रमवासिनः प्रत्यवेक्ष्योपावर्ते। तावद् आर्द्रपृष्ठाः क्रियन्तां वाजिनः[2]।

सूत : तथा (इति निष्क्रान्तः)।

राजा : (परिक्रम्यावलोक्य च) इदम् आश्रमद्वारं। यावत् प्रविशामि (प्रविश्य निमित्तं[3] सूचयन्)।

it was necessary to strew it with the blades of this grass. The officiating Brāhmaṇas were purified by sitting on it, and by rubbing it between their hands. Its sanctifying qualities were very various, see Manu, ii, 43, 75, 182; iii, 208, 223, 255, 256; iv, 36; v, 115; xi, 149; and Viṣṇu Purāṇa, p. 106. The leaves of this grass are very long, with tapering points of which the extreme acuteness is proverbial among the Hindūs; whence the expression *kuśāgra-buddhi* [Raghuvaṁśa, v., 4] 'a person whose intellects are as sharp as the point of a *kuśa*-leaf.' Sir W. Jones quotes a passage from the Atharva-veda, in which this grass is addressed as a god. 'Thee, O Darbha! the learned proclaim a divinity, not subject to age or death; thee they call the armour of Indra, the preserver of regions, the destroyer of enemies,' etc. vol. v., p. 79. According to the Commentators this verse and the last afford an example of the *anumānālaṅkāra*, or figure called 'Inference.'

1. Compare Manu, viii, 2.

2. Literally, 'let the horses be made wet-backed,' *i.e.*, let them be watered and refreshed. Let their fatigue be removed by giving them water and by rubbing their backs. [Śaṅkara.]

3. 'Acting an omen,' or 'acting as if he observed an omen,' literally, 'manifesting a sign.' *Nimittam* is any omen or sign, such as the throbbing of the arm or eyelid. If this was felt on the right side it was a good omen in men; if on the left, a bad omen. The reverse was true of women.

शान्तम् इदम् आश्रमपदं स्फुरति च बाहुः कुतः फलम् इहास्य।
अथवा भवितव्यानां द्वाराणि भवन्ति सर्वत्र[1] ।। 16 ।।

नेपथ्ये : इदो इदो सहीओ।

नेपथ्ये : इत इतः सख्यौ।

राजा : (कर्णं दत्त्वा) अये। दक्षिणेन[2] वृक्षवाटिकाम् आलाप इव श्रूयते। यावद् अत्र गच्छामि (परिक्रम्यावलोक्य च) अये। एताम् तपस्विकन्यकाः स्वप्रमाणानुरूपैः सेचनघटैर्[3] बालपादपेभ्यः पयो दातुम् इत एवाभिवर्तन्ते (निरूप्य) अहो मधुरम् आसां दर्शनम्।

शुद्धान्तदुर्लभम् इदं वपुर् आश्रमवासिनो यदि जनस्य।
दूरीकृताः खलु गुणैर् उद्यानलता वनलताभिः[4] ।। 17 ।।

1. 'This hermitage is tranquil, [*i.e.*, a peaceful spot, undisturbed by passion or emotion] and yet my arm throbs; whence can there be any result of this in such a place? But yet the gates of destiny are everywhere.' A quivering sensation in the right arm was supposed to prognosticate union with a beautiful woman. See Raghuvaṁśa, xii, 90. Bhaṭṭi, i, 27, Vikramorvaśīya, Act 2.

2. 'To the right of the grove of trees.' *Dakṣiṇena* governs the acc. case as well as the genitive. See Pāṇini, ii, 3, 31; and v., 3, 35.

3. 'With watering-pots (of a size) proportioned to their strength,' or 'with watering-pots suited to their size,' *i.e.*, not too large for a woman to carry.

4. 'If this (beautiful) figure of people living in a hermitage is rarely met with [of difficult to be found] in the inner apartments of palaces [*i.e.*, in harmas], then indeed the shrubs of the garden are distanced in good qualities [in beauties] [left behind, surpassed] by the (wild) shrubs of the forest.' Sir W. Jones translates, 'the garden-flowers must make room for the blossoms of the forest, which excel them in colour and fragrance.' The *Śuddhānta* is the *antaḥpura* or 'inner suite of apartments, appropriated to women;'

Verse 16. *Āryā* or *Gāthā*. (*See* Verse 2.)
— ⏑ ⏑ | ⏑ — ⏑ | ⏑ ⏑ — ‖ ⏑ ⏑ ⏑ ⏑ | — — | ⏑ — ⏑ | ⏑ ⏑ — | ⏑
⏑ ⏑ — | ⏑ ⏑ — | — — ‖ — — | ⏑ ⏑ — | ⏑ | — — | ⏑

Verse 17. *Āryā* or *Ghāthā* . (*See* Verse 2.)
— — | ⏑ — ⏑ | ⏑ ⏑ — ‖ ⏑ ⏑ — | ⏑ ⏑ — | ⏑ — ⏑ | ⏑ ⏑ — | ⏑
— — | ⏑ — ⏑ | ⏑ ⏑ — ‖ — — | ⏑ ⏑ — | ⏑ | ⏑ ⏑ — | —

यावद् इमां छायाम् आश्रित्य प्रतिपालयामि (इति विलोकयन् स्थितः)

[ततः प्रविशति यथोक्तव्यापारा[1] सह सखीभ्यां शकुन्तला]

शकुन्तला : इदो इदो सहीओ।

शकुन्तला : इत इतः सख्यौ।

अनसूया : हला सउन्दले। तुवत्तोबि तादकस्सबस्स अस्सम रुक्खआ

अनसूया : हला शकुन्तले। त्वत्तोऽपि तातकाश्यपस्य आश्रम वृक्षाः

पिअदरेत्ति तक्केमि। जेण णोमालिआकुसुमपेलवाबि तुम एदाणं

प्रियतरा इति तर्कयामि। येन नवमालिकाकुसुमपेलवापि[2] त्वम् एतेषाम्

आलवालपूरणे णिउत्ता।

आलवालपूरणे[3] नियुक्ता।

शकुन्तला : हला अणसूए। ण केवलं तादणिओओ एव्व। अत्थि मे

शकुन्तला : हला अनसूये। न केवलं तातनियोग एव। अस्ति मे

सोदरमिणेहोबि एदेसु (इति वृक्षमेक्षमं निरूपयति)।

सोदरस्नेहोऽपि एतेषु (इति वृक्षसेचनं निरूपयति)।

राजा : कथम् इयं सा कण्वदुहिता। असाधुदर्शी खलु तत्रभवान् काश्यपः। य इमाम् आश्रमधर्मे नियुंक्ते।[4]

called also the *avarodha* or 'private quarter,' shut out from the rest of the house and strictly guarded. *Haram* is the equivalent Arabic word.

1. 'Occupied in the manner described.' An elegant Bahuvrīhi compound.

2. *Mālikā* or *mallikā is* a kind of double jasmine with large flowers, sometimes called 'Arabian jasmine' (*Jasminum zambac*); from its delicious perfume, and abundant nectar, much frequented by bees. See Raghuvaṁśa, xvi, 47.

3. *Ālavāla*, 'the basin for water round the root of a tree.' [Raghuvaṁśa, i, 51.] See also Vikramorvaśīya, end of Act 2 [*taror mūlālavālam.*]

4. 'Truly his reverence Kāśyapa is (a man) of little discrimination, inasmuch as he appoints her to the duties (manner of life) of the hermitage (*i.e.*, imposes upon her a hermitage-life; a mode of life such as is usual in a hermitage].' The sage Kaṇva is here called 'a descendant of Kāśyapa.' As a sage and Brāhmaṇa he might especially claim this celebrated personage as his progenitor; but

इदं कि किलाव्यजमनोहरं वपुस्
तप:क्षमं साधयितुं य इच्छति।
ध्रुवं स नीलोत्पलपत्रधारया
शमीलतां छेत्तुम् ऋषिर् व्यवस्यति[1] ।। 18 ।।

भवतु। पादपान्तरित एव विश्वस्तां तावद् एनां पश्यामि (इति तथा करोति)।

शकुन्तला : सहि अणसूए। अहिपिणद्धेण बक्कलेण पिअंवदाए णिअन्तिदम्हि। सिढिलेहि दाव णं।

शकुन्तला : सखि अनसूये। अतिपिनद्धेन वल्कलेन प्रियंवदया नियन्त्रितास्मि। शिथिलय तावद् एनम्।

अनसूया : तह (इति शिथिलयति)।

अनसूया : तथा (इति शिथिलयति)।

Kāśyapa, who was the son of Marīci (who was the son of Brahmā, and one of the seven Prajāpatis] was a progenitor on rather a magnificent scale, as he is considered to have been the father of the gods, demons, man, fish, reptiles, and all animals, by Aditi, and twelve other daughters of Dakṣa. He is supposed by some to be a personification of the race who took refuge in the central Asiatic chain, in which traces of his name may be found, as Koh-kas (or Caucasus), the Capian, Kashmir, etc., [Wilson's Hindū Theatre, vol. ii, p. 12).

1. 'The sage who expects to make this artlessly-charming form capable of (enduring) penance, certainly attempts to cut a branch of the hard *śamī* wood with the edge of the blue lotus-leaf.' *Avyāja-manoharam* 'that which captivates without art or ornament,' 'naturally beautiful.' For an account of the different orders of Ṛsis or sages, see the word 'saint' in the English and Sanskrit Dictionary. The *śamī* tree is a kind of Acacia (*Acacia suma*), the wood of which is very hard, and supposed by the Hindūs to contain Fire. *[śamī abhyantara-līna-pāvakā,* Raghuvaṁśa, iii, 9, see also Manu, viii., 247.] The Hindūs employ it to kindle their sacred fire by rubbing two dreid pieces together. The legend is that Purūravas generated primeval fire, by rubbing together two branches of the Śamī and Aśvattha tree. [Wilson's Hindū Theatre, p. 190.]

Verse 18. *Vaṁśasthavila* (variety of *Jagatī*) containing twelve syllables to the half-line, each half-line being alike.

◡ — ◡ — — ◡ ◡ — ◡ — ◡ — ||

प्रियंवदा : (सहासं) एत्थ पओहरवित्थारइत्तअं अत्तणो जोव्वणं उबालह।
प्रियंवदा : (सहासं) अत्र पयोधरविस्तारयितृकं आत्मनो यौवनम् उपालभस्व।
मं किं उबालम्भेसि।
मां किम् उपालभसे।
राजा : सम्यग् इयम् आह–

इदम् उपहितसूक्ष्मग्रन्थिना स्कन्धदेशे
स्तनयुगपरिणाहाच्छादिना वल्कलेन।
वपुर् अभिनवम् अस्याः पुष्यति स्वां न शोभां
कुसुमम् इव पिनद्धं पाण्डुपत्रोदरेण[1] ।। 19 ।।

अथवा कामम् अननुरूपम् अस्या वपुषो वल्कलं। न पुनर् अलङ्कारश्रियं न पुष्यति।[2]
कुतः–

1. 'This blooming [or youthful] body of hers, by (reason of) the bark dress fastened with delicate knots upon her shoulder (and) covering the orbs of her two breasts, does not exhibit (the fulness of) its own charms, like a flower enveloped by a calyx of brown leaves.' The first meaning of *push*, like *bhṛ*, is 'to nourish, or be nourished.' Thence, like *bhṛ*, it passes into the sense of 'maintain,' 'support,' 'bear'' and thence into that of 'possess,' 'enjoy,' 'exhibit,' 'make to appear.' In these last senses it may be used actively, though in the 4th conjugation. [See Manu, ix, 37. Rāmāyaṇa, ii, 94, 10. Raghuvaṁśa, xvi., 58. Mahābhārata, vol. ii, p. 186, 2607.] It is curious that our English word *exhibition* may have the sense of 'maintenance' (*Cf.* latin *exhibeo*). Two Mumbai MSS. read *svābhikhyām* instead of *svām na śobhām:* the meaning would then be 'maintains its own beauty' [*abhikyā* is so used, Raguvaṁśa, i, 46]; and this reading would be more consistent with what follows, but by the next word *athavā,* as the Commentators observe, *svoktam ākṣipati,* he corrects his previous remark.

2. 'Or rather, granted that the bark-dress be ill suited to her figure, yet it does not not [*i.e.*, it really does] possess the charm of an embellishment;' or less literally, 'it really does act as an embellishment to set off the beauty of her person.' This is not the only instance to be found in Kālidāsa of two negatives employed to strengthen an affirmative. See Meghadūta, 106.

Verse 19. *Mālinī* or *Māninī* (variety of *Ati-Śakkarī*). *See* Verse 10.

सरसिजम् अनुविद्धं शैवलेनापि रम्यं
मलिनम् अपि हिमांशोर् लक्ष्म लक्ष्मीं तनोति।
इयम् अधिकमनोज्ञा वल्कलेनापि तन्वी
किमिव हि मधुराणां मण्डनं नाकृतीनाम्[1] ।। 20 ।।

शकुन्तला : (अग्रतोऽवलोक्य) एसो वादेरिदपल्लवङ्गुलीहिं तुवरेदि

शकुन्तला : (अग्रतोऽवलोक्य) एष वातेरितपल्लवाङ्गुलीभिस् त्वरयाति।

1. 'The lotus, though intertwined [or overspread] with the *śaivala* is charming; the speek, though dark, heightens [*lit.*, extends] the beauty of the moon; this graceful one even with her bark-dress is more lovely; for what is not an embellishment of sweet forms? [*i.e.*, everything serves as an ornament to heighten the beauty of a figure which is naturally beautiful.'] *Sarasi-jam*, *lit.*, 'that which is born in a pool,' a name applicable to any aquatic plant, but especially to the different kinds of lotus (*Nelumbium* or *Nymphaea*). This beautiful plant—the varieties of which, blue, white, and red, are numerous, bears some resemblance to our water-lily. It is as favourite a subject of allusion and comparison with the Hindū poets, as the rose with the Persian. It is often figuratively used to express beauty, as 'lotus-face,' or the 'lotus of the face,' 'lotus-hands,' 'lotus-feet' [Git. Gov. *passim*]. It is also used by women as an ornament [Act 3 of this play], and as a cooling remedy [Ratnāvalī, Act 2]. The Śaivala (Vallisneria) is an aquatic plant which spreads itself over ponds, and interweaves itself with the lotus. The interlacing of its stalks is compared in the Śṛṅgāra-tilaka (verse i) to braided hair (*dhammilla*). *See* Sir W. Jones' Works, vol. iv, p. 113. The spots on the moon were thought to resemble those on an antelope, and hence one of the moon's names, *hariṇa-kalaṅka* 'deer-spotted.'

The following verse, which is found in the Bengālī MSS. immediately after verse 20, and has been adopted by the Kolkata edition, is omitted in all the Devanāgarī MSS., and in the commentaries of Śaṅkara and Kāṭavema. It is probably spurious, as it repeats the same sentiment with much harshness and some obscurity of expression :—

Verse 20. *Mālinī* or *Māninī* (variety of *Ati-Śakkarī*.) *See* Verse 10.

विअ मं केसररुक्खओ। जावणं सम्भावेमि (इति परिक्रामति)

इव मां केशरवृक्षकः। यावद् एनं सम्भावयामि[1] (इति परिक्रामति)।

प्रियंवदा : हला सउन्दले। एत्थ एव्व दाव मुहुत्तअं चिट्ठ।

प्रियंवदा : हला शकुन्तले। अत्र एव तावन् मुहूर्तं तिष्ठ।

शकुन्तला : किणिमित्तं।

शकुन्तला : किन्निमित्तं।

प्रियंवदा : जाव तुए उबगदाए लदासणाहो विअ अअं केसररुक्खओ।

प्रियंवदा : यावत् त्वया उपगतया लतासनाथ[2] इव अयं केशरवृक्षकः।

कठिनमपि मृगाक्ष्या वल्कलं कान्तरूपं
न मनसि रुचिभङ्गं स्वल्पम् अप्यादधाति।
विकचसरसिजायाः स्तोकनिर्मुक्तकण्ठं
निजम् इव कमलिन्याः कर्कशं वृन्तजालम्।।

'The bark-dress though rough, is beautiful on this fawn-eyed one. It does not in one's mind cause the slightest impairment of her beauty [or, of my liking for her]; just as its own rough tissue of stalks on the lotus-bed whose lotuses have expanded, so as slightly to release the neck-of-the-flower' [*i.e.*, the pedicle, or that part of the stalk immediately under the flower].

1. 'The Keśara-tree, with its fingers of young shoots set in motion by the wind bids me hasten as it were (towards it). I will just go and pay my respects to it.' The Keśara-tree [*Mimuspos elengi*] is the same as the Bakula or Vakula, frequent mention of which is made in some of the Purāṇas, and in the Ratnāvalī [Act 3]. It bears a strong-smelling flower, which, according to Sir W. Jones, is even placed among the flowers of the Hindū paradise. The tree is very ornamental in pleasure-grounds. *Sambhū* in the caus. generally means 'to honour, or pay one's respects to another in person.' Motion towards the object seems usually, though not always, implied. Thus, *sambhāvayāmorājarṣim*, Vikramorvaśīya, Act 1; and Raghuvaṁśa, v, 2; x, 56.

2. 'Possessed of a creeper.' This use of *sa-nātha* is noticeable. The literal meaning of the expression is, 'having a lord or master,' and in this sense it is used towards the end of this Act, where the devotees are said to be *sa-nāthāḥ* 'possessed of a guardian' in

पडिभादि।

प्रतिभाति।

शकुन्तला : अदोक्खु पिअंवदासि तुमं।

शकुन्तला : अतः खलु प्रियंवदासि त्वम्।[1]

राजा : प्रियमपि तथ्यम् आह शकुन्तलां प्रियंवदा। अस्याः खलु–

अधरः किसलयरागः कोमलविटपानुकारिणौ बाहू।
कुसुममिव लोभनीयं यौवनम् अङ्गेषु सन्नद्धम्[2] ।। 21 ।।

Duṣyanta. A compound verb *sa-nāthīkṛ*, 'to cause to be possessed of a master' is also used in the 2nd Act of this play, and in the Hitopadeśa [line 797]. But in the present passage, *sa-nātha* is simply equivalent to *sahita, dvitīya, yukta,* 'accompanied,' 'joined,' 'furnished with.' The transition of the word into such an acceptation may be easily understood by referring to a passage in the 6th. Act of this play, and to a parallel one in the 2nd Act of the Vikramorvaśīya, where the same expression is applied to an arbour (*maṇḍapa*) which is said to be *maṇi-śilāpaṭṭa-sanātha,* 'having a slab of marble as its master,' *i.e.,* 'in which the most prominent and striking object is a marble seat;' or in plain words, 'an arbour furnished with a marble seat.' It is used again similarly in the 2nd Act of this play, where the surface of a stone seat (*śilā-talam*) is said to be *vitāna-sanātham,* 'furnished with a canopy' by the shade of a tree. It occurs twice again in the 4th Act of the Vikramorvaśīya, where the King is said to be *Lakṣmī-sanātha,* 'possessed of Fortune;' and the hair of Urvaśī is said to be *kusuma-sanātha,* 'decked with flowers' and once in the 5th Act, where the youth Āyus is said to be *sanātha* with reference to *dhanurveda*. See also Mālatī-mādhava, p. 58, 1. 2, Meghadūta, verse 97, Mālavikāgnimitra, p. 5, 1. 9.

1. 'Hence most truly art thou (named) Priyaṁvadā,' (*i.e.,* Kindly-speaking). The name is made up of two words—*priyam,* 'what is agreeable,' and *vada,* 'one who speaks.' Chēzy compares the Greek μελιφθογγος.

2. 'Though agreeable (still it is) the truth (that) Priyaṁvadā

Verse 21. *Āryā* or *Ghāthā*. (*See* Verse 2.)

◡◡— |◡◡◡◡|——‖—◡◡| ◡◡—|◡—◡|——|—
◡◡◡◡| ◡—◡ |——‖—◡◡| —— | ◡ |——|—

अनसूया : हला सउन्दले। इअं सअंवरवहू सहआरस्स तुए किदणामहेआ

अनसूया : हला शकुन्तले। इयं स्वयंवरवधू सहकारस्य त्वया कृतनामधेया

वणजोसिणित्ति णोमालिआ। णं विसुमरिदासि।

वनज्योत्स्नेति नवमालिका। एनां विस्मृतासि।[1]

शकुन्तला : तदा अत्ताणम्पि विसुमरिस्सं (लताम् उपेत्यावलोक्य च)

शकुन्तला : तदात्मानमपि विस्मरिष्यामि (लताम् उपेत्यावलोक्य च)

हला। रमणीएक्खु काले इमस्स लदापाअबमिहुणस्स वइअरोसंवुत्तो।

हला। रमणीये खलु कालेऽस्य लतापादपमिथुनस्य व्यतिकर: संवृत्त:।

says to Śakuntalā. Truly her under lip has the colour of a young bud, her two arms resemble flexible stalks. Attractive youth like the blossom pervades her limbs.' *Sannaddham=sarvato vyāpakam.* Schol.

1. 'Here is the young Mālikā [a kind of double jasmine, see page 22, note 2] named by you the Light of the Grove, the self-elected wife of the Sahakāra.' The Sahakāra is a fragrant sort of Mango-tree. Its union with other plants seems a favourite idea with Kālidāsa; for in the Raghu-vaṁśa allusion is made to its marriage with the Phalinī or Priyaṅgu [viii., 60]. It is said to be a great favourite with the bees [Raghu-vaṁśa, vi, 69]. In the Ratnāvalī, p. 11, 1. 7, it has the epithet *maṇḍalāyamāna,* forming a circle.' *Svayaṁvara-vadhū* 'a wife by self-election.' The *Svayaṁvara* or 'selection for one's self,' (*svayam* 'by one's self,' *vara* 'choice') was a form of marriage in which a princess made a free public choice of a husband from a number of assembled suitors. In very early times, the princesses of India seem to have enjoyed this singular privillage. It is not mentioned amongst the forms of marriage in Manu, iii, 21, etc.; but the provision which is made in Manu, ix, 90, proves that a similar custom prevailed at that period. When marriageable, she is there told to wait for three years; and after that time, if she fail to obtain a suitable husband, she is to choose for herself; [*samāna-jāti-guṇaṁ varaṁ svayaṁ vṛṇīta.* Schol.] She is then called *svayaṁvarā.* In the Mahābhārata we have a beautiful account of the *Svayaṃvara* of Damayantī (who chooses Nala), and Draupadī (who chooses Arjuna, p. 52); and in the Raghuvaṁśa, chap. vi, of the *Svayaṁvara* of Indumatī, sister of Bhoja, king of Vidarbha (who chooses Aja, the son of Raghu). See also Nalodaya, i, 30. Even the goddess Lakṣmī

णवकुसुमजोव्वणा वणजोसिणी। बद्धपल्लवदाए उबभोअक्खमो सहसारो।

नवकुसुमयौवना वनज्योत्स्ना। बद्धपल्लवतया उपभोग क्षमः सहकारः।[1]

(इति पश्यन्तो तिष्ठति)

(इति पश्यन्ती तिष्ठति)

प्रियंवदा : (सस्सितं) अणसूए। जाणासि किणिमित्तं सउन्दला

प्रियंवदा : (सस्मितं) अनसूये। जानासि किन्निमित्तं शकुन्तला

वणजोसिणिं अदिमेत्तं पेक्खदित्ति।

वनज्योत्स्नाम् अतिमात्रं प्रेक्षत इति।

अनसूया : णक्खु विभावेमि। कहेहि।

अनसूया : न खलु विभावयामि। कथय।

is said to have exercised this privilege. See the allusion to the *Lakṣmī-svayaṁvara* at the beginning of the 3rd Act of the Vikramorvaśīya.

1. 'At a charming season, indeed, has the union between this pair, the (Mālikā or jasmine) creeper and the (Sahakāra) tree, taken place. The Light of the Grove (has) youthfulness by (its) fresh blossoms, [*i.e.*, its fresh blossoms give it all the bloom of a young bride] and the Sahakāra is capable of enjoyment by reason of (its) young shoots (just) formed.' *Vyatikara* is properly 'mutual action,' 'co-operation;' hence 'union,' 'blending,' 'intertwining,' 'intermingling.' [See Meghadūta, 15] So also *vyatikara-sukham*, 'mutual enjoyment.' The prepositions *vi* and *ati* in composition imply both reciprocity and contrariety : hence, in the Hitopadeśa, line 2319, *vyatikara* signifies 'reverse,' 'turn in affairs.' *Baddha-pallavatayā*, 'by its state of young shoots formed on it.' This is a very idiomatic use of the instrumental case of the abstract noun ending in *tā*, to denote 'by reason of,' 'on account of.' The root *bandh* has often the sense of 'to form,' 'produce;' thus, *badhnanti phalam* [Raghuvaṁśa, xii., 69]. *Drumeṣu svayaṁ phalaṁ baddham* [Kumāra-sam., v. 60]. *Upabhoga-kṣama* is found in the prologue of this play in connection with *grīṣma-samaya* [page 5, note 2], and in the 3rd Act of the Vikramorvaśīya with *avakāśa*. The first meaning of *kṣama* is 'patient,' 'enduring.' In this compound, and many others, it is equivalent to *yogya*, 'fit,' 'capable,' 'suitable;' so *dṛṣṭi-kṣama*, 'capable of being seen,' 'visible.'

प्रियंवदा : जह वणजोसिणी अणुरूबेण पाअबेण सङ्गदा। अबिणाम
प्रियंवदा : यथा वनज्योत्स्ना अनुरूपेण पादपेन सङ्गता। अपि नाम[1]
एव्वं अहम्पि अत्तणो अणुरूबं वरं लहेअंत्ति।
एवम् अहमपि आत्मनोऽनुरूपं वरं लभेयेति।

शकुन्तला : एसो णूणं तुह अत्तगदो मणोरहो (इति कलशम्
शकुन्तला : एष नूनं तव आत्मगतो मनोरथः (इति कलशम्
आवर्जयति)।
आवर्जयति)।

राजा : अपि नाम कुलपतेर् इयम् असवर्णक्षेत्रसम्भवा स्यात्।[2]
अथवा कृतं सन्देहेन।[3]

असंशयं क्षत्रपरिग्रहक्षमा
यद् आर्यम् अस्याम् अभिलाषि मे मनः।

1. *Api nāma*, 'would that.' In this sense it occurs also in the 3rd Act of the Vikramorvaśīya, *api nāma purūravā bhaveyam*, 'would that I were Purūravas!'

2. 'Can this (lady) possibly be sprung from a wife dissimilar in class (to that) of the father of the family.' *Api nāma* is here equivalent to 'may be,' 'can it possibly be,' 'I wonder whether,' expressive of some doubt [*evaṁ sambhāvyate.* Schol.] *Kṣetra=kalatra,* 'a wife;' *asavarna=asamāna-jātīya* 'of a different (and inferior) tribe or caste.' A Brāhmaṇa might marry a Kṣatriyā, *i.e.*, a woman of the military or kingly class next below him [Manu, iii., 13], and the female offspring of such a marriage would belong to the mixed class called *mūrddhābhiṣikta* or *mūrddhāvasikta* 'head-anointed' [Manu, x, 6], and would be a suitable object of affection for a Kṣatriya, who in his kingly character was a *mūrddhābhiṣikta* also. But if Śakuntalā were a pure Brāhmaṇī woman, both on the mother's and father's side, she would be ineligible as the wife of a Kṣatriya [Manu, iii., 13].

3. 'But, have done with [away with] doubt.' *Athavā* is used to correct a previous thought [*pakṣāntare*]. *Kṣtam* when used adverbially is like *alam*, and requires the instrumental case.

सतां हि सन्देहपदेषु वस्तुषु
प्रमाणम् अन्तःकरणप्रवृत्तयः[1] ।। 22 ।।

1. 'Without any doubt she is capable of marriage with a Kṣatriya, since my honourable soul has a longing towards her: for in matters that are subjects of doubt, the tendencies [inclinations, promptings] of the hearts of good men are an authoritative guide (to the truth.') The meaning is, If this damsel be the daughter of a Brāhmaṇa by a Brāhmaṇī or woman of the same caste, then why should I be conscious of such a sudden liking for one whom I could never hope to marry. This feeling of attraction and sympathy would not arise spontaneously in the breast of an honourable man, excepting twoards a legitimate object of affection: for in such matters, the secret prompting [inner voice] of the heart is decisive.' He therefore concludes that she must have been of mixed origin, with some Kṣatriya or regal blood in her veins; and discovers afterwards that she was, in fact, the daughter of the Rājarṣi Viśvāmitra (who was originally of the Kṣatriya or regal tribe) by an Apsarās. Duṣyanta, as a king, belonged of course to the Kṣatriya or military caste. This caste came next to the Brāhmaṇical and according to Manu [i, 87] sprang from the arm of Brahmā. They wore a girdle of *mūrvā* and a sacrificial cord of hemp [Manu, ii, 42, 44], and were entirely concerned with warfare and military affairs. The Mahābhārata relates that they were exterminated 'by Paraśurāma, the representative of the Brāhmaṇical tribe, in revenge for the murder of his father, sage Jamadagni, by the sons of Kārtavīrya. This fable is founded on the historical fact that, at some period or other, struggles, arising out of mutual jealousy of each other's encroachments, took place between the military and sacerdotal classes; and that the former did in the end succumb to the superior power and intelligence of the priests. The example of Viśvāmitra proves that it was possible for a Kṣatriya, by the practice of religious austerities, to raise himself to the rank of a Brāhmaṇa. There are also other anomalies of caste to be found; for the Viṣṇu-Purāṇa makes mention of a number of men, half-warriors, half-priests, Kṣatriyas by birth, and Brāhmaṇas by profession, called

---

Verse 22. *Āryā* or *Ghāthā*. (*See* Verse 2.)

तथापि तत्त्वत एवैनाम् उपलप्स्ये।[1]

शकुन्तला : (ससम्भ्रमं) अम्मो मलिलमेअसम्भमुग्गदो णोमालिअं

शकुन्तला : (ससम्भ्रमं) अहो सलिलसेकसम्भ्रमोद्गतो नवमालिकाम्[2]

उज्झिअ वअणं मे महुअरो अहिवट्टइ (इति भ्रमरबाधां नाटयति)

उज्झित्वा वदनं मे मधुकरो[3]ऽभिवर्तते[4] (इति भ्रमरबाधां नाटयति)

राजा : (सस्पृहं विलोक्य) साधु बाधनमपि रमणीयम् अस्याः[5]

Āṅgirasas or descendants of Aṅgiras, who were said to have sprung from Nabhāga [Viṣṇu Pur., p. 359. Mahābh. Selections, p. 23.] Kings, however, were never chosen from the Brāhmaṇical class, but were properly Kṣatriyas [Manu, vii, 2]; though there was no positive law against their belonging to the two inferior classes of Vaiśyas and Śūdras, or even to the three mixed classes [*Śaṅkaras*] formed by intermarriage with the others, *viz.*, Mūrddhābhiṣiktas, Māhiṣyas and Karaṇas [Manu, x, 6]. One dynasty of kings of the line of Nanda were actually Śūdras, and kept the Kṣatriyas in subjection [Viṣṇu Purāṇa, p. 467.] In fact, the king was but a high officer appointed to train the army, instruct in military exercises, administer justice, and execute the laws. These onerous duties were sufficient to deter the Brāhmaṇas from desiring a rank or privileges which were inconsistent with their love of dignified repose. *Āryam=samaryādam,* 'correct,' 'upright' [Schol.] *Pramāṇam,* 'that by which any thing is measured;' hence, 'a criterion or standard of truth, 'asure guide', an authority *pramākāraṇam*, a cause of true knowledge,' [Schol.]. In this sense it is usually found in the singular number, neuter gender, though in opposition. To a masculine or feminine noun, or even to a noun in the plural number, as here. Thus, also *Vedāḥ pramāṇam* 'the Vedas are an authority.' See also Hitopadeśa, lines 169, and 1465. *Pravṛtti,* 'continuous flow;' hence, 'a course of action,' 'tendency,' 'inclination.'

1. 'Nevertheless [however the suggestions of my heart are to be relied upon]

I will accurately ascertain about her.' *Upalapsye=jñāsye,* 'I will inform myself.' Schol.

2. See note 2, page 22.

3. *Madhukara,* 'a honey-maker,' mellificus, mellifer, *i.e.*, 'a bee.'

4. Literally, 'turns towards,' 'attacks,' 'assaults.'

5. 'Good! even her repulse is charming.'

यतो यतः षट्चरणोऽभिवर्त्तते
ततस् ततः प्रेरितलोललोचना।
विवर्त्तितभ्रूर् इयम् अद्य शिक्षते
भयाद् अकामापि हि दृष्टिविभ्रमम्[1] ।। 23 ।।

अपिच (सासूयमिव)

चलापाङ्गां दृष्टिं स्पृशसि बहुशो वेपथुमतीं
रहस्याख्यायीव स्वनसि मृदु कर्णान्तिकचरः।
करं व्याधुन्वत्याः पिबसि रतिसर्वस्वम् अधरं
वयं तत्त्वान्वेषान् मधुकर हतास् त्वं खलु कृती[2] ।। 24 ।।

1. 'In whichever direction the bee turns towards (her), from that quarter her rolling eye is darted: bending her brows through fear, she is already learning conquettish-movements of the eye even though (as yet) uninfluenced-by-love.' *Yatas* and *tatas* are properly 'whence' and 'thence' *tatas=tasmāt sthānāt*, 'from that place.' Śaṅkara. *Ṣaṭ-caraṇa*, 'a six-footed insect,' 'a bee.' *Dṛṣṭi-vibrama*, 'conquettish play of the eye,' 'amorous or sidelong glances' 'rolling motion of the eyes, indicative of amorous feelings.' [*dṛṣṭi-vilāsa*. Śaṅkara.]

2. 'Thou touchest repeatedly her quivering eye, whose outer-corner moves (playfully); going close to her ear, thou art softly humming as if whispering a secret (of love); thou art drinking the lower lip, containing all the treasures of delight, of her waving her hand; (whilst) we O bee! through (the necessity for) inquiring into the truth (of her origin), are disappointed (of immediate fruition), thou indeed art in the full enjoyment (of the desire). In other words, 'Whilst I am kept in suspense by the necessity of ascertaining whether she be a Brāhmaṇī woman or a Kṣatriya woman, thou art in the act of enjoying her charms.' *Vyādhunvatyāḥ* genitive case of the pres. part. fem. agreeing with *asyāḥ* understood. *Dhū* with *vi* and *ā* 'to shake about.' The 5th conjugation rejects the nasal in this participle, Pāṇini, vii, 1, 80. *Rati-sarva-svam=rati-nidhānam*, 'entirely made up, or constituted, of delight,' 'whose whole essence is delight.' So *khaḍga-sarva-svaḥ*, 'one whose whole property consists

---

Verse 23. *Vaṁśasthavila* (variety of *Jagatī*). *See* Verse 18, 22.
Verse 24. *Śikhariṇī* (variety of *Atyaṣṭi*). *See* Verse 9.

शकुन्तला : ण एसो धिट्ठो विरमदि। अणदो गमिस्सं (पदान्तरे स्थित्वा
शकुन्तला : न एष धृष्टो विरमति। अन्यतो गमिष्यामि। (पदान्तरे स्थित्वा
सदृष्टिक्षेपं) कहं इदोबि आअच्छदि। हला परित्ताअध परित्ताअध मं
सदृष्टिक्षेपं) कथम् इतोऽपि आगच्छति। हला परित्रायध्वं परित्रायध्वं माम्
इमिणा दुव्विणीदेण दुट्ठमहुअरेण अहिहूअमाणं।
अनेन दुर्विनीतेन[1] दुष्टमधुकरेण अभिभूयमानां।

उभे : (सस्मितं) काओ वअं परित्तादुं। दुस्सन्दं अक्कन्द। राअ रक्खिदाइं
उभे : (सस्मितं) के आवां परित्रातुं।[2] दुष्यन्तम् आक्रन्द। राज रक्षितानि
तबोवणाइं णाम।
तपोवनानि नाम।

राजा : अवसरोऽयम् आत्मानं प्रकाशयितुं। न भेतव्यं (इत्यर्द्धोक्ते स्वगतं) राजभावस् त्वभिज्ञातो भवेत्। भवतु। एवं तावद् अभिधास्ये।

of a sword.' *Adhara,* 'the lower lip,' in contradistinction to *oṣṭha,* 'the upper lip.' *Adharam pivasi,* 'thou art drinking the moisture of) the lower lip.' Compare *adharam pātum pravṛttā* [Vikramorvaśīya, Act 4], and *adhara-madhu* (the nectar of the lip) *pivanti.* [Bhartṛ-Hari, i, 26.] *Hata* is here equivalent to *mano-hata,* 'disappointed,' or rather 'kept in anxious suspense.' *Kṛti=kṛtārtha* or *kṛta-kṛtya* 'one who has gained the object of his desire, and is in full enjoyment of it.'

1. Literally, 'ill-trained;' hence 'ill-behaved,' 'ill-mannered.'

2. 'Who are we to rescue you?' Who are we that we should be able to rescue you? What power have we to rescue you? [*āvayoḥ ko dhikāra,* Śaṅkara.] In a passage further on in this Act, where the pronoun *ka* is similarly used (*kā tvam visraṣṭavyasya,* etc.) it is explained by Kāṭavema to mean *na prabhu, avāsa,* 'not having the power.' All the Devanāgarī MSS. read *parittādum* [Sans. *paritrātum*], but the Bengālī read *partittāṇe* [Sans. *partitrāṇ*], and the Kolkata *kā sattī amhe parittāṇe.* There is no difficulty in admitting the infinitive, which may well stand for the dative *paritrāṇāya* [see page 14, note 1], especially in Prākṛt, which possesses no dative. A precisely similar construction occurs in the Mālavikāgnimitra, p. 55, 1. 13, *kā vyam jetum;* and again, p. 40. 1. 16, *ke āvām parigrahāya* [Prākrit *pariggahassa,* the genitive being put for the Sanskṛt dative.]

शकुन्तला : (पदान्तरे स्थित्वा) कहं इदोबि मं अणुसरदि।
शकुन्तला : (पदान्तरे स्थित्वा) कथम् इतोऽपि माम् अनुसरति।
राजा : (सत्वरम् उपसृत्य)

क: पौरवे वसुमतीं शासति शासितरि दुर्विनीतानाम्।
अयम् आचरत्यविनयं मुग्धासु तपस्विकन्यासु[1]।। 25।।

[सर्वा राजानं दृष्ट्वा किञ्चिदिव सम्भ्रान्ता:]

अनसूया : अज्ज। णक्खु किम्पि अच्चाहिदं। इअं णो पिअसही महुअरेण
अनसूया : आर्य। न खलु किमपि अत्याहितं।[2] इयं नौ प्रियसखी मधुकरेण
अहिहूअमाणा कादरीभूदा (इति शकुन्तलां दर्शयति)।
अभिभूयमाना कातरीभूता (इति शकुन्तलां दर्शयति)।
राजा : (शकुन्तलाभिमुखो भूत्वा) अपि तपो वर्धते।[3]

[शकुन्तला साध्वसाद् अवचना तिष्ठति]

1. 'Who is this that is practising rudeness towards the gentle maidens of the hermits, (and that too) whilst a descendant of Puru [see page 15, note 1] a chastiser of the ill-behaved, is governing the earth?' *Śāsati,* loc. ca. of the pres. part., used here absolutely, and liable in this root and in roots of the 3rd. conjugation to be confounded with the 3rd pers. plur. of the present tense. *Mugdhāsu=aprauḍāsu, apragalbhāsu,* 'gentle,' 'timid,' 'modest,' 'innocent:' Schol.

2. *Atyāhitam=mahābhīti,* 'great cause of fear:' Amarakośa. Wilson adds another meaning, *viz.,* 'daring action;' but, according to Dr. Boehtlingk, the meaning here rather is 'great crime,' 'punishable offence.' The word occurs in the beginning of the 4th. and 5th Acts of the Vikramorvaśī. *Cf.* also Mālavik., 55, 19; 56, 4.

3. 'I trust your devotion prospers,' 'does your devotion prosper? 'is all well with your acts of devotion?' This was the regular formula of salutation on meeting a Brāhmaṇa. According to Manu, the word *kuśalam* should be then used, which implies an inquiry respecting the well-being of his acts of penance, at all times liable to be obstructed by evil spirits and demons. Manu, ii, 127. See aslo Rāmāyaṇa, I, lii, 4.

Verse 25. *Āryā* or *Ghāthā*. (*See* Verse 2.)

— — |⏑ — ⏑|⏑ ⏑ —‖— ⏑ ⏑|— ⏑ ⏑|⏑ — ⏑|— —|—
⏑ ⏑ —|⏑ — ⏑|⏑ ⏑ —‖ — — |⏑ ⏑ —| ⏑ |— —|⏑

अनसूया : दाणिं अदिधिविसेसलाहेण। हला सउन्दले। गच्छ उडअं।

अनसूया : इदानीम् अतिथिविशेषलाभेन।[1] हला शकुन्तले। गच्छ उटजम्।

फलमिस्सं अग्घं उबहर। इदं पादोदअं भविस्सदि।

फलमिश्रम् अर्घम्[2] उपहर। इदं पादोदकं भविष्यति।[3]

राजा :: भवतीनां सूनृतयैव[4] गिरा कृतम् आतिथ्यम्।

1. 'Now (indeed it does prosper) by the reception of a distinguished guest.' The rites of hospitality were enforced amongst the Hindūs by very stringent regulations. The observance of them ranked as one of the five great sacraments (*mahā-yajñāḥ*), under the title of *nṛ-yajña* or *manuṣya-yajña* 'the man-sacrament.' Brahmā, Prajāpati, Indra, Fire, the Vasus and the Sun were supposed to be present in the person of a guest, and to partake of the food that was given to him [Viṣṇu Purāṇa, p. 306]. No wonder then that reverence of him was said to be conducive to wealth, to fame, to life, and to a heavenly reward. [Manu, iii, 106.] On the other hand, no punishment was thought too severe for one who violated these rites. If a guest departed disappointed from any house, his sins were to be transferred to the householder, and all the merits of the householder were to be transferred to him. [Viṣṇu Purāṇa, p. 305. Hitopadeśa, line 361.] Some of the things which were to be offered to a guest by even the poorest man were food, potherbs, water for the feet, and if he could do no more, ground on which to lie. [Manu, iii., 101. Viṣṇu Purāṇa, 308.]

2. The *argha* or *arghya* was a respectful offering to Brāhmaṇas of rice, *Dūrbā*-grass, flowers, fruit, etc., with water in a small boat-shaped vessel. *Cf.* Rāmāyaṇa, I, xx, 9, 10. See also Wilson's note to Meghadūta, verse 4. *Upahara=ānīya prayaccha*, 'having fetched, present.'

3. 'This (which we have brought with us for watering our plants) will serve as water for the feet.' Water for the feet was one of the first things invariably presented to a guest in all Eastern countries. Should a guest arrive, a seat is to be offered to him, and his feet are to be washed and food is to be given him. [Viṣṇu Purāṇa, page 305. Compare also Luke also Luke vii, 44.] *Idam* i.e., *vṛkṣārtham ānītam udakam.* Schol.

4. *Sūnṛtā gir* 'kind yet sincere language,' 'complimentary and friendly words without flattery' (*priyaṁ satyaṁ ca vacanam*). This is

प्रियंवदा : तेण हि इमस्सिं पच्छाअसीअलाए सत्तबणवेदिआए मुहुत्तअं

प्रियंवदा : तेन हि अस्यां प्रच्छायशीतलायां सप्तपर्णवेदिकायां मुहूर्तम्

उबविसिअ परिस्समविणोदं करेदु अज्जो।

उपविश्य परिश्रमविनोदं करोतु [1]आर्यः।

राजा : नूनं यूयम् अप्यनेन कर्मणा परिश्रान्ताः।

one of the four things with which even the poorest man was to greet a guest. 'Grass and earth to sit on, water to wash the feet, an fourthly, friendly yet sincere speech (*vāk sūnṛtā*) are never refused in the houses of the good, even though they be poor.' Manu, iii, 101. Hitopadeśa, line 301.

1. 'On the raised-seat under the *Saptaparṇa*-tree, cool with much shade, having sat down for a short time, let your honour cause removal of fatigue.' According to Śaṅkara, *prachāya = prakṛṣṭā yā chāyā*, 'excessive shade.' The other Commentators explain it by *prakṛṣṭā chāyā yatra deśaḥ*, 'a place where there is excessive shade,' and by *prakṛṣṭā chāyā yasyāḥ*, 'having excessive shade.' A parallel passage occurs in the Mālavikāgnimitra, page 3, line 20, *'pracchāya-śītale śilāpaṭṭake nisannā,'* etc. It seems clear that the effect of *pra* in this word is to give intensity to the original idea. It is is needless to regard it either as a Tatpuruṣa or Karmadhāraya compound, although it is in such compounds especially that *chhāyā* becomes *chhāya*. [See page 5, note 2, and Raghu-vaṁśa, iv, 20; xii, 50. Meghadūta, verse 103. Pāṇini, ii, 4, 22. 25.] *Saptaparṇa*, 'a tree having seven leaves on a stalk' (*Echites scholaris*), called also *viṣama-chada*, 'having an odd number of leaves,' and *viśāla-tvac*, 'having a broad bark' [Raghu-vaṁśa, iv., 23.] *Vedikā=viśrāma-sthānam*, 'place of repose or rest.' Schol. It was probably a quadrangular raised-seat, something in the form of an altar, and covered with a roof supported by pillars, used as a kind of arbour or summer-house, for sitting or standing under. In this case it seems to have been erected under a *Saptaparṇa*-tree. *Sapta-parṇa-nāmno vṛkṣasya tale nirmitā yā vedikā.* Śaṅkara. Sir W. Jones [vol. v, p. 102] observes that this tree, when full-grown, is very large; when young, light and elegant. *Muhūrta* is properly an Indian hour of forty-eight minutes or two *daṇḍas*, but is used for any short space of time.

अनसूया : हला सउन्दले। उइदं णो पज्जुबासणं अदिधीणं। एत्थ

अनसूया : हला शकुन्तले। उचितं नः पर्युपासनम् अतिथीनां। अत्र

उबविसन्ह। (इति सर्व उपविशन्ति)।

उपविशामः। (इति सर्व उपविशन्ति)।

शकुन्तला : (आत्मगतं) किं णुक्खु इमं जणं पेक्खिअ तबोवणवि-

शकुन्तला : (आत्मगतं)[1] किं नु खलु इमं जनं प्रेक्ष्य तपोवनवि-

रोहिणो विआरस्म गमणीअम्हि संवुत्ता।

रोधिनो विकारस्य गमनीयास्मि संवृत्ता।[2]

राजा : (सर्वा विलोक्य) अहो समवयोरूपरमणीयं भवतीनां सौहार्दम्।

प्रियंवदा : (जनान्तिकं) अणसूए। को णुक्खु एसो। चउरगम्भी-

प्रियंवदा : (जनान्तिकं[3]) अनसूये। को नु खलु एषः। चतुरगम्भी-

1. *Ātma-gatam* and *sva-gatam (lit.*, 'gone to one's self') are used in theatrical language like the English 'aside' to denote that the words which follow are supposed to be spoken privately, as if to the speaker's self, and not in the hearing of any one but the audience. [*Ananya-prakāśam* : Schol.] *Gata*, 'gone,' at the end of a compound is used loosely to express realationship and connexion without any necessary implication of motion. It may mean simply 'in connexion with,' 'in relation to;' or, as here, 'with exclusive reference to,' 'addressed exclusively to.'

2. 'How now! can it really be that, having looked upon this man, I am become susceptible of [*lit.*, accessible to] an emotion inconsistent with a grove devated to penance *Vikāra* is any alteration or transition from the natural and quiescent state of the soul; hence any emotion, whether of joy, grief, anger, etc. *Kim* is used *kutsāyām*, 'disdainfully,' and is equivalent to *katham eva jātam*, 'How can it have happened;' Schol.

3. *Janāntikam*, 'aside to a person standing near.' This is a theatrical direction something similar to *ātma-gatam*, but denotes that the speech which follows is supposed to be audible by one other person, to whom a private signal is made. 'That which is spoken apart from the rest, with a signal, such as holding up three fingers of the hand (*tripatāka*), being a mutual speech (between two), is called *janāntikam*.' Śankara and Sāhit.-Darp., 177.

राकिदी महुरं आलबन्तो पहावबन्दो विअ लक्खीअदि।

राकृतिर् मधुरम् आलपन् प्रभाववान् इव लक्ष्यते।[1]

अनसूया : सहि। ममबि अत्थि कोदूहलं। पुच्छिस्सं दाव णं ।। प्रकाशं।।

अनसूया : सखि। ममापि अस्ति कौतूहलं। प्रक्ष्यामि तावद् एनं।। प्रकाशम्।।[2]

अज्जस्स महुरालाबजणिदो विस्सासो मं मन्ताबेदि।

आर्यस्य मधुरालापजनितो विश्वासो मां मन्त्रयति।

कदमो अज्जेण राएमिवसो अलङ्करीअदि। कदमो वा विरहपज्जु-

कतम आर्येण राजर्षिवंशोऽलङ्क्रियते।[3] कतमो वा विरहपर्यु-

स्सुअजणो किदो देसो। किस्मिमित्तं वा सुउमारदरोवि तबोवण-

त्सुकजनः[4] कृतो देशः। किन्निमित्तं वा सुकुमारतरोऽपि तपोवन-

1. 'Who can this be (who being) lively (yet) dignified in mien, appears as if endowed with majesty (while) speaking to us sweetly.' *Catura,* 'lively, 'sprightly,' 'animated;' may perhaps mean here, 'polite,' 'courteous,' in relation to *madhuram ālapan. Gambhīra,* 'profound,' is used metaphorically for one whose thoughts and feelings are deep or suppressed, 'reserved' 'dignified,' 'not betraying emotion.' The oldest MS. reads *mahuram;* the others *mahuram piam;* but *piam* belongs properly to the margin.

2. *Prakāśam,* 'aloud,' another theatrical direction denoting that the words which follow are to be made audible to all, those which precede having been spoken aside.

3. 'What race of royal-sages is adorned by your honour?' A Rājarṣi is a king or man of the Kṣatriya and military class who has attained to the rank of a *Ṛṣi* or saint by the practise of religious austerities. Such were Ikṣvāku, Purūravas, Duṣyanta, etc. There are six other classes of Ṛṣis. [See the word 'Saint' in the English and Sanskṛt Dictionary.] The Rājarṣi is inferior to the Brahmarṣi or 'Brāhmaṇa-saint,' but it was possible for a Rājarṣi to raise himself to the rank of the latter, and therefore to the state of a Brāhmaṇa, by very severe penance, as exemplified in the story of the celebrated Viśvāmitra, son of Gādhi, and father of Śakuntalā [See Rāmāyaṇa, I, xx, 20; lxv, 18. Astra-śikṣā, 118.].

4. 'With its people regretful by separation' *i.e.*, by your absence.

गमणपरिस्सस्स अत्ता पदं उबणीदो।

गमनपरिश्रमस्य आत्मा पदम् उपनीतः।[1]

शकुन्तला : **आत्मगतं।। हिअअ। मा उत्तस्स। एसा तुए चिन्दिदं**

शकुन्तला : आत्मगतं।। हृदय। मा उत्ताम्य। एषा त्वया चिन्तितम्

अणसूआ मन्तेदि।

अनसूया मन्त्रयते।[2]

राजा : (आत्मगतं) कथम् इदानीम् आत्मानं निवेदयामि। कथं वात्मापहारं करोमि।[3] भवतु। एवं तावद् एनां वक्ष्ये।। प्रकाशं।। भवति।[4] यः पौरवेण राज्ञा धर्माधिकारे नियुक्तः सोऽहम् अविघ्नक्रियोपलम्भाय धर्मारण्यम् इदम् आयातः।[5]

1. 'On what account has your person even though very delicate [unaccustomed to hardships] been brought to the point of (undergoing) the fatigue of visiting this grove of penance?'

2. 'O my heart! be not uneasy, this Anasūyā is giving utterance to all thy thoughts,' *i.e.*, is making inquiry about all those points about which thou art anxious (such as, who this stranger is, whence he has come; *etc*. Schol.).

3. 'Or how shall I make concealment of myself?' *i.e.*, How shall I hide my real character? how shall I dissemble? *Apahāra* is equivalent to *vañcanam*, 'deception,' [Kāṭava.] or rather to *nihnava* or *saṅgopanam*, 'concealment,' 'dissimulation.' This is a very unusual sense of the word, but all lthe Devanāgarī MSS. agree in reading *apahāra*. The Bengālī have *parīhāra*, which is also explained by *saṅgopanam*. The oldest Bengālī MS. [1060, E. I. House] omits the words from *katham vā* to *karomi*.

4. 'O lady!' voc. case of *bhavatī*. According to Manu, a Brāhmaṇa is to be accosted with the respectful pronoun *bhavat*, and to any woman not related by blood, the address *bhavati* or *subhage bhagini* is to be used [ii, 128, 129].

5. 'I, that very person who was appointed by his majesty, the descendant of Puru, for the administration of justice, have arrived at this sacred grove, for the purpose of ascertaining whether the (religious) rites are free from obstruction.' The religious rites and sacrifices of holy men were often disturbed by certain evil spirits or goblins called Rākṣasas, who were the determined enemies of piety and devotion. No great sacrifice or religious ceremony was

अनसूया : सणाहा दाणिं धम्मचारिणो।

अनसूया : सनाथा[1] इदानीं धर्म्मचारिण:।

।। शकुन्तला शृङ्गारलज्जां निरूपयति।।

सख्यौ : उभयोर् आकारं विदित्वा जनान्तिकं।। हला सउन्दले। जइ

सख्यौ : उभयोर् आकारं[2] विदित्वा जनान्तिकं।। हला शकुन्तले। यदि

एत्थ अज्ज तादो सस्सिहिदो भवे।

अत्र अद्य तात: सन्निहितो भवेत्।

शकुन्तला : (सरोषं) तदो किं भवे।

शकुन्तला : (सरोषं) तत: किं भवेत्।[3]

सख्यौ : इमं जीविदसव्वस्सेणबि अदिधिविसेमं किदत्थं करिस्सदि।

सख्यौ : इमं जीवितसर्वस्वेनापि अतिथिविशेष कृतार्थं करिष्यति।[4]

ever carried on without an attempt on the part of these demons to impede its celebration; and the most renowned saints found it necessary on such occasions to acknowledge their dependence on the strong arm of the military class, by seeking the aid of warriors and heroes. The inability of holy men, who had attained the utmost limit of spiritual power, to cope with the spirits of evil, and the superiority of physical force in this respect is very remarkable. [See Rāmāyaṇa, I. xx, xxi, xxxii, and the end of Act 3 of this play].

1. See page 26. note 2.

2. 'Understanding the gesures of both,' *i.e.*, of Śakuntalā and Duṣyanta. *Ākāra=ceṣṭā* or *iṅgitam*, 'a gesture,' 'sign,' or rather the state of mind as evidenced by gestures and outward appearances, such as change of colour, etc.

3. 'What if he were (near at hand)?' *i.e.*, If he were near at hand, what would he do? Schol.

4. 'He would make this distinguished guest happy [possessed of the object of his desire] with all the substance of his life,' *i.e.*, He would do worldly honour to his guest by offering him the best of his substance and property. See page 33, note 2. There is here evidently a *double-entendre*. Śaṅkara explains *sarva-svam* by *phala-mūlādikam*, 'fruits, roots, and other necessaries of life.' Fruits and roots were the chief food of anchorites and constituted their whole substance and worldly treasure. With an offering of these they were

शकुन्तला : तुम्हे अबेध। किम्पि हिअए करिअ मन्तेध। ण वो वअणं सुणिस्सं।

शकुन्तला : युवाम् अपेतं। किमपि हृदये कृत्वा मन्त्रयेथे।[1] न वां वचनं श्रोष्यामि।

राजा : वयमपि तावद् भवत्यौ सखीगतं[2] किमपि पृच्छामः।

सख्यौ : अज्ज। अणुग्गहो विअ इअं अब्भत्थणा।

सख्यौ : आर्य। अनुग्रह इव इयम् अभ्यर्थना।

राजा : भगवान् काश्यपः शाश्वते ब्रह्मणि वर्त्तते।[3] इयं च वः सखी तदात्मजेति कथम् एतत्।

अनसूया : सुणादु अज्जो। अत्थि कोबि कोसिओत्ति मोत्तणामहेओ

अनसूया : शृणोतु आर्यः। अस्ति कोऽपि कौशिक इति गोत्रनामधेयोमधेयो

commanded to honour every one who came to their hermitage. [Rāmāyaṇa, I, lii, 16, and lxi; 4. Manu, vi, 7] The allusion, however, evidently is to Śakuntalā, who might be regarded as the holy father's most valuable possession and treasure.

1. 'Get off with you! having formed some (idea) in your heart, you are speaking.' *Hṛdaye* or *manasi kṛ* is not an unusual idiom for 'to turn or cogitate in the mind.' [*See* Rāmāyaṇa, II, 64, 8] *Apetam* is the 2nd pers. du. imp. *i*, 'to go,' with *apa*.

2. *Sakhī-gatam*, 'relating to your friend.' [*Śakuntalā-viṣayakam* : Schol.] This use of *gata* is noticeable, *see* the note to *ātmagata*, p. 38, note 1. Only one Devanāgarī MS. reads *bhavatyau;* but this is supported by the oldest Bengālī, which also adds *kimapi.*

.3. 'His reverence Kāśyapa [see note 4, p. 22] lives in the constant practice-of-austerities.' *Brahman* is properly the Supreme Spirit or Being from which all created things are supposed to emanate and into which they are absorbed. The dictionary gives three other senses—1. The practice of austerities; 2. The Vedas; 3. Holy knowledge. The first is the one here required. Śaṅkara explains it by *tapas, i.e.,* the practice of bodily mortification and penance; Kāṭavema by *brahmacaryam,* 'the practice of continence.'

महप्पहावो राएसी।

महाप्रभावो राजर्षिः।[1]

1. 'There is a certain Rājarṣi (or royal-sage, *i.e.*, both king and saint) of great majesty, whose family name (patronymic) is Kauṣika.' This was the great Viśvāmitra (a descendant of Kuśa or Kauśika), whose story—he being the preceptor of Rāma-candra—is told in the Rāmāyaṇa, I, li, lxv, and xxxv. He is there said to be the son of Gādhi (a prince of the Lunar dynasty, king of Gādhipur, or the ancient Kanouj) who is said to be the son of Kuśa-nātha, who is the son of Kuśa or Kuśa or Kuśika. According to the Viṣṇu Purāṇa the following is the pedigree of Viśvāmitra. One of the sons of Purūravas, a prince of the Lunar dynasty (*see* Vikramorvaśīya) was Amāvasu. Thence in direct succession came Bhīma, Kāñcana, Jāhnu, Sumantu, Ajaka, Valākaśva and Kuśa. The latter had two sons, Kuśāmba and Kuśa-nātha, but Gādhi was the son of Kuśāmba, and was said to be an incarnation of Indra (who is hence sometimes called Kauśika); for Kuśāmba had engaged in great penance, to obtain a son who should be equal to Indra, and the latter being alarmed, took upon himself the character of Kuśāmba's son. Gādhi had a daughter, Satyavatī, who married a Brāhmaṇa named Ṛcīka, son of Bhṛgu. This Ṛcīka—with the view of securing to himself a son who should be an illustrious Brāhmaṇa, and to his father-in-law, a son of great prowess—made two messes of food, one for his own wife, and the other for the wife of Gādhi; infusing into one the qualities suited to a Brāhmaṇa, and into the other the properties of power and heroism. The two wives exchanged messes, and so it happened that the wife of Gādhi had a son, Viśvāmitra, who, though a Kṣatriya, was born with the inclinations of a Brāhmaṇa; and the wife of Ṛcīka had a son, the sage Jamadagni, who was the father of the warrior-priest Paraśu-rāma, she having by her entreaties induced her husband to transfer the effects of the exchange of food from her son to her grandson. There is something like anachronism in the history of Viśvāmitra. Satyavatī, his sister, was the grandmother of Paraśurāma, and it was not till the close of the latter's career that Rāmacandra appeared on the field and became the pupil of Viśvāmitra. At any rate the *Ṛṣi* must have been very old. Indeed, in the Rāmāyaṇa he is stated to have mortified himself for two thousand years before he attained the rank of a *Ṛṣi*; for

राजा : अस्ति। श्रूयते।

अनसूया : तं णो पिअमहीए पहवं अवगच्छ। उज्झिआए सरीरसंवड्ढणा-

अनसूया : तं नौ प्रियसख्याः प्रभवम् अवगच्छ। उज्झितायाः शरीरसंवर्धना-

दीहिं तादकस्सबो से पिदा।

दिभिस् तातकाश्यपोऽस्याः पिता।[1]

राजा : उज्झितशब्देन जनितं मे कौतूहलं। आमूलाच् छ्रोतुम् इच्छामि।

अनसूया : सुणादु अज्जो। गोदमीतीरे पुरा किल तस्स राएसिणो उग्गे

अनसूया : श्रृणोतु आर्यः। गौतमीतीरे पुरा किल तस्य राजर्षेर् उग्रे

तवसि वट्टमाणस्स किम्पि जादसङ्केहिं देवेहिं मेणआ णाम अच्छरा पेसिदा

तपसि वर्तमानस्य किमपि जातशङ्कैर् देवैर् मेनका नाम अप्सराः प्रेषिता

णिअमविग्घकारिणी।

नियमविघ्नकारिणी।[2]

many years more before his cohabitation with Menakā, which led to the birth of Śakuntalā; and for many thousand years more before he became a Brāhmaṇa. It was not till after this period that he became the preceptor of Rāma-candra, but no chronological inconsistency is too great for Hindū mythology.

1. 'Know him to be the father of our friend; but father Kaṇva is the (reputed) father of her, through the fostering of her body, etc., when deserted. *Prabhava=janma-hetu,* 'the operative cause of being,' *i.e.,* a father. Schol.

2. 'The story of Viśvāmitra, as told in the Rāmāyaṇa, is briefly this. On his accession to the throne in the room of his father Gādhi, in the course of a tour through his dominions, he visited the hermitage of the Muni Vaśiṣṭha one of the ten Brahmādikas or Prajāpatis, sons of Brahmā. There the cow-of-plenty excited his cupidity. He offered the Muni untold treasures in exchange for the cow, but being refused, prepared to take it by force. A long war ensued between the King and the Muni (symbolical of the struggles between the Kṣatriya and Brāhmaṇical classes) which ended in the defeat of Viśvāmitra, whose vexation was such, that he devoted himself to austerities in the hope of attaining the condition of a Brāhmaṇa. The Rāmāyaṇa goes on to recount how by gradually increasing the rigour of his bodily mortification through thousands

राजा : अस्त्येतद् अन्यसमाधिभीरुत्वं देवानाम्।[1]

अनसूया : तदो वसन्तोदारसमए मे उस्सादइत्तअं रूबं पेकिषुअ।

अनसूया : ततो वसन्तावतारसमयेऽस्या उन्मादयितृकं रूपं प्रेक्ष्यम्।[2]

of years, he successively earned the title of Rājarṣi [I., lviii., 5], *Ṛṣi* [lxiii., 2], Maharṣi [lxiii.,12], and finally, Brahmarṣi [ixv., 18]. It was not till he had gained this last title that Vaśiṣṭha consented to acknowledge his equality with himself, and ratify his admission into the Brāmaṇical state. It was at the time of Viśvāmitra's advancement to the rank of a *Ṛṣi*, and whilst he was still a Kṣatriya, that Indra and the inferior gods, jealous of his increasing power—as exhibited in his transporting King Triśanku to the region of the stars, and in saving Śunaḥśephas, the son of his won brother-in-law Ṛcīka, out of the hands of Indra, to whom he had been promised by King Ambarī as a victim in a sacrifice—sent the nymph Menakā, to seduce him from his life of mortification and continence. The Rāmāyaṇa records him from his life of mortification and continence. The Rāmāyaṇa records his surrender to this temptation, and relates that the nymph was his companion in the hermitage for ten years, but does not allude to the birth of Śakuntalā, during that period. It only informs us that at the end of ten years the *Ṛṣi* having come to himself. extricated himself from this hindrance (*niyama-vigha*), and abandoning the the nymph, departed into another region.

1. 'Such is the fear which there is to the (inferior) gods of the devotion of other !' It may be remarked here that, according to the Hindū system, Indra and the other inferior deities were not the possessors of *Svarga*, or heaven, by inalienable and indefeasible right. They accordingly viewed with jealousy and even alarm, any extraordinary persistency by human being in acts of penance, as it raised him to a level with themselves; and if carried beyound a certain point, enabled him to dispossess them of paradise. Indra was therefore, the enemy of exceessive devotion, and had in his servies numerous nymphs [Apsarās], such as Menakā, Rambhā, and Urvaśī, who were called his 'weapons' [*Indrasya praharaṇāni*, Vikram., Act I] and whose business it was to impede by their reduction, the devotion of holy men.

2. 'Then at the season of the descent of Spring, having looked upon the intoxicating beauty [form] of that (nymph).' The

[इत्यर्द्धोक्ते लज्जया विरमति]

राजा : परस्ताद् अवगम्यत एब।[1] सर्वथाप्सर:सम्भवैषा।

अनसूया : अहइं।

अनसूया : अथ किम्।[2]

राजा : उपपद्यते।

मानुषीषु कथं वा स्याद् अस्य रूपस्य सम्भवः।
न प्रभातरलं ज्योतिर् उदेति वसुधातलात्[3] ।। 26 ।।

[शकुन्तलाधोमुखी भूत्वा तिष्ठति]

commentators consider *vasantodāra* to be a compound of *vasanta* and *udāra;* but *odāra* is a legitimate Prākṛt contraction for *avatara,* although *avadāra* would be equally correct. Compare *odaṁsayanti* for *vataṁsayanti* [p. 5, note 4], *hodi* for *havadi* or *bhavati, jedi* for *jayadi* or *jayati,* etc. Lassen,'s Instit. Prāk., p. 176. *Avatāra* is derived from *avatṛī,* 'to descend,' and applies especially to the descent of a god from heaven. There can be nothing inappropriate in connecting it with *Vasanta,* 'the Spring,' often personified as a deity. See a passage in the 2ndAct of the Vikramorvaśīya, *pekkadu bhavam vasantāvadārasūidam assa ahirāmattaṇam pamadavaṇassa,* 'let your honour observe the delightfulness of this pleasure-garden manifested by the descent of Spring.' *unmādayitṛkam* [Kāṭavema] is for *unmādayitṛ,* the neuter of the causal noun of agency, 'that which causes to go mad or be intoxicated' [*adhairya-janakam,* 'causing unsteadiness,' Schol.]

1. 'What (happened) afterwards is quite understood' [or guessed by me.] According to Pāṇini (v. 3. 27) the affix *tāt,* in words like *parastāt, adhastāt,* may stand for the nominative case, as well as for the ablative and locative. Hence *parastāt* is equivalent to *para-vṛttāntaḥ,* 'the rest of the story,' 'the subsequent particulars.

2. 'Exactly so,' 'how can it be otherwise ?' *Athakim* is a particle of assent.

3. 'It is fitting (that she should be the daughter of an Apsarās). How otherwise could there be the birth of this beautiful-form amongst mortal females ? The tremulously-radiant flash does not rise from the surface of the earth (but descends from the skies).'

Verse 26. *Śloka* or *Anuṣṭubh. See* verses 5, 6, 11.

राजा : (आत्मगतं) लब्धावकाशो मे मनोरथः।[1] किन्तु सख्याः परिहासोदाहृतां वरप्रार्थनां श्रुत्वा धृतद्वैधीभावकातरं मे मनः।[2]

प्रियंवदा : (सस्मितं शकुन्तलां विलोक्य नायकाभिमुखी भूत्वा) पुणोवि

प्रियंवदा : (सस्मितं शकुन्तलां विलोक्य नायकाभिमुखी भूत्वा)[3] पुनरपि

वत्तुकामो विअ अज्जो।

वक्तुकाम इव आर्यः।

Apsaraḥ-sambhavatvam is the nominative case to *upapadyate,* School. According to Kāṭavema, *prabhā-taralaṁ* [*prabhayā cañcalam*] *jyotis,* is a periphrasis for *vidyut.* 'lightning;' but Śaṅkara applies it also to the beams of the sun and moon. The comparison of the unearthly beauty of a nymph to the radiance of lighting is appropriate. See Meghadūta, verse 40.

1. 'My desire has found (free) scope,' *i.e.,* 'Since it is certain that she is not a Brāhmaṇī woman, [*asavarnatva-niścayāt,* from the certainty of her not being of the same class with the holy father], it is clear that my desire is directed towards an attainable object.' *Avakāśa* means 'free course, 'range,' 'ower of expatiating.' A similar phrase occurs later in this Act, *labdhāvakāśā me prārthanā*. Kāṭavema there explains it by *labdhāśrayaḥ* or *sārtho me manorathaḥ.*

2. 'Nevertheless, having heard the prayer for a husband uttered in joke by her female-friend [see page 30, line 4], my heart is held in suspense and anxious,' *i.e.,* anxious to know the truth, as to whether she is really destined for marriage, or for an ascetic life; and fearful least at some former time her husband may have been decided upon (*pūrvam asyā varo nirnīito na vā.* Kāṭav.). Śaṅkara interprets *vara-prārthanā* by *svāmyabhilāṣa,* 'wish for a husband.'*Dhṛta-dvaidhī-bhāva-kātaram* is a complex Dvandva compound. *Dvaidhibhāva,* 'a state of difference, distraction, doubt.'

3. 'Looking with a smile at Śakuntalā, (and then) turning her face towards the hero-of-the-poem;' [*lit.,* having become with her face turned, etc.] All the Devanāgarī MSS. have this latter clause. *Nāyaka,* in erotic poetry, is the lover, husband, or rather the hero of the poem, and *nāyikā,* the heroine or female who is the object of his admiration and love. So Romeo, in Shakspere, would be the *nāyaka,* and Juliet the *nāyīkā.* According to Śaṅkara and Kāṭavema, in every Hindū play there is also a *prati-nāyaka,* or 'antagonist of the hero,' and an *upa-nāyaka,* or 'sub-hero.'

[शकुन्तला सखीम् अङ्गुल्या तर्जयति][1]

राजा : सम्यग् उपलक्षितं भवत्या। अस्ति नः सच्चरितश्रवणलोभाद् अन्यदपि प्रष्टव्यम्।[2]

प्रियंवदा : अलं विआरिअ। अणिअन्तणाणुओओ तबस्सिअणो णाम

प्रियंवदा : अलं विचार्य। अनियन्त्रणानुयोगस् तपस्विजनो नाम[3]

राजा : सखीं ते ज्ञातुम् इच्छामि।

वैखानसं किम् अनया व्रतम् आप्रदानाद्
व्यापाररोधि मदनस्य निषेवितव्यम्।
अत्यन्तम् आत्मसदृशेक्षणवल्लभाभिर्
आहो निवत्स्यति समं हरिणाङ्गनाभिः[4] ।। 27 ।।

1. 'Śakuntalā threatens [reproves] her friend with her finger,' *i.e.*, makes a threatening or chiding gesture, as if she were angry with her friend for leading Duṣyanta to pursue his interrogatories, and were ashamed at the revelation of the particulars of her history. (*Ātmano vrīḍā-janaka-svavṛttāntodyhātanam.* Kāṭavema.) According to Śaṅkara, this is an example of the coquettish gesture called *lalitam*, *i.e.*, though she was really eager to hear all that her lover had to say, yet by her outward gestures she appeared to be the reverse. *priyajana-kathā-śuśrūṣur api vahis tad-anyathā*. Śaṅkara.

2. 'It has been rightly judged by your ladyship; from an eagerness to hear (all the particulars of) her good history, there is still something (that remains) to be asked by us.'

3. 'Enough of deliberating; surely persons (who lead the life) of hermits may be questioned unreservedly' [freely]. *Aniyantraṇānuyoga* is equivalent to *aniyama-praśna*, 'one to whom a question may be put without any restraint or ceremony.' Kāṭavema *Alam*, in the sense of prohibiting or forbidding, is more usually found with the instrum case of the noun, but, like *khalu*, it may sometimes be used in this sense with the indeclinable participles in *tvā and ya*, thus alam *dattvā*, enough of giving, or 'having given, it is enough;' and so *khalu pītvā*, 'having drunk, hold!' Wilkins' Grammar, rule 737. The Bengālī MSS. read *'alam vicāritena.'*

4. 'I wish to ascertain (respecting) your friend—Is this monastic vow (so) opposed to the ways of love, to be observed by her (merely)

Verse 27. *Vasantatilakā* (a variety of Śakkarī). *See* Verse 8.

प्रियंवदा : अज्ज। धम्मचरणेबि परबसो अअं जणो। गुरुणो उण से

प्रियंवदा : आर्य। धर्म्मचरणेऽपि परवशोऽयं जनः। गुरोः पुनर् अस्या

अणुरूबवरप्पदाणे सङ्कप्पो।

अनुरूपवरप्रदाने सङ्कल्पः।[1]

until her gift-in-marriage; or, on the contrary (*āho*), will she live to the end (of her life) along with the female deer, her favourites (from) having eyes like her own ?' Dr. Boehtlingk remarks that *sakhī te jñātum icchāmi kim anayā*, etc., is equivalent to *jñātum icchāmi kiṁ sakhyā te*, etc., 'I wish to know whether this vow is to be observed by thy friend,' etc. He gives instances of a similar construction in Draup., iv, 5. Mahābh., iii., 269. *Vaikhānasa*, anything relating to a *Vikhānasa* or hermit, *tena kṛtam proktam vā vratam vaikhānasam, tattu niyatāraṇya-vāsa-rūpam*, the vow which is performed or enjoined by him is called *vaikhānasa*, and that consists in always living in the woods.' Śaṅkara. *Apradānāt =pradāna-paryantam*, or *āvivāhāt*, 'up to the period of her marriage.' In the time of Manu every Hindū girl was given away in marriage before the season of maturity (*ṛtoḥ prāk pradānakāla)*, and that father incurred great disgrace who did not so give her away. It was deemed highly represhensible if the betrothed husband did not take her to his own house, when the marriageable period of life arrived. See Manu, ix, 4, with commentary. *Vyāpāra-rodhi madanasya=kāma-kriyā-nivārakam*, 'hindering amatory actions.' According to Kāṭavema *ātma-Sadṛśekṣana-vallabhābhir* 'may be optionally resolved into *ātma-sadṛśekṣana-vallabhā ābhir*. '*Āho*, a particle of doubt or asking, is said by the commentators to be used *pakṣāntare* or *vikalpe, i.e.*, antithetically, or, in stating an opposite alternative.

1. 'Even in the practice of religious duties this person [Śakuntalā] is dependant on (the will of) another [*viz*., Kaṇva]; nevertheless, it is the purpose of the Guru to give her away to a suitable husband,' According to Manu (ix, 2, 3), women were to never to be deemed fit for independence. Day and night they were to be held by their protectors in subjection. But in certain matters, such as lawful recreations, and if they chose to enter upon a religious life, they were to be left at their own disposal. It seems that even in those matters Śakuntalā was not her own mistress. The holy father had enjoined a life of penance upon her, but had resolved that her residence in the hermitage should not be perpetual. *Api śabdena dharmā-caraṇasya sva-chanda-karaṇīyatvaṁ sūcitam*, 'by the word 'even' it is indicated that the duties of religion are generally to be

राजा :: (आत्मगतं) न दुरवापेयं खलु प्रार्थना।[1]

भव हृदय साभिलाषं सम्प्रति सन्देहनिर्णयो जातः।

आशङ्कसेयद् अग्निं तद् इदं स्पर्शक्षमं रत्नम्[2] ।। 28 ।।

शकुन्तला : सरोषमिव।। अणसूए अहं गमिस्सं।

शकुन्तला : सरोषमिव।। अनसूये अहं गमिष्यामि।

अनसूया : किणिमित्तं।

अनसूया : किन्निमित्तम्।

शकुन्तला : इमं असम्बद्धप्पलाबिणिं विअंवदं अज्जाए गोदमीए

शकुन्तला : इमाम् असम्बद्ध[3]प्रलापिणीं प्रियंवदाम् आर्यायै गौतम्यै

performed as a voluntary act.' Kāṭavema. Amara-Sinha explains *saṅkalpa* by *mānasaṁ karma*, 'a mental act or resolution.' The rule of Vararuci (i., 22) by which the Sanskṛt *guru* becomes *garua* in Prākṛt, only applies to the adjective.

1. 'This prayer is not difficult or realization,' *i.e.*, A suitable husband, about whom there is this wish, is not difficult to be obtained; *prārthanā-śabdena tad-viṣayo varo lakṣyate :* Kāṭavema. According to this, it would appear that the word *Prārthanā* refers to the prayer supposed to have been made by Kaṇva, that he might find a suitable husband for his foster-child.

2. 'O (my) heart ! become hopeful [possessed of desire]; now the certainty (of what was a matter) of doubt has come to pass. That which thou suspectedst (to be) fire, the same (is) a gem capable of being touched.' *Sandeha-nirṇaya*, 'arriving at positive certainty on a doubtful point.' This was the boubt mentioned before, at page 30, line 9, with p. 31 note 1. The word *antaḥ-karaṇa* p. 31 [line 2], is there used for *hṛdaya. Yad* [*Śakuntala-rūpaṁ vastu*] *agnim tarkayasi*, 'The thing, [*viz.*, Śakuntalā] which thou imaginedst fire :' Śaṅkara. The power of a Brāhmaṇa, especially if exhibited in anger, is compared to fire [Verse 41 of this play. Bhaṭṭi, i, 23. Mahābh., I, 3010.] There may be some allusion to this here, or it may simply mean that, supposing Śakuntalā to have been a Brāhmaṇī woman, she would have been as inapproachable to a Kṣatriya as a flame of fire. *Sparśa-kṣamam=samparka-yogyam* [*see* page 29, note 1, at end].

3. *Asambaddha*, properly 'unconnected;' hence, 'absurd,' 'nonsensical.' *Abaddha* is used with the same acceptation.

Verse 28. *Āryā* or *Ghāthā*. (*See* Verse 2.)

⏑⏑⏑⏑|⏑—⏑|——‖—⏑⏑ |——|⏑—⏑|——|—

— — |⏑—⏑|——‖⏑⏑—|——| ⏑ |——|—

णिवेदइस्सं।

निवेदयिष्यामि।

अनसूया: महि। ण जुत्तं ते अकिदसक्कारं अदिहिविसेसं विसज्जिअ

अनसूया: सखि न युक्तं तेऽकृतसत्कारम् अतिथिविशेषं विसृज्य

मच्छन्ददो गमणं। (शकुन्तला न किञ्चिद् उक्त्वा प्रस्थितैव)

स्वच्छन्दतो गमनम्।[1] (शकुन्तला न किञ्चिद् उक्त्वा प्रस्थितैव)

राजा : (ग्रहीतुम् इच्छन् निगृह्यात्मानम्[2] आत्मगतं) अहो चेष्टाप्रतिरूपिका कामिनो मनोवृत्तिः। अहं हि–

अनुयास्यन् मुनितनयां सहसा विनयेन वारितप्रसरः।

स्थानाद् अनुच्चलन्नपि गत्वेव पुनः प्रतिनिवृत्तः[3] ।। 29 ।।

1. Compare note 1, page 36. Śaṅkara quotes an aphorism of Bhṛgu, 'Whosoever does not reeverently honour an unknown guest, weary with travelling, and hungry and thirsty, him they call (equal in guilt to) the slayer of a Brāhmaṇa.

2. 'Wishing [making a movement] to arrest (her departure, but) checking himself.' The above is the reading of all the Devanāgarī MSS. The Bengālī have, *Utthāya jighṛkṣur iva icchām nigṛhya,* 'Rising up as if desirous of seizing her (and then) restraining his intention.' It is clear from what follows that, although Duṣyanta did not advance towards Śakuntalā, yet he must have indicated what was passing in his mind by some gesture. It appears from page 38, line 4, that the whole party were seated. The Bengālī reading supposes that, with the idea of arresting her departure, he started up and then checked himself.

3. 'Ah! the thoughts passing in the mind [the state of the mind] of a lover have their counterpart in his gestures : for, being desirous of following the hermit's daughter, all at once I have been restrained from advancing by decorum; although not (really) moving from my place, as if having gone, I have turned back again,' *i.e.,* 'I feel just as if I had gone and turned back. My feelings and my gestures correspond : I had a desire to follow her, and seemed to myself to do so; but as I felt checked by decorum, so I did not move from my

---

Verse 29. *Āryā* or *Ghāthā*. (*See* Verse 2.)

⏑ ⏑ — | — ⏑ ⏑ | ⏑ ⏑ — ‖ ⏑ ⏑ — | ⏑ ⏑ — | ⏑ — ⏑ | — ⏑ ⏑ | —
— — | ⏑ — ⏑ | — ⏑ ⏑ ‖ — — | ⏑ ⏑ — | ⏑ | ⏑ ⏑ — | —

प्रियंवदा : (शकुन्तलां निरुध्य) हला ण दे जुत्तं गन्तुं।

प्रियंवदा : (शकुन्तला निरुध्य) हला न ते युक्तं गन्तुम्।

शकुन्तला : सभ्रूभङ्गं।। किणिमित्तं।

शकुन्तला : सभ्रूभङ्गं।।[1] किन्निमित्तम्।

प्रियंवदा : रुक्खसेअणाइं दुवे धारेसि मे। एहि दाव। अत्ताणं मोचिअ तदो गमिस्समि (इति बलाद् एनां निवर्तयति)

प्रियंवदा : वृक्षसेचने द्वे धारयसि मे।[2] एहि तावत्। आत्मानं मोचयित्वा ततो गमिष्यसि (इति बलाद् एनां निवर्तयति)

राजा : भद्रे। वृक्षसेचनादेव परिश्रान्ताम् अत्रभवतीं लक्षये।

तथा ह्यस्याः

स्रस्तांसाव् अतिमात्रलोहिततलौ बाहू घटोत्क्षेपणाद्
अद्यापि स्तनवेपथुं जनयति श्वासः प्रमाणाधिकः।
बद्धं कर्णशिरीषरोधि वदने घर्माम्भसां जालकं
बन्धे स्रंसिनि चैकहस्तयमिताः पर्याकुला मूर्द्धजाः[3] ।। 30 ।।

place.' *Vinayena=kula-maryādayā* : [Śaṅkara] and *sauśīlyena* : [Kāṭav.], 'by family honour,' by honourable, gentlemanly feeling.' *Vārita-prasara=niruddha-gamana.*

1. 'With a frown.' The *bhrū-bhaṅga,* or 'bending of the brow,' was one of the acts of femine coquetry called *su-kumāra,* 'very delicate.' Under this head are included all coquettish glances of the eye : Śaṅkara. *See* page33, note 1, and Meghadūta, verse 73.

2. 'Thou owest me two waterings of trees,' or according to Sir W. Jones, 'You owe me the labour, according to our agreement, of watering two more shrubs.' The commentaries have *mahyam* for *me. Dhṛ* in the causual, in the scense of 'to owe,' requires a dative of the person.

3. 'For her her arms have shoulders drooping, and the lower part [fore arm] excessively red through tossing the watering-pot. Even now her unnaturally-strong breathing causes a heaving of her breast; a collection of drops of perspiration, impeding (the play of) the Śirīṣa in her ears, has formed upon her face : her dishevelled locks, the fillet (that confined them) having given way [fallen], are held together with one hand.' *Bāhu* is the arm from the shoulder-joint [*aṁśa*] to the wrist, and does not include the *Karabha,* or part

Verse 30. *Śārdūlavikrīḍita* (variety of *Atidhṛti*). *See* Verse 14.

तद् अहम् एनाम् अनृणां करोमि ।। इत्यङ्गुलीयं[1] दातुम् इच्छति ।।

[उभे नाममुद्राक्षराण्यनुवाच्य परस्परम् अवलोकयतः][2]

राजा : अलम् अस्मान् अन्यथा सम्भाव्य राज्ञः प्रतिग्रहोऽयमिति राजपुरुषं माम् अवगच्छथ ।[3]

from the wist to the fingers. It is divided into parts, the upper arm, *pragaṇḍa*, or that part of the arm from the elbow to the shoulder; and the lower arm, *prakoṣṭha*, commonly called the fore-arm, extending from the elbow to the wrist [see Amarakoṣa, pp. 149, 150]. *Atilohita-talau* is a Bahuvrīhi compound, in agreement with *bāhū; talau* cannot, therefore, be translated by the palms of the hands.' Wilson gives 'fore-arm' as one meaning of *tala*, and Śaṅkara explains it by *bhujodara*. It may possibly mean the under-surface of the arms, which would be reddened by the exertion of lifting and tossing the watering-pot. *pramāṇādhika=svābhavika-mānād adhika*, 'more than natural,' 'undue.' *Baddham* 'formed' [*see* page 29, note 1]. *Jālakam*, properly a 'net-work'—hence, 'a collection' *[samūha*, Schol.] or assemblage of anything.' Śaṅkara observes that her face was spotted with drops of perspiration so as to resemble net-work. So *svedam ānana-vilagna-jālakam* : Raghu-vaṁśa ix, 68. *Karṇa-śirīsha-rodhi* [*see* page 5, note 4]. The drops of perspiration would prevent the play of the pendent flower by causing it to adhere to her cheek [*Sthirī-karaṇāt* : Śaṅkara. *Saṁśleṣa-kārtvāt* : Kaṭav.] A similar idea occurs in the Megha dūta, verse, 28, wherethe lotus of the ears is described as faded by the act of removing the perspiration from the cheeks in the hot weather. The lotus-flower, or one of its petals, seems to have furnished as common an ornament for the ear as the *śirīṣa* : [Meghadūta, verse 69, 46.] *Paryākulāḥ=vikīrṇaḥ*, 'scattered.'

1. This is probably the ring which was afterwards given to Śakuntalā, and served as the *abhijñāna* or token of recognition.

2. 'Both, reading the latters of the seal with the name (of Duṣyanta stamped on it), look at each other;' [*Asau rājā iti kṛtvā*, 'Thinking to themselves,' 'This is the king'. Kāṭavema]. All the Devanāgari MSS. read *nāmamudrākṣarāṇi. Mudrā* is here not a 'seal-ring,' 'but the seal *or* engraved stone on the ring;' *nāma-mudra, lit.*, 'name-seal' is a seal with a name engraved on it, a signet-seal. So in the Mālavikāgnimitra, [p. 5, l. 9, and 48, 4] *nāga mudrā-sanātham*, and *sarpa-mudrakam aṅgulīyakam*, 'a ring possessed of a snake-seal,' *or* 'snake-stone seal.' *Anuvācya= paṭitva*, 'having read,' having decyphered.' *Vac* and *anvac* in the causal have generally this sense in dramatic composition.

3. 'Enough of considering me to be different (from what I am);

प्रियंवदा : तेण हि णारिहदि[1] एदं अङ्गुलीअअं अङ्गुलीविओअं। अज्जस्स
प्रियंवदा : तेन हि नार्हति एतद् अङ्गुलीयकम् अङ्गुलीवियोगम्। आर्यस्य
बअणेण अणिरिणा दाणिं एसा (किञ्चिद्विहस्य) हला सउन्दले मोइदासि
वचनेन अनृणा इदानीम् एषा (किञ्चिद्विहस्य) हला शकुन्तले मोचितासि
अणुअम्पिणा अज्जेण अहवा महाराएण। गच्छ दाणिं।
अनुकम्पिना आर्य्येण अथवा महाराजेन। गच्छ इदानीम्।

शकुन्तला : (आत्मगतं) जइ अत्तणो पहविस्सं।। प्रकाशं।। का तुमं
शकुन्तला : (आत्मगतं) यदि आत्मनः प्रभविष्यामि।। प्रकाशं।। का त्वं
विसज्जिदव्वस्स रुन्धिदव्वस्स वा।
विस्रष्टव्यस्य रोद्धव्यस्य वा।[2]

राजा : (शकुन्तलां विलोक्य आत्मगतं) किं नु खलु यथा वयम् अस्याम् एवम् इयमप्यस्मान् प्रति स्यात्। अथवा लब्धावकाशा मे प्रार्थना।[3] कुतः।[4]

this (ring) is a present (received) from the king : therefore understand me to be the king's officer.' *Alam anyathā sambhāvya= alam anyathā sambhāvanayā,* [*see* page 48, note 3] 'Do not imagine me to be the king himself; I am only the king's servant, and this is his ring, which he has given me to serve as my credentials.' *Pratigraho yam, i.e., idam aṅgurīyakaṁ mayi dattam :* Śaṅkara. The verb *pratigrah* signifies especially 'to receive a gift.' and reqires a genitive case : thus, *Rājñaḥ* [or *nṛpasya*] *na pratigṛhṇīyāt,* 'Let him not receive any gift from the king.' Manu iv., 84. *Pratigraha* is 'that which is received [*pratigṛhyate*]; hence, any gift.

1. All the MSS. have either *ṇāruhadi* or *ṇāluhadi* for the Sanskṛt *nārhati,* but the above is correct according to Lassen's Instit., Prāk., p. 193, 10.

2. 'Who are you (in respect) of what is to be allowed to go and what it is to be held back ?' *i.e.,* 'What power have you to send me away or keep me back ?' *Kā=na prabhuḥ, avaśa :* [Kāṭav.] *i.e.,* 'You have no right or powr.' [*see* page 34, note 2] This use of the genitive case for the dative, and of the future pass. part. for the verbal noun, is peculiar to Prākṛt. The idiom of Sanskṛt would require, *viṣarjanāya rodhanāye vā,* 'for loosing or binding.'

3. 'My wish has found (free) scope,' *i.e.,* I am at liberty to indulge it. *Prārthanā=manoratha :* Kāṭav. [*See* p. 47, note 1].

4. *Kutus,* 'Whence ?' 'Why so ?' This expression is frequently used where a reason is about to be given in verse for some previous statement. It may be translated by 'because.'

वाचं न मिश्रयति यद्यपि मे वचोभिः
कर्णं ददात्यभिमुखं मयि भाषमाणे।
कामं न तिष्ठति मदाननसम्मुखी सा
भूयिष्ठम् अन्यविषया न तु दृष्टिर् अस्याः[1] ।। 31 ।।

नेपथ्ये : भो भोस् तपस्विनः। सन्निहितास् तपोवनसत्त्वरक्षायै भवत।[2] प्रत्यासन्नः किल मृगयाविहारी पार्थिवो दुष्यन्तः।

तुरगखुरहतस् तथा हि रेणुर्
विटपविषक्तजलार्द्रवल्कलेषु।
पतति परिणतारुणप्रकाशः
शलभसमूह इवाश्रमद्रुमेषु[3] ।। 32 ।।

अपि च–

1. 'Although she mingles not her speech with my words, (nevertheless) she place her car directly opposite to me speaking [When I speak]. Granted that she does not stand with her face towards my face, (still) her eye for the most part is not fixed on any object.' Thus, says the Scholiast, he was free to indulge his hopes, without being actually certain of their realization. *Dadāti* [*nikṣipati* : Kāṭav.] *karṇam, i.e., avahitā, tatparā asti,* 'she is very attentive :' Śaṅkara. *Kāmam,* 'Well!' 'Granted!' explained by *atyartham* and *niścitam : see* page 24, line 10.

2. 'Be ye near at hand to protect the animals of the penance-grove,' *Sattva=jantu,* 'an animal :' Śaṅkara. Boetlingk translates it by *vesen,* 'being,' 'existence,' 'weal,' which is a legitimate acceptation of the word.

3. 'For the dust, raised by the hoofs of the horses, like a swarm of locusts shining in the fading glow of sun-set, falls on the frees of the hermitage, having bark-garments, moist with water, suspended (to dry) on the branches.' For *valkaleṣu see* page 18, note 1. *Aruṇa* is the glow either explained by Kāṭavema, is the evening (sayantana) redness of the sun, in of sun-rise or sun-set, more usually the former. *Pariṇatāruṇa* as contradistinction to the *aruṇodaya* or dawn. *Śalabha-samūha-pataṅga-nivaha,* 'an assemblage of grasshoppers.'

Verse 31. Vasantatilakā (a variety of *Śakkarī*). *See* Verses 8, 27.

Verse 32. *Puṣpitāgrā,* containg twenty-five syllables to the line, each line being alike, the first and third half-lines ending at the twelfth syllable.

⏑⏑⏑⏑⏑⏑—⏑—⏑——‖⏑⏑⏑⏑—⏑⏑—⏑—⏑—⏓

तीव्राघातप्रतिहततरुस्कन्धलग्नैकदन्तः
पादाकृष्टव्रततिवलयासङ्गसञ्जातपाशः।
मूर्त्तो विघ्नस् तपस इव नो भिन्नसारङ्गयूथो
धर्मारण्यं प्रविशति गजः स्यन्दनालोकभीतः[1] ।। 33 ।।

।। सर्वाः कर्णं दत्त्वा किञ्चिदिव सम्भ्रान्ताः।।

राजा : [आत्मगतं] अहो धिक् पौरा अस्मदन्वेषिणम् तपोवनम् उपरुन्धन्ति। भवतु। प्रतिगमिष्यामस् तावत्।

सख्यौ : अज्ज इमिणा आरणअवुत्तन्तेण पज्जाउलम्ह। अणुजाणाहि णो उडअगमणस्स।[3]

सख्यौ : आर्य अनेन आरण्यकवृत्तान्तेन[2] पर्याकुलाः स्मः। अनुजानीहि न उटजगमनाय।

1. 'An elephant, terrified at the sight of the (king's) chariot, enters the sacred grove, searing the herd of deer, a corporeal interruption, as it were, of our penance; having a (kind of) tether, caused by the clinging of the hedge of creepers dragged along by his feet; having one of his tusks fixed in the trunk of a tree, struck back with a violent blow.' Such is the reading of all the Devanāgarī MSS. The Bengālī have *tīvrāghātād abhimukha-taru-skandha-bhagnaika-danta*, 'with a violent blow having broken one tusk against the trunk of a tree standing in his way.' For *pāda* Kāṭavema reads *kroḍa*, 'the breast' *Valaya=veṣṭana*, 'anything that surrounds and encloses as a hedge, a fence : *'vratati-valaya* is the hedge of creeprers surrounding the hermitage. *Pāśa=bandhana-rajju*, 'a binding-rope :' Schol. *Mūtro=mūrtimān*, 'possessed of a body, incarnate :' as oppesed to the spiritual obstruction caused by evil spirits, etc. *Bhinna-sāraṅga-yūthaḥ* is a Bahuvrīhi compound, in agreement with *gajaḥ*, *i.e.* an elephant (*yena*) by whom (*sāraṅga-yūtham*) the herd of deer (*bhinnam*) has been scattered [*vikīrṇam*]. Kāṭavema observes that it may be inferred that this was a wild elephant [*vanya-gaja*], and not an elephant belonging to the king, from its being frightened at the sight of the royal chariot [*syandana*]. Compare a scene in the Ratnāvali, page 27.

2. 'By this forest-incident.' *Vṛttānta* often has the sense of 'incident,' 'event,' occurrence.'

3. There is no dative case in Prākṛt, the genitive is used to supply its place.

Verse 33. *Mandākrāntā* (variety of *Atyaṣṭi*). *See* Verse 15.

राजा : (ससम्भ्रमं) गच्छन्तु भवत्यः। वयमप्याश्रमपीडा यथा न भविष्यति तथा प्रयतिष्यामहे।

[सर्व उत्तिष्ठन्ति]

सख्यौ : अज्ज असम्भाविदादिहिसक्कारं भूओबि पेक्खणणिमित्तं

सख्यौ : आर्य असम्भावितातिथिसत्कारं भूयोऽपि प्रेक्षणनिमित्तं

लज्जेमो अज्जं विस्णबिदुं।

लज्जामहे आर्यं विज्ञापयितुम्।[2]

राजा : मा मैवं। दर्शनेनैव भवतीनां पुरस्कृतोऽस्मि।[2]

शकुन्तला : अणसूए। अहिणवकुससूईए परिक्खदं मे चलणं। कुर-

शकुन्तला : अनसूये। अभिनवकुशसूच्या[3] परिक्षतं मे चरणम्। कुर-

वअसाहापरिलग्गं च वक्कलं। दाव परिपालेध मं। जाव णं मोआबेमि।।

वक[4]शाखापरिलग्नं च वल्कलम्। तावत् परिपालयतं माम्। यावद् एनन् मोचयामि।।

1. *Vijñāpayitum* is properly, 'to make a respectful representation,' as from an inferior to a superior. Here it governs two accusatives, like verbs of telling, informing, etc. The phrase *sambhāvitātithisatkāro bhūyo prekṣaṇa-nimittam*, 'Adequate hospitality to a guest is a cause of seeing (him) again,' was probably a proverb. The two friends, wishing to quote this proverb as an argument for a second visit from Duṣyanta, said that they were ashamed to do so, as the hospitality they shown to their guest had been *asambhāvita*, inadequate.' Translate—'We are ashamed to represent inadequate hospitality to a guest as a reason for seeing (him) again.

2. 'Nay, not so; I have received all the honours (of a guest) by the mere sight of you ladyships.' *Puraskṛta=satkṛta*, 'hospitably entertained.'

3. 'By the point of a young *kuśa* (leaf).' Sūcsi, 'a needle,' is here used for the long tapering point of the leaf of the *kuśa* grass. The needle-like sharpness of the blades of this grass has been already noticed, *see* page 19, note 1.

4. A species of Jhinti or Barleria, with purple flowers and covered with sharp prickles.

इति राजानम् एवावलोकयन्ती सव्याजं विलम्ब्य सह सखीभ्यां निष्क्रान्ता।।

इति राजानम् एवावलोकयन्ती सव्याजं विलम्ब्य[1] सह सखीभ्यां निष्क्रान्ता।।

राजा : मन्दौत्सुक्योऽस्मि नगरगमनं प्रति। यावद् अनुयात्रिकान् समेत्य नातिदूरे तपोवनस्य निवेशयामि।[2] न खलु शक्नोमि शकुन्तलाव्यापाराद्[3] आत्मानं निवर्तयितुम्। मम हि–

गच्छति पुरः शरीरं धावति पश्चाद् असंस्तुतं चेतः।
चीनांशुकमिव केतोः प्रतिवातं नीयमानस्य[4]।। 34।।

[इति निष्क्रान्ताः सर्वे]

।। प्रथमोऽङ्कः।।

1. 'Pretendedly delaying,' *i.e.,* Making some pretext for lingering.

2. 'I am become indifferent about returning to the city. Meanwhile having joined my followers, I will make (them) encamp at not great distance from the penance-grove.' *Manda,* in composition, has the sense of 'little.' The verb *ni-viś,* 'to enter,' 'take up a station,' is often used in reference to the encampment of an army. Manu, vii, 188; Raghuvaṁśa, v., 42.

3. 'From occupying myself about Śakuntalā.' *Śakuntalā-gocara-pravartanāt :* K. *Śakuntalā-vividha-ceṣṭitatvāt :* Ś.

4. '(My) body goes forward (towards my retinue); (my) heart, not being in harmony (with my body), runs back (towards Śakuntalā), like the silken flag of a banner borne against the wind.' *Puraḥ, i.e., Agrataḥ senām prati,* 'Forward toward (my) army.' *Paścāt, i.e., Pṛṣṭhataḥ śakuntalām prati :* K. *Asaṁstutam=aparicitam, avaśam,* 'unacquainted, unrelated, not under the control (of the body).' The verb *saṁ-stu* is properly 'to sing or praise in chorus.' Hence, *asaṁstuta* probably means, 'not harmonizing,' 'not in concert.' The Bengālī MSS. read *asaṁsthitam* (=*avyavastham*) 'restless, unstable, illregulated.' *Cīnānssukam=cīna-deśa-bhava-vastra-viśeṣaḥ,* 'a kind of cloth produced in China,' 'silk,' 'muslin.

Verse 34. *Āryā or Ghāthā.* (*See* Verse 2.)

— ⏑⏑| ⏑—⏑ |——||—⏑⏑|——|⏑— ⏑|——|—
— —|⏑⏑⏑⏑|——||⏑⏑—|— —| ⏑ |——|—

ACT - II

अथ द्वितीयोऽङ्कः

।। ततः प्रविशति विषणो विदूषकः ।।

विदूषक : (निःश्वस्य) भो दिट्ठं। एदस्स मिअआसीलस्स रणो वअस्स-

विदूषक[1] : (निःश्वस्य) भो दिष्टम्। एतस्य मृगयाशीलस्य राज्ञो वयस्य

---

1. The word *Vidūṣaka* means 'a witty, merry, facetious person;' 'a good-natured jolly fellow.' In dramatic language it is the title given to the jocose companion and confidential friend of the *nāyaka*, or hero of the piece. This character acts the same part towards the king or prince who is the hero, that her female companions and confidantes do towards the heroine of the play. He is his constant attendant, and by a curious regulation, is to be a Brāhmaṇa, that is to say, of a caste higher than that of the king himself; and yet his business is to excite mirth by being ridiculous in person, age, and attire. Śaṅkara says that he is to be grey-haired (*palitaḥ*), hump-backed (*kubjaḥ*), lame (*khañjuḥ*), and with ugly features (*vikṛtānanaḥ*); that the chief part of all that he says is to be humorous and nonsensical; and that he is to be allowed access to the female apartments (*antaḥ-pura-caraḥ;* see Wilson's Dramatic System, page xliii). In fact, he is a species of buffoon. His attempts at with which are never very successful, and his allusions to the pleasure of the table, of which he is a confessed votary, are absurdly contrasted with the sententious solemnity of the despairing hero, crossed in the prosecution of his love-suit. The shrewdness of the heroine's confidantes never seems to fail them under the most trying circumstances; but the clumsy interference of the Vidūṣaka in the intrigues of his friend, only serves to augment his difficulties, and occasions many an awakward dilemma. As he is the universal butt, and is allowed in return full liberty of speech, he fills a character which is very necessary for the enlivement of the otherwise dull

भावेण णिव्विणोन्हि। अअं मिओ। अअंवराहो। अअं सद्दूलोत्ति
भावेन निर्विणोऽस्मि। अयं मृगः। अयं वराहः। अयं शार्दूल इति
मज्झणेबि गिम्हविरलपाअबच्छआसु वणराईसु आहिण्डीअदि अडवीदो
मध्याह्नेऽपि ग्रीष्मविरलपांदपच्छायासु वनराजिषु आहिण्ड्यत अटव्या
अडविं। पत्तसङ्करकसाआणि कडुआणि गिरिणईजलाणि पीअन्ति।
अटवीम्।[1] पत्रसङ्करकषायाणि कटूणि गिरिनदीजलानि पीयन्ते।

monotony of a Hindū drama. He is called by Śaṅkara the *upanāyaka* of the piece, or the *nāyakasya upanāyakaḥ,* a kind of sub-hero, or assistant to the hero: *see* page 47, note 3. Kāṭavema says. The Vidūṣaka is the name for a ridiculous childish man (*māṇavaka*), who is always at the side of the hero (*nāyaka-pārśva-parivartī*). He is the companion of his sports and promoter of his amusement (*hāsya-kāri-narma-suhṛd,* or, *narma-saciva*). In effecting the three objects of human life, *viz.*, merit, wealth, and pleasure; the family priests assist the king in the first; the young prince *(yuva-rājua),* ane the army in the second; the Vidūṣaka,the parasite (*pīṭamarda*), and the pimp (*viṭa*), in the third.' For an account of the Viṭa, see Wilson's Dramatic System of the Hindūs, page xlvii.

1. 'Oh (my evil) destiny! I am worn out by being the associate of this king, who is so addicted to the chase. 'Here's a deer,' 'There's a boar,' Yonder's a tiger :' (in the midst of) such (cries), even at mid-day, is it wandered about from forest to forest, in the paths of the woods, where the shade of the trees is scanty in the hot season.' *Vayasya* is properly, 'an associate or companion of about the same age (*vayas*). *Iti,* 'so saying,' here, rather, 'so crying out.' *Vana-rāji* sometimes denotes 'a fine tree,' 'one that beautifies the woods:' [*see* Wilson's Dict.] Bopp, in his Glossary, observes that *rāji,* in composition, signifies 'region,' and that *vana-rāji* in this passage may be translated 'region of the woods.' The only other compound I can call to mind in which *rāji* occurs, in *nīla-rājayaḥ,* 'dark lines or rows (of clouds) :' [verse 2 of the Ṛtu-saṁhāra.] As most of the synonyms for *rāji,* such as *paddhati, saraṇi, āli,* etc.—signify 'road,' 'path,' as well as 'line,' a similar sense may be given to *rāji. Āhiṇḍyate,* pres. pass. of *hiṇḍ* or *hiḍi,* with prep. *ā,* 'to wander about:' a very uncommon root: understand *asmābhiḥ,* 'by us.' The Prākṛt, and not the Sanskṛt, is answerable for the collection of words in this sentence.

अणिअदवेलं सुल्लमंसभूइट्ठो आहारो अण्हीअदि। तुरगाणुधावणकण्डिद-
अनियतवेलं शूल्यमांसभूयिष्ठ आहारोऽश्यते।[1] तुरगानुधावनकण्डित-
सन्धिणो रत्तिम्मिबि णिकामं सइदव्वं णत्थि। तदो महन्ते एव्व पच्चूसे दासीए
सन्धे रात्रावपि निकामं शयितव्यं नास्ति।[2] ततो महति एव प्रत्यूषे दास्याः
पुत्तेहिं सउणिलुद्धएहिं वणग्गहणकोलाहलेण पडिबोधिदोम्हि। एत्तएण
पुत्रैः शकुनिलुब्धकैर् वनग्रहणकोलाहलेन प्रतिबोधितोऽस्मि।[3] इयता -
दाणिम्पि पीडा ण णिक्कमदि। तदो गण्डस्स उबरि पिण्डिआ संवुत्ता। हिओ
इदानीमपि पीडा न निष्क्रामति। ततो गण्डस्य उपरि पिटका संवृत्ता[1]। ह्यः

1. 'Bad-smelling [pungent] water of mountain-streams, astrigent from the mixture of leaves, is drunk. At irregular hours, food, (consisting) chiefly of meant roasted on spits, is eaten.' *Kaṭu*, 'pungent,' 'ill-scented.' *Śūlyamāṁsa*, 'roast meat,' 'meat cooked on a spit.' *Bhūyiṣṭha;* see page 3, note 2.

2. 'Even in the night it cannot be slept peacefully (by me) having (my) joints strained by running along side of (his) horse.' Such is the reading of all the Devanāgarī MSS. The Bengālī have *turaga-gānam ca sadena,* 'by the noise of horses and elephants.' *Anu* is either 'after' or 'by the side of.' *Kaṇḍa* or *kaṇḍi,* 'to break, tear, separate,' is not so common as *khaṇḍ;* but the latter would be too strong a word in this passage. The genitive *mama,* 'of me,' must be supplied after *śayitavyam.* The instrum. case is more usual after the fut. pass. part., but not more correct.

3. 'Then at the very earliest dawn, by the sons of slaves hunting the birds, I am awakened by the din of taking the forest.' *Mahati-pratyūṣe, lit.,* 'at great dawn.' Compare *mahā-rātra,* 'mid-night,' and the French 'de grand matin.' *Dāsyāḥ-putraiḥ* stands for *dāsī-putraiḥ,* and is to be regarded as one compound. Śaṅkara quotes a note of Pāṇini [vi. 3. 22.] to the effect that the genitive case in this compound is used *ākrośe* in abusing and reviling. So also in *vṛṣalyāḥ-putraiḥ* for *vṛṣalī-putraiḥ. Vana-grahaṇa* denotes 'surrounding and taking possession of a wood for the purpose of hunting the animals it contains [*mṛga-grahaṇārtham :* K.]'. Those who do so are called, further on in this Act, *vana-grāhiṇaḥ,* which Kāṭavema explains by *vanāvarodhakāḥ,* 'those who inclose a wood and obstruct the points of egress.'

किलअम्हेसु ओहीणेसु तत्तभवदो मिआणुसारेण अस्समपदं पविट्ठस्सताबस-
किलअस्मासु अवहीनेषु तत्रभवतो मृगानुसारेण आश्रमपदं प्रविष्टस्यतापस-
कणआ सउन्दला णाम मम अधणदाए दंसिदा। सम्पदं णअरगमणस्स
कन्यका शकुन्तला नाम मम अधन्यतया दर्शिता।[2] साम्प्रतं नगरगमनाय
मणं कहम्पि ण करेदि। अज्जबि तस्स तं एव्व चिन्तअन्तस्स अच्छीसु पभादं
मनः कथमपि न करोति। अद्यापि तस्य ताम् एव चिन्तयतोऽक्ष्णोः प्रभातम्
णासि। का गदी। जाव णं किदाचारपरिकम्मं पेक्खामि।। इति परिक्रम्या-
आसीत्।[3] का गतिः। यावद् एनं कृताचारपरिकर्म्माणं प्रेक्षे।। इति परिक्रम्या-
वलोक्य च।। एसो वाणासणहत्थाहिं जवणीहिं वणपुप्फमालाधारिणीहिं
वलोक्य च।। एष वाणासनहस्ताभिर् यवनीभिर् वनपुष्पमालाधारिणीभिः
परिवुदो इदो एव्व आअच्छदि पिअवअस्सो। भोदु। अङ्गभङ्गविअलो विअ
परिवृत इत एव आगच्छति प्रियवयस्यः। भवतु। अङ्गभङ्गविकल इव

1. 'Even by all this my trouble does not come to an end; (for) afterwards upon the (old) boil, (another small) boil is produced.' *Iyatā = etāvatā,* 'by this much,' 'by so much.' *Niṣkrāmati = śāmyati,* 'Cases.' *Piṭakā visphoṭaka,* 'a pustule,' 'a small boil,' 'a pimple.' This was probably a proverbial phrase, as we have it also in Mudrārākṣasa, page 120, line 14; *ayam aparo gaṇḍasya upari visphoṭaḥ.*

2. 'For indeed yesterday, while we were left behind, a hermit's daughter, named Śakuntalā, through my ill-luck was presented to the view of his highness, who had entered the grounds of the hermitage in pursuit of a deer.' *Asmāsu avahineṣu = paścāt patiteṣu,* 'dropped behind :' Ś.

3. 'Even to-day (the light of) dawn (broke) upon the eyes (of him) thinking of that very (damsel);' that is, according to Candra-śekhara, *jāgrata eva rajanī nirgatā,* 'the night passes away whilst he was still awake.' Kāṭavema remarks, 'By this it may be inferred that, with thinking of her, he had not closed his eyes all night.' *Akṣṇoḥ, i.e. dṛīsor unmīlatoḥ satoḥ,* 'on his eyes being (still) open.' The word *satoḥ* in the commentary indicates that *akṣṇoḥ* is in the locative case dual.

भविअ चिट्ठिस्सं। जइ एव्वम्पि णाम विस्समं लहेअं।। इति दण्डकाष्ठम्

भूत्वा स्थास्यामि।[1] यदि एवमपि नाम विश्रमं लभेय।। इति दण्डकाष्ठम्

1. 'What is to be done? Meanwhile I will (be on the look out to) see him, when he has performed (his) usual toilet. Here is my dear friend coming in this very direction, surrounded by Yavana women, having bows in their hands, and wearing garlands of wild-flowers. Be it so; I will stand as if crippled by paralysis of my limbs.' *Kā gatiḥ*, lit., 'what resource,' *i.e.*, 'what remedy, what expedient can be devised?' This is a common phrase in Prākṛt; it occurs again in the 5th Act. *Kidācāra-parikammam* [Sanskṛt, *kṛtācāra-parikarmāṇam*]. This is the reading of one of the oldest MSS. [East-India House, 1060], and of Candra-śekhara. Kāṭavema reads *pratikarmāṇam;* but *parikarma* and *pratikarma* have the same sense, *viz.*, 'decoration after purification of the body,' 'rubbing it with perfumes after bathing.' Most of the Devanāgarī MSS. have *parikkamam* for *parikramam,* 'circumambulation.' *Yavanī,* properly a Muhammadan woman, a native of *Yavana* or Arabia, but applied also to a native of Greece. Wilson, in his translation of the Vikramorvaśīya, where the same word occurs [Act 5, page 261], remarks that Tartarian or Bactrian women may be intended. However this may be, it is plain that the business of these attendants was to act as the bearers of the king's bow and arrows. At the end of Act 6. a Yavanī enters again; *śārṅga-hastā,* 'carrying a horn-bow.' Chézy quotes the following gloss; *Yavanī yuddha-kāle rājño'stram dadāti.* 'The Yavanī in the time of war gives weapons to the king.' Kāṭavema says, *Yavanī śastradhāriṇī,* 'The Yavanī is the weapon-bearer.' *Aṅga-bhaṅga,* properly 'palsy or paralysis of the limbs.' Kāṭavema observes that the Vidūṣaka here acts the *Viṣkambha,* which he defines as an *Adhama-praveśaka* or inferior intoductory scene, coming between the acts (*aṅkayor-madhya-vartī*), and performed by inferior actors (*nīca-pātra-prayojitaḥ*). Its object is to connect or bind together the story of the drama and the sub-divisions of the plot (*kathāsaṅghaṭṭanārtham*), by concisely alluding to what has happened in the intervals of the acts, or what is likely to happen at the end *(bhūtānām bhāviṇām api sankṣepeṇa sūcanāt).*

अवलम्ब्य स्थितः।।

अवलम्ब्य[1] स्थितः।।

[ततः प्रविशति यथानिर्दिष्टपरिवारो राजा]

राजा :

कामं प्रिया न सुलभा मनस्तु तद्भावदर्शनाश्वासि।
अकृतार्थेऽपि मनसिजे रतिम् उभयप्रार्थना कुरुते[2] ।। 35 ।।

(स्मितं कृत्वा) एवम् आत्माभिप्रायसम्भावितेष्टजनचित्तवृत्तिः[3] प्रार्थयिता विडम्ब्यते।। तद्यथा–

1. 'Leaning on a staff.' *Daṇḍa-kāṣṭha = yaṣṭi,* 'a stick, a staff of wood.'

2. 'Granted my beloved is not easy to gain, still my heart encourages (itself) by observing her gestures (of love). Even though love has not accomplished the desire (of us) anticipates enjoyment.' *Kāmam; see* note 4, page 54. *Na sulabhā, i.e.,* from her relationship to the *Ṛṣi* : K. *Tad-bhāva-darśanāśvāsi;* such is the reading of all the Bengālī MSS., and of Śaṅkara. The Devanāgarī read *tad-bhāva-darśanāyāsi* where *āyāsi* properly means 'active,' 'kept in activity,' 'stimulated to exertion,' *i.e.,* exerting exerting itself to obtain her. But it may be questioned whether *āsvāsi* be not preferable, especially as Kāṭavema, though he writes *āyāsi,* explains it by *santuṣyati,* 'is cheered,' and by *āśvāsitam,* 'consoled.' *Bhāva = śṛṅgāra-ceṣṭā,* 'the expression of amorous sentiments by gestures.' The gestures here referred to are described in the next verse, beginning *snigdham,* etc. *Darśana* is either 'seeing, looking at,' [*avalokana* : Ś.] or, 'exhibiting, showing.' [*sākṣāt-karaṇa,* K.] In the latter case, translate 'by her exhibition of amorous gestures.' *Ubhaya, i.e., nāyaka-nāyikayoḥ* or *strī-puruṣayoḥ. Prārthanā = abhilāṣa,* 'longing.'

3. This is a long Bahuvrīhi compound, agreeing with *prārthayitā.* Translate 'Thus the suitor [lover] who judges of the state of feeling of his beloved one by his own desires, is deluded.' *Evam, i.e., vakṣyamaṇaprakāreṇa,* 'in the following manner, in the way about to be mentioned :' K. *Abhiprāya = abhilāṣa. Sambhāvita = kalpita,* 'imagined,' or *śaṅkita,* 'suspected.' *Iṣṭa-jana = manogata-vyakti,* 'the

---

Verse 35. *Āryā* or *Ghāthā.* (*See* Verse 2.)

— — | ⏑ — ⏑ | ⏑ ⏑ — ‖ ⏑ — ⏑ | — — | ⏑ — ⏑ | — — | ⏑
⏑ ⏑ — | — ⏑ ⏑ | ⏑ ⏑ — ‖ ⏑ ⏑ ⏑ ⏑ | — — | ⏑ | — ⏑ ⏑ | —

स्निग्धं वीक्षितम् अन्यतोऽपि नयने यत् प्रेरयन्त्या तया
यातं यच्च नितम्ब्योर् गुरुतया मन्दं विलासादिव।
मा गा इत्यवरुद्धया यदपि सा सासूयम् उक्ता सखी
सर्वं तत् किल मत्परायणम् अहो कामी स्वतां पश्यति[1] ।। 36 ।।

विदूषक : (तथा स्थित एव) भो वअस्स। ण मे हत्था पसरन्ति। ता वाआमेत्तेण जआबीअसि।

विदूषक : (तथा स्थित एव[2]) भो वयस्य। न मे हस्तौ प्रसरतः। तद् वाचामात्रेण जाप्यसे।[3]

individual in one's thoughts.' *Prārthayitā* = *kāmukaḥ* or *yācakaḥ*. *Viḍambyate* = *apahāsyate*, 'is mocked,' 'is made a fool of;' supply *kāmena*, 'by love.' The direction *smitam kṛtvā*, implies that, whilst saying this, he is to smile at his own folly in supposing that she was as fond of him as he was of her, merely because her gestures were conquettish.

1. 'Whereas by her, even though casting her eyes in another direction, a tender glance was given [*lit.*, it was looked tenderly]; and whereas by the weight of (her) hips she moved [*lit.*, it was moved by her] slowly, as if from dalliance; and whereas by (her) detained in these (words) 'Do not go,' [*see* page 52, line 2], that friend was addressed with disdain; all the certainly had reference to me. Ah! (how) a lover discovers (what is) his own!' *Vīkṣitam* is here the pass. past part, and *snigdham* an adver: Ś. *Avaruddhayā*, or, according to same MSS., *uparuddhayā* = *kṛta-gamana-bādhayā* or *kṛta-gativyāghātayā*. *Mat-parāyaṇam* = *mad-viṣayaka*, 'relating to me.' *Aho* here denotes wonder. [*āścarye* : K.] *Svatām* = *ātmīyatām* or *svakīyatām*, *i.e.*, *mat-kṛtaṁ sarvam idam*, 'All that was done on my account.' 'Although her gestures appeared to be unfavourable, yet it was easy to refer them to myself.' [*ātma-viṣayatvāropa iti mantavyam* : K.]

2. 'Still in the same position,' *i.e.*, leaning on his stick, as if *aṅga-bhaṅgavikala*, 'crippled by a paralysis of the limbs.' *See* page 64, line 2.

3. 'My hands are not capable of extension [*lit.*, do not go forward], therefore, by words merely are you wished victory [*lit.*, are you made to be victorious],' *i.e.*, 'I cannot greet you with the usual *añjali* or salutation made by joining the hands and applying

---

Verse 36. *Śārdūlavikrīḍita* (variety of *Atidhṛti*). *See* Verses 14, 30.

राजा : कुतोऽयं गात्रोपघातः।

विदूषक : कुदो किल सअं अच्छी आउलीकरिअ अस्सकारणं

विदूषक : कुतः किल स्वयम् अक्षिणी आकुलीकृत्य अश्रुकारणं

पुच्छेसि।

पृच्छसि।[1]

राजा : न खल्ववगच्छामि। भिन्नार्थम्[2] अभिधीयताम्।

विदूषक : भो वअस्स। जं वेदसो खुज्जलीलं विडम्बेदि तं किं अत्तणो

विदूषक : भो वयस्य। यद् वेतसः कुब्जलीलां विडम्बयति तत् किम् आत्मनः

पहावेण णं णईवेअस्स।

प्रभावेण ननु नदीवेगस्य।[3]

them to the forehead; you must therefore be contented with the salutation *Jayatu!* or *Vijayī bhava!'* This is the reading of the oldest MSS. [East-India House, 1060; Bodleian, 233]. The Kolkata edition, without the support of any MS. in my possession, adds *'jayatu, jayatu bhavān,* 'Let your majesty be victorious.' This is sufficiently implied in *jāpyase,* which I cannot agree in deriving from *jap,* 'to repeat or mutter,' but rather from the causal of *ji,* 'to conquer.' If referred to *jap* the meaning could only be 'you are caused to mutter,' which does not suit the context; whereas the sense of *jāpyase,* as the 2nd per. sing. pres. pass. of the causal of *ji,* is quite suitable, and is, moreover, agreeable to the interpretation of Kāṭavema [*vijayi bhava*], and to that of the Kolkata edition [*jayārho'si*]. Lassen considers *jāpyase* to be the proper Sanskrit equivalent for the Prākṛt *jaābiasi,* although, with Chezy, he refers it to *jap* (Instit. Ling. Prāk., p. 361]. Most of the Devanāgarī MSS. read: *jīābaissam for jivayishyāmi,* 'I will cause to live,' 'I will wish life,' *i.e.,* I will statue you with *chiram jīva,* 'Long life to you!' Compare page 68, line 12.

1. 'Why indeed, having yourself troubled (my) eyes, do you inquire the cause of (my) tears.' Thus explained by Śaṅkara : *yathā ko'pi kasyacin netrayor aṅgulyādikaṁ praveśya pṛcchati bhavataś cakṣuṣokr aśru katham āyāti tathā tvam api,* 'You are like a person who, after thrusting a finger etc., into the eyes of any one, asks, How doses a tear come into your eyes ?' The Vidūṣaka probably here quotes some proverb, and the king observes in the next line that he does not understand its application in the present case.

2. *Bhinnārtham=sphutārtham,* 'clearly,' 'intelligibly :' Candra-śekhara.

3. 'When the reed imitates the character [gait] of the Kubja

राजा : नदीवेगस् तत्र कारणम्।

विदूषक : ममबि भवं।

विदूषक : ममापि भवान्।

राजा : कथमिव।

विदूषक : एव्वं राअकज्जाणि उज्झिअ एआरिसे अमांणुससञ्चारे

विदूषक : एवं राजकार्याणि उज्झित्वा एतादृशे अमानुषसञ्चारे

आउलप्पदेसे वणचरवुत्तिणा तुए होदव्वं। जं सच्चं पच्चहं साबदा-

आकुलप्रदेशे वनचरवृत्तिना त्वया भवितव्यम्। यत् सत्यं प्रत्यहं श्वापदा-

णुसरणेहिं सङ्खोहिअसन्धिबन्धाणं मम गत्ताणं अणीसोम्हि संवुत्तो।

नुसरणैः मङ्खोभितसन्धिबन्धानां मम गात्राणाम् अनीशोऽस्मि संवृत्तः।

ता पसादइस्सं विसज्जिदुं मं एक्काहम्पि दाव विस्समिदुं।

तत् प्रसादयिष्ये विस्रष्टुं माम् एकाहमपि तावद् विश्रमितुम्[1]।

(plant), is that by its own power ? (or) is it not (by the force) of the current of the river.' *Vetasa,* a large reed or cane [*calamus rotang*] which grows in Indian rivers. *Kubja* or *Kubjaka,* properly 'hump-backed,' but also the name for a croocked aquatic plant [*trapa bi-spinosa*], called also *vāri-kubja* and *jala-kubja.* Śaṅkara says, it is sometimes called *kuvalaya,* a name usually applied to a species of water-lily. He also mentions a reading *kuñja,* 'an arbour,' instead of *kubja.* Possibly this is the reading to which the *kujja* of the Devanāgarī MSS. is to be referred, as, according to Vararuci (II. 33), *khujja* is the Prākṛt equivalent for *kubja.* There is doubtless a double-entendre in the word, but the first allusion is to the Kubja plant. In order to apprehend the full force of the Vidūṣaka's pleasantry in comparing himself to an upright reed, accidentally transformed into a crooked plant, it must be remembered that his natural form was that of a lame, hump-backed man. [*see* page 59, note 1.]

1. 'By you, having thus relinquished the affairs of your kingdom, it is to be lived as a forester [*lit.,* it is to be become with the manner of life of a forester], in a wild unfrequented region like this. Since (then) I truly am become no (longer) master of my own limbs, whose joints are shaken about by daily chases after wild beasts, therefore I will beg you as a favour to let me go just for one

राजा : (स्वगतं) अयं चैवम् आह। ममापि काश्यपसुताम् अनुस्मृत्य मृगयाविक्लवं[1] चेतः। कुतः।

न नमयितुम् अधिज्यम् अस्मि शक्तो
धनुर् इदम् आहितसायकं मृगेषु।
सहवसतिम् उपेत्य यैः प्रियायाः
कृत इव मुग्धविलोकितोपदेशः[2] ।। 37 ।।

विदूषक : (राज्ञो मुखं विलोक्य) अत्तभवं किम्पि हिअए करिअ मन्तेदि। अरणे मए रुदिअं आसि।

विदूषक : (राज्ञो मुखं विलोक्य) अत्रभवान् किमपि हृदये कृत्वा मन्त्रयते[3]। अरण्ये मया रुदितम् आसीत्।[4]

राजा : (सस्मितं) किम् अन्यत्। अनतिक्रमणीयं मे सुहृद्वाक्यमिति स्थितोऽस्मि।[5]

day to rest myeslf.' *Amānuṣa-sañcāre, lit.*, 'untrodden by man :' Taylor MS. *Sandhi-bandha* or *sandhi-bandhana,* properly 'the ligament or tendon which binds the joints together,' *Pra-sad* in the causal ātm., is 'to beg a favour [*prasāda*] from any one.'

1. *Viklava,* according to Kāṭavema=*vihvala, parāṅgmukha,* 'averse to,' 'turning from,' 'disinclined.' Some read *nirutsuka,* 'indifferent.'

2. 'I am not able to bend this strung bow, having-the-arrow-fixed-on-it, against the deer, by whom, possessing (the privilege of) dwelling in the society of (my) beloved, instruction in beautiful glances is as it were given (to her).' *Adhijya, see* page 9, note 4. *Āhita-sāyaka*=arpita-sāyaka : Ś. *Upetya, lit.*, 'having undergone,' [*prāpya,* Ś.]; hence *upeta,* 'possessed of.'

3. Compare the same expression, page 42, note 1.

4. 'By me a cry has been made in the wilderness,' *i.e.*, I have spoken in vain, no one listen to me [*ko' pi na śṛnoti* : Ch.] This was a kind of proverbial phrase : Compare Mahābhārata, I., 3022 : *Aham idam śūnye raumi, kim na śṛino hi me* : Also Amaruśataka, 76.

5. 'What else (ought I to have in my mind ?) The words of a friends ought not to be disregarded by me : So (thinking to myself)

Verse 37. *Puṣpitāgrā*, in which each whole line is alike. *See* Verse 32.
First and third half-line. Second and fourth half-line.

◡◡◡◡◡◡—◡—◡——|◡◡◡◡—◡◡—◡—◡——

विदूषक : चीरं जीव (इति गन्तुम् इच्छति)

विदूषक : चिरं जीव (इति गन्तुम् इच्छति)

राजा : वयस्य। तिष्ठ। शृणु सावशेषं मे वचः।

विदूषक : आणबेदु भवं।

विदूषक : आज्ञापयतु भवान्।

राजा : विश्रान्तेन भवता ममाप्येकस्मिन्न् अनायासे कर्मणि सहायेन भवितव्यम्।

विदूषक : किं मोद अखज्जिआए।

विदूषक : किं मोदकखादिकायां।[1]

राजा : यत्र वक्ष्यामि।

विदूषक : गहीदो खणः

विदूषक : गृहीतः क्षणः[2]

राजा : कः कोऽत्र भोः।

दौवारिक : (प्रविश्य) आणबेदु भट्टा।

दौवारिक : (प्रविश्य) आज्ञापयतु भर्ता[3]।

I stand here,' After *'kim anyat'* understand *hṛdaye heridaye kartavyam;* and afer *'iti' hṛdye kṛtvā.*

1. 'Is it in eating sweetmeats (that you require my assistance) ? The Kolkata edition and my own Mumbai Devanāgarī MS. read *khañjiāe,* which might equally stand for the Sanskṛt *khādikāyām,* but the above is the reading of the oldest MSS. *Khādikāyam* is given on the authority of Candra-śekhara and the Bodleian MS. (233). According to Vārttika, I. on Pāṇini, III., 3. 108., *khādikā* is an admissible form.

2. *Lit.,* 'The opportunity is taken,' *i.e.,* 'Now is a good opportunity : now is the time : I am all attention : [*avadhānaṁ kṛtam* : Ch.] I have nothing else to do but to listen.' Amara gives as one of the meanings of *kṣaṇa; nirvyāpāra-sthiti* or *vyāpārāntara-rahita-sthiti,* 'the state of having no other occupation,' *i.e.,* 'leisure, opportunity.' The above is the reading of the oldest MS. and of Kāṭavema. Śaṅkara has *gṛhītaḥ praṇayaḥ,* and the Devanāgarī MSS. *sugṛhīta ayaṁ janaḥ.*

3. Śaṅkara quotes an aphorism of Bharata, as follows : 'An universal monarch is to be addressed by his attendants with the title of *Bhaṭṭa* [*Bhartā*].' Boehtlingk compares Sāhityadarpaṇa, page 178. Kāṭavema remarks that the inferior attendants only ought to use this title; the others, *svāmin* or *deva.*

राजा : रैवतकः। सेनापतिस्। तावद् आहूयताम्।।

दौवारिक : तह।। इति निष्क्रम्य सेनापतिना सह पुनः प्रविश्य।।

दौवारिक : तथा।। इति निष्क्रम्य सेनापतिना सह पुनः प्रविश्य।।

एसो अणाबणुक्कण्ठो भट्टा इदो दिणदिट्ठी एव्व चिट्ठदि। उबसप्पदु

एष आज्ञापनोत्कण्ठो भर्त्ता इतो दत्तदृष्टिर् एव तिष्ठति[1]। उपसर्पतु

अज्जो।

आर्यः।

सेनापति : (राजानम् अवलोक्य) दृष्टदोषापि स्वामिनि मृगया केवलं गुण एव संवृत्ता।[2] तथा हि देवः–

अनवरतधनुर्ज्यास्फालनक्रूरपूर्वं
रविकिरणसहिष्णु क्लेशलेशैर् अभिन्नम्।
अपचितमपि गात्रं व्यायतत्वाद् अलक्ष्यं
गिरिचर इव नागः प्राणसारं बिभर्त्ति[3] ।। 38 ।।

1. 'There stands his Majesty eager to give (some) order, casting a look in this direction.' According to Kāṭavema *utkaṇṭha=udgrīva,* 'having the neck erect with expectation.' It is here equivalent to *udyata,* 'ready,' 'in the act,' 'on the point.'

2. 'Though observed to have evil effects, the chase has proved only an advantage in (the case of) our master.' *Dṛṣṭa-doṣā* may perhaps be translated 'regarded as a fault :' *See* the end of note 5, page 71. One MS. reads *adṛṣṭadoṣāpi,* 'certainly hunting shows not ill-effects in our master,' etc.

3. 'For truly his Majesty, like a mountain-roving elephant exhibits [bears, possesses] a body, whose fore-part is hardened by the incessant friction of the bow-string, patient of the rays of the sun, not affected [broken, weakened] by the slightest fatigue, though losing flesh [reduced in bulk] not (in a manner) to be observed, by reason of (increased) muscular development, (and) all life and energy.' *Asphālana=karṣaṇa,* 'rubbing,' 'drawing :' The idea generally implied is that of moving or flapping backwards and forwards. *Pūrva=pūrva-bhāga. Kleśa-leśair;* this reading is given on the authority of Śaṅkara and the oldest East-India House MS. (No. 1060).

Verse 38. *Mālinī* or *Māninī* (variety of *Ati-Śakkarī.*) *See* Verses 10, 19, 20.

(उपेत्य) जयतु स्वामी। गृहीतश्वापदम् अरण्यं। किमिति स्थीयते।[1]

राजा : मन्दोत्साहः कृतोऽस्मि मृगयापवादिना माठव्येन।[2]

सेनापति : (जनान्तिकं) सखे। स्थिरप्रतिबन्धो भव।[3] अहं तावत् स्वामिनश् चित्तवृत्तिम् अनुवर्तिष्ये।। प्रकाशं।। प्रलपत्येष वैधेयः।[4] ननु प्रभुरेव निदर्शनं। पश्यतु देवः।

मेदश्छेदकृशोदरं लघु भवत्युत्थानयोग्यं वपुः
सत्त्वानामपि लक्ष्यते विकृतिमच् चित्तं भयक्रोधयोः।
उत्कर्षः स च धन्विनां यद् इषवः सिध्यन्ति लक्ष्ये चले
मिथ्यैव व्यसनं वदन्ति मृगयाम् ईदृग्विनोदः कुतः[5] ।। 39 ।।

Kāṭavema passes it over. All the others road *seda-leśair*. It may be suspected that *sveda* was accidentally written for *kheda*, the synonym for *kleśa*. *Vyāyatatvād=kṛta-vyāyāmatwāt* [Ch.] and *dṛḍhatvāt* [K.] It is the state produced by *vyāyāma*, 'athletic and manly exercise of the muscles of the body.' *Alakṣya=na vibhāvya*, 'imperceptible.' Compare in the begining of Act 6, *kṣīṇo' pi nālakṣyate*, and Act 7, *avatīrno' pi na lakṣyate* : also Hitopadeśa, line 2631, *kāyaḥ kṣīyamāṇo na lakṣyate*. *Prāṇa-sāram*, 'whose whole essence or substance consists of life and spirit.' Compare *vajara-sāra*, page 14, line 4. *Bibharti*, see page 24, note 1.

1. 'The forest has its beasts of prey tracked, Why then is it staid ?' *i.e.*, Why do you delay ?' The first clause follows the reading of the Devanāgarī MSS.; the second is adopted from the oldest MS. (East-India House, 1060), supported by Kāṭavema. *Kimiti, Cf.* Hitopadeśa, line 2618; Gīta Gov., ix, 7. *Gṛhīta=jñāta*, 'found out,' discovered.' The Bengālī MSS. insert *pracāra-sūcita*, 'indicatd by their tracks,' after '*gṛhīta*.'

2. *Māṭhavya* is the name of the Vidūṣaka. In the Bengālī MSS., it is written *Mādhavya*.

3. 'Be firm in your opposition,' 'Persevere in throwing obstacles in his way.'

4. *Pralap=yadvā tadvā bhāṣ*, 'to talk nonsense,' 'to talk idly.' *Vaidheya=mūrkha*, ' fool,' 'blockhead.'

5. 'The body (of the hunter) having the waist [belly, abdomen] attenuated by the removal of fat becomes light (and) fit for exertion; moreover the spirit of living creatures is observed (to be) affected

---

Verse 39. *Śārdūlavikrīḍita* (variety of *Atidhṛti*). See Verses 14, 30, 36.

विदूषक : (सरोषं) अबेहिरे उच्छाहहेतुअ। अत्तभवं पकिदिं आपणो।

विदूषक : (सरोषं) अपेहि रे उत्साहहेतुक।[1] अत्रभवान् प्रकृतिम् आपन्नः।।

तुमं दाव अडवीदो अडविं आहिण्डन्तो णरणासिआलोलुबस्स जिणरिच्छस्स

त्वं तावद् अटव्या अटवीम् आहिण्डन् नरनासिकालोलुपस्य जीर्णर्क्षस्य

कस्मबि मुहे पडिस्ससि।

कस्यापि मुखे पतिष्यसि।[2]

with various emotions, through fear and anger; and that is the glory of the archers when the arrows fall true on the moving mark. Falsely indeed do they call hunting a vice; where (is) there such a recreation as this ?' *Medas,* 'adeps or fat,' or rather *sthaulya-janaka-dhātu,* ' serous secretion causing fatness :' K. It performs the same functions to the flesh that the marrow does to the bones; its proper seat is in the belly [*udaram*] : hence the flesh is called *medas-kṛt,* 'the maker of adeps.' *Cheda=nāśa,* 'destruction,' 'removal,' 'reduction.' *Cf. Gharmacheda,* 'the cessation of the heat :' Vikramorvaśīya, Act 4. *Utthāna-yogyam;* the Bengālī MSS. read *utsāha-yogyam,* but *utsāha* is merely a synonym for *utthāna,* which is applied to any kind of manly exertion. Kāṭavema says, the word here refers especially to the act of mounting on horse-back. *Sattvānām, i.e., jantūnāṁ sinhādīnām,* 'animals such as lions, etc.' It probably refers both to the hunters and the hunted. *Vikṛtimat,* 'affected with *vikṛti* or *vikāra, i.e.,* any emotion which causes a change from the *prakṛti,* or natural and quiescent which [*parityakta-prakṛtikam* : K.]; *See* page 38, note 2. *Bhaya-krodayḥ* [*satoḥ*]=*bhaye krodhe ca.* Śaṅkara explains *utkarṣa* by *pratiṣṭhā,* 'fame, honour.' *Vyasanam :* In Manu, vii., 47. 50, hunting is designated as one of the ten vices [*vyasanāni*] of kings, and is, moreover, included amongst the four most pernicious [*kaṣṭatama*].

1. *Utsāha-hetukaḥ,* 'One who encourages or incites to exertion :' opposed to *utsāha-bhaṅga-karaḥ,* 'One who damps another's zeal :' Hitopadeśa, line 1987.

2. 'His Majesty has returned to his natural state [*i.e.,* is no longer eager after the excitement of hunting]; but thou, wandering from forest to forest, wilt probably fall into the jaws of some old bear, gready after a human nose.' *prakṛti,* 'the natural, quiescent, state of the soul,' as opposed to *vikṛti; see* above. *Āhiṇḍan* : *see* p. 60, 3. 4: *Daśa-kumāra.* : p. 151, 1. 6. *Nara-nāsikā:* Kāṭvavema in explanation

राजा : भद्र सेनापते। आश्रमसन्निकृष्टस्थिताः स्मः। अतस् ते वचो नाभिनन्दामि। अद्य तावत्–

गाहन्तां महिषा निपानसलिलं शृङ्गैर् मुहुस् ताडितं
छायाबद्धकदम्बकं मृगकुलं रोमन्थम् अभ्यस्यतु।
विश्रब्धं क्रियतां वराहततिभिर् मुस्ताक्षतिः पल्वले
विश्रामं लभताम् इदं च शिथिलज्याबन्धम् अस्मद्धनुः[1] ।। 40 ।।

says, *bhallūkā manuṣyāṇām nāsikāṁ gṛhṇanti,* 'bears seize the human nose.' The Bengālī read *śṛgāla-mṛga-lolupasya,* 'eager after a jackal or deer.' *Richcassa* is the Prākṛt for *ṛkṣasya,* in accordance with Vararuchi. III, 30.

1. 'Let the buffaloes agitate-by-their-plunges the water of the tanks, repeatedly struck with their horns : let the herd of deer, forming groups under the shade, busy themselves in rumination; let the bruising of the Mustā grass be made in (undisturbed) confidence by the lines [herbs] of boars in the pool; and let this may bow, having the fastening of its string-loose get repose *Gāhantām=lolayantu,* 'Let them agitate, stir :' K. : hence *lulāpa* is one of the names for a buffalo. *Gāh* is properly, 'to plunge into,' or 'plunge about in.' *Nipāna=āhāva,* 'a reservoir near a well [*upakūpa*] : Amara. *Romantham=adhara-calanam,* 'The moving of the lower lip :' K. and *bhuktasya punar ākṛṣya* or *udgīrya carvaṇam,* 'The chewing of what has been eaten after drawing or vomiting it up again :' Ś. *and* Ch. : *i.e.,* chewing the cud.' *Abhyasyatu=paunaḥpunyena karotu,* 'Perform again and again :' Ch. *Tatibhir=yūthaiḥ,* 'By herds.' The Bengālī read *varāha-patibhir,* 'By the chiefs of the boars.' There is no difficulty in *tatibhir;* many herds of animals form lines in moving from one place to another, or in grazing. *Mustā,* a sort of fragrant grass [*Cyperus rotundus*] of which swine are fond, and are hence called *mustāda. Kṣati=vidāraṇam,* 'tearing, uprooting :' K. : and *luṇṭhanam,* 'rolling :' Ś. The grass would probably be bruised by their trampling and rolling on it, as well as by their eating it. *Śithila-jyā-bandha=avaropita-guṇa.* Śaṅkara and Candraśekhara observe that the above verse furnishes an example of the figure called *Jāti* or *Svabhāvokti, i.e.,* 'Descripition of living objects by circumstances or acts suited to their character.' They also animadvert on the somewhat unusual change of construction from the nominative to the instrumental in the third line, and its resumption in the fourth.

Verse 40. *Śārdūlavikrīḍita* (variety of *Atidhṛti*). *See* Verses 14, 30, 36, 39.

सेनापति : यत् प्रभविष्णवे[1] रोचते।

राजा : तेन हि निवर्तय पूर्वगतान् वनग्राहिण:।[2] यथा न मे सैनिकास् तपोवनम् उपरुन्धन्ति तथा निषेद्धव्या:। पश्य।

शमप्रधानेषु तपोधनेषु
गूढं हि दाहात्मकम् अस्ति तेज:।
स्पर्शानुकूला इव सूर्यकान्तास्
तद् अन्यतेजोभिभवाद् वमन्ति[3] ।। 41 ।।

1. *Prabhaviṣṇu,* 'The Mighty one.' This more nearly corresponds to our expression 'His Majesty' than the other common titles *svāmin, bhartṛ,* etc.

2. *Vana-grāhiṇaḥ=vanāvarodhakān* : see page 62, note 1.

3. In ascetics with whom stoicism [a passionless state] is predominant (over all other qualities), there lies concealed a consuming energy [fire]. That (energy), like sun-crystals, (which are) grateful [cool] to the touch, they put forth, from (being acted upon by) the opposing-influence of other forces :' *i.e.,* The inhabitants of this hermitage, however passionless they may be, and however agreeable as associates when unprovoked, contain within themselves a latent energy, which, when roused by opposing influences, will be put forth to the destruction of those who molest them : as a crystal lens, however cool to the touch in its natural state, will emit a burning heat when acted upon by the rays of the sun. *Śoma-pradhāneṣu,* 'to whom stoicism is everything;' who regard exemption from all passion and feeling as the *summum bonum. Śūryakānta, lit.,* 'beloved by the sun,' also called *sūrya-maṇi,* 'the sun-gem,' and *dīptopala,* shining stone,' was a stone resembling crystal. Wilson calls it a fabulous stone with fabulous properties, and mentions a fellow-stone called *candra-kānta,* 'moon-beloved,' or *candra-maṇi,* 'moon-gem.' It may be gathered from this passage that its properties resembled those of a glass lens, and it may be presumed that this instrument was not unknown to the Hindūs at the time when this play was written. The following parallel

Verse 41. *Upajāti* or *Ākhyānakī* (variety of *Triṣṭubh*), each half-line being either *Upendra-vajrā* or *Indra-vajrā;* the former only differing from the latter in the first syllable.

⏓—◡——◡◡—◡|——||

सेनापति : यद् आज्ञापयति स्वामी।

विदूषक : गच्छ भो दासीएपुत्त। धंसिदो दे उच्छाहवुत्तन्तो।

विदूषक : गच्छ भो दास्याःपुत्र।[1] ध्वंसितस् ते उत्साहवृत्तान्तः।[2]

[निष्क्रान्तः सेनापतिः]

राजा : (परिजनं विलोक्य) अपनयन्तु भवत्यो[3] मृगयावेशं (रैवतक) त्वमपि स्वं नियोगम् अशून्यं कुरु।[4]

परिजन : जं देवो आणबेदि (इति निष्क्रान्तः)।

परिजन : यद् देव आज्ञापयति (इति निष्क्रान्तः)।

विदूषक : किदं भवदा दाणिं णिम्मच्छिअं। सम्पदं इमस्सिं पादब-

विदूषक : कृतं भवता इदानीं निर्मक्षिकं।[5] साम्प्रतम् अस्मिन् पादप-

sentiment is from Bhartṛhari, II., 30 : *Yad acetano' pi pādaiḥ spṛṣṭaḥ prajvalati savitur atikāntaḥ, tat tejasvī puruṣaḥ para-kṛta-nikṛtam kathaṁ sahate,* 'Since even the lifeless (stone) beloved of the sun, when touched by its rays, burns; how then can the man of spirit put up with an injury inflicted by another ?' *Abhibhava=tiraskāra,* 'insult:' K. The sun's rays, disturbing the natural state of the stone, are compared to the hunter's disturbing the hermitage and provoking its inhabitants. *Vamanti :* this is the reading of all the Devanāgarī MSS. and of Kāṭavema. The Bengālī read *sparsānukūlā api sūrya-kāntās, te hyanya-tejo-bhibavāda dahanti,* 'Although the sun-crystals be grateful to the touch, yet, from the influence of other they burn.'

1. This is inserted on the authority fo Kāṭavema, and one MS. [East-India House, 2696.] The Bengālī read, *bho utsāha-hetuka niṣkrama.*

2. 'Your arguments for exertion (in the chase) have fallen (to the ground)', *i.e.,* All that you have alleged in praise of hunting, with the view of rousing the king's ardour, has been in vain.

3. Some read *bhavanto;* but the feminine *bhavatyo* (which is supported by Kāṭavema) seems more correct, as the female attendants, called Yavanī, are intended. *See* page 63, note 1, in middle.

4. 'Fulfil your office (of a door-keeper),' *i.e., dvāra-stho bhava,* 'Stand at the door :' Ch.

5. '(The place) has now been made clear of flies by your Majesty,' *i.e.,* We are now left alone, and no one can interrupt us.

च्छआविरइदविदाणसणाहे सिलाअले उबविसदु भवं जाव अहम्पि सुहासीणो
च्छायाविरचितवितानसनाथे शिलातले[1] उपविशतु भवान् यावद् अहमपि सुखासीनो
होमि।
भवामि।

राजा : गच्छाग्रत:।

विदूषक : एदु भवं।

विदूषक : एतु भवान्।

[उभौ परिक्रम्योपविष्टौ]

राजा : माठव्य। अनवाप्तचक्षु:फलोऽसि येन त्वया द्रष्टव्यानां परं न दृष्टम्।[2]

विदूषक : णं भवं अग्गदो मे वट्टदि।

विदूषक : ननु भवान् अग्रतो मे वर्तते।

राजा : सर्व: कान्तम् आत्मीयं पश्यति। अहं तु ताम् एवाश्रमललामभूतां शकुन्तलाम् अधिकृत्य ब्रवीभि।[3]

Nirmakṣikam=nirjanam, 'free from people :' Ś. *and* Ch. According to Pāṇini II., 1. 6, *nirmakṣikam* is an Avyayībhāva compound; but it is here used adjectively. The Prākṛt equivalent follows Vararuci III, 30. The phrase occurs again in the beginning of the 6th Act. Has *makṣikam* here at all the sense of the French *mouchard,* 'a spy,' which is derived from *mouche,* ' a fly ?'

1. On this stone-seat, furnished with a conopy,' etc. *See* page 26, note 2.

2. *Lit.,* 'Thou hast not obtained the fruit of thy eyes, since the best of things worthy to be seen has not been seen by thee;' *i.e.,* Until you have seen Śakuntalā, you may consider your eyes as barren, and created in vain : when they have fallen upon this object, they may then be said to have yielded some fruit. So in the Viramorvaśīya, Act 1, the King, speaking of Urvaśī, says, *yasyu netrayor abandhyayoḥ* [not barren] *pathi sthitā tvam. Cf.* also Gīta-Gov. ix, 6 : *Harim avalokaya sa-phalaya nayane,* 'look upon Hari (and) make thy eyes fruitful.

3. Every one regards his own as beautiful; but I speak in reference to that same Śakuntalā who is the ornament of the hermitage.' *Ātmīyam* is given in one Mumbai MS. [East-India

विदूषक : (स्वगतं) होदु। मे अवसरं ण दाइस्सं।। प्रकाशं।। भो

विदूषक : (स्वगतं) भवतु।। अस्य अवसरं न दास्यामि।।[1] प्रकाशं।। भो

वअस्स। जइ सा तबस्सिकणआ अणब्भत्थणीआ ता किं ताए दिट्ठआए।

वयस्य। यदि मा तपस्विकन्यका अनभ्यर्थनीया तदा किं तया दृष्टया।[2]

राजा : सखे। न परिहार्ये वस्तुनि पौरवाणां मनः प्रवर्तते।[3]

सुरयुवतिसम्भवं किल मुनेर् अपत्यं तदुज्झिताधिगतम्।
अर्कस्योपरि शिथिलं च्युतमिव नवमल्लिकाकुसुमम्[4] ।। 42 ।।

House, 1858], and supported by Kāṭavema. *Lalāna=alaṅkāra. Adhikṛtya*, see page 5, note 2. *Cf.* Mālavik., page 49, line 11 : *Mudrām adhikṛtya bravīmi* : aslo Raghu-vaṁśa, xi, 62; Kumāra-sam., iv. 38.

1. 'I will not give him an opportunity (of speaking about her).' *Se* may stand for either *asya* or *asyāḥ;* Kāṭavema here interprets it by the former *Avasaram=vāg-avasaram.* I will not hold a conversation with him respecting Śakuntalā : Ś.

2. 'If she be a hermit's daughter, she is not (fit) to be wooed (by you); what (good) then will you get) by her seen ?' This reading in adopted from the Bengālī MSS.

3. 'The heart of the descendants of Puru does not engage in (the pursuit of) a forbidden object :' *See* page 31, note 1. The Bengālī MSS. and two of the Devanāgarī [East-India House, 2696, and my own] insert the following curious verse before the above sentence : *Mūrkha, Nirākṛta-nimeṣābhir netra-paṅktibhir unmukhaḥ Navām indu-kalāṁ lokaḥ kena bhāvena paśyati,* 'O fool ! with what idea do people look at a new digit of the moon, turning up their faces with a row of eyes free from winking.

4. '(Although the reputed) offspring of the sage, she is really sprung from a celestial nymph, (and was) found (by him when) deserted by her; like a severd flower of the Navamallikā [*see* page 22, note 2] fallen on the Sun plant' [swallow-wort, gigantic Asclepias, or Calotropis gigantea]. The Nava-mallikā was a delicate

---

Verse 42. *Āryā* or *Ghāthā*. (*See* Verse 2.)

⏑⏑⏑⏑|⏑—⏑|—⏑⏑|| ⏑—⏑ | — — |⏑— ⏑|—⏑⏑|—
—— |—⏑⏑|⏑⏑—||⏑⏑⏑⏑|⏑⏑—| ⏑ |— ⏑⏑|—

विदूषक : (विहस्य) जह कस्सबि पिण्डखजूरेहिं उव्वेजिदस्स
विदूषक : (विहस्य) यथा कस्यापि पिण्डखर्जूरैर् उद्वेजितस्य
तिन्तिडिआए अहिलासो भवे। तह अन्तेउरइत्थिआरअणपरिभाविनो भवदो
तिन्तिडिकायाम् अभिलाषो भवेत्। तथा अन्तेपुरस्त्रीरत्नपरिभाविनो भवत
इअं अब्भत्थणा।
इयम् अभ्यर्थना।[1]

राजा : न तावद् एनां पश्यसि। येनैवम् अवादीः।

विदूषक : तंक्खु रमणिज्जं। जं भवदोबि विन्हअं उप्पादेदि।

विदूषक : तत्खलु रमणीयं। यद् भवतोऽपि विस्मयम् उत्पादयति।

राजा : वयस्य। किं बहुना।

and tender plan [*atikomala-puṣpa-bheda* : Ch.] which, as a creeper, depended on some other tree for support; the *arka* was a large and vigorous one [*see* Sir W. Jones, vol. v, page 102] : hence the former is compared to Śakuntalā, the latter to the sage Kaṇva. Śaṅkara explains *arkopari* by *raver upari,* 'upon the sun :' but, according to Sir W. Jones, *ravi* may be a synonym for the swallow wort; and Śaṅkara himself hints that some interpret *arka* by *arka-puṣpa.* Kāṭavema, explains the first line of the verse, but dismisses the second as too clear for any remark. *Sura-yuvati; 'see* page 44, note 2. According to Kāṭvema, *kila* is used *vārtāyam,* 'it is said,' 'it is reported;' but Śaṅkara interprets it by *niścitam,* 'certainly.' *Śithilam=vṛntāc cyutam,* 'fallen from the stalk :' Ch. The correspondence of the words in the first line with those in the second is noticeable; *sura-yuvati* with *nava-mallikā, muni* with *arka, apatya* with *kusuma, ujjhita* with *śithila, adhigata* with *cyuta.*

1. 'Just as to any one [*lit.*, of any one] having lost his relish for dates, there may be a great desire for the tamarind; so is this desire of your majesty (for Śakuntalā), slighting the jewels of women in (your own) haram.' *Piṇḍa-kharjūa,* 'a kind of Kharjūra, or date-tree,' here probably used for the fruit, and therefore in the neuter. *Tintiḍikā* or *tintiḍī,* 'the tamarind-tree.' *Udvejita=vaimanasyam prāpita,* 'brought to a change of mind or feeling.' *Itthiā, itthikā* and *itthī* are the regular Prākṛt equivalents for *strī. See* Lassen's Inst. Prāk., page 182, note.

चित्रे निवेश्य परिकल्पितसत्त्वयोगा
रूपोच्चयेन मनसा विधिना कृता नु।
स्त्रीरत्नसृष्टिर् अपरा प्रतिभाति सा मे
धातुर् विभुत्वम् अनुचिन्त्य वपुश्च तस्याः[1] ।। 43 ।।

1. Was she endowed with the properties of life by the Creator after delineating her [placing her] in a picture; or was she rather formed by the mind by a conncentration [assemblage, selection] of lovely forms. She appears to me like a matchless [the last] creation of the loveliest of women [*or* like another creation of the goddess of beauty], when I recollect [recollecting] the omnipotence of the Creator, and her (graceful) person :' *i.e.,* When I call to mind the divine power of Brahmā, I cannot help regarding her as some faultless picture which he has painted and endowed with breath and life; when I reflect on her sylph-like figure, I am inclined to think she must have been formed in his mind by an ideal selection of the most beautiful forms. Or, it may simply mean—Whatever was the method of her creation, whether she was formed by the hand, by first painting a beautiful figure and then breathing into it the principle of life; or by the mind, by collecting into one ideal model a combination of various exquisite forms; it is clear that when I reflect on the omnipotence of the Creator, and upon her loveliness, I must regard her as an unequalled beauty (or, as another creation of the goddess Lakṣmī). *Strī-ratna* is explained by Śaṅkara and Candraśekhara to mean Lakṣmī; but it may be better to refer it to the *antepura-strī-ratna* mentioned before, as *aparā=apūrvā,* 'matchless,' 'peerless,' 'without a fellow;' *na vidyate parā* : K. *and* Ś. *Citre=ālekhye. Niveśya=vinyasya,* 'having placed, fixed, committed.' *Parikalpita=sampādita,* or *sampanna,* 'endowed with,' 'provided with :' K. *Yoga,* at the end of a compound, is used somewhat vaguely; *sattva-yoga* may mean 'a combination of the various properties of being and life.' Kāṭavema observes that, 'as an object is lovely, so is it capable of being represented in a picture,' and refers to the verse in the 6th Act, beginning *Yadyat sādhu na citre syāt.* This, he says, is tantamount to asserting that the figure of Śakuntalā was faultless. *Rūpoccaya=candrādya-upamāna-vastu-samuccaya, i.e.,* 'collecting together such models of beauty as the

---

Verse 43. *Vasantatilakā* (a variety of *Śakkarī*). *See* Verses 8, 27. 31.

विदूषक : जइ एव्वं। पच्चादेसो दाणिं रूबवदीणं।

विदूषक : यदि एवं। प्रत्यादेश[1] इदानीं रूपवतीनाम्।

राजा : इदं च मे मनसि वर्तते।

अनाघ्रातं पुष्पं किसलयम् अलूनं कररुहैर्
अनाविद्धं रत्नं मधु नवम् अनास्वादितरसम्।
अखण्डं पुण्यानां फलमिव च तद् रूपम् अनघं
न जाने भोक्तारं कम् इह समुपस्थास्यति विधिः[2] ।। 44 ।।

moon, etc., for the purpose of forming one ideal perfect form, by a selection from each K. *Manasā kṛ*, or *kalp*, ' to form by means of the mind;' hence often simply, 'to imagine;' and hence, *mano-kalpitam*, ' an idea.' There may be an allusion here to the mind-born sons of Brahmā. *Vidhinā=vidhātra.* Kāṭavema observes that, 'being dissatisfied with the thought contained in the first line, he asserts in the second that her limbs were too delicate to have been fashioned by the hand in a picture; they must, therefore, have been formed in the mind.' *Strī-ratna=strī-śreṣtha* : Ch. *Jātau jātau yad utkṛṣtaṁ taddhi ratnaṁ pracakṣate*, 'whatever is best of its kind that indeed they call *ratna*, a gem :' Ch. The connection of *anucintya* with the dative case *me* is unusual, but not without precedent. The Bengālī MSS. read *citte* for *citre.*

1. 'The supplanter.' The verb *praty-ā-diś=nirākṛ, i.e.*, 'to reject,' 'remove,' 'set aside,' and *pratyādeśa*, 'rejection,' is here used for 'the cause of rejection;' *i.e.*, anything which, by its superiority, supplants and brings into contempt what was before highly priced. *Tayā nija-saundarya-mahimnā' nyarūpoavatī-rūpaṁ khaṇḍitam* : Ś. So also, in the beginning of the Vikramorvaśīya, Urvaśī is called '*pratyādeso rūpa-gorvitāyāḥ śri-gauryāḥ.*'

2. 'This faultless form (is) like a flower not (yet) smelt, a tender-shoot unplucked [uncut, unhurt] by the nails, and unperforated jewel, fresh honey whose flavour (is yet) untasted, and the full [unalloyed] reward of meritorious deeds. I know not to what possessor [enjoyer] here [of this form] Destiny will resort;' *i.e.*, I know not whom Destiny intends to be the enjoyer of her beauty. *Alūnam, i.e., śākhāvasthitam*, 'Still remaining on the branch.' *Anāviddham=asamutkīrṇam*, 'unperforated :' K. Cf. Raghuvaṁśa, i,

Verse 44. *Śikhariṇī* (variety of *Atyaṣṭi*) *See* Verses 9, 24.

विदूषक : तेण हि लहु परित्ताअदु णं भवं। मा कस्सबि तबस्सिणो

विदूषक : तेन हि लघु परित्रायताम् एनां भवान्। मा कस्यापि तपस्विन

इङ्गुदीतेल्लचिक्कणसीसस्स हत्थे पडिस्सदि।

इङ्गुदीतैलचिक्कणशीर्षस्य हस्ते पतिष्यति।[1]

राजा : परवती खलु तत्रभवती। न च सन्निहितोऽत्र गुरुजनः।

विदूषक : अध भवन्तं अन्तरेण कीदिसो से दिट्ठिराओ।

विदूषक : अथ भवन्तम् अन्तरेण कीदृशोऽस्या दृष्टिरागः।[2]

राजा : निसर्गाद् एवाप्रगल्भस् तपस्विकन्याजनः। तथापि तु–

4, where he speakes of *maṇau vajra-samutkīrṇe sūtrasya gatiḥ*, 'the entrance of a thread into a gem perforated by the adamant.' The Bengālī MSS. read *anāmukta=aparihitam, ākarād ānīta mātram*, 'not yet put on, only drawn from the mine :' Ś. *phalaṁ puṇyānām, i.e.*, 'the fruit of many virtuous acts in various former births come to its maturity' *(pariṇatī bhūtam)* : Ś. *Akhaṇḍa=sampūrṇa*, 'unimpaired,' 'entire.' The consequences of good deeds performed in former birhts is sometimes mixed with evil; but, in this comparison, it is said to be unalloyed : hence the form of Śakuntalā is called *anagham*, 'faultess,' *i.e., pratyavāya-hetu-rahitam* : K. *Iha, i.e., asmin rūpa-viṣaye*, 'with reference to this form :' K. *Samupasthāsyati=samprāpsyati*, 'will attain,' 'arive at.' This verse affords an example of the figure called 'Rūpaka,' *i.e.*, A description of one object under the form of another, animate or imanimate, which it is poetically supposed to resemble. There are various modification of this figure.

1. 'Therefore let your highness quickly rescue her, lest she fall into the hands of some devout-rustic, whose head is greasy with the oil of Ingudī.' See page 19, note 1. *Mā=yathā na* : K.

2. 'Towards your honour what of feeling (was displayed) by her eyes ?' *Atha* is used in asking a question : Ś. *Bhavantam antareṇa=bhavan-nimittam* : Ch. :=*bhavan-madhye* : Ś. The same expression occurs in the third Act of the Vikramorvaśīya, where the interpretation given is, *bhavantam uddiśya, i.e.*, 'towards or with regard to you,' *Antareṇa* is similarly used in the Mālavikāgn. page 5, line 7. It governs an accusative case, by Pāṇini II., 3, 4 *Dṛṣṭi-rāga=cakṣuḥ prīti*, 'the love of the eyes :' K. The above is the reading of all the Devanāgarī MSS., supported by K. and Ś.; but he Bengālī read *citta-rāga*.'

अभिमुखे मयि संहृतम् ईक्षितं
हसितम् अन्यनिमित्तकृतोदयम्।
विनयवारितवृत्तिर् अतस् तया
न विवृतो मदनो न च संवृतः[1] ।। 45 ।।

विदूषक : णंक्खु दिट्ठमेत्तस्स तुह अङ्कं आरोहदि।।

विदूषक : ननु खलु दृष्टमात्रस्य तव अङ्कम् आरोहति।[2]

राजा : मिथःप्रस्थाने पुनः शालीनतयापि ममाविष्कृतो भावस् तत्रभवत्या।[3] तथा हि–

दर्भाङ्कुरेण चरणः क्षत इत्यकाण्डे
तन्वी स्थिता कतिचिदेव पदानि गत्वा।
आसीद् विवृत्तवदना च विमोचयन्ती
शाखासु वल्कलम् असक्तमपि द्रुमाणाम्[4] ।। 46 ।।

1. 'When I stood fecing her, her glance was withdrawn, a smile was (feigned to be) raised from some other cause (than love); hence love, whose course was checked by modesty, was not (fully) displayed by her, nor (yet) concealed.' *Anya-nimitta, i.e.,* some other cause than love, which was the true one; [*abhilāṣa-vyatirikta* : K.] 'By this her love was concealed :' K. The Bengālī have *kathodayam. Vinaya-vārita-vṛttir* is to be taken with *madano* : K. *Cf.* page 50, note 3.

2. 'Is it really (to be expected) that she will seat herself on the lap of you, barely seen ?' *i.e.,* Do you expect to gain her all at once, without some effort ?

3. 'Again, at our mutual departure, her feeling towards me was betrayed by her ladyship, although with modesty.' *Sakhībhyām* before *mithaḥ* is not supported by the commentators or by the best Devanāgarī MSS.

4. 'For, having proceeded only a few steps (that) slim one stopped without any (real) occasion, saying, '(My) foot is hurt by a blade of kuśa-grass' [p. 57, l. 10]; and remained with her face turned back (towards me), whilst (pretending to be employed in) releasing

---

Verse 45. *Druta-Vilambita* (variety of *Jagatī*), containing twelve syllables to the halfl-line, each half-line being alike.

◡◡◡—◡◡—◡◡—◡—||

Verse 46. *Vasantatilakā* (variety of *Sakkrī*). *See* Verses 8, 27, 31. 43.

विदूषक : तेण हि गहीदपाहेओ होहि। किदं तुए उववणं तबोवणंत्ति पेक्खामि।

विदूषक : तेन हि गृहीतपाथेयो भव। कृतं त्वया उपवनं तपोवनमिति प्रेक्षे।[1]

राजा : सखे। तपस्विभिः कैश्चित् परिज्ञातोऽस्मि। चिन्तय तावत् केनापदेशेन पुनर् आश्रमपदं गच्छामः।

विदूषक : को अबरो अबदेसो। णं भवं राआ।

विदूषक : कोऽपरोऽपदेशः। ननु भवान् राजा।

राजा : ततः किम्।

विदूषक : णीवारच्छट्ठभाअं अन्हाणं उबहरन्तुत्ति।

विदूषक : नीवारषष्ठभागम्[2] अस्माकम् उपहरन्त्विति।

राजा : मूर्ख। अन्यम् एव भागधेयम् एते तपस्विनो निर्वपन्ति यो रत्नराशीनपि विहायाभिनन्द्यते।[3] पश्य।

her bark-dress, although not (really) entangled in the branches of the shrubs.' *Darbhāṅkureṇa* : see page 57, note 3 : page 19, note 1. *Iti* : *see* page 53, line 4. *Akāṇḍe=akasmāt* : K.:=*animittam* : Ś :=*anavasaram* : Ch. One sense of *kāṇḍa* is 'occasion,' 'opportunity.' *Vivṛtta-vadanā, i.e., mad-avalokanāya,* 'for a look at me :' Ś. This verse affods an example of the '*Samādhi alaṅkāra* :' Ś.

1. 'Therefore be provided with a stock of provender : I see that you have made the penance-grove a pleasure-grove [pleasure-garden].' *Gṛhīta-pātheya,* 'one who has provided himself with provender or the necessaries for a journey.' According to Kāṭavema it is here equivalent to *sannaddho,* 'equipped', 'prepared,' *i.e.* for rambling in the precincts of the harmitage in quest of Śakuntalā. The Vidūṣaka is characteristically anxious about the provisions.

2. According to Manu (vii, 131-133), a king might take a sixth part of liquids, flowers, roots, fruits, grass, etc.; but, even though dying with want, he was not to receive any tax from a Brāhmaṇa learned in the Vedas.

3. 'These hermits pay another (kind of) tribute, which, leaving behind heaps of jewels, is welcomed [rejoiced in] :' *i.e.,* which is welcomed more than heaps of jewels. This is the reading of the

यद् उत्तिष्ठति वर्णेभ्यो नृपाणां क्षयि तत् फलम्।
तपः षड्भागम् अक्षय्यं ददत्यारण्यका हि नः[1] ।। 47 ।।

नेपथ्ये : हन्त सिद्धार्थौ स्वः।[2]

राजा : (कर्णं दत्त्वा) अये धीरप्रशान्तस्वरैस् तपस्विभिर् भवितव्यम्।[3]

दौवारिक : (प्रविश्य) जेदु जेदु भट्टा। एदे दुवे इसिकुमारआ पडिहार-भूमिं उवट्ठिदा।

दौवारिक : (प्रविश्य) जयतु जयतु भर्ता। एतौ द्वौ ऋषिकुमारकौ प्रतिहार-भूमिम्[4] उपस्थितौ।

राजा :: तेन ह्यविलम्बितं प्रवेशय तौ।

दौवारिक : एसो पवेसेमि। (इति निष्क्रम्य ऋषिकुमाराभ्यां सह प्रविश्य)

दौवारिक : एष प्रवेशयामि।[5] (इति निष्क्रम्य ऋषिकुमाराभ्यां सह प्रविश्य)

oldest Bengālī MSS., and seems preferable to that of the Devanāgarī *anyad bhāgadheyaṁ eteṣām rakṣaṇe nipatati,* 'another tribute accrues (to me) for their protection.' According to Amara (II, III, 1.27) bhagadheya in this sense is masculine. Śaṅkara and some of the Bengālī have *puṇya* for *anya.*

1. 'That tribute which arises to kings from the (four) classes is perishable; but hermits [inhabitants of the woods] offer us a sixth part of (the merit of their) penance, (which is) imperishable.' *Varṇebhyaḥ,* 'the four classes of Brāhmaṇas, Kṣatriyas, Vaiśyas, and Śūdras :' K., Ś., and Ch. Hence, it would appear that the Brāhmaṇas were liable to some kind of tribute as well as the other classes, though it is clear from Manu that they were in most cases exempt. The Bengālī have *dhanam* for *phalam. Dadati;* the third conjugation rejects the nasal in the third person plural.

2. 'We have accomplished our object,' *i.e.,* in gaining an audience of the king : Ś. *Hanta,* an exclamation of pleasure : Ś.

3. 'Oh ! it is to be by the hermits, [it mst surely be the hermits by their deep (yet) calm voices,' *i.e.,* to judge by their deep, yet suppressed, tone, the voices which I hear must be those of some of the hermits.

4. Properly 'the ground near the gate of the palace' [*rāja-dvāra-pradeśa :* Ś.], but here simply the station of the porter [*dvāram* : Ch.]

5. The present for the future is not uncommon. Compare page 12, line 1.

Verse 47. *Śloka* or *Anuṣṭubh. See* Verses 5, 6, 11, 26.

इदो इदो भवन्ता।

इत इतो भवन्तौ।

[उभौ राजानं विलोकयतः]

प्रथम : अहो दीप्तिमतोऽपि विश्वसनीयतास्य वपुषः। अथवा उपपन्नम् एतद् अस्मिन् ऋषिकल्पे [1]राजनि। कुतः।

अध्याक्रान्ता वसतिर् अमुनाप्याश्रमे सर्वभोग्ये
रक्षायोगाद् अयमपि तपः प्रत्यहं सञ्चिनोति।
अस्यापि द्यां स्पृशति वशिनश् चारणद्वन्द्वगीतः
पुण्यः शब्दो मुनिरिति मुहुः केवलं राजपूर्वः[2] ।। 48 ।।

1. 'Oh! the confidence (inspired by the sight) of his person, majestic though (it be) ! But this is quite natural in this king (who) is very little inferior to a *Ṛṣi*.' *Dīptimat=tejasvin*, 'splendid,' hence 'majectic.' *Viśvasanīyata*, 'the state of being confided in.' *Upapanna*, 'fit.' 'proper,' 'agreeable to reason.' *Cf.* Vikramorvaśīya, Act 2, *upapannaṁ viśeṣaṇam asya vāyoḥ*. *Ṛṣi-kalpe*, 'resembling a *Ṛṣi*, but with a degree of inferiority;' such is the force of *kalpa* in composition. Duṣyanta was a Rājarṣi, and therefore one degree below a *Ṛṣi* : See page 44, in the middle; and page 39, note 3. The Devanāgarī' reading is *ṛshibhyo nātibhinne rājani*, but the Bengālī is here preferable.

2. 'Because, by him also (in the manner of a *Ṛṣi*) a residence has been entered upon in (this) hermitage open to the enjoyment of every one : (and because) he also day by day accumulates the-merit-of-penance through the act of protecting (his subjects). Of him also having-his-passions-in-subjection, the (same) sacred title of Muni [or *Ṛṣi*], but (with this difference that it is) proceded by Rāja, [*i.e.*, Rājarṣi] repeatedly ascends to heaven, being chanted by pairs of (celestial) minstrels.' *Adhyākrānta=svī-kṛta* 'appropriated,' 'taken possession of :' K. *Āśrame=dharmācaraṇa-sthāne* ' a place for the practice of religion :' K.:=*gārhasthye*, 'the order of a householder :' Ś. and Ch. It is difficult to see how this last sense can apply. *Rakṣā-yogād* : See p. 79, line 1. *Cf.* Manu, vii, 144. 'The highest virtue of a king is the protection of his subjects.' *Cāraṇa-dvandva=gandharba-mithuna*, 'pair of Gandharbas, or celestial choristers.' These being

---

Verse 48. *Mandākrāntā*, variety of *Atyaṣṭi*. *See* Verse 15, 33.

द्वितीय : गौतम। अयं स बलभित्सखो[1] दुष्यन्तः।

प्रथम : अथ किं।

द्वितीय : तेन हि

नैतच् चित्रं यद् अयम् उदधिश्यामसीमां धरित्रीम्
एकः कृत्स्नां नगरपरिघप्रांशुबाहुर् भुनक्ति।
आशंसन्ते समितिषु सुराः सक्तवैरा हि दैत्यैर्
अस्याधिज्ये धनुषि विजयं पौरुहूते च वज्रे[2] ।। 49 ।।

were the musicians or minstrels of Indra's heaven, just as the Apsarās were the dancers and actresses : and their business was to amuse the inhabitants of *Svarga* by singing the praises of gods, saints and heroes. *Cāraṇa* is any bard or herald. According to Kāṭavema *kevalam=eva,* 'certainly.' This verse affords an example of the figure called 'Vyatireka,' *i.e.,* A description of the difference of two things compared in some respects to each other : Ś.

1. 'The friend of Indra.' *Bala-bhit,* 'Indra' who crushes armies with his thunder-bolt. *Sakhi* at the end of a compound (like *rātri, akṣi,* etc.) changes its final to *a,* and becomes a noun of the first class. Pāṇ. V., 4, 87, 91, 98, 102. Indra is the chief of the *Suras* or secondary gods, being inferior to the gods of the Triad; and corresponds to the Jove or Jupiter Tonans of classical mythology. In his lordship over *Svarga,* or paradise, he might be supplanted by any one who could perform a hundred *Āśva-medhas* or horse-sacrifices : *see* p. 45, note 1. He and the other *Suras* were for ever engaged in hostilities with their half-brothers, the demons called *Asuras* or Daityas, the giants or Titans of Hindū mythology, who were the children of Kaśyapa by Diti, as the *Suras* were by Aditi : *see* p. 22, note 4. One such occasions the gods seem to have depended much upon the assistance they received from the heroes of the earth, such a Duṣyanta, Purūravas, etc.

2. 'This is not wonderful, that he whose arm is an long as the bar of a city (gate), should alone govern the entire earth, having the ocean as its dark [green] boundary [*i.e.,* as far as the very ocean]. The gods, rooted in their enmity with the demons, in their battles

---

Verse 49. *Mandākrāntā,* (variety of *Atyaṣṭi*). *See* Verses 15, 33, 48.

उभौ : (उपगम्य) विजयस्व[1] राजन्।

राजा : (आसनाद् उत्थाय) अभिवादये भवन्तौ।

उभौ : स्वस्ति भवते (इति फलान्युपहरतः)।

राजा : सप्रणामं परिगृह्य (आज्ञाम् इच्छामि)।

उभौ : विदितो भवान् आश्रमसदाम् इहस्थः।[2] तेन भवन्तं प्रार्थयन्ते।

expect victory through [in] his strung-bow and the thundrbolt of Indra.' *Parigha=argala,* 'the bar or bolt which fastens a gate.' In a city-gate it was both massive and long (*styāna-dīrgha* : Ch.) and therefore an object of comparison highly significant of muscular strength. It should be borne in mind that length and vigour of arm were prime requisites in the ancient hero, whose fame depended on the ease with which he managed his bow. Hence, the appositeness of such epithets as *mahā-bāhu* and *prāṁśu-bāhu,* 'long-armed.' *Bhunakti=pālayati* : Ch. *Bhuj,* applied to a king in the sense of ruling and protecting the earth, is common. *Cf. kṛtsnāṁ pṛthivīṁ bhuṅkte.* Manu, vii, 148. Raghu., viii, 7; iii, 4. *Āśaṁsante=icchanti,* 'wish for,' 'hope for :' in this sense *ā-śans* is conjugated in the ātm. *Samitiṣu surāḥ,* etc.: this is the Bengālī reading; the Devanāgarī have *sura-yuvatayo baddha-vairā,* etc. *Daityair,* See the last note. *Adhijye;* see page 9, note 2. The loc. c. has sometimes the force of the instrumental. *Pauru-kūta=aindra,* belonging to Indra :' *Puru-hūta,* 'much-worshipped' is one of Indra's thousand names. This verse is an example of the figure called 'Dīpaka' or 'illustration :' Ś. : its use is to throw light, as it were, upon an idea by some apposite illustration.

1. The root *ji,* 'to conquer,' with *vi* is rightly conjugated in the ātm. according to Pāṇini, I, 3, 19, but this rule is not always observed.

2. 'Your highness is known to the inhabitants of the hermitage (to be) staying here.' *Āśrama-sad=āśrama-vāsin,* 'a dweller in a hermitage,' 'a hermit :' so *nāka-sad,* 'a dweller in paradise,' 'a god :' hence *sadana,* 'a house.' *Vidita* with a present signification, in construction with the gen. c., is noticeable. *See* Pāṇini, iii, 2, 188; ii, 3, 67. See also Raghuvaṁśa, x, 40, *viditaṁ tapyamānaṁ tena me bhuvana-trayam,* 'the three worlds are known to me (as) being harassed by him.'

राजा : किम् आज्ञापयन्ति।

उभौ : तत्रभवतः कण्वस्य महर्षेर् असान्निध्याद् रक्षांसि[1] न इष्टिविघ्नम् उत्पादयन्ति। तत् कतिपयरात्रं[2] सारथिद्वितीयेन[2] भवता सनाथोक्रियताम्[2] आश्रम इति।

राजा : अनुगृहीतोऽस्मि।

विदूषकः (अपवार्य) एसा दाणिं अनुजला देअब्भत्थणा।

विदूषकः (अपवार्य) एषा इदानीम् अनुकूला तेऽभ्यर्थना।

राजा : (स्मितं कृत्वा) रैवतक। मद्वचनाद् उच्यतां सारथिः। सवाणासनं रथम् उपस्थापयेति।

दौवारिक : जं देवो आणबेदि।। इति निष्क्रान्तः।।

दौवारिक : यद् देव आज्ञापयति।। इति निष्क्रान्तः।।

उभौ : (सहर्षं)

अनुकारिणि पूर्वेषां युक्तरूपम् इदं त्वयि।
आपन्नाभयसत्रेषु दीक्षिताः खलु पौरवाः[3] ।। 50 ।।

राजा : (सप्रणामं) गच्छतां पुरो भवन्तौ। अहमप्यनुपदम् आगत एव।

उभौ : विजयस्व (इति निष्क्रान्तौ)।

1. The neuter *rakṣas* has the sense as *rākṣasa* : *see* page 40, note 5.

2. *Rātram* : *see* page 86, note 1. *Dvitīyena* : *see* page 13, note 1. *Sanāthī-kriyatām* : *see* page 26, note 2.

3. 'This is a becoming trait in you, an emulator of (your) ancestors. Truly the descendants of Puru are ordained (for officiating) in the sacrifices of (giving) exemption from fear to the distressed;' *i.e.*, Whilst we Brāhmaṇas are consecrated to officiate in real sacrifices, the highest duty of kings is the protection of their afflicted subjects : *See* page 85, note 2. The above is the reading of all the Devanāgarī and some of the Bengālī MSS. The old Bengālī [Bodleian 234] has *satreṇa*, and some begin the verse with *upakāriṇi sarveṣām*, 'the helper of all.' *Yukta-rūpam* : *Cf.* page 16, line 1. *Āpannābhaya-satreṣu=āpad-gatānāṁ bhaya-trāṇe* : Ś *Dīkṣitāḥ=kṛta-pratiṣṭhāḥ*, 'consecrated.'

Verse 50. *Śloka* or *Anuṣṭubh. See* Verses 5, 6, 11, 26.

राजा : माठव्य। अप्यस्ति[1] शकुन्तलादर्शन कुतूहलम्।

विदूषक : पढमं सपरिवाहं आसि। दाणिं रक्खसवुत्तन्त्रेण विन्दूबि णावसेसिदो।

विदूषक : प्रथमं सपरिवाहम् आसीत्। इदानीं राक्षसवृत्तान्तेन विन्दुरपि नावशेषितः।[2]

राजा : मा भैषीः। ननु मत्समीपे वर्तिष्यसे।

विदूषक : एस तव चक्करक्खीभूदोम्हि।

विदूषक : एष तव चक्ररक्षीभूतोऽस्मि।[3]

दौवारिक : (प्रविश्य) सज्जो रधो भट्टिणो विजयअप्पत्थाणं अवेक्खदि। एस उण णअरादो देवीणं आणत्तिहरओ करभओ आअदो।

दौवारिक : (प्रविश्य) सज्जो रथो भर्तुर् विजयप्रस्थानम् अपेक्षते। एष पुनर् नगराद् देवीनाम् आज्ञप्तिहरः करभक आगतः।[4]

1. *Api* may be used *praśne* 'in asking a question' : Cf. page 35, line 11.

2. 'At first it was overflowing; (but) now, by the account of the Rākṣasas, not even a drop is left :' this is the reading of the Devanāgarī MSS. supported by K. *Parivāha* is either 'an inundation,' or 'a channel for carrying off an excess of water :' the Bengālī have *aparibādham,* 'unchecked.' *Vṛttāntena=nāma-grahaṇena,* 'by the mention.'

3. 'I shall indeed then be protected [am protected] by the discus' : so reads the oldest MS., supported by Ś. and C.; the Devanāgarī have *esa rakkhasādo rakkhidomhi,* 'I am protected from the Rākṣasa.' The *cakra* is the discus or circular missile weapon of Viṣṇu, and often employed by him against the demons, as he is their great enemy; whence his titles 'Daityāri,' 'Asuraśatru' : the attribution of this weapon to Duṣyanta by the Vidūṣaka is probably meant as a humourous compliment.

4. 'The equipped chariot awaits our Majesty's advance to victory; but here is Karabhaka just arrived from the city, bearing a message from the Queen-mother.' *Devīnām* is here in the respectful plural; so *ambābhiḥ* two lines below : this latter word is peculiar to dramatic language.

राजा : (सादरं) किम् अम्बाभिः प्रेषितः।

दौवारिक : अहइं।

दौवारिक : अथ[1] किम्।

राजा : ननु प्रवेश्यताम्।

दौवारिक : (तह इति निष्क्रम्य करभकेण सह प्रविश्य) एसो भट्टा।

दौवारिक : (तथा इति निष्क्रम्य करभकेण सह प्रविश्य) एष भर्ता।

उबसप्प।

उपसर्प।

करभक : जेदु जेदु भट्टा। देवी आणबेदि। आआमिणि चउत्थदिअहे

करभक : जयतु जयतु भर्ता। देवी आज्ञापयति। आगामिनि चतुर्थदिवसे

पुत्तपिण्डपालणो णाम उबवासो भविस्सदि। तहिं दीहाउणा अवस्सं अम्हे

पुत्रपिण्डपालनो नाम उपवासो भविष्यति। तत्र दीर्घायुषा अवश्य वयं

सम्भावइदव्वत्ति।

सम्भावयितव्या[2] इति।

1. *Atha kim* (*=vāḍham,* 'yes') is used *aṅgīkṛtau* : See page 46, note 2.

2. 'On the fourth day, (which is now) coming, [*i.e.,* on the fourth day after to-day] the ceremony [fast] named *'Putra-piṇḍa-pālana'* [*i.e.,* cherishing of the body of a son] will take place : thereat [on that occasion] certainl we ought to be honoured-with-a-visit by the long-lived-one [by your Majesty, long may you live !]' Most of the Bengālī MSS. read *putra-piṇḍa-pāraṇa;* but Ch. substitutes *pālana,* and interprets the phrase by *pura-deha-puṣṭi prada* : Ś. gives the same interpretation, but reads *paryupāsana* for *pālane* : *'Piṇḍa, deha-mātre iti Medinī,'* 'According to Medinī, *piṇḍa* has the sense of body' : Ś. and Ch. : and this sense is given by Wilson. *Putra* refers to the king in his relation to the queen-mother. The Devanāgarī reading of this passage [*pravṛtta-pāraṇa upavās,* 'fast which has come to an end.'] is not very satisfactory. *Upavāsa=vrata,* 'a religious ceremonial accompanied with fasting, but not necesarily a fast': K. and Ch. observe that one name for this ceremonial was *putra-rāja,* and that it consisted in offering various presents to the young king of sweetmeats, clothes, etc., just as might be done in the present day

राजा : इतस् तपस्विकार्यं। इतो गुरुजनाज्ञा। द्वयम् अप्यनतिक्रमणीयं। किमत्र प्रतिविधेयम्।[1]

विदूषक : तिमङ्कू विअ अन्तरा चिट्ठ।

विदूषक : त्रिशङ्कुर् इव अन्तरा तिष्ठ।[2]

राजा : सत्यम् आकुलीभूतोऽस्मि।

on the occasion of a birth-day. *Dīrghāyuṣā* : *See* page 8, note 2. *Vayam* is used by the same rule that the plural *devīnām* is employed above. *Śambhāvayitavyā* : See page 26, note 1, at end.

1. 'In this direction the business of the hermits, in the other the command of a venerable parent (calls me). Both are not to be neglected. How, in such a case, can an arrangement be effected ?' *Dvayam api,* 'both the one and the other :' *api* is often affixed to *dvau* in this sense : *See* Amara., II, 1, 5; Mālavik., page 16, line 22 : In Hitop., line 2048, *dvayam* without *api* has the sense of 'both.'

2. 'Stand in the middle, like Triśaṅku.' The story of this monarch is told at length in the Rāmāyaṇa, I., LVII. to LX. [see also page 42, note 1, of this book]. He is there described as a just and pious prince of the solar race, who aspired to celebrate a great sacrifice, hoping thereby to ascend to heaven in his mortal body. He first requested the sage Vaśiṣṭha to officiate for him; but, being refused, he then applied to the sage's hundred sons, by whom he was cursed and degraded to the condition of a Cāṇḍāla. In this pitiable state he had recourse to Viśvāmitra, who undertook to conduct the sacrifice, and invited all the gods to be present; they, however, refused to attend. Upon this the enraged Viśvāmitra, by his power, transported Triśaṅku to the skies, whither he had no sooner arrived than he was hurled down again, head-formost by Indra and the gods, but, being arrested in his downward course by Viśvāmitra, remained suspended *between heaven and earth,* forming a constellation in the southern hemsiphere. The story is differently told in some of the Purāṇas [Wilson's translation of the Viṣṇu-P., page 371, note.] They and the Harivaṁśa describe Triśaṅku as a wicked prince, guitly of three heinous sins [*śaṅku*]. Śaṅkara adopts this view of his character, and calls him *Kṛta-bahutara-malina-karmā rāja. Antarā=tapovana-sva-nagarayou madhye,* 'between the hermitage and the city.' The facetious allusion to Triśaṅku is quite charateristic of the Vidūṣaka and affords an example of the 'Vyāhāra alaṅkāra :' Ś. and Ch.

कृत्ययोर् भिन्नदेशत्वाद् द्वैधीभवति मे मनः।
पुरः प्रतिहतं शैलैः स्रोतः स्रोतोवहं यथा[1] ।। 51 ।।

(विचिन्त्य) सखे। त्वम् अम्बया पुत्र इति प्रतिगृहीतः। अतो भवान् इतः प्रतिनिवृत्य मां तपस्विकार्यव्यग्रमानसम् आवेद्य तत्रभवतीनां पुत्रकृत्यम् अनुष्ठातुम् अर्हति।[2]

विदूषक : णंक्खु मं रक्खोभीरुअं गणेसि।

विदूषक : ननु खलु मां रक्षोभीरुकं गणयसि।

राजा : (सस्मितं) भो महाब्राह्मण कथमेतद् भवति सम्भाव्यते।[3]

विदूषक : जह राआणुण्ण गन्तव्वं तह गमिस्सं।

विदूषक : यथा राजानुजेन गन्तव्यं तथा गमिष्यामि।[4]

राजा : ननु तपोवनोपरोधः परिहरणीय इति सर्वान् अनुयात्रिकांस् त्वयैव सह प्रस्थापयामि।

1. 'Verily I am embarrassed. From the difference of the places of the two duties [*i.e.*, account of the distance between the place where the two duties have to be performed] my mind is divided in two, as the stream of a river driven back [made to recoil] by rocks (lying) before it.' *Purah=agre*, 'in front,' 'ahead.' *Pratihataṁ śaile*, which has struck on a rock,' is the reading of the Bengālī MS. [Bodleian, 233] and if all the Devanāgarī : The other Bengālī and Śaṅkara read *śailaḥ*, which I think preferable : Compare the suntiment at page 58. *Srotovaham=nadī-sambandhi*, 'belonging to a *srotovahā* or river,' [K., Ś., and Ch.] and is therefore an adjective agreeing with *srotaḥ :* the Devanāgarī read *srotovaho*, genitive case of a subtantive, *srotovah* : Wilson gives only *srotovahā*, but has the adjective. The above furnishes an example of the 'Yothopamā alaṅkāra,' or comparison by the use fo the conjuction *yathā*.

2. 'You have been recerived by the Queen-mother as a son; therefore let your honour, having returned from hence and having announced that my mind is intent of [zealous for] the business of the hermits, have the goodness to discharge the office of a son towards her Majesty.' *Putra iti pratigṛhītaḥ, i.e., tvaṁ poṣita-putro bhavasi*, 'Your are an adopted son :' Ś.: have *putratvam* for *putra-kṛtyam*.

3. 'How is this possible in your honour ?' *Bhavati*, locative case of *bhavat*. *Sambhāvyate* may mean, 'is fitting,' is consistent.'

Verse 51. *Śloka* or *Anuṣṭubh*. *See* Verses 5, 6, 11, 12, 26, 47, 50, 51.

विदूषक : (सगर्व्वं) तेण हि जुवराओम्हि दाणिं संवुत्तो ।

विदूषक : (सगर्व्वं) तेन हि युवराजोऽस्मि[1] इदानीं संवृत्तः ।

राजा : (आत्मगतं) चपलोऽयं वटुः ।[2] कदाचिद् अस्मत्प्रार्थनाम्[3] अन्तःपुरेभ्यः कथयेत् । भवतु । एनम् एवं वक्ष्ये (विदूषकं हस्ते गृहीत्वा प्रकाशं) वयस्य । ऋषिगौरवाद्[4] आश्रमं गच्छामि । न खलु सत्यम् एव तापसकन्यकायां शकुन्तलायां ममाभिलाषः । पश्य ।

क्व वयं क्व परोक्षमन्मथो मृगशावैः समम् एधितो जनः ।
परिहासविजल्पितं सखे परमार्थेन न गृह्यतां वचः[5] ।। 52 ।।

विदूषक : अहइं ।

विदूषक : अथ किम् ।

।। इति निष्क्रान्ताः सर्वे ।।
।। द्वितीयोऽङ्कः ।।

4. 'I will go, as it should be gone by the younger brother of a king.'

1. *Yuva-rāja,* 'the young prince,' who was the heir-apparent and generally associated with the reigning monarch in the throne.

2. *Vaṭu,* 'a youth,' 'a lad :' here it is equivalent to 'fellow,' 'chap.'

3. *Prārthanā=abhilāṣitam,* 'desire,' 'pursuit :' *i.e., Śakuntalā-viṣayānu-sandhāna-rūpa-kathām,* 'the story of my pursuit of Śakuntalā :' Ś.

4. 'On account of my veneration for the *Ṛṣi,*' *lit.,* 'from the venerableness of the *Ṛṣis.*'

5. 'Where are we, (and) where a person brought up with fawns out of sight of love ? O friends ! let not a speech uttered in jest be taken in earnest.' '*Kva-dvayam atyantāsambhāvanāyām,*' 'The two *kvas* are expressive of excessive incompatibility : Ś. *See* page 13, note 2. '*Nāgarikāranya-janayoḥ sambandho nopapadyate iti bhāvaḥ,*' 'The meaning is that a connection between a town-bred person and a forester is not possible :' K. *Parokṣa-manmatha=apratyakṣa-manmatha* or *ajñāta-manmatha* or *agocara-kāma,* 'one who has had no perception or experience of love,' 'one who is out of the reach of its influence.' *Parihāsa-vijalpitam=hāsya-bhāṣitam* : K.=*kautuka-bhāṣitam* : Ś. the Bengālī read *vikalpita,* 'invented :' *Cf. parihāsa-vijalpa* in the 6th act. *Paramārthena=tattvena.*

Verse 52. *Vaitālīya,* containing twenty-one syllables to the line, each line being alike, the first and third half-lines ending at the tenth syllable.

◡◡—◡◡—◡—◡—‖◡◡——◡◡—◡—◡—

।। अथ तृतीयाङ्कादौ विष्कम्भः ।।

[ततः प्रविशति कुशान् आदाय[1] यजमानशिष्यः]

शिष्य : अहो महाप्रभावो **राजा** :दुष्यन्तः। येन प्रविष्टमात्र एवाश्रमं तत्रभवति[2] निरूपप्लवानि नः कर्म्माणि संवृत्तानि।

का कथा बाणसन्धाने ज्याशब्देनैव दूरतः।
हुङ्कारेणेव धनुषः स हि विघ्नान्[3] अपोहति।। 53 ।।

1. 'The pupil of the sacrificing-(brāhmaṇa) bearing *kuśa*-grass.' *Yajamāna* is for *yajvan*, 'a sacrificer :' *See* Raghu-v, xviii, 11 : in Telugu it has acquired the sense of 'master :' Compare *tataḥ praviśati Bharata-śiṣyau* : Vikram., Act 3. Dr. B. reads *yajamānaḥ śiṣyaḥ* on the authority of only one MS. The translation must then be 'a pupil occupied about a sacrifice.' The pupil, or religious student, certainly, did not officiate himself. *Śiṣya,* in fact, denotes a Brahmacārī, or young brāhmaṇa in that state of pupilage through which every brāhmaṇa had to pass, living in the house of some superior brāhmaṇa, who was his preceptor; and who, in return for instruction given, required his assistance in various menial offices, in collecting the materials for sacrifice, and in asking alms. 'Let the student carry water-pots, flowers, cow-dung, fresh earth and *kuśa*-grass, as much as may be useful to his preceptor; let him bring wood for the oblation to fire; let him go begging through the whole district,' etc. Manu, ii, 176 *et seq. Kuśān* : *see* page 19, note 1.

2. 'Since on his highness having merely entered the hermitage, our rites have become free from molestation.' So read the oldest MSS. supported by K. The others *praviṣṭa evāśramaṁ tatrabhavati,* etc. The student need hardly be reminded that *praviṣṭa-mātre,* etc. is in the loc. case absolute.

3. 'What mention of fitting the arrow (to the bow) ? for by the mere sound of the bow-string from afar, as if by the roar of the bow, he dispels the obstacles.' *Kā kathā,* 'what account ?' *i.e.,* What necessity for fitting the arrow ? the expulsion of the demons who impede our rites is effected by the mere twanging of the bow,

Verse 53. *Śloka* or *Anuṣṭubh. See* Verses 5, 6, 11, 12, 26, 47, 50, 51.

यावद् इमान् वेदिसंस्तरणार्थं[1] दर्भान् ऋत्विग्भ्य[2] उपहरामि (परिक्रम्यावलोक्य च।
आकाशे)।[3] प्रियंवदे। कस्येदम् उशीरानुलेपनं मृणालवन्ति च नलिनीपत्राणि नीयन्ते।।[4]

without the use of the arrow, (*śara-sandhānam antareṇa* : Ś.) in the same manner as a threatening roar often suffices to scare those who hear it. *Cf. Pratiśabdo hi harer hinasti nāgān.* Vikram. Act I. *Huṅkāra* is the roar of any fierce animal. The figure by which the sound of the bow is thus designated is called Utprekṣā, or hyperbolical compariosn : Ś. and Ch. So Bhaṭṭi (x, 41) in giving an example of this figure, describes a mountain as stretching out its huge *body* between heaven and earth to protect the land from the inroads of the sea.

1. 'For strewing on the altar,' or on the ground near it : see note 1, p. 19.

2. *Ṛtvij,* 'a priest,' but expecially 'an officiating priest,' a sacrificer,' derived from *ṛtu,* 'a season', and *yaj,* 'to sacrifice;' 'one who sacrifices at the prescribed time.' *Anṛtvig yajñaṁ na gacchet* 'one ought not to go to (perform) a sacrifice unattended by an officiating brāhman.' Manu, iv, 57; ii, 143.

3. 'In the air, ' *i.e.* speaking in the air. This is an example of *ākāśa-bhāṣitam* or *ākāśa-vākyam,* which is defined by Śaṅkara to be *dūra-stha-bhāṣaṇam,* 'speech at a distance,' or *aśarīram nivedanam,* 'bodiless statement :' and by Kāṭavema as *apraviṣṭaiḥ ṣa ālāpaḥ,* 'conversation with (characters) not on the stage.' It is, in fact, a speech addressed to some person outside or off the stage, the actor at the same time fixing his eyes in the air, or on some object only visible to himself. Hence, in Kāṭavema *ākāśa* is followed by the words *lakṣam* or *lakṣyaṁ baddhvā,* 'fixing his gaze.' Cf. *Ākāśa-baddha-lakṣaḥ.* Vikram. Act 4, and Mudrā-rākṣ., p. 6, 1. 19; p. 31, 1. 3. The answer which is supposed to be given is also *ākāśa-bhāṣitam,* and is not heard by the audience. The actor on the stage pretending to listen (*śrutim abhinīya*) repeats the imaginary reply, always introducing it with the words, *kiṁ bravīṣi* : Sāhit.-darp., p. 177, at end.

4. 'For whom are brought this *uśīra*-ointment and lotus-leaves, with fibres attached ?' *Uśīra=vīraṇa-kanda,* the root of *vīraṇa,* a fragrant grass *[Andropogon muricatum]* with which a cooling ointment was made. *Nalini* is used for lotus as well as *nalina,* but rather denotes the entire plant : *See* page 25, note 1. *Mṛṇāla=visa,* 'the fibres of the stalk of the lotus.'

(श्रुतिम् अभिनीय) किं ब्रवीषि। आतपलङ्घनाद् बलवद् अस्वस्था शकुन्तला:[1] तस्या: शरीरनिर्वापणायेति। प्रियंवदे यत्नाद् उपचर्य्यताम्। सा हि तत्रभवत: कुलपतेर् उच्छ्वसितम्। अहमपि तावद् वैतानिकं शान्त्युदकम् अस्यै गौतमीहस्ते विसर्जयिष्यामि[2] ।। इति निष्क्रान्त:।।

।। विष्कम्भ:।।[3]

1. 'Śakuntalā is excessively indisposed, from injury inflicted by the heat [from a stroke of the sun]; is it for the cooling of her body that you say (they are brought) ?' *Laṅghanāt=āghātat* : K.: *=abhibhavāt* : Ś. :*=paribhavāt* : Ch. The root-*laṅgh*, the first sense of which is 'to over,' often signifies 'to inflict some injury, hurt, or insult.' *Nir-vap*, 'to extinguish a fire,' 'to put out a light.' *Nirvāpaṇa*, 'a refrigerant remedy :' Wilson.

2. 'Let her be nursed with care; for she is the (very) breath of his reverence (Kaṇva), the head of (our) society. I also will just deliver into the hands of Gautamī for her the soothing water consecrated in the sacrifice.' *Upacar*, 'to wait upon a sick person,' 'administer remedies,' etc. *Ucchvasitam=prāṇāḥ*, 'breath : '*=jīvanam*, 'life,' *i.e.*, as precious as his own life : Compare Lam. iv, 20, 'The breath of our nostrils, the anointed of the Lord, was taken,' etc.; also Kumāra-s., vii, 4. *Vaitānika=vitānakya-yāga-sambandhi* 'belonging to the sacrifice called *Vitāna*,' 'sacred,' 'holy.' *Vitāna* is also 'the sacrificial hearth on which the sacred fire was kept.' The *śāntyudakam* may have been a kind of holy water, like the 'eau bénite' of the Roman Catholics. *Gautamī*, the name of the sister of Kaṇva : K.

3. The Viṣkambha or Viṣkambhaka, according to the Sāhitya-darpaṇa (p. 146), and Kāṭavema's commentary on the opening speech of the 2nd Act of this play, is an introductory monologue or dialogue, so called from its concisely compressing [root *skambh* with *vi*] into a short space an account of those subordinate parts of the plot, which are not enacted before the audience, but are to be taken for granted as having happened before the Act, or as about to happen after it; and a knowledge of which is essential to the comprehending of the action of the remainder of the play : [*Vṛtta-vartiṣyamāṇām kathānāṁ nidarśakaḥ, saṅkṣiptārthastu viṣkambhaḥ* : See also page 63, note 1 at end.]. In the case of a monologue, it may be suspected that these terms may be indentified with the speaker, but when more than one actor is concerned, the direction at the

end [*niṣkrāntau, viṣkambhakaḥ*] would seem to indicate that the terms belongs to the dialogue itself, and not to the speaker of it. The Viṣkambha may occur at the beginning of any of the Acts, even of the 1st immediately after the Prastāvanā [*ādāv aṅkasya darśitaḥ*]. It may be spoken by two out of the three sets of characters into which the *dramatis-personae* of an Indian play are divided, *viz.*, the inferior [*nīca*] who speak Prākṛt *anudāttoktyā* 'in the low tone'; and the middling [*madhya, madhyama*] who speak Sanskṛt *udāttoktyā* 'in the high tone'; but not by the chief [*pradhāna*], such as the hero, etc. Again, it may be spoken by one character in the form of a soliloquy, or by two in the form of a dialogue; and either by characters of the middle class only, when it is called *Śuddha, i.e.*, pure; or by those of the middle and lower combined, when it is called Miśra or Saṅkīrṇa, *i.e.*, mixed : [*Madhyena madhyamābhyāṁ vā pātrābhyāṁ samprayojitaḥ śuddhaḥ syāt tu saṅkīrṇo nīca-madhyama-kalpitaḥ*]. Sometimes the characters are exclusively those of the inferior class, who speak Prākṛt; sometimes more than two appear on the stage at once, in which cases it is properly called Praveśaka. It must, however, be borne in mind that the terms Praveśaka and Viṣkambhaka are regarded as indentical by the MSS. and Commen-tators [*Viṣkambha eva suvyaktaiḥ praveśaka iti smṛtaḥ* : K. *praveśeka eva viṣkambhakaḥ* : Ś.]; although the Sāhitya-darpaṇa restricts the former titile to the cases above specified, and limits it still further by applying it to an interlude only [*Praveśako anudāttoktyā nīca-pātra-prayojitaḥ, aṅka-dvayāntar vijenyaḥ śesham viṣkambhake yathā*]. There can be little doubt, too, that the term Praveśaka, like Viṣkambhaka, may be sometimes applied to the speaker in the case of a monologue. From the circumstance that the opening speech in the 2nd Act of this play is called a Praveśaka by K. (unsupported, however, by the MSS.), we may infer that the speaker was not obliged to leave the stage at the end of the scene. It is possible, however, that he might have withdrawn and re-entered, as in the 5th Act of the Vikramorvaśī, where the opening soliloquy in the one play, as in the other. According to the rule thus propounded by the Sāhit.-darp., the present monologue is a Śuddha-Viṣkambha. In the Bengālī MSS. it is termed a Praveśaka. Dr. Boehtlingk justly remarks that the modern epithet Śuddha should be omitted in the text.

ACT - III

।। अथ तृतीयोऽङ्कः ।।

[ततः प्रविशति समदनावस्थो राजा]

राजा : (सचिन्तं निःश्वस्य)

जाने तपसो वीर्यं सा बाला परवतीति मे विदितम्।
न च निम्नाद् इव सलिलं निवर्त्तते मे ततो हृदयम्[1] ।। 54 ।।

भगवन् कुसुमायुध। त्वया चन्द्रमसा च विश्वसनीयाभ्याम् अतिसन्धीयते कामिजनसार्थः। कुतः।

तव कुसुमशरत्वं शीतरश्मित्वम् इन्दोर्
द्वयम् इदम् अयथार्थं दृश्यते मद्विधेषु।
विसृजति हिमगर्भैर् अग्निम् इन्दुर् मयूखैम्
त्वमपि कुसुमवाणान् वज्रसारीकरोषि[2] ।। 55 ।।

1. 'I know the efficacy of penance : it is (also) known to me that that maiden is subject to another [is in a state of tutelage]. But as water does not turn back from the valley, (neither) does my heart from that (Śakuntalā).' The Devanāgarī MSS., unsupported by the commentators, substitute the following for the second line of the above verse, *Alam asmi tato hṛdayaṁ tathāpi nedaṁ nivartayitum,* 'Nevertheless, I am not able to turn back this heart from that (damsel).' *Jāne* etc., *i.e.,* I know that if I attempt to carry her off by force or by stealth, the power acquired by penance is such, that the *Ṛṣi* will effect my destruction by a curse, etc. [*śāpādinā nāśaṁ vidhāsyati* : Ś.] *Nimnād, i.e., deśāt,* 'from low land :' *see* Hitop., 1. 2651.

2. 'O divine flower-armed (god), by thee and by the moon, who

---

Verse 54. *Āryā* or *Ghāthā*. (*See* Verse 2.)

— — |⏑ ⏑ —| — — ‖ — — |— ⏑ ⏑|⏑ — ⏑|— ⏑ ⏑|—
⏑ ⏑ —|— ⏑ ⏑|⏑ ⏑ —‖⏑ — ⏑| — — | ⏑ |— ⏑ ⏑|—

Verse 55. *Mālinī* or *Māninī* (variety of *Ati-Śakkarī*.) *See* Verses 10, 19, 20. 38.

भगवन् कामदेव न ते मय्यनुक्रोशः (मदनबाधां निरूप्य) कुतम् ते कुसुमायुधस्य मतं तैक्ष्ण्यम् एतत्। आं ज्ञातम्

अद्यापि नूनं हरकोपवह्निस्
त्वयि ज्वलत्यौर्व इवाम्बुराशौ।

(seem) to be worthy of confidence, the whole company of lovers is deceived. Why so ? of thee, (there is said to be) the property of having flowers for arrows, of the moon the property of having cold beams; both these (properties) are observed to be untrue in such as me : (for) the moon emits fire with rays charged with cold; thou also makest (thy) flower-arrows hard as adamant.' The Hindū Cupid or Kāmadeva, 'god of love,' is the son of Viṣṇu or Kṛṣṇa by Lakṣmī, who is then called Māyā or Rukmiṇī. He is armed with a bow made of sugar-cane, the string consisting of bees, and with five arrows, [whence his name Pañca-vāṇa] each tipped with the blossom of a flower, which pierce the heart through the five senses. The names of the five arrows (according to Bharata, cited by Ś.) are—1. *Harṣaṇa*, Gladdener;' 2. *Prahasana*, 'Exhilarater;' 3. *Mohana*, Fascinater :' 4. *Mūrcchana*, 'sense-destroyer :' 5. *Vikarṣaṇa*, Distracter.' According to Kāṭavema, the names of the five flowers which form the points of these arrows, and which may be supposed to possess properties similar to that impiled in the names of the arrows themselves, are—1. the Aravinda, a kind of lotus *[Nymphaea Nelumbo]*; 2. the Aśoka; 3. the Śirīṣa; 4. the Cūta or Āmra, *i.e.*, the Mango; 5. the Utpala or blue lotus. But according to Sir W. Jones [Hymn to Kāmadeva, vol. xiii., p. 239] they are—1. the Campaka; 2. the Cūta or Āmra; 3. the Keśara or Nāga-keśara; 4. the Ketaka; 5. the Vilva or Bela. In both lists the Cūta occurs, and is considered the favourite arrow of the god; hence the frequent allusions to it in the Gīta-govinda (iii., 12; iv, 6), and hence in Act VI its epithet *pañcābhyadhika* 'chief of the five.' This epithet is explained by Śaṅkara to mean 'a sixth arrow, in addition to the five,' which interpretation is more in accordance with passage in the 2nd Act of the Vikramorvaśīya, *kimuta upavana-sahakārair*, etc. It is clear that some authorities do not include the Mango in the list. The Gīta-govinda (x, 14) mentions five other flowers as occasionally employed by the god, *viz.*, the Badhūka, the Madhūka, the blue Lotus, the Tila, and the Kuṇḍa. Another account includes the Mallikā or Jasmin amongst the five; so that it is difficult to fix the names with any certainty. In Hindū erotic poetry, cooling properties are always attributed to the rays of the moon, which are said to

त्वम् अन्यथा मन्मथ मद्विधानां
भस्मावशेष: कथम् इत्थम् उष्ण:[1] ।। 56 ।।

distil nectar; hence some of his names—*śīta-mayūkha, hima-raśmi, hima-kara, amṛta-sū, sudhā-nidhi*, etc. On the other hand, the heating effect of these rays on the lover is often alluded to, thus, *śītāṁśus tapanaḥ* : Gīt.-Gov. ix., 10; vi., 7; v. 3 : Compare in the Vikramorvaśīya, *nandana-vana-vātāḥ śikhina iva* [Act 2]; and *pādās te śaśinaḥ sukhayanti*, etc. [end of Act iii.] *Sārtha=samūha;* properly, a caravan : Hitopadeśa, 1. 2574. *Ayathārtham=viparīta-kriyam,* 'having a contrary effect.' *Dvayam* : *see* p. 91, note 1. *Garbhair* : *see* p. 18, 1. 3. *Vajra-sārī* : *see* p. 14, 1. 4.

1. 'Verily, even now the fire of Śiva's wrath burns in thee like the submarine fire in the ocean : otherwise how couldst thou, O agitator of the soul ! with nothing left but ashes, be so scorching towards such as me ?' The story of the incineration of Kāmadeva by a beam of fire darted from the central eye of Śiva is thus told in the Rāmāyaṇa (I, xxv, 10). "Kandarpa, whom the wise call Kāma (Cupid), had formerly a body. He once approached Śiva, the husband of Umā (Pārvatī), soon after his marriage, that he might influence him with love for his wife. Śiva happened then to be practising austerities, and intent on a vow of chastity. He therefore cursed the god of love in a terrible voice, and at the same time a flash from his terrific eye caused all the limbs of his body to shrivel into ashes. Thus Cupid was made incorporeal [whence, as some say, is his power over the minds of men] by the anger of the great god, and from that time has been called *Anaṅga*, 'the bodiless one.'" *Aurva*, 'submarine fire,' called *baḍava* or *bāḍava*, and personified as the son of the saint Urva. The fable is told in the Harivaṁśa (ch. xlv), and is noticed in Troyer's Rāja-taraṅgiṇī (iii., 170). The Ṛṣi Urva, who had gained great power by his austerities, was pressed by the gods and others to beget children that he might perpetuate his rece. He consented, but warned them that his offspring would consume the world. Accordingly, he created from his thigh a devouring fire, which as soon as it was produced, demanded nourishment, and would have destroyed the whole earth, had not Brahmā appeared and assigned the ocean as its habitation, and the

Verse 56. *Upajāti* or *Ākhyānkī* (variety of *Triṣṭubh*), each half-line being either *Indra-vajrā* or *Upendra-vajrā*, the former only differing from the latter in the length of the first syllable. *See* Verse 41.

अथवा।

अनिशमपि मकरकेतुर् मनसोरुजम् आवहन्न् अभिमतो मे।
यदि मदिरायतनयनां ताम् अधिकृत्य प्रहरतीति[1] ।। 57 ।।

भगवन् कन्दर्प। एवम् उपालब्धस्य ते न मां प्रत्यनुक्रोशः।

वृथैव सङ्कल्पशतैर् अजस्रम्
अनङ्ग नीतोऽसि मया विवृद्धिम्।
आकृष्य चापं श्रवणोपकण्ठे
मय्येव युक्तं तव वाणमोक्षः[2] ।। 58 ।।

waves as its food. The spot where it entered the sea was called *Baḍavā mukha,* 'the mare's mouth.' Doubtless the story was invented to suit the phenomenon of some marine *jvāla-mukhi* or volcano, which probably exhaled through the water bitumenous inflammable gas, and which, perhaps in the form of a horse's mouth, was at times visible above the sea. Langlois, conjecturally, places the position of it on the coast north of Malabar.

1. "Nevetheless, the fish-bannered (god) even though incessantly bringing mental anguish, (will be) acceptable to me, if employing (as the subject about which he inflicts pain) that (maiden) with long intoxicating eyes he or strike (me).' *Makara-ketu,* a name of Cupid, is derived from the *makara,* or marine monster, subdued by him, which was painted from on his banner [*ketu*]. 'By the mention fo this title, his invincibleness is indicated :' Ś. *Adhikṛtya=uddiśya,* 'with reference to :' Ś. and Ch. : See page 5, note 1; and p. 76, note 3, also Ragh-v. xi, 62, *śāntim adhikṛtya anvayuṅkta.*

2. 'In vain, truly, O bodiless (god), hast thou perpetually been brought by me to growth by hundreds of vows. Is it becoming of you, drawing your bow to your very ear, (to) discharge (your) arrows even upon me (your votary) ?' Vows were to the bodiless god of love, what the oblation (upon which they were supposed to feed and fatten) were to the other gods. *Saṅkalpa=icchā,* 'wish.' *Śravaṇopakaṇṭa ākṛṣya=karnāntikam ānīya,* 'drawing the string of the

---

Verse 57. *Āryā* or *Ghāthā.* (*See* Verse 2.)

⏑⏑⏑⏑|⏑⏑⏑⏑| —— ‖⏑⏑--|⏑⏑—|⏑—⏑|⏑⏑—|—
⏑⏑⏑⏑| —⏑⏑ |⏑⏑—‖—⏑⏑| —— | ⏑ |⏑⏑—|⏑

Verse 58. *Upajāti* or *Ākhyānkī* (variety of *Triṣṭubh*). *See* Verses 41, 56.

(सखेदं परिक्रम्य) क्व नु खलु संस्थिते कर्मणि सदस्यैर् अनुज्ञातः श्रमक्लान्तम् आत्मानं विनोदयामि[1] (निःश्वस्य) किं नु खलु मे प्रियादर्शनाद् ऋते शरणम् अन्यत्। यावद् एनाम् अन्विष्यामि (सूर्यम् अवलोक्य) इमाम् उग्रातपां वेलां प्रायेण लतावलयवत्सु मालिनीतीरेषु ससखीजना शकुन्तला गमयति।[2] तत्रैव तावद् गच्छामि ।। परिक्रम्यावलोक्य च ।। अनया बालपादपवीथ्या सुतनुर् अचिरं गतेति तर्कयामि। कुतः।

सम्मीलन्ति न तावद् बन्धनकोषाम् तयावचितपुष्पाः।
क्षीरस्निग्धाश् चामी दृश्यन्ते किंशलयच्छेदाः[3] ।। 59 ।।

bow back as far as the ear.' *Upakaṭṇṭha* near,' *lit.*, 'near the neck :' *Cf.* Raghu-v., ix., 57, *ākarṇa-kṛṣṭaṁ vāṇam. Yukta=ucita.* The passage from *Bhagavan Kāmadeva* (page 100) to *vāṇamokṣa* is given on the authority of the Taylor and my own Mumbai Devanāgarī MS., supported by Śaṅkara and Candra-śekhara, and by all the Bengālī MSS. The Mackenzie MS. has part of the passage, but Colerbrooke's omits it altogether.

1. 'Where, indeed, at the conclusion of the rite being permitted (to depart) by those who were present at the sacrifice,' etc. *Sadasya*, 'any assistant or by-stander at a sacrifice.' The Bengālī have *nirasta-vighnais-tapavibhir*, 'by the hermits whose obstacles have been removed.'

2. 'Śakuntalā along with her female friends is passing [*lit.*, causing to go] this intensely hot time of the day probably on the banks of the Mālini, possessed of inclosures of creepers.' *Valaya*, properly an 'inclosure or hedge :' *see* p. 56, note 1 in middle; here it may mean a bower, or arbour affording shade.

3. 'I conjecture that the very delicate one has not long since passed by this avenue of young trees, because the cavities of the flower-stalks whose flowers have been plucked off by her, do not yet close up, and these fragments of tender-shoots are seen (still) unctuous with milky-juice.' *Vithi=paṅkti. Sammīlanti=saṅkucanti*, 'contract.' *Bandhana=prasava-bandhana=vṛnta*, ' flower-stalk :' Ś. *Bandhana-koṣās=vṛntabhyan' tarāṇi* : Ś :=*vṛnta-garbhāṇi* : Ch. *Amī*, these,' *i.e*, *puro-vartinaḥ*, 'lying in front of us.' *Kiśalaya-chedāḥ=*

Verse 59. *Āryā* or *Ghāthā*. (*See* Verse 2.)

— — | — ⏑ ⏑ | — — ‖ — ⏑ ⏑ | — — | ⏑ — ⏑ | ⏑ ⏑ — | —
— — | — — | — — ‖ — — | — ⏑ ⏑ | ⏑ | — — | —

(स्पर्शं रूपयित्वा) अहो प्रवातसुभगोऽयम् उद्देशः।[1]

शक्यम् अरविन्दसुरभिः कणवाही मालिनीतरङ्गाणाम्।
अङ्गैर् अनङ्गतप्तैर् अविरलम् आलिङ्गितुं पवनः[2] ।। 60 ।।

(परिक्रम्यावलोक्य च) अस्मिन् वेतसपरिक्षिप्ते लतामण्डपे सन्निहितया तया भवितव्यम्। तथा हि (अधो विलोक्य)

pallava-khaṇḍāḥ. Kṣīra-snigdhāś=dugdha-cikkaṇāḥ. When a stalk has been some time broken off, in contracts and the milk dries up. 'The duty of gathering flowers and cutting stalks for sacrificial purposes would be entrusted by the hermits to Śakuntalā : hence, it would be inferred that she had passed that way. This is an example of the Anumāna-alaṁkāra :' Ś. and Ch. Some of the Devanāgarī MSS. omit the above couplet.

1. 'Oh ! how delightful is this spot by (reason of) the fresh breeze!' *Aho* an exclamation implying approbation (*prasaṁsāyām*) : Ś. *Pravāta=prakriṣṭa-vāta* : K.=*Praśasta-vāta*, 'a good breeze :' Ś. : see note 1, page 37.

2. 'The breeze fragrant with the lotuses (and) wafting the spray [particles] of the waves of the Mālinī, is able to be closely embraced by (my) limbs inflamed by the bodiless one.' *Śakya* (like *yogya* and sometimes *yukta*) gives a passive sense to the infinitive. The Bengālī MSS. and the Kolkata edition read *śakyo* in the nominative case agreeing with *pavanah,* which would appear at first sight to be the better reading. But Kāṭavema expressly states that *śakyam* is here used adverbially, and quotes a parallel passage from the Rāmāyaṇa, sakyam *añjalibhiḥ pātum vātāḥ,* 'the breezes are able to be drunk by the hollowed palms.' Two other passages may be added, one from the Hitopadeśa (edit. Johnson) *vibhūtayaḥ śakyam avāptum,* 'great successes are able to be obtained;' and the other from Mālavikāg. verse 58, *na sakyam upekṣitum kupitā* : see also Mahābh., I., 769. *Aravinda,* 'a kind of lotus' (Nymphaea) : see p. 25, note 1. *Kaṇa-vāhī=śīkara-vāhaka* : Ś. 'Wafting cool spray.' *Anaṅga,* 'the bodiless god :' *see* p 100, note 1. *Avirala, lit.,* 'having no interstices,' 'close.' The Bengālī read *nirdayam=dṛḍham.*

Verse 60. *Āryā* or *Ghāthā*. (*See* Verse 2.)

— ⏑ ⏑ | ⏑ — ⏑ | ⏑ ⏑ — ‖ ⏑ ⏑ — | — — | ⏑ — — ⏑ | — — | —
— — | ⏑ — ⏑ | — — ‖ ⏑ ⏑ ⏑ ⏑ | — — | ⏑ | — ⏑ ⏑ | —

अभ्युन्नता पुरस्ताद् अवगाढा जघनगौरवात् पश्चात्।
द्वारेऽस्य पाण्डुसिकते पदपङ्क्तिर् दृश्यतेऽभिनवा[1] ।। 61 ।।

(यावद् विटपान्तरेणावलोकयामि)[2] परिक्रम्य। तथा कृत्वा। सहर्षम्।। अये लब्धं नेत्रनिर्वाणम्।[3] एषा मे मनोरथप्रियतमा सकुसुमास्तरणं शिलापट्टम् अधिशयाना सखीभ्याम् अन्वास्यते।[4] भवतु। श्रोष्याम्यासां विश्रम्भकथितानि।। इति विलोकयन् स्थितः।।

[ततः प्रविशति यथोक्तव्यापारा सह सखीभ्यां शकुन्तला]
[सख्यावुपवीजयत][5]

1. 'At the entrance of it where-there-is-white-stand, a fresh line of foot-steps is seen, raised in front, depressed behind through the weight or (her hips.' *Avagādhā=nimnā. Pāṇḍu-sikate (=dhavala bāluke)* is a Bahuvrīhi compound agreeing with *dvāre*. The weight of the hips of a beautiful female is a favourite subject of allusion. Compare *paścān-natā guru-nitambatayā asyāḥ pada-paṅktiḥ* : Vikram., Act 4 : and *Śroṇi-bhārād alasa-gamanā* : Megh., verse 81. Hence, one of the names of a lovely woman is *nitambinī*, having large and handsome hips and loins.' Chēzy compare the epithet 'Callipyge' applied to a celebrated statue of Venus.

2. 'Through the branches.' The Kolkata edition has *viṭapāntarito*, 'concealed by the branches.'

3. 'The highest object of my eye-sight,' 'the full bliss of my eyes :' [*netrā-nanda* : K. *nayana-nirvṛti, cakṣuḥ-sukha* : Ś.] *Nirvāṇa* or *apavarga*, is properly 'final beatitude, consisting in emancipation from further transmigration.'

4. 'Yonder the best-beloved object of my wishes, reclining on a stone-seat strewed with flowers, is attended by her two friends.' *Manorathapriyatamā* : 'most dear by desire;' not be actual possession or by any other method : K. *Śilā-paṭṭam=pāṣāṇā-khaṇḍam* : *see* p. 76, note 1. *Anvās* 'to sit near' (*anu, ās.*).

5. 'Are in the act of fanning her. ' *Vīj* with *upa*, 'to fan.' Hence, *vyajana*, 'a fan.'

Verse 61. *Āryā* or *Ghāthā*. (*See* Verse 2.)

— — | ⏑ — ⏑ | — — ‖ ⏑ ⏑ — | — ⏑ ⏑ | ⏑ — ⏑ | — — | —
— — | ⏑ — ⏑ | ⏑ ⏑ — ‖ ⏑ ⏑ — | — — | ⏑ | — ⏑ ⏑ | —

सख्यौ : (उपवीज्य। सस्नेहं) हला सउन्दले। अवि सुहाअदि दे
सख्यौ : (उपवीज्य। सस्नेहं) हला शकुन्तले। अपि सुखायते ते
णलिणीपत्तवादो।
नलिनीपत्रवातः।[1]

शकुन्तलाः किं वीजअन्ति मं महीओ।

शकुन्तला : किं वीजयतो मां सख्यौ।

(सख्यौ विषादं नाटयित्वा परस्परम् अवलोकयतः)

राजा : बलवद् अस्वस्थशरीरा शकुन्तला दृश्यते (सवितर्कं) ततः किम् अयम् आतपदोषः स्यात्। उत यथा मे मनसि वर्तते[2] (साभिलाषं निर्वर्ण्य) अथवा कृतं सन्देहेन।

स्तनन्यस्तोशीरं प्रशिथिलमृणालैकवलयं
प्रियायाः साबाधं तदपि कमनीयं वपुर् इदम्।
समस् तापः कामं मनसिजनिदाघप्रसरयोर्
न तु ग्रीष्मस्यैवं सुभगम् अपराद्धं युवतिषु[3] ।। 62 ।।

1. 'Is this wind from the (fan) of lotus-leaves agreeable to thee ?' see p. 89, note 1; p. 25, note 1, in middle. Some of the Devanāgarī read *suhā adi* for *sukhayati,* but the above is supported by K. and the oldest MSS.

2. 'Can this be the fault of the heat ? or as is passing in my mind ?' *i.e.,* or is love, as I conjecture, the true cause ?

3. 'This form of my beloved, having the Usīra applied to the bosom, and having only one armlet (and that formed) of lotus-fibres hanging-loose, (is certainly) disordered, but even so is lovely. Granted that the heat of the two influences of love and the hot season [*or* the heat induced by the prevalence either of love or of the sultry weather] be equal, still disorder is not inflicted on maidens by the hot weather in such a charming manner :' *i.e.,* Since the disorder apparent in the person of Śakuntalā only contributes to her beauty, it is clearly not caused by the hot weather, but by love. *Usīra* : *see* p. 95, note 4, and Sir W. Jones, vol v, p. 154. Two other names for this plant are *jalāśaya,* 'growing in water,' and *avadāha,* 'allaying fever;' the slender fibres of it are now known by the name

---

Verse 62. *Śikhariṇī* (variety of *Atyaṣṭi*) *See* Verses 9, 24, 44.

प्रियंवदा : (जनान्तिकं) अणसूए। तस्स राएसिणो पढमदंसणादो
प्रियंवदा : जनान्तिकं।। अनसूये। तस्य राजर्षेः प्रथमदर्शनाद्
आरहिअ पज्जुस्सुआ विअ सउन्दला। किं णुक्खु मे तणिमित्तो अअं आतङ्को
आरभ्य पर्युत्सुका इव **शकुन्तला** : किं नु खलु अस्यास् तन्निमित्तो ऽयम् आतङ्को
भवे।
भवेत्।

अनसूया : **महि। ममबि ईदिसी आसङ्का हिअअस्स। होदु। पुच्छिस्सं**
अनसूया : सखि। ममापि ईदृशी आशङ्का हृदयस्य। भवतु। प्रक्ष्यामि
दाव णं। (प्रकाशं) सहि। पुच्छिदव्वासि किम्पि। बलिअं क्खु दे मन्दाबो।
तावद् एनाम्।। प्रकाशम्।। सखि। प्रष्टव्यासि किमपि। बलीयान् खलु ते सन्तापः।

शकुन्तला : (पूर्व्वार्द्धेन शयनाद् उत्थाय) हला। किं वत्तुकामासि।
शकुन्तला : पूर्व्वार्द्धेन शयनाद् उत्थाय।। हला। किं वक्तुकामासि।
अनसूया। हला सउन्दले। अणब्मन्तरा खु अन्हे मदणगदस्स वुत्तन्तस्म।
अनसूया। हला शकुन्तले। अनभ्यन्तरे खलु आवां मदनगतस्य वृत्तान्तस्य।
किन्दु। जादिसी इदिहासणिबन्धेसु कामअमाणाणं अवत्था सुणीअदि
किन्तु। यादृशी इतिहासनिबन्धेषु कामयमानानाम् अवस्था श्रूयते
तादिसिं दे पेक्खामि। कहेहि। किणिमत्तं दे सन्दाबो। विआरंक्खु परमत्थदो
तादृशीं ते प्रेक्षे। कथय। किन्निमित्तं ते सन्तापः। विकारं खलु परमार्थतो-

of Khaskhas and are used in India in trellises for cooling the air. *Prasithila=adṛḍha* : Ś.=*komala*, 'withered :' Ch. 'Her body was so enfeebled that she could not bear the weight of two armlets or bracelets; she therefore had only one, and that made, not of gold, but of lotus-fibres [*mṛṇāla-ghaṭita*] tied loosely round the arm :' Ś. *Sābādham=sapīḍam* : Ch.:=*sa-vyadham* : K. 'diseased,' 'deranged.' *Tadapi*, 'even so;' even in this manner or under these disadvantages : *tad* is here used adverbially. This reading is supported by the oldest MSS. and by K. The Devanāgarī have *kimapi ramaṇīyam*, 'somewhat pleasing.' *Kāmam* : *see* p. 55, note 3. *Prasarayoḥ*, literally, 'of the two prevalences :' *prasara=prasaṅga*, 'attachment,' 'connection :' Ś : but the simple meaning is 'spreading,' 'prevalence.'

अजाणिअ अणारम्भो पडिआरस्स।

ऽज्ञात्वा अनारम्भः प्रतिकारस्य।[1]

राजा : अनसूययापि मदीयस् तर्कोऽवगतः।

शकुन्तला : (आत्मगतं) बलिअंक्खु मे अहिणिवेसो। सहसा एदाणं

शकुन्तला : । आत्मगतम्।। बलीयान् खलु मेऽभिनिवेशः।[2] सहसा एतयोर्

ण मक्कणोमि णिवेदिदुं।

न शक्नोमि निवेदितुम्।

प्रियंवदा : सहि सउन्दले। सुट्ठु एसा भणादि। किं अत्तणो आतङ्कं

प्रियंवदा : सखि शकुन्तले। सुष्ठु एषा भणति। किम् आत्मन आतङ्कम्

उबेक्खसि। अणुदिअहंक्खु परिहीअमि अङ्गेहिं। केवलं लावणमई छाआ

उपेक्षसे। अनुदिवसं खलु परिहीयसे अङ्गैः। केवलं लावण्यमयी छाया

तुमं ण मुञ्चदि।

त्वां न मुञ्चति।[3]

राजा : अवितथम् आह प्रियंवदा। तथा हि–

1. 'We are not indeed intimately conversant with matters relating to love; but as the condition of lovers is heard of (by us) in legendary tales, of such a kind I perceive is thy (condition). Say, from what cause (is) thy disorder ? (for) indeed without being accurately acquainted with the desease, (there) can be no application of the remedy.' *Anabhyantara,* nom. c. du. fem. of a compound adjective or Bahuvrīhi formed from the substantive *abhyantara,* 'interior,' 'inside,' by prefixing the privative *an,* in the same manner as *anantara,* 'uninterrupted,' from *antara, Anabhyantara* is, literally 'one not admitted to the inside.' Compare *gaṇabhyantara,* 'one who is a member of any private association :' Wilson's Dict. *Madanagatasya : see* p. 37, note 1. *Itihāsa=purā-vṛtta : Ś. Nibandha,* 'a composition,' 'a narrative;' whence *nibandhṛ,* 'an author.'

2. 'My attachment [affection] is strong.' *Abhiniveśa* [here= *abhilāṣa* implies firm attachment to or intense pursuit of any object. *Dānimapi,* 'even now,' which the Devanāgarī give at the end of this sentence, does not appear in K., or in the Bengālī MSS.

3. 'Thy limbs are wasting away [*lit.,* thou art abandoned by thy limbs]. Thy lovely complexion alone deserts the not.'

क्षामक्षामकपोलम् आननम् उरः काठिन्यमुक्तस्तनं
मध्यः क्लान्ततरः प्रकामविनताव् अंसौ छविः पाण्डुरा।
शोच्या च प्रियदर्शना च मदनक्लिष्टेयम् आलक्ष्यते
पत्राणामिव शोषणेन मरुता स्पृष्टा लतामाधवी[1] ।। 63 ।।

शकुन्तला : सहि। कस्स वा अणस्स कहइस्सं। किन्दु आआमइत्तिआ
शकुन्तला : सखि। कस्य वा अन्यस्य कथयिष्यामि।[2] किन्तु आयासयित्री
दाणिं वो भविस्सं।
इदानीं वां भविष्यामि।

उभे : अदो एव्वक्खु णिब्बन्धो। सिणिद्धजणसंविभत्तं हि दुक्खुं
उभे : अत एव खलु निर्बन्धः। स्निग्धजनसंविभक्तं हि दुःखं

1. 'For, indeed her face has its checks excessively emaciated, her bosom has its breasts destitute of firmness, her waist is more slender, her shoulders are quite drooping, her complexion is pale; she being tormented by love appears both deplorable and (yet) lovely, like Mādhavi-creepr touched by the wind, the scorcher of (its) leaves.' *Kṣāma-kṣāma-kapola=atikṛśa-gaṇḍa* : Ś. The repetition of *kṣāma* may imply 'becoming gradually every day more and more emaciated;' as Priyaṁvadā had said *anudivasaṁ parihīyase aṅgaiḥ*. *Kāṭhinya-mukta* : the Bengāli have *yukta*, but the *loss* of firmness in the breasts would rather be sign of debility. *Prakāma* : Ś. interprets this by *atyartham*, 'excessively.' So, the commentator on Gīt.-Gov., iv, 17; vii., 10, explains *nikāmam* by *atiśayena*. Similarly *kāmam* has the sense of *niścitam*, 'certainly.' May the meaning not be 'stoop of their own accord,' *i.e.*, 'languidly,' 'listlessly,' from their being allowed to fall without any effort being made to raise them ? *Śoṣaṇena=śoṣakena, i.e.*, By the wind that dries up the leaves and causes them to fall : [*patra-pātaka-vāyunā*] K., Ś. *Mādhavī*, a large and beautiful creeper bearing white fragrant flowers, *[Gaertnera recemosa]* to which constant allusion is made in the plays : see page 113, note 2.

2. 'To whom else shall I relate it (if not to you, my two friends ?)' *Yadi kathanīyaṁ tadā bhavatībhyām* : Ś.

Verse 63. *Śārdūla-vidrīḍita* (variety of *Atidhṛti*). *See* Verses 14, 30, 36, 39, 40.

सज्झवेदणं होदि।
सह्यवेदनं भवति।[1]

राजा :

पृष्ट्य जनेन समदुःखसुखेन बाला
नेयं न वक्ष्यति मनोगतम् आधिहेतुम्।
दृष्टो विवृत्य बहुशोऽप्यनया सतृष्णम्
अत्रान्तरे श्रवणकातरतां गतोऽस्मि[2] ।। 64 ।।

शकुन्तलाः सहि। जदो पहुदि मम दंसणपहं आअदो सो तवो-
शकुन्तला : सखि। यतः प्रभृति मम दर्शनपथम्[3] आगतः स तपो-

1. 'Our impotunity is on this very account. Grief shared with affectionate friends becomes supportable suffering.' *Nirbandha,* 'urgency,' 'pressing solicitation.'

2. This maiden being questioned by the persons who are the partners of her sorrows and joys, will most certainly declare the cause of her anguish (now) concealed in her breast. Although (I was) looked upon longingly by her repeatedly turning round, I (nevertheless) at the present moment experience an uneasy-anxiety for hearing (her reply).' *Jana=sakhi-jana;* though used in the singular, it may have a plural signification. *Sama-duḥkha-sukha,* 'one who has the same joys and sorrows : *Cf. sama-duḥkha-sukhaḥ pīyate locanābhyām* : Vikramorvaśīya, Act I. *Bālā* properly 'a girl sixteen years of age :' Ś. *Na na vakṣyati=vakṣyati eva* : Ś. : two negatives give intensity to the affirmative [*dvau niṣedhau prakṛtam artham gamayataḥ* : Ś.] : *see* page 24, note 2. *Mano-gatam=hṛdaya-stham* : *see* page 37, note 1. *Atrāntare=asminn avasare* : K. *Śravaṇa-kātaratām=Sakuntalā-prativacana-śravaṇa-bhīrutaām.* According to Bharata, the four ways by which a maiden encouraged the advances of her lover were *Lekha pasthāpana,* 'sending a letter :' *Śnigdha-vīkṣita,* 'a loving glance;' *Mṛdubhāṣita,* 'soft speech;' and *Dūtī-sampreṣaṇa,* 'sending a messenger :' Ś. Although Śakuntalā had favoured her lover with one of these tokens, yet he was fearful that, when about to reply to her friends, she might through carelessness [*pramādatas*] confess to an affection for some other person : Ś.

3. 'Met my eye,' 'crossed my sight,' *lit.,* 'came across the path [range] of my sight.' A not uncommon idea : Compare *yasya netrayoḥ*

Verse 64. *Vasantatilakā* (variety of *Śakkarī*). *See* Verses 8, 27, 31, 43, 46.

वणरक्खिदा राएसी (इत्यर्द्धोक्तेन लज्जां नाटयति)

वनरक्षिता राजर्षिः (इत्यर्द्धोक्तेन लज्जां नाटयति)

उभे : कधेदु पिअसही।

उभे : कथयतु प्रियसखी।

शकुन्तला : तदो पहुदि तग्गदेण अहिलासेण एतदवत्थन्हि संवुत्ता।

शकुन्तला : ततः प्रभृति तद्गतेन अभिलाषेण एतदवस्थास्मि संवृत्ता।

राजा : (सहर्षं) श्रुतं श्रोतव्यम्।

स्मर एव तापहेतुर् निर्वापयिता स एव मे जातः।

दिवस इवाभ्रश्यामस् तपात्यये जीवलोकस्य[1] ।। 65 ।।

शकुन्तला : तं जइ वो अणुमदं तह वट्ठह जह तस्स राएसिणो

शकुन्तला : तद् यदि वाम् अनुमतं तथा वर्तेथां यथा तस्य राजर्षेर्

pathi sthitā twam : Vikramorvaśīya, Act I.

1. 'Love, indeed, the cause of my fever, has himself become the cooler of it : as, on the passing off of the heat, a day dark with clouds (which was at first hot, becoms afterwards the cooler) of living creatures.' *Smara,* one of the names of the god of love, 'The ideal one' [page 101, note 1] derived from *smṛ,* 'to recollect.' *Nirvāpayitā, lit.,* 'the extinguisher'=sukha-hetuḥ, 'the cause of pleasure :' Ś. According to Kāṭavema *tapātyaye=grīshmānte,* 'at the end of the hot season :' He and Śaṅkara observe that a cloudy day at the end of the hot season and at the approach of the rains, is very sultry, until by the rising of clouds it brings coolness in place of the heat which itself had caused : and quote a parallel passage from the Ratnāvalī [p. 64] *Tapati prāvṛṣi nitarām abhyarṇa-jalāgamo divasaḥ,* 'In the rainy season when the rain is near at had the day is expecially hot.' Some of the Devanāgarī read *arddha-śyāma,* 'half-obscured,' which is not supported by any of the commentators, nor by the oldest MSS.

Verse 65. *Āryā* or *Gāthā*. (*See* Verse 2.)

◡◡— |◡—◡|——|| —— |◡◡—|◡—◡|——|—

◡◡◡◡| —— |——||◡—◡| —— | ◡ |——|◡

अणुकम्पणिज्जा होमि। अणहा अवस्सं सिञ्चह मे तिलोदअं।
अनुकम्पनीया भवामि। अन्यथा अवश्यं सिञ्चतं मे तिलोदकम्।[1]

राजा : संशयच्छेदि वचनम्।

प्रियंवदाः (जनान्तिकं) अणसूए। दूरगअवस्सहा अक्खमा इअं
प्रियंवदा : (जनान्तिकं) अनसूये। दूरगतमन्मथा अक्षमा इयं
कालहरणस्स। जस्सिं बद्धभावा एसा सो ललामभूदो पोरवाणं। ता जुत्तं से
कालहरणस्य।[2] यस्मिन् बद्धभावा एषा स ललामभूतः पौरवाणां।[3] तद् युक्तम् अस्या

1. 'Then if (it be) approved by you, so act, that I may be commiserated by the royal sage. Otherwise most certainly (it will happen that you will have to) pour out for me water with sesamum-seed;' *i.e.,* That you will have to celebrate my funeral obsequies. Oblations to the manes of the deceased were offered by the nearest surviving relations soon after death, and were repeated once, or, according to some, twice in every year. They were supposed to be necessary to secure the residence of the souls of the dead in the world appropriated to the manes. The ceremony itself was called *Śrāddha,* and generally consisted in offering a cake made of rice and milk [*piṇḍa-nirvāpana*]; or in pouring out water [*udaka-dāna, udaka-kriyā*]; or water and sesamum-seed mixed. In the latter case it was called *tilodaka-dāna, tila-tarpaṇa,* etc. The ceremony as performed by Brāhmaṇas is described in Manu, iii, 203, etc.; see especially iii, 223 : *Dattvā sapavitraṁ tilodakam,* ' Having poured out water with sesamum-seed and *kuśa*-grass.' Kāṭavema refers in illustration to a verse towards the end of the 6th Act of this play, where Duṣyanta says *Nūnaṁ prasūti-vikalena mayā prasiktam, dhautāśru-śeṣaṁ udakaṁ pitaraḥ pivanti,* 'In all probability my (deceased) ancestors are (now) drinking the only offering-of-water that is left to them (consisting of) glistening tears poured forth by me destitute of posterity.' *Siñcatam=nirvapatam* : K. *Vartethām; vṛt* may have the sense of 'to behave,' 'to act.'

2. 'She is far gone in love, and unable to bear loss of time,' *i.e.,* Her love has reached that point which brooks no delay. Compare *dūrarūḍho' syāḥ praṇayaḥ :* Vikramorvaśīya, Act 4., at beginning *Vammaha* or *bammaha* is the proper Prākṛt equivalent for *manmatha,* according to Vararuci ii, 38; iii, 43. Lassen, Instit. Prāk., p. 245, although the MSS. give *mammaha*

3. 'He on whom she has fixed her affections is the ornament of

अहिलासो अहनन्दिदुं।।
अभिलाषोऽभिनन्दितु।

अनसूया : तह। जह भणासि।
अनसूया : तथा। यथा भणसि।

प्रियंवदा : (प्रकाशं) सहि। दिट्ठिआ। अणुरूबो से अहिणिवेसो। साअरं
प्रियंवदा : (प्रकाशं) सखि। दिष्ट्या। अनुरूपोऽस्या अभिनिवेशः। सागरं
वज्जिअं कहिं वा महाणई ओदरइ। को दाणिं सहआरं अन्तरेण अदिमुत्तलदं
वर्जयित्वा कुत्र वा महानदी अवतरति। क इदानीं सहकारम् अन्तरेण अतिमुक्तलतां
पल्लविदं सहेदि।
पल्लवितां सहते[1]।

राजा : किमत्र चित्रं यदि विशाखे शशाङ्कलेखाम् अनुवर्तेते।[2]

the Pauravas [p. 15, note 2], therefore her love is fit to be approved;' or it is proper that her love should meet with our approval. *Yuktam* is here used like *śakyam* : p. 103, note 2. *Baddha-bhāvā* : Compare in the beginning of Act 3 of Vikramorvaśiya, *Yasmin baddha-bhāva'si tvam.*

1. 'Where should a great river end its course excepting at the ocean ? What (tree) excepting the Sahakāra [Mango] can support the Atimukta [Mādhavī creeper] with (its) new sprouts ?' *Ava-tṛ* (properly 'to descend,' or alight') is here applied to the disemboguing of a river into the ocean. *Yathā mahā-nadī samudraṁ praviśati, tathā rūpavatī tvam duṣyante evānuraktā* : Ś. The Sahakāra is described p. 28, note 1. The Atimukta is the same as the Mādhavī or vernal creeper, called also Vāsantī and Puṇḍraka, and noticed before : p. 108, note 1. 'The beauty and fragrance of the flower of this creeper give them a title to all the praises which Kālidāsa and Jayadeva bestow on them. It is a gigantic and luxuriant climber; but when it meets with nothing to grasp, it assumes the form of a sturdy tree, the highest branches of which display, however, in the air, their natural flexibility and inclination to climb :' Sir W. Jones, vol. v, p. 124.

2. 'Why need we wonder at this, since the constellation Viśākhā courts [goes after] the young-moon ?' *i.e.*, If the constellation Viśākhā [or the sixteenth lunar asterism, which is sometimes written in the dual Viśākhe, as containing two stars] is eager for an union with the Moon, why need we wonder at Śakuntalā's desire to be united

अनसूया : को उण उबाओ भवे। जेण अविलम्बिअं णिहुअं अ सहीए

अनूसया : कः पुनर् उपायो भवेत्। येन अविलम्बितं निभृतं च सख्या

मणोरहं सम्पादेन्ह।

मनोरथं सम्पादयावः।

प्रियंवदा : णिहुअंत्ति चिन्तणिज्जं भवे। सिग्घंत्ति सुअरं।

प्रियंवदा : निभृतम्। इति चिन्तनीयं भवेत्। शीघ्रम् इति सुकरम्।[1]

a prince of the lunar race ? *Śaśāṅka-lekhā* is properly 'a digit of the moon,' or the moon in its most beautiful form when quite young. A complete revolution of the moon, with respect to the stars, being made in twenty-seven days, odd hours; the Hindūs divide the heavens into twenty-seven constellations [asterisms] or lunar stations, one of which receives the moon for one day in each of his monthly journeys. As the Moon [Candra] is considered to be a masculine deity, the Hindūs fable these twenty-seven contellations as his wives, and personify them as the daughters of Dakṣa. Of these twenty-seven wives (twelve of whom give names to the twelve months) Candra is supposed to show the greatest affection for the fourth (Rohiṇī) but each of the others, and amongst them Viśākhā, is represented as jealous of this partiality, and eager to secure the Moon's favour for herself. Duṣyanta probably means to compare himself to the Moon (he being of the lunar race : p. 15, note 2) and Śakuntalā to Viśākhā. The selection fo Viśākhā, rather than Rohiṇī, may perhaps be explained by a reference to p. 5, 1. 5, where we learn that the summer-season had barely set in at the period when the events of the drama were supposed to be taking place. If therefore the season corresponded to the middle of May, the month would probably be Vaiśākha, and Viśākhā would, therefore, be appropriately chosen before Rohiṇi. This passage may also be interpreted, but not so consistently with the fable, by referring *viśākhe* to the two female friends and *śaśāṅka-lekhā* to Śakuntalā. The meaning would then be, 'It is not to be wondered at that these two friends should follow Śakuntalā and assist in carrying out her schemes, any more than that the two stars of Viśākhā should go after the young moon.' *Anuvartete=anusarataḥ* : K. Compare in Vikram., Act 1, *Citralekhā-dvitīyaṁ priya-sakhim Urvāśīṁ gṛhītvā viśākhā-sahita iva bhagavān soma upasthitaḥ sa rājarṣiḥ.*

1. '(Your) "unobservedly" will require thought, (your)

अनसूया : कहं विअ।

अनसूया : कथम इव।

प्रियंवदाः णं सो राएसी इमस्सिं सिणिद्धदिट्ठीए सूइदाहिलासो इमाइं दिअहाइं पज्जाअरकिसो लक्खीअदि।

प्रियंवदा : ननु स राजर्षिर् अस्यां स्निग्धदृष्ट्या सूचिताभिलाष इमानि दिवसानि प्रजागरकृशो लक्ष्यते।

राजा : (आत्मानम् अवलोक्य) सत्यम् इत्थम्भूत एवास्मि। तथा हि–

इदम् अशिशिरैर् अन्तस्तापाद् विवर्णमणीकृतं
निशि निशि भुजन्यस्तापाङ्गप्रवर्त्तिभिर् अश्रुभिः।
अनतिलुलितज्याघाताङ्कं मुहुर् मणिबन्धनात्।
कनकवलयं स्रस्तं मया प्रतिसार्यते[1] ।। 66 ।।

"quickly" (is) easy.' This use of *iti* in quoting previous words is noticeable.

1. 'For this golden bracelet, having its jewels sullied by the ears (rendered) scorching from internal fever night after night flowing from the outer-corner-of-my-eye which rests on my arm, slipping slipping down [*i.e.*, as it constantly slips down] from the wrist, without pressing on [catching on, hitching on] the sears (that are caused) by the friction of the bow-string, is repeatedly pushed back by me.' *Āpānya* = *netra-prānta. Pravarttibhiḥ=skhaladbhiḥ. Atilulita=atisakta,* 'closely adhering :' K : = *nābhilupta:* S. and Ch. The same word occurs at the end of this act, where allusion is made to the flowery couch of Śakuntalā, *śarīra-lulitā,* which her body had pressed:' One sense of the root *lul* is certainly to 'adhere,' 'stick,' 'cleave:' The Devanāgarī all have *anabhilulita* with the same meaning, unsupported by K. and the other scholiasts, and the oldest Bengālī MSS. Through emaciation and disuse of the bow (*Cf.* p. 70, 1. 10, with p. 68, 1. 3) the callosities on the fore-arm usually caused by the bow-string, were not sufficiently prominent to prevent the bracelet from slipping down from the wrist to the elbow, when the

---

Verse 66. *Hariṇī* (variety of *Atyaṣṭi*) containing seventeen syllables to the half-line, each half-line being alike.

⏑⏑⏑⏑⏑ – – | – – – – | ⏑ – ⏑⏑ – ⏑ – ||

प्रियंवदा : (विचिन्त्य) हला । मअनलेहो से करीअदु । इमं देवदासेसाब-

प्रियंवदा : (विचिन्त्य) हला। मदनलेखोऽस्य क्रियताम्। इमं देवताशेषाप-

देसेण सुमणोगोबिदं करिअ मे हत्थअं पाबइस्सं।

देशेन सुमनोगोपितं कृत्वा अस्य हस्तं प्रापयिष्यामि।[1]

अनसूयाः रोअद् मे सुउमारो पओओ। किं वा सउन्दला भणादि।

अनसूया : रोचते मे सुकुमारः प्रयोगः। किं वा शकुन्तला भणति।

शकुन्तलाः सहीणिओओबि विकप्पीअदि।

शकुन्तला : सखीनियोगोऽपि विकल्प्यते।[2]

arm was raised to support the head. This is a favourite idea with Kālidāsa to express the attenuation caused by love. Compare Meghadūta, verse 2: *Kanaka-valaya-bhraṁśa-rikta-prakoṣṭhaḥ,* 'having the fore-arm bare by the falling of the golden bracelet.' The Bengālī have *anatilulita-jyā ghātāṅkād*, agreeing with *maṇi-bandhanāt*, which would appear at first sight to be tbe better reading. I have followed Kāṭavema and the Devanāgarī MSS. in making this compound agree with *valayam,* and I believe there is no other way of translate it satisfactorily. It may, however, as Kāṭavema observes, be taken adverbially. *Maṇibandhana* 'the wrist,' 'the place of binding jewels.'

1. 'Let a love-letter be composed for him. Having hidden it [made it hid] in a flower, I will deliver it into [cause it to reach] his hand under the pretext of [as if it were] the remains (of an offering presented) to an idol.' *Madana-lekha = anaṅga-lekha:* Ch. :=*smara-bhāva-sūcakam lekham* : Ś. *Sumano-gopitam=kusuma-saṅguptam* : Ś. *Devatā-śeṣāpadeśena;* the Bengālī read *devatā-sevāpadesena,* 'under pretext of honouring a divinity,' supported by Ś. Kāṭavema reads *devatā-vyapadeśena,* with the word *prasāda* inserted in the margin. *Devatā-śeṣa* is supported by Ch., and explained by him as *nirmālyam,* 'the remains of an offering of flowers presented to an idol.' Garlands of flowers were sometimes so offered. A love-letter was one of the four recognized modes of enouraging a lover : *see* page 109, note 2.

2. 'This very injuction [suggestion] of my friend is weighed (in my mind),' *i.e.,* I must consider before I can consent to it. This is the reading of the two oldest MSS. One, however, has *sahi* for *sahī.*

प्रियंवदा : तेण हि अत्तणो उबणासपुव्वं चिन्तेहि दाव किम्पि ललिवपदबन्धणं।

प्रियंवदा : तेन हि आत्मन उपन्यासपूर्वं चिन्तय तावत् किमपि ललितपदबन्धनम्।[1]

शकुन्तला : हला। चिन्तेमि अहं। अवहीरणभीरुअं पुणो वेबइ मे हिअअं।

शकुन्तला : हला। चिन्तयामि अहं। अवधीरणभीरुकं पुनर् वेपते मे हृदयम्।

राजा : (सहर्षं)

अयं स ते तिष्ठति सङ्गमोत्सुको
विशङ्कसे भीरु यतोऽवधीरणाम्।
लभेत वा प्रार्थयिता न वा श्रियं
श्रिया दुरापः कथम् ईप्सितो भवेत्[2] ।। 67 ।।

1. 'Therefore just think of some pretty composition in verse, accompanied by an allusion to yourself.' *Upanyāsa-pūrvam, lit.*, 'preceded [headed] by an allusion.' *Lalita-pada-bandhanam* : Compare *lalitārtha-bandham* : Vikramorvaśīya, Act 2.

2. 'That very one, O timid one, from whom thou apprehendest a refusal, stands pining for an union with thee. The lover may or may not win Fortune, (but) how, being beloved (by her), should he be difficult-to-be-won by Fortune?' *Śrī = Lakṣmī,* 'the goddess of beauty and fortune,' here identified with Śakuntalā or with the object of the lover's hopes and aspirations. The commentators do not throw light on this passage. The meaning seems to be, 'There is always a doubt whether the suitor will gain favour with Fortune, or with the beautiful maiden who may be the object of his love, but when it is certain that he is beloved by her, how can *she* have any difficulty in gaining *him*? for there surely will be no doubt of his being willing to accept her favours, however uncertain may be her encouragement of his advances.' The verse which follows this in the Bengālī MSS. is omitted in all the Devanāgarī, and is most probably spurious.

Verse 67. *Vaṁśasthavila* (variety of *Jagatī.*) *See* Verses 18, 22, 23.

सख्यौ : अयि अत्तमुणावमाणिणि। को दाणिं मरीरणिव्याबइत्तिअं

सख्यौ : अयि आत्मगुणावमानिनि। क इदानीं शरीरनिर्वापयित्रीं

सारदिअं जोसिणिं पडन्तेण वारेदि।

शारदीं ज्योत्स्नां पटान्तेन वारयति।[1]

शकुन्तला : (सस्मितं) णिओइदा दाणिंम्हि।। इत्युपविष्टा

शकुन्तला : सस्मितम्।। नियोजिता इदानीम् अस्मि।।[2] इत्युपविष्य

चिन्तयति।

चिन्तयति।

राजा : स्थाने खलु विस्मृतनिमेषेण चक्षुषा प्रियाम् अवलोकयामि। यतः–

उन्नमितैकभ्रूलतम् आननम् अस्याः पदानि रचयन्त्याः।
कण्टकितेन प्रथयति मय्यनुरागं कपोलेन[3] ।। 68 ।।

1. 'O thou undervaluer of thine own excellencies, who now would ward off with the skirt of a garment the autumnal moonlight, the cooler of his body?' *i.e.*, according to Śaṅkara, This prince is too sensible to be averse to an union with one so beautiful as thou art. *Nirvāpayitrīm* : *see* p. 95, note 5. *Paṭāntena* : Compare in Act V. *Paṭāntena mukham āvṛtya roditi.*

2. 'I am now (acting) under (your) directions,' *i.e.*, It is by your orders that I do this: *Niyojitāsmi bhavatībhya gīti-karaṇe*, 'I am directed by you to compose verses:' Ś. : I am only following your directions, therefore you are responsible, if I meet with a repulse : Ś.

3. 'Fitly, indeed, do I gaze on my beloved with an eye that forgets to wink, because the countenance of her composing [whilst she is in the act of composing] verses has one eyebrow raised; (and) by her thrilling cheek she discloses her affection for me.' *Vismṛta-nimeṣeṇa* is very expressive of a fixed, earnest gaze. Chēzy translates, 'O spectacle enchanteur! dont je serais jalous que le moindre clignement d'oeil me privāt un instant!' *Kaṇṭakita, lit.*, 'having the downy hair of the cheek erect like thorns.' The Bengālī have *pulakācitena*, and the Kolkata edition *pulakāñcitena*, meaning the same. Horripilation, or the erection of the hair of the body (*pulaka*,

---

Verse 68. *Āryā* or *Ghāthā*. (*See* Verse 2.)

— ⏑ ⏑ | — — | — ⏑ ⏑ || — ⏑ ⏑ | — — | ⏑ — ⏑ | ⏑ ⏑ — | —
— ⏑ ⏑ | — — | ⏑ ⏑ ⏑ ⏑ || — ⏑ ⏑ | — — | ⏑ | — — | ⏑

शकुन्तला : हला। चिन्तिदा मए गीदिआ। ण क्ख सणिहिदाणि उणलेहणसाहणाणि।
शकुन्तला : हला। चिन्तिता मया गीतिका। न खलु सन्निहितानि पुनर् लेखनसाधनानि।[1]

प्रियंवदाः इमस्सिं सुओदरसुअमारे णलिणीपत्ते णहेहिं णिक्खित्तवणं करेहि।
प्रियंवदा : अस्मिन् शुकोदरसुकुमारे नलिनीपत्रे नखैर् निक्षिप्तवर्णं कुरु।[2]

शकुन्तला : (यथोक्तं रूपयित्वा) हला। सुणुह दाणिं सङ्गदत्थं ण वेत्ति।
शकुन्तला : (यथोक्तं रूपयित्वा) हला। शृणुतम् इदानीं सङ्गतार्थं न वेत्ति।

उभे : अवहिदन्ह।
उभे : अवहिते स्वः।
शकुन्तला : (वाचयति)
शकुन्तला : (वाचयति)
तुज्झ ण आणे हिअअं मम उण कामो दिवाबि रत्तिम्पि।
तव न जाने हृदयं मम पुनः कामो दिवापि रात्रिमपि।

---

roma-kaṇṭaka, romāñcana) is considered by the Hindūs to be an indication of exquisite delight or pleasurable emotion. The Dictionary does not give this sense to *kaṇṭaka*, but it is so used in Vikramorvaśīya, Act I., *mama aṅgaṁ sa-roma-kaṇṭakam aṅkuritam.*

1. 'But the writing-materials indeed are not at hand' Most of the MSS. have *hu* for Sanskrit *khalu*. Lassen (Instit. Prāk., p. 192) shows that *kkhu* is the proper form after a short vowel.

2. 'Engrave the letters [make engraving of the letters] with your nails on this lotus-leaf smooth as a parrot's breast.' *Śukodara* : In Vikramorvaśīya, Act IV., the colour of a scarf is compared to the same thing [*śukodaraśyāmaṁ stanāṁśukam*] and in Mahābh. ii, 1035, the colour of horses [*śukodra-samān hayān*]. The Prākṛt is answerable for *nikṣipta-varṇaṁ kuru*. This is the reading of all the Devanāgarī; the Bengālī have *padacheda-bhaktyā nakhair ālikhyatām*.

णिग्घिण तबेइ बलिअं तुइ वुत्तमणोरहाइ अङ्गाइं ।। 69 ।।

निर्घृण तपति बलीयस् त्वयि वृत्तमनोरथाया अङ्गानि[1] ।। 69 ।।

राजा : (सहसोपसृत्य)

तपति तनुगात्रि मदनस् त्वाम् अनिशं मां पुनर् दहत्येव ।
ग्लपयति यथा शशाङ्कं न तथा हि कुमुद्वतीं दिवसः[2] ।। 70 ।।

सख्यौ : (विलोक्य सहर्षम् उत्थाय) साअदं अविलस्विणो मणो-रहस्स ।

सख्यौ : (विलोक्य सहर्षम् उत्थाय) स्वागतम् अविलम्बिनो मनो रथस्य ।[3]

1. 'Thy heart I know not, but day and night, O cruel one, Love vehemently inflames the limbs of me, whose desires are centred in thee.' Such is the reading of the Taylor MS. and my own. The other Devanāgarī agree, but give *maṇorahāiṃ* for *manorathāni* in concord with *aṅgāni. Maṇorahāi* and *maṇorahae* may both stand for the Sanskṛt gen. fem. *manorathāyāḥ* (in concord with *mama*), and both are equally admissible into the metre: Lassen's Instit. Prāk., pp. 304, 305, 147. The interpretation of Ch. supports this reading [*niṣkṛpa tapayati balīyas tvad-abhimukha-manorathāyā aṅgāni*]. This verse is called by Kāṭavema, the *upanyāsa* : compare p. 116, note 1.

2. 'Thee, O slender-limbed one, Love inflames; but me he actually consumes incessantly: for the Day does not so cause the lotus to fade as it does the moon.' *Kumuda* or *kumudvatī* is a kind of lotus, which blossoms in the night and fades by day [*kumudvatī candra-viraheṇa santaptā bhavati* : Ś.] here compared to Śakuntalā. *Kumudvatī* is usually a 'grop of lotuses,' but I cannot agree with Dr. Boehtlingk in restricting it to this acceptation. *Śaśāṅka* : see p. 25, note 1 at end : Duṣyanta again compares himself to the moon : Compare p. 113, note 1. This and the preceding verse, according to Śaṅkara and Candraśekhara, afford an example of the figure Uttarottaram.

3. 'Welcome to the speedy (fulfilment of thy) desire !' *or*

Verse 69. *Gīti* or *Upagāthā. See* Verse 4.
— ⏑ ⏑ | — — | ⏑ ⏑ — ‖ ⏑ ⏑ ⏑ ⏑ | — — | ⏑ — ⏑ | — — | —
— ⏑ ⏑ | ⏑ — ⏑ | ⏑ ⏑ — ‖ ⏑ ⏑ — | ⏑ ⏑ — | ⏑ — ⏑ | — — | —

Verse 70. *Āryā* or *Gāthā. See Verse* 2.
⏑ ⏑ ⏑ ⏑ | ⏑ — ⏑ | ⏑ ⏑ — ‖ — ⏑ ⏑ | — — | ⏑ — ⏑ | — — | —
⏑ ⏑ ⏑ ⏑ | ⏑ — ⏑ | — — ‖ ⏑ ⏑ — | ⏑ ⏑ — | ⏑ | — ⏑ ⏑ | —

(शकुन्तला अभ्युत्थातुम् इच्छति)

राजा : अलम् अलम् आयासेन।

संदष्टकुसुमशयनान्याशुक्लान्तविसभङ्गसुरभीणि।

गुरुपरितापानि न ते गात्राण्युपचारम् अर्हन्ति[1] ।। 71 ।।

अनसूया : इदो सिलातलेक्कदेसं अणुमेण्हदु वअस्सो।

अनसूया : इतः शिलातलैकदेशम् अनुगृह्णातु वयस्यः।[2]।

[राजोपविशति। शकुन्तला सलज्जा तिष्ठति]

प्रियंवदा : दुवेणम्पि वो अणोणाणुराओ पच्चक्खो। सहीसिणेहो उण मं पुणरुत्तवादिणिं करेदि।

प्रियंवदा : द्वयोरपि युवयोर् अनयोनयानुरागः प्रत्यक्षः। सखीस्नेहो पुनर् मां पुनरुक्तवादिनीं करोति।[3]

'Welcome to the object of thy desire which does not delay (its appearance).' The Bengālī insert *samīhita-phalasya* or *cintita-phalasya*.

1. 'Thy limbs, which closely press the couch of flowers, (and are) fragrant by the crushing of the quickly-faded lotus-fibres, being grievously inflamed, do not deserve (to perform) obeisance;' *i.e.*, 'are excused the usual salutation.' 'In consideration of the state of your bodily frame, you are privileged to keep your recumbent posture even before me.' *Upacāram, i.e., mat-kṛte vinayādi-rūpam. San-daṁś, lit.*, 'To press the teeth closely together;' hence *sandaṣṭa*, 'coming in close contact with.' *Cf.* Raghu-v., xvi., i65, *Sandaṣṭa-vastreṣu nitambeṣu* 'On (their) hips to which garments were closely fitted.' Our English word 'bite' has the same acceptation. *Āśu-klānta*, etc. The Bengālī have *āśu-vimardita-mṛṇāla-valayāni* or *āśu-vivarṇita* (=*mlānī-bhūta* : Ch.) etc. 'Having bracelets of lotus-fibres that have quickly faded (from the heat of her limbs).' Compare p. 105, note 3.

2. Compare page 76, 1. 2. *Anugṛhiṇātu*, 'let him favour,' is the reading of Kāṭavema. The stone-seat served also for the couch of Śakuntalā : Ś.

3. 'But affection for my friends prompts me to be the speaker of something superfluous' *i.e.*, of what has been so often repeated

---

Verse 71. *Āryā* or *Gāthā*. (*See* Verse 2.)

— — |⏑ ⏑ ⏑ ⏑|⏑ ⏑ —‖— —|— ⏑ ⏑|⏑ — ⏑|⏑ ⏑ —|⏑
⏑ ⏑ ⏑ ⏑| — — |⏑ ⏑ —‖— —|⏑ ⏑ —| ⏑ | — — |—

राजा : भद्रे। नैतत् परिहार्यं। विवक्षितं ह्यनुक्तम् अनुतापं जनयति।[1]

प्रियंवदा : आबणस्स विसअवासिणो जणस्स अत्तिहरेण रणा होदव्वंत्ति

प्रियंवदा : आपन्नस्य विषयवासिनो जनस्य आर्त्तिहरेण राज्ञा भवितव्यम्

एसो वो धम्मो।

इति एष वो धर्म्मः।[2]

राजा : नास्मात् परम्[3]।

प्रियंवदा : तेण हि इअं णो पिअसही तुमं उद्दिसिअ इमं

प्रियंवदा : तेन हि इयम् आवयोः प्रियसखी त्वाम् उद्दिश्य इदम्

अवत्थन्तरं भअवदा मअणेण आरोबिदा। ता अरुहसि अब्भुबबत्तीए जीविदं

अवस्थान्तरं भगवता मदनेन आरोपिता।[4] तद् अर्हसि अभ्युपपत्त्या जीवितम्

---

as to be already sufficiently well-known. *Punar-ukta* which properly means 'said again,' 'said twice,' 'frequently repeated,' has in dramatic composition, acquired the acception of 'notorious,' 'well-known,' and hence 'superfluous, 'unnecessary,' 'over and above what is wanted;' and hence sometimes simply 'additional.' Thus in the Vikramorvaśīya, Act 3. the torches are said to be *punar-uktāḥ candrikāyām,* 'rendered superfluous in the moonlight;' and in Act 5 of that play, tears dropping from the eyes on the breast are said to cause *muktāvalī-viracanaṁ punar-uktam,* 'the formation of a superfluous [additional] necklace of pearls. Compare also *kiṁ punar-uktena* : Mālavikāg, p. 63, 1. 5. *Sakhī-viṣayaka-praṇayaḥ.*

1. 'That (which you have to say) ought not to be suppressed [omitted], for that-which-was-intended-to-be-spoken and is not spoken, produces subsequent regret.' *Anu-tāpa, lit.,* 'after-pain,' *i.e.,* repentance.]

2. 'It is to be become by the king [the king ought to be] the remover of the suffering of a person engaged in the affairs of life, who has fallen into trouble : Such is your duty.' The Bengālī have *āśrama-vāsino* for *viṣaya-vāsino*. The latter reading is supported by K., and the compound is given by Wilson.

3. 'No other than this.' *i.e.,* Nothing short of this; this is exactly my duty.

4. 'Therefore, (know that) this our dear friend has been reduced to this altered condition by the divinity Love on thy account.'

मे अवलम्बिदुं।

अस्या अवलम्बितुम्।

राजा : भद्रे। असाधारणोऽयं प्रणयः।[1] सर्वथानुगृहीतोऽस्मि।

शकुन्तलाः (प्रियंवदाम् अवलोक्य) हला किं अन्तेउरविरहपव्जुस्सुअस्स राएसिणो उबरोहेण।

शकुन्तला : (प्रियंवदाम् अवलोक्य) हला किम् अन्तःपुरविरहपर्युत्सुकस्य राजर्षेर् उपरोधेन।[2]

राजा : सुन्दरि।

इदम् अनन्यपरायणम् अन्यथा
हृदयसन्निहिते हृदयं मम।
यदि समर्थयसे मदिरेक्षणे
मदनवाणहतोऽस्मि हतः पुनः[3] ।। 72 ।।

अनसूया : वअस्स। बहुवल्लहा राआणो सुणीअन्ति। जह णो पिअसही

अनसूया : वयस्य। बहुवल्लभा राजानः श्रूयन्ते। यथा नौ प्रियसखी

Uddiśya 'aiming at,' 'regarding :' *see* p. 101, note 1. *Avasthāntaram, lit.*, 'another state;' *i.e.*, an alteration from the natural and healthy state. *Āropitā=prāpitā* : Ś.

1. Compare, in the Vikramorvaśiya, Act 2, *Sādhārano yam ubhayoḥ praṇayaḥ*.

2. 'What (can you mean) by detaining the Rājarṣi, who is pining (by reason of) separation from his royal-consorts ?' *Antaḥpura*, 'the inner part of the palace,' 'the female apartments,' here put for the occupants.

3. 'O thou that art near my heart, if this heart of mine which is devoted to no other, thou judgest to be otherwise, (then) O lovely-eyed one, being (already) slain by Love's shafts, I am slain again,' *i.e.*, I suffer a second death. Compare Bhartṛhari, i, 63 [*hatamapi nihantyeva madanaḥ*]. *Hṛdaya-sannihite=man-manovasthāyini*, 'O thou that abidest in my heart : Ś :=*cittārūḍhe* : Ch. *Madirā*, 'wine,' as applied to *ikṣana*, 'the eyes,' is said by Śaṅkara to be equivalent to *sundara*, 'beautiful;' or to *iṣad-ghūrṇana-śīla*, 'slightly inclined to roll about.' Wine-eyed may mean 'one whose eyes intoxicate like wine.'

1. 'Even in the multitude of (my) wives [however numerous

Verse 72. *Druta-Vilambita* (variety of *Jagatī*). *See* Verse 45.

बन्धुअणसोअणिज्जा ण होइ। तह णिव्वाहेहि।

बन्धुजनशोचनीया न भवति। तथा निर्वाहय।

राजा : भद्रे। किं बहुना।

परिग्रहबबहुत्वेऽपि द्वे प्रतिष्ठे कुलस्मे।
समुद्ररसना चोर्वी सखी च युवयोर् इयम्[1] ।। 73 ।।

उभे : णिव्वुदन्ह।

उभे : निर्वृते खः।[2]

प्रियंवदा : (सदृष्टिक्षेपं) अणसूए। जह एसो इदो दिणदिट्ठी

प्रियंवदा : (सदृष्टिक्षेपं) अनसूये। यथा एष इतो दत्तदृष्टिर्

उस्सुओ मिअपोदओ मादरं अणेसदि। एहि। सञ्जोएम णं।। (इत्युभे प्रस्थिते)।

उत्सुको मृगपोतको मातरम् अन्विष्यति। एहि। संयोजयाव एनम्[3]। (इत्युभे प्रस्थिते)।

may be my wives] there (will be) but two chief-glories of my race, the sea-girt earth on the one hand [*ca*] and on the other [*ca*] this friends of yours :' *i.e.,* There will be but two sources of glory to my race, *viz.,* the sea-girt earth and Śakuntalā. *Pratiṣṭhā=utkarṣa-hetu,* ' a cause of renown,' 'a distinguished ornament :' Ś. : properly 'a cause of stability,' 'a prop.' 'a support,' 'a stay.' *Parigraha-bahutve=kalatra-bāhulye.* The Devanāgarī MSS. read *samudra-vasanā,* 'clothed in the ocean,' 'having the ocean for its garments' [*Samudra eva vastrāṇi yasyāḥ* : Ś.] The Bengālī all have *samudra-rasanā,* which is literally 'sea-girt' [*rasanā=mekhalā*] and seems to be the better-reading. Compare Hitop., 1. 2542. Confusion between *rasanā* and *vasanā* may easily have arisen. *Ca ca* : see page 13, note 2.

2. In the Bengālī MSS., the dialogue which follows these words has several interpolations.

3. Literally. 'Let us cause it to join (its mother)' 'let us lead it to its mother :' *Mātrā saha iti anuṣaṅga* : Ś. Some word like *paśya,* 'See !' may be supplied before *yathā* in the sentence preceding.

Verse 73. *Śloka* or *Anuṣṭubh. See* Verses 5, 6, 11, 12, 26, 47, 50, 51, 53.

शकुन्तला : हला। असरणन्हि। अणदरा वो आअच्छदु।

शकुन्तला : हला अशरणास्मि। अन्यतरा युवयोर् आगच्छतु।

उभे : पुहवीए जो सरणं। सो तुह समीबे वट्टइ। (इति निष्क्रान्ते)

उभे : पृथिव्या यो शरणम्। स तव समीपे वर्तते।। इति निष्क्रान्ते।।

शकुन्तला : कहं गदाओ एव्व।

शकुन्तला : कथं गते एव।

राजा : अलम् आवेगेन नन्वयम् आराधयिता जनस् तव समीपे वर्तते।[1]

किं शीतलैः क्लमविनोदिभिर् आर्द्रवातान्
सञ्चारयामि नलिनीदलतालवृन्तैः।
अङ्के निधाय करभोरु यथासुखं ते
संवाहयामि चरणाव् उत् पद्मताम्रौ[2] ।। 74 ।।

1. 'Does not this person, thy humble-servant [thy adorer] remain near thee ?' *i.e.*, Am not I here to wait upon thee, in place of thy friends ?' The Bengālī add *sakhī-bhūmau. Ārādhayitā=paricārakaḥ,* 'an attendant,' 'a servant' : Ś., but it is also 'the worshipper of a deity,' and therefore implies adoration as well as service. There is designedly a double-entendre.

2. 'Shall I set in motion moist breezes by (means of) cool lotus-leaf-fans which-remove langour ? or placing thy feet, brown as the lotus, O round-thighed (maiden), in (my) lap shall I rub them soothingly.' *Karabhoru*, voc. c. of *karabhorū.* According to Pāṇini, IV, i, 69, *Uru,* 'a thigh or hip,' at the end of this and some other compounds becomes *ūrū* and is declined like *vadhū;* and *karabhorūh* is said to be equivalent to *vṛttorūḥ strī*, 'a woman with round thighs.' *Karabha* is 'the thick part of the hand,' 'the part between the wrist and the fingers;' it is also 'a young elephant.' Dr. Boehtlingk considers that the comparison is taken from the first of these senses. It may with more reason be taken from the other : for from the following gloss of Candraśekhara, it seems probable that as *kara* stands for both the human hand and the trunk of an elephant, and *karabha* for the upper part of the hand, so the latter word may be taken for the same part of an elephant's trunk. *Karabhaḥ prāṇyangam* ['is part of an animal'] *tadiva ūrur yaṣyāḥ śubha-lakṣaṇam idam tad uktam, hasti-hasta-nibhair* ['like an elephant's trunk'] *vṛttair* ['round']

Verse 74. *Vasantatilakā* (variety of *Śakkarī*). *See* Verses 8, 27, 31, 43, 46, 64.

शकुन्तलाः ण माणणीएसु अत्ताणं अबराहइस्सं।। इत्युत्थाय गन्तुम्

शकुन्तला : न माननीयेषु आत्मानम् अपराधयिष्यामि[1]।। इत्युत्थाय गन्तुम्

इच्छति।

इच्छति।

राजा : सुन्दरि। अपरिनिर्वाणो दिवसः।[2] इयं च ते शरीरावस्था।

उत्सृज्य कुसुमशयनं नलिनीदलकल्पितस्तनावरणम्।

कथम् आतपे गमिष्यसि परिबाधापेलवैर् अङ्गैः[3] ।। 75 ।।

(इति बलाद् एनां निवर्तयति)

शकुन्तला : पोरव। रक्ख विणअं। मअणसन्तत्ताबि ण हु अत्तणो

शकुन्तला : पौरव। रक्षाविनयं। मदनसन्तप्तापि न खलु आत्मनः

asthābhaiḥ karabhopamaiḥ prāpnuvantyūrūhiḥ śaśvat striyaḥ sukham anaṅgajam. The epithet may therefore mean 'having thighs gracefully tapering like the trunk of an elephant.' Compare *karabhopamorūḥ* : Raghuvaṁśa, vi, 83. 'This is confirmed by Bhaṭṭi-kāvya, iv, 17, where the epithet *dvirada-nāśorūḥ* is applied to female. *Saṁvāhayāmi=mardayāmi* : *Śam-vāḥ* is applied especially to the rubbing, kneading, or shampooing of the limbs. *Padma-tāmrau* : Chēzy observes that the Hindū women extracted a rosy-coloured dye from a plant called *Lawsonia Inermis*, with which they dyed their nails and fingers, as well as their feet. Cf. *Strī-nakha-pāṭalam kuruvakam* : Vikramorvaśīya, Act 2.

1. 'I will not make myself in fault with those whom I am bound to respect [towards those who are worthy of respect]' *i.e.*, with my foster-father and others.

2. 'The day is not (yet) cool. *Aparinirvāṇa=anapagata-tīvrātapaḥ*, 'having its great heat not yet passed off.' 'It was still noon :' Ś. Some MSS. have *anirvāṇa*, and others *apa-nirvāṇa [=anirvāṇa, nirvāṇa-rahita*].

3. 'Having left the couch of flowers (and) the covering of thy bosom formed of lotus leaves, how wilt thou go in the heat, with thy limbs (too) delicate for hardships ?' *Paribādha-pelava= duḥkhāsahiṣṇu*, 'incapable of bearing hardship.' The Bengālī have *komala* for *pelava*.

Verse 75. Āryā *or* Gāthā. (*See* Verse 2.)

— — | ◡ ◡ ◡ ◡ | ◡ ◡ — ‖ ◡ ◡ — | ◡ ◡ — | ◡ — ◡ | — ◡ ◡ | —

◡ ◡ — | ◡ — ◡ | — ◡ ◡ ‖ ◡ ◡ — | — — | ◡ | — — | —

पहवामि।

प्रभवामि।[1]

राजा : भीरु। अलं गुरुजनभयेन। दृष्ट्वा ते विदितधर्मा तत्र-भवान् नात्र दोषं ग्रहीष्यति कुलपति:।[2] अपि च

गान्धर्वेण विवाहेन बह्व्यो राजर्षिकन्यका:।
श्रूयन्ते परिणीतास् ता: पितृभिश् चाभिनन्दिता:[3] ।। 76 ।।

शकुन्तला : मुञ्च दाव मं। भूओबि सहीजणं अणुमाणइस्सं।

शकुन्तला : मुञ्च तावन् माम्। भूयाऽपि सखीजनम् अनुमानयिष्यामि।[4]

1. 'Even though inflamed by Love, I have not the power (of disposing) of myself.' *i.e., yena tvam-manoratha-pūraṇaṁ kriyate,* 'so that your wishes may be fulfilled :' Ś.

2. 'Having seem it, his reverence the head-of-your-society who knows-the-law will not take (it as a) fault in you,' *i.e.,* will not attribute blame to you in this matter.' *Dṛṣṭvā te* is supported by the concurrent authority of the Taylor, Mackenzie, and Colebrooke MSS. I have note ventured to follow Dr. Boehtlingk in reading *Diṣṭyā te.* My own Mumbai MS. omits the words entirely, but a blank space indicates that something is left out. *Vidita-dharmā* : *see* Pā. V. 4, 124. *Dharma* at the end of a Bahuvrīhi compound becomes *dharman. Cf. Yuvāṁ Kṣatriya-dharmāṇau* : Hitop., 1. 2473.

3. 'Many daughters of Rājarṣis [p. 44, notes 1 and 2] are heard to have been married by the marriage (called) Gāndharva, and (even) they have received the approval of their fathers [been approved by their fathers].' The Gāndharva marriage is one of the forms of marriage described in Manu, iii, 22, *et seq.* It is a marriage proceeding entirely from love [*kāma-sambhava*] or the mutual inclination [*anyonyecchā*] of a youth and maiden, and concluded without any ceremonies and without consulting relatives : see especially Manu, iii, 32. *Gāndharva=paraspara-bhāṣayā kṛto vivāha* : K. The long scene which follows this verse in the Bengālī MSS. is omitted in all the Devanāgarī, and must be regarded as an interpolation.

4. 'I will again take counsel with may female friends.' *Anuman*

Verse 76. *Śloka* or *Anuṣṭubh. See* Verses 5, 6, 11, 12, 26, 47, 50, 51, 53, 73.

राजा : भवतु। मोक्ष्यामि।

शकुन्तला : कदा।

शकुन्तला : कदा।

राजा :

अपरिक्षतकोमलस्य तावत्

कुसुमस्येव नवस्य षट्पदेन।

अधरस्य पिपासता मया ते

सदयं सुन्दरि गृह्यते रसोऽस्य[1] ।। 77 ।।

[इति मुखम् अस्याः समुन्नमयितुम् इच्छति। शकुन्तला परिहरति नाट्येन]

नेपथ्ये : चक्कवाकबहुए आमन्तेहि सहअरं। उबट्ठिदा रअणी।

नेपथ्ये : चक्रवाकवधुके आमन्त्रयस्व सहचरम्। उपस्थिता रजनी।[2]

in the causal may mean 'to ask the consent of,' 'to cause or to induce to assent.'

1. '(As) by the bee (the honey) of the fresh, untouched tender blossom, (so) now by me eager-to-allay-my-thirst must the nectar of this under-lip of thine be gently stolen, O fair one, (ere I can let thee go.') *Apariksata, lit.*, 'unhurt,' 'uninjured,' applied to a virgin. *Adharasya* : compare p. 33, note 2.

2. '[*Behind the scenes.*] O female-cakravāka, bid farewell to thy mate : the night is at hand [arrived].' *Cakravāka-vadhukā* [Pāṇini, VII., 4, 13] *i.e.,* the Cakravākī or female of the Ruddy goose, commonly called the Brāhmaṇī duck (Anas Casarca). The male and female of these birds keep together during the day (whence one of their names, *dvandva-cara,* 'going in pairs') and are, like turtle-doves, patterns of constancy and connubial affection; but the legend is that they are doomed to pass the night apart (whence the name *rātri-viśleṣa-gāmin*) in consequence of a curse pronounced upon them by some saint whom they had offended. Accordingly, as soon as night commences, they take up their station on opposite banks of a river, and call to each other in piteous cries. The name *rathāṅga* or *ratha-pāda,* 'chariot-footed,' sometimes given to them, indicates

---

Verse 77. *Aupacchandasika*, containing eleven syllables to the first half-line, and twelve to the second, each whole line being alike.

◡◡—◡◡—◡—◡—— ‖ ◡◡——◡◡—◡—◡——

शकुन्तला : (ससम्भ्रमं) पोरव। असंसअं मम सरीरवुत्तन्तोबल-
शकुन्तला : ससम्भ्रमम्।। पौरव। असंशयं मम शरीरवृत्तान्तोपल-
म्भस्स अज्जा गोदमी इदो एव्व आअच्छदि। दाव विडबन्तरिदो
म्भाय[1] आर्या गौतमी इत एव आगच्छति। तावद् विटपानतरितो[2]
होहि।
भव।

राजा : तथा (इत्यात्मानम् आवृत्य तिष्ठति)

[ततः प्रविशति पात्रहस्ता[3] गौतमी सख्यौ च]

सख्यौ : इदो इदो अज्जा मोदमो।

सख्यौः इत इत आर्या गौतमी।

गौतमी : (शकुन्तलाम् उपेत्य) जादे। अबि लहुसन्दांबाइं दे
गौतमी : (शकुन्तलाम् उपेत्य) जाते। अपि लघुसन्तापानि ते
अङ्गाइं।
ऽङ्गानि।

शकुन्तला : अज्जे अत्थि मे विसेसो।

शकुन्तला : अर्य्य अस्ति मे विशेषः।[4]

some peculiar formation of the feet. Constant allusion is made to their habits : thus in the Vikram., Act 4, *Sahacarīṁ dūre matvā samutsukaḥ. Cf.* also Meghadūta, verse 82, and Raghuvaṁśa, viii, 55.

1. 'To ascertain the state of my bodily health.' Prākṛt has no dative, but gives the force of that case to the genitive.

2. 'Concealed by the branches :' see page 104, note 2.

3. 'With a vessel in her hand.' One MS. has *udaka-pātra-hastā,* 'with a vessel of water in her hand.'

4. 'O venerable mother ! there is a change for the better in me.' *Nairujyaṁ kiñcid idānīṁ vṛttam,* 'There is now some freedom from pain :' Ś. *Ajje* is the reading of the oldest MSS. supported by Ś. and Ch. *Viśeṣa* is 'a change for the better,' in contradistinction to *vikāra,* 'a change for the worse.' The very same expression occurs in Mālavikāg., p. 46, 1. 9.

गौतमी : इमिणा इब्भोदएण णिराबाधं एव्व दे सरीरं भविस्सादि।।
गौतमी : अनेन दर्भोदकेन[1] निराबाधम् एव ते शरीरं भविष्यति।।
(शिरसि शकुन्तलाम् अभ्युक्ष्य) वच्छे। परिणदो दिअहो। एहि। उडजं
(शिरसि शकुन्तलाम् अभ्युक्ष्य) वत्से। परिणतो दिवसः। एहि। उटजम्
एव्व गच्छन्ह [इति प्रस्थिताः]
एव गच्छामः [इति प्रस्थिताः]।

शकुन्तला : (आत्मगतं) हिअअ। पढमं एव्व सुहोबणदे मणोरहे
शकुन्तला : आत्मगतम्।। हृदय। प्रथमम् एव सुखोपनते मनोरथे
कादरभावं ण मुञ्चसि। साणुसअविहडिअस्स कहं दे सम्पदं सन्दाबो (पदान्तरे
कातरभावं न मुञ्चसि। सानुशयविघटितस्य कथं ते साम्प्रतं सन्तापः।। पदान्तरे
स्थित्वा। प्रकाशं) लदावलअ सन्दाबहारअ। आमन्तेमि तुमं भूओबि
स्थित्वा। प्रकाशम्।। लतावलय सन्तापहारक। आमन्त्रये त्वां भूयोऽपि
परिभोअस्स।
परिभोगाय।[2]

[दुःखेन निष्क्रान्ता शकुन्तला सहेतराभिः]

राजा : (पूर्वस्थानम् उपेत्य। सनिःश्वासं) अहो विघ्नवत्यः प्रार्थितार्थसिद्धयः। मया हि–

मुहुर् अङ्गुलिसंवृताधरोष्ठं
प्रतिषेधाक्षरविक्लवाभिरामम्।

1. 'With this Darbha-water,' *i.e.*, water and Kuśa-grass, mixed and used for the *śāntyudakam*, mentioned at p. 96, 1. 3; *see* also p. 19, note 1 in middle.

2. 'O heart, even before, when the object-of-thy-desire readily presented itself, thou didst not abandon (thy) anxiety. How (great) now (will be) the anguish of thee regretful (and) dispirited ! [*After advancing a step, standing still again, aloud*] O bower of creepers, remover of my suffering, I bid thee adieu, (hoping) to occupy (thee) again [to have enjoyment of thee again].' *Prathamam eva*, etc. : see page 119, line 7. *Sukhopanate* : compare *yad upanatam duḥkham sukham tat* : Vikram., end of Act 3. *Vighaṭita*, 'broken,' distracted with grief.' *Paribhoassa* : see page 128, note 1. *Paribhogāya* : Compare *paribhukta* : page 130, line 3.

मुखम् अंशविवर्ति पक्ष्मलाक्ष्याः
कथमप्युन्नमितं न चुम्बितं तु[1] ।। 78 ।।

क्व नु खलु सम्प्रति गच्छामि। अथवा। इहैव प्रियापरिभुक्तमुक्ते लतावलये मुहूर्तं स्थास्यामि[2] (सर्वतोऽवलोक्य)।

1. 'Alas ! the fulfilment of desired object has hindrances [there are many obstacles in the way of the accomplishment of one's wishes]; for by me the face of the lovely-eye-lashed-eyed (maiden), having its upper and lower lip repeatedly protected by (her) fingers, beautiful in stammering out the syllables of denial, tuning (away from me) towards the shoulder, was with some difficulty raised but not kissed.' *Aṅguli-saṁvṛta=aṅgulibhyāṁ pihita* : Ś. *Adharoṣṭha* : *see* p. 33, note 2, in middle. *Pratishedhākṣare, i.e., na mamādharaṁ cumbanīyam* [*unnamanīyam*] 'my lip must not be kissed :' Ś. Ch. *Alam alaṁ mā iti prabhṛtbhiḥ,* 'by such expresssions as 'enough,' 'enough,' 'don't :' K. Some of the Devanāgarī MSS. read *pratiṣedhāntara. Akṣara* is 'a syllable,' as well as 'a letter :' see *ekākṣara* in Wilson's Dictionary. *Aṅśavivarti=tiryak-kṛtam,* 'turned on one side :' Ch. It may, however, also mean 'revolving on the shoulders' [*aṁśayor vivarti*]. Śaṅkara mentions another reading, *aṅga-vivarti=kroḍa-ghūrṇamānam. Pakṣmalākṣī=cāru-bahu-pakṣma-yuktam,* or *praśasta-pakṣma-yuktam akṣi yasyāḥ,* 'who has eyes with beautiful eye-lashes :' Ś., and Ch. : *i.e.,* 'Whose eye-lashes are brown like the leaf of a lotus :' Ch. The Hindū women used collyrium to darken the eye-lashes and eye-brows. *Pakṣmala* is properly, 'possessed of eye-lashes' [*pakṣmavat*] an adjective formed from *pakṣman* as *sidhmala* from *sidhman* : Pāṇini, v., 2, 97. *Utpakṣmala,* 'having upturned eyelashes,' occurs about the middle of the second Act of the Vikramorvaśīya. *Kathamapi,* 'somehow or other,' 'hardly :' compare page 127, lilne 9. *Na cumbitaṁ tu* is the reading of the Kolkata edition and the Sāhityadarpaṇa, [page 116], supported by Candraśekhara.

2. 'Or rather, I pied, (but now) abandoned by my beloved.' *Athavā* : *see* page 30, note 3; and page 24, note 1, at end. *Paribhukta* : Compare *paribhogāya,* page 130, note 2 at end. *Muhūrtam* : *see* page 37, note 1, at end.

Verse 78. *Aupacchandasika*. *See* Verse 77.

तस्याः पुष्पमयी शरीरलुलिता शय्या शिलायाम् इयं
क्लान्तो मन्मथलेख एष नलिनीपत्रे नखैर् अर्पितः।
हस्ताद् भ्रष्टम् इदं विसाभरणम् इत्यासज्यमानेक्षणो
निर्गन्तुं सहसा न वेतसगृहाच् छक्तोऽस्मि शून्यादपि[1] ।। 79 ।।

आकाशे : राजन्–

सायन्तने सवनकर्मणि सम्प्रवृत्ते
वेदीं हुताशनवतीं परितः प्रकीर्णाः।
छायाश् चरन्ति बहुधा भयम् आदधानाः
सन्ध्यापयोदकपिशाः पिशिताशनानाम्[2] ।। 80 ।।

राजा : अयम् अयम् आगच्छामि। (इति निष्क्रान्तः)

[तृतीयोऽङ्कः]

1. 'Here on the stone-seat is her flowery couch impressed by her form; here is the faded love-letter committed to the lotus-leaf with her nails; here is the lotus-fibre bracelet slipped from her hand—having my eyes fixed on such (objects as these) I am not able to tear myself away [go out hastily] from the Vetasa-arbour, even though deserted (by her).' *Śarīra-lulitā=dehāsaṅghṛṣṭā,* rubbed by the body :' *see anatilulilta,* p. 114, note 1. *Śilāyām* : see page 104, note 4, and page 120, note 2. *Klānta* : Śaṅkara and the Bengālī MSS. read *kānta,* 'charming,' 'dear.' *Visābharaṇa=mṛnālavalaya* : see p. 106, note 3. *Āsajyamānekṣaṇo=āropyamānekṣaṇo. Vetasa gṛhat=latā-maṇḍapāt,* 'from the arbour of creepers :' see p. 103, line 4.

2. '[*In the air.*] The evening sacrificial rite being commenced, the shadows of the Rākṣasas, brown as evening clouds, scattered around the altar which bears the consecrated fire, are flitting about in great numbers, producing consternation.' *Akāśe* : see p. 95, note 3. *Savana-karmaṇi=homa-karmaṇi Sampravṛtte=upakṛānte. Prakīrṇāḥ* is the reading of the oldest MSS. : Śaṅkara reads *vistīrṇāḥ* : the Devanāgarī, *prayastāḥ,* 'striving,' 'using effort.' *Hutāśanavatīm= āhitāgnim. Bhayam ādadhānāḥ=trāsam utpādayantyaḥ. Piśitāśanānām= rākṣasānām.* The Rākṣasas [see p. 40, note 5] were so called from their appetite for raw flesh [*piśita*].

Verse 79. *Śārdūla-vikrīḍita* (variety of *Atidhṛti*). *See* Verses 14, 30, 36, 39, 40, 63.
Verse 80. *Vasanta-Tilakā* (variety of *Śakkarī*). *See* Verses 8, 27, 31, 43, 46, 64, 74.

।। अथ चतुर्थाङ्कादौ विष्कम्भः[1] ।।

[ततः प्रविशतः कुसुमावचयम् अभिनयन्त्यौ सख्यौ]

अनसूया : हला पिअंवदे। जइबि गन्धव्वेण विवाहविहिणा णि-
अनसूया : हला प्रियंवदे। यद्यपि गान्धर्वेण विवाहविधिना नि-
व्वुत्तकल्लाणा सउन्दला अणुरूबभत्तुमामिणी संवुत्तेत्ति णिव्वुदं मे हिअअं
वृत्तकल्याणा शकुन्तला अनुरूपभर्तृगामिनी संवृत्तेति निर्वृत्तं मे हृदयं
तहबि एत्तिअं चिन्तणिज्जं।
तथापि इयच् चिन्तनीयम्।[2]

प्रियंवदा : कहं विअ।
प्रियंवदा : कथम् इव।

अनसूया : अज्ज सो राएसी इट्ठिं परिसमाबिअ इसीहिं विसज्जिओ
अनसूया : अद्य स राजषिर् इष्टिं परिसमाप्य ऋषिभिर् विसर्जित
अत्तणो णअरं पविसिअ अन्तेउरसमागदो इदोगदं वुत्तन्तं सुमरदि वा
आत्मनो नगरं प्रविश्य अन्तःपुरसमागत इतोगतं वृत्तान्तं स्मरति वा
ण वेत्ति।
न वेति।

प्रियंवदा : वीसद्धा होहि। ण तादिसा आकिदिविसेसा गुणविरोहिणा
प्रियंवदा : विश्रब्धा भव। न तादृशा आकृतिविशेषा गुणविरोधिनो

1. *See* the note on the term Viṣkambha, page 96, note 3.

2. 'Although my heart is comforted by the thought that Śakuntalā has become completely happy in being united to a husband worthy of her by a Gāndharva marriage; nevertheless, there is still some cause for anxiety [there is still something to be thought about].' *Gāndharveṇa* : *see* p. 126, note 3. *Anurūpa-bhartṛ-gāminī* : the Bengālī have *anurūpa-bhartṛ-bhāginī. Iti* may often be translated by 'so thinking.' *see* p. 138, note 2.

होन्ति। किन्दु तादो दाणिं इमं वुत्तन्तं सुणिअ ण आणे किं पडिबज्जिस्स
भवन्ति। किन्तु तात इदानीम् इमं वृत्तान्तं श्रुत्वा न जाने किं प्रतिपत्स्यत
दित्ति।
इति।[1]

अनसूया : जह अहं देक्खामि। तह तस्स अणुमदं भवे।

अनसूया : यथा अहं पश्यामि। तथा तस्य अनुमतं भवेत्।

प्रियंवदा : कहं विअ।

प्रियंवदा : कथम् इव।

अनसूया : गुणवदे कणआ पडिबादणिज्जेत्ति अअं दाव पढमो
अनसूया : गुणवते कन्या प्रतिपादनीया इति अयं तावत् प्रथमः
सङ्कप्पो। तं जइ देव्वं एव्व सम्पादेदि। णं अप्पाआसेण किदत्थो
सङ्कल्पः[2]। तं यदि दैवम् एव सम्पादयति। ननु अल्पायासेन कृतार्थो
गुरुअणो।
गुरुजनः।

प्रियंवदा : (पुष्पभाजनं विलोक्य) सहि। अवइदाइं बलिकम्मपज्जत्ताइं
प्रियंवदा : (पुष्पभाजनं विलोक्य) सखि। अवचितानि बलिकर्मपर्याप्तानि
कुसुमाइं।
कुसुमानि।

1. 'Such distinguished characters as these do not become enemies to virtue [do not treat virtuous women with contumely]. But I know not now what reply the father will make when he has heard this intelligence.' *Ākṛti* properly 'from,' 'figure.' *Kintu* is inserted by the Mackenzie MS., supported by K. *Pratipatsate=abhidhāsyati* : Ś. :=*prativakti* : K. : Westergaard gives 'respondere' as one sense of *pratipad*. Compare *tac chrutvā tatheti pratyapadyata* : Rāmāy., I, 10, 15. 'What he will do,' or 'whether he will ratify it,' would be an equally correct translation.

2. ' "The maiden is to be given to a worthy (husband) :" such was the first purpose-of-his-heart.' *Saṅkalpa=manoratha* : Ś. : properly 'a resolve,' 'mental determination :' *see* p. 49, line 4, with note 1 at end.

अनसूया : णं पिअसहीए सउन्दलाए सोहग्गदेवआ अच्चणीआ।

अनसूया : ननु प्रियसख्याः शकुन्तलायाः सौभाग्यदेवता अर्चनीया।[1]

प्रियंवदा : जुज्जदि (इति तदेव कर्मारभेते)

प्रियंवदा : युज्यते। (इति तदेव कर्मारभेत)

नेपथ्ये : अयम् अहं भोः।[2]

अनसूया : (कर्णं दत्त्वा) सहि। अदिधिणा विअ णिवेदिदं।।

अनसूया : (कर्णं दत्त्वा) सखि। अतिथिना इव निवेदितम्।[3]

प्रियंवदा : णं उडजसणिहिदा सउन्दला (आत्मगतं) अज्ज हिअएण असणिहिदा।

प्रियंवदा : ननु उटजसन्निहिता शकुन्तला। (आत्मगतं) अद्य पुनर् हृदयेन असन्निहिता।[4]

1. 'It not the guardian-deity of our dear friends Śakuntalā to be honoured (with an offering) ?' *Saubhāgya-devatā,* 'the tutelary deity,' 'the deity who watches over the fortune and welfare of any one.' The Bengālī read *devatāḥ,* 'deities,' and Śaṅkara adds *Ṣaṣṭikā-gaurī-prabhṛtayaḥ,* 'such as Ṣaṣṭikā [Durgā], Gaurī, etc.'

2. '[*Behind the scenes.*] It is I, ho there !' *Nepathye* : *see* p. 3, note 1. *Ayam aham āgatosmi iti arthaḥ : Ś. see* Manu, ii., 122, etc. 'After salutation, a Brāhmaṇa must address an elder saying, 'I am such an one' [*asaunāmāham*] pronouncing his own name. If any persons (through ingorance of Sanskṛt) do not understand the form of salutation (in which mention is made) of the name, to them should a learned man say, 'It is I' (*aham iti*), and in that manner should he address all women. In the salutation he should utter the word *bhoḥ* [*bhoḥ-śabda*], for the particle *bhoḥ* is held by sages to have the same property with names (fully expressed).'

3. '(It seems) as if an announcement were made by a guest [as if a guest were announcing himself].' This is the reading of the Bengālī, the Devanāgarī have *atithīnām.*

4. 'With her heart she is not near,' *i.e.*, her heart is absent with Duṣyanta.

अनसूया : होदु। अलं एत्तिएहिं कुसुमेहिं।
अनसूया : भवतु। अलम् इयद्भिः कुसुमैः।

[इति प्रस्थिते]

नेपथ्ये : आ अतिथिपरिभाविनि।

विचिन्तयन्ती यम् अनन्यमानसा
तपोधनं वेत्सि न माम् उपस्थितम्।
स्मरिष्यति त्वां न स बोधितोऽपि सन्
कथां प्रमत्तः प्रथमं कृतामिव[1]।। 81।।

प्रियंवदा : हद्धी हद्धी। अप्पिअं एव्व संवुत्तं। कस्सिंपि पूआरुहे
प्रियंवदा : हाधिक् हाधिक्। अप्रियम् एव संवृत्तम्। कस्मिन्नपि पूजार्ह
अबरद्धा सुणहिअआ सउन्दला (पुरोऽवलोक्य) ण हु जस्सिं
ऽपराद्धा शून्यहृदयं शकुन्तला (पुरोऽवलोक्य) न खलु यस्मिन्
कस्सिंपि। एसो दुव्वासो सुलहकोबो महेसी। तह सबिअ वेअचहु-
कस्मिन्नपि। एष दुर्वासाः सुलभकोपो महर्षिः। तथा शप्त्वा वेगचटु-
लुप्फुल्लदुव्वाराए गईए पडिणिवुत्तो। को अणो हुदवहादो दहिदुं
लोत्फुलदुर्वारया गत्या प्रतिनिवृत्तः।[2] कोऽन्यो हुतवहाद् दहितुं

1. 'Woe ! thou that art disrespectful to a guest ! that (man) of whom (thou art) thinking to-the-exclusion-of-every-other-object-from-thy-mind, (so that) thou perceivest not me, rich in penance, to have approached, shall not recall thee to his memory, even being reminded; as a drunken-man (does not recall) the talk [speech] previously made (by himself).' *Atithi-paribhāvini* : see p. 36, note 3 : the Bengālī have *katham atithim paribhavasi. Vetsi=vibhā-vayasi* : Ś. *Bodhito=smāritaḥ* : Ś. *Kṛtam, i.e., ātmanaiva* : Ś. *Kathām kṛ* is equivalent to the root *kath*, 'to speak,' 'tell,' 'say;' and *kathām kṛtām* to *kathitām*, 'What is spoken,' 'said.'

2. 'A very unpleasant thing has occurred. Śakuntalā, in her absense of mind, has comitted an offence against some person deserving of respect. [*Looking on in front.*] Not, indeed, against some (mere ordinary) person : (for I see that) it is the great *Ṛṣi* Durvāsas, easily-provoked to anger. After uttering such a curse, he has turned back with a step tremulous, bounding and difficult to be checked through its impetuosity.' *Śūnya-hṛdayā lit.*, 'empty-hearted,' one

Verse 81. *Vaṁśasthavila* (variety of *Jagatī*.) *See* Verses 18, 22, 23, 67.

पहविस्सदि।

प्रभविष्यति।[1]

अनसूया : गच्छ। पादेसु पणमिअ णिवत्तेहि णं जाव अहं अग्घोदअं

अनसूया : गच्छ। पादयोः प्रणम्य निवर्तय एनं यावद् अहम् अर्घ्योदकम्

उबकप्पेमि।

उपकल्पयामि।[2]

whose heart is engrossed with some other object. *Vega-caṭula,* etc. : This is the reading of the Mackenzie MS., and seems to have been that of K. All the Devanāgarī have *upphulla,* for the Sanskṛt *utphula* from the root *sphul,* 'to leap,' allied to *sphur. Utphāla* from the same root is given by Wilson, and both *sphula* and *sphura,* but not *utphula,* which is a legitimate word. As to the Prākṛt *upphulla,* it may be observed that many consonants in Prākṛt are too weak to sustain themselves singly, and that if elision does not take place, the consonant is sometimes doubled. Thus *sukkha,* or *suha* may be written for the Sanskṛt *sukha,* and *nīhitta* or *nīhia* for *nīhita* : Lassen's Instit. Prāk., p. 276, 3. The oldest Bengālī MS. has *avirala-pādoddhārayā,* and the Calcutta edition *avirala-pāda-tvarayā gatyā.* As to Durvāsas, he is a Saint or Muni, represented by the Hindū poets as excessively choleric, and inexorably severe. The Purāṇas and other poems contain frequent accounts of the terrible effects of his imprecations on various occasions, the slightest offence being in his eyes deserving of the most fearful punishment. On one occasion he cursed Indra, merely because his elephant let fall a garland which he had given to this god; and in consequence of this imprecation all plants withered, men ceased to sacrifice, and the gods were overcome in their wars with the demons : see Viṣṇu-Purāṇa., p. 70. With regard to the titile Maharṣi : see p. 39, note 3, and p. 44, note 2.

1. 'Who beside Fire will have have (such) power to consume ?' Śaṅkara has *tathā* [*taha*] at the end of this sentence, but I have not ventured to insert it, without other authority. The wrath of a Brāhmaṇa is frequently compared to fire : see p. 74, note 3, and p. 50 note 2.

2. 'Therefore, bowing down at his feet, persuade him to return, whilst I prepare a propitiatory offering and water.' The Bengālī have *patitvā,* 'having fallen' for *praṇamya. Arghyodakam* : *see* p. 36, notes 2 and 3.

प्रियंवदा : तह (इति निष्क्रान्ता)।

प्रियंवदा : तथा (इति निष्क्रान्ता)।

अनसूया : (पदान्तरे स्खलितं निरूप्य) अम्मो। आवेअक्खलिदाए गई ए

अनसूया : (पदान्तरे स्खलितं निरूप्य) अहो। आवेगस्खलितया गत्या

पब्भट्ठं मे हत्थादो पुप्फभाअणं। (इति पुष्पोच्चयं रूपयति)

प्रभ्रष्टं मे हस्तात् पुष्पभाजनं (इति पुष्पोच्चयं रूपयति[1])।

प्रियंवदा : (प्रविश्य) सखि। पकिदिवक्को सो कस्स अणुणअं पडि-

प्रियंवदा : (प्रविश्य) सखि। प्रकृतिवक्रः स कस्य अनुनयं प्रति-

गेण्हदि। किम्पि उण साणुक्कोसो किदो।

गृह्णाति। किमपि पुनः सानुक्रोशः कृतः।[2]

अनसूया : (सस्मितं) तस्सिं बहु एदम्पि। कहेहि।

अनसूया : (सस्मितं) तस्मिन् बहु एतदपि। कथय।[3]

प्रियंवदा : जदा णिवत्तिदुं ण इच्छदि। तदा विणबिदो मए। भअवं।

प्रियंवदा : यदा निवर्तितुं न इच्छति। तदा विज्ञापितो मया। भगवन्।

पढमंत्ति पेक्खिअ अविणादतबप्पहावस्स दुहिदुजणस्स भअवदा एक्को

प्रथममिति प्रेक्ष्य अविज्ञाततपः प्रभावस्य दुहितृजनस्य भगवता एको-

अबराहो मरिसिदव्वोत्ति।

ऽपराधो मर्षयितव्य इति।[4]

1. 'She acts the gathering up of the flowers.' *Uccaya* has the same sense as *samuccaya,* 'collecting together in a heap :' see p. 79, line 2.

2. 'Whose freindly-persuasion will this crooked-tempered (person) accept ? however, he was somewhat softened [he was made a little merciful].' *Prakṛti-vakra,* 'one whose disposition is crooked or harsh,' 'ill-temered,' 'cross-grained.'

3. 'Even this (somewhat) was much for him : say on.'

4. 'Considering (it is) the first-time, this one offence of the daughter, who is unaware of the potency of penance, it to be pardoned by your reverence.' *Prathamam iti* : The Bengālī, supported by K., have *prathama-bhaktim avekṣya,* 'in consideration of her former devotion.

अनसूया : तदो तदो।

अनसूया : ततस् ततः।

प्रियंवदा : तदो मे वअणं अणहाभविदुं णारिहदि। किन्दु अहिणाणा-

प्रियंवदा : ततो मे वचनम् अन्यथाभवितुं नार्हति। किन्तु अभिज्ञाना-

भरणदंसणेण साबो णिवत्तिस्सदित्ति मन्तअन्तो सअं अन्तरिहिदो।

भरणदर्शनेन शापो निवर्तिष्यत इति मन्त्रयमाणः स्वयम् अन्तर्हितः[1]।

अनसूया : शक्कं दाणिं अस्ससिदुं अत्थि। तेण राएसिणा सम्पत्थिदेण

अनसूया : शक्यम् इदानीम् आश्वसितुम् अस्ति। तेन राजर्षिणा सम्प्रस्थितेन

सणामहेअङ्किअं अङ्गुलीअअं सुमरणीअंत्ति मअं पिणद्धं। तस्सिं

स्वनामधेयाङ्कितम् अङ्गुलीयकं स्मरणीयम् इति स्वयं पिनद्धम्। तस्मिन्

माहीलोबाआ सउन्दला भवस्सदि।

स्वाधीनोपाया शकुन्तला भविष्यति।[2]

प्रियंवदा : सहि। एहि। देवकज्जं दाव णिव्वत्तेम्ह।

प्रियंवदा : सखि। एहि। देवकार्यं तावन् निर्वर्तयावः।

[इति परिक्रामतः]

प्रियंवदा : (अवलोक्य) अणसूए। पेक्ख दाव। वामहत्थोबहिदवअणा

प्रियंवदा : (अवलोक्य) अनसूये। प्रेक्षस्व तावत्। वामहस्तोपहितवदना

1. '"My word must not be falsified : but at the sight of the jewel-of-recognition, the curse shall cease :" so speaking, he withdrew himself from sight [vanished.]' *Abhijñānā-bharaṇa, lit.*, 'the recognition-ornament,' 'the tokenring :' see p. 3, note 3. *Ṇārihadi* : *see* p. 54, note 1. *Svayam antarhitaḥ, lit.*, 'he became self-hidden.'

2. 'A ring stamped with his name was by that Rājarṣi himself at his departure, fastened on (her finger) as a souvenir. In that [with that], Śakuntalā will be possessed-of-a-resource-in-her-own-power.' *Sva-nāma-dheyānkitam* : *see* p. 53, notes 1 and 2. *Smaraṇīyam iti* : properly, 'Saying, "It is a remebrance :"' *Iti* often involves the sense of 'saying,' 'thinking,' etc. : *see* p. 60, note 1. The Bengālī add *Śakuntalā-haste,* but I have not ventured to do so, without the authority of the Devanāgarī or K. *Tasmin* : Ś. has *tasmāt*.

आलिहिदा विअ पिअमही। भत्तुगदाए चिन्ताए अत्ताणम्पि ण एसा
आलिखिता इव प्रियसखी।[1] भर्तृगतया चिन्तया आत्मानमपि न एषा
विभावेदि। किं उण आअन्तुअं।
विभावयति। किं पुनर् आगन्तुकम्।

अनसूया : पिअंवदे। दुवेण एव्व णो मुहे एसो वुत्तन्तो चिट्ठदु।
अनसूया : प्रियंवदे। द्वयोर् एव नौ मुखे एष वृत्तान्तस् तिष्ठतु।
रक्खणीआ खु पकिदिपेलवा पिअसही।
रक्षणीया खलु प्रकृतिपेलवा प्रियसखी।[2]

प्रियंवदा : को दाणिं उण्होदएण णोमालिअं सिञ्चेदि।
प्रियंवदा : क इदानीम् उष्णोदकेन नवमालिकां सिञ्चति।

[इत्युभे निष्क्रान्ते]

।। विष्कम्भः।।

1. 'Our dear friend, her face resting on her left hand, (is motionless) as if in a picture :' *see* p. 6, note 2.

2. 'Let this circumstance remain in the mouth of us two only. Our dear friend being of a delicate nature must be spared [preserved],' *i.e.,* She must not be told about this imprecation, lest her feeling be so hurt, that her delicate constitution be injured. *Vṛttāntaḥ, i.e., śāpa-vṛttāntaḥ* : Ś.

ACT - IV

।। अथ चतुर्थोऽङ्कः ।।

[ततः प्रविशति सुप्तोत्थितः[1] शिष्यः]

शिष्य : वेलोपलक्षणार्थम् आदिष्टोऽस्मि तत्रभवता प्रवासाद् उपावृत्तेन काश्यपेन। प्रकाशं निर्गतं तावदृ अवलोकयामि कियद् अवशिष्टं रजन्या इति[2] (परिक्रम्यावलोक्य च) हन्त प्रभातं। तथा हि–

यात्येकतोऽस्तशिखरं पतिर् ओषधीनाम्
आविष्कृतारुणपुरःसर एकतोऽर्कः।
तेजोद्वयस्य युगपद् व्यसनोदयाभ्यां
लोको नियम्यत इवात्मदशान्तरेषु[3] ।। 82 ।।

1. 'Arisen from sleep,' *i.e., suptānantaram utthitaḥ,* 'just arisen after sleep,' 'just aroused from sleep :' Ś.

2. 'I am commisioned by his reverence Kāśyapa (who has just) returned from his pilgrimage [residence abroad], to observe the time of day. Having gone out into the open air, I will just see how much of the night remains.' *Pravāsāt, i.e., somatūthāt' : see* p, 17, note 1. *Kāśyapena : see* p. 22, note 4. *Prakāśam=vivṛta-pradeśa,* 'an open spot :´K.=*catwara,* 'a courtyard : ' Ś.

3. 'On the one side the lord of the plants [the Moon] descends to the summit of the western mountain; on the other side (rises) the Sun, whose forerunner Aruṇa [the Dawn] has just become visible. By the contemporaneous setting and rising of the two luminaries, human beings are guided as it were through their different states :' *i.e.,* by the alternations of these luminaries, the vicissitudes to be expected in human life are indicated. One of the names of the Moon is *Oṣadhī-patiḥ,* 'lord of the annual or medicinal plants.' He is so called from some influence which he is supposed to exercise over the growth of such plants. Compare Deut., xxxiii, 14, 'The precious fruits brought forth by the sun, and the precious

---

Verse 82. *Vasanta-tilakā* (variety of *Śakkarī*). *See* Verses 8, 27, 31, 43, 46, 64, 74, 80.

अपि च।

अन्तर्हिते शशिनि सैव कुमुद्वती मे
दृष्टिं न नन्दयति संस्मरणीयशोभा।
इष्टप्रवासजनितान्यबलाजनस्य
दुःखानि नूनम् अतिमात्रसुदुःसहानि[1] ।। 83 ।।

things put forth by the moon.' *Oṣadhī* is explained in Manu, i, 46, as *phala-pākāntā*, 'a plant which dies after the ripening of its fruit.' *Asta* is the name for the mountain in the West, behind which, in Hindū poetry, the sun and moon are always supposed to set, as *Udaya* is the name of that over which they are supposed to rise. *Arka* is a name of the god Sūrya, 'the Sun.' He is represented in Hindū mythology, as seated in a chariot drawn by seven green horses, or by one horse with seven heads [whence his name *Saptāśva*], and before him is a lovely youth without legs, who acts as his charioteer, and who is called Aruṇa, or the Dawn personified. *Aruṇa* is the son of Kaśyapa and Vinatā, and elder brother of Garuḍa. His imperfect form may be allusive to his gradual or partial appearance, his legs being supposed to be lost, either in the darkness of the departing night, or in the blaze of the coming day. The sentiment expressed in this verse is paralleled by the speech of the Cāṇḍāla in Mṛcchakaṭika [p. 321, 1. 4], thus translated by Prof. Wilson, 'In heaven itself the sun and moon are not free from change [*vipattiṁ labhete*] : how should we poor weak mortals hope to escape it in this lower world ? One man rises but to fall, another falls to rise again,' etc.

1. 'The moon having disappeared, even the lotus no longer gladdens my sight, its beauty being now only a matter of remembrance. The sorrows produced by the absensce of a lover are beyond measure hard to be supported by a tender-girl.' Some species of the lotus-plant (especially the white esculent kind) open their petals during the night and close them during the day, whence the Moon is often called the Friend, Lover, or Lord of the lotuses [*Kumuda-bāndhava, kumudinī-nāyikā, Kumudeśa*]. *Abalā-janasya :* The Bengālī have *abalā-janena*.. The genitive is equally admissible. Compare *śriyo durāpaḥ*, which is the Bengālī reading for *śriyā-durāpaḥ* at p. 117, 1. 13, and *svabhāvas tasya duratikramaḥ* : Hitop. 1. 1945.

Verse 83. *Vasanta-tilakā* (variety of *Śakkarī*). *See* Verses 8, 27, 31, 43, 46, 64, 74, 80, 82.

अनसूया : (प्रविश्य पटाक्षेपेण) एवं णाम विसअपरम्मुहस्सबि

अनसूया : (प्रविश्य पटाक्षेपेण[1]) एवं नाम विषयपराङ्मुखस्यापि

इमस्स जणस्स ण एदं ण विदिअं। तेण रणा सउन्दलाए अणज्जं

अस्य जनस्य न एतन् न विदितम्। तेन राज्ञा शकुन्तलायाम् अनार्य्यम्

1. 'With a hurried toss of the curtain.' *Paṭākṣepeṇa* (so read all the Devanāgarī MSS., and K.) is from *Paṭa,* with the same sense as *apaṭī, i.e.,* 'the curtain separating the stage from the *nepathya*' [see p. 3, note 1] and *ākṣepa,* 'tossing aside.' The Bengālī reading is *apaṭī-kṣepeṇa. Paṭākṣepeṇa=yavanikāpanodanena* : K.:=*akasmāt*, 'suddenly :' Ś. 'The entrance of an actor under the influence of flurry caused by joy, sorrow, or any other emotion [*harṣa-śokādi-janita-sambhrama-yuktasya*] is made with a toss of the curtain :' K.

The following verses have not the authority of the Devanāgarī MSS., nor of K., but are given immediately after verse 83 in the Bengālī MSS., and in the Kolkata and French editions, supported by Ś. :—

अपि च।

कर्कन्धूनाम् उपरि तुहिनं रञ्जयत्यग्रसन्ध्या
दार्भं मुञ्चत्युटजपटलं वीतनिद्रो मयूरः।
वेदिप्रान्तात् खुरविलिखिताद् उत्थितश्चैष यद्यः
पश्चाद् उच्चैर्भवति हरिणः स्वाङ्गम् आयच्छमानः।।

अपि च।

पादन्यासं क्षितिधरगुरोर् मूद्र्ध्नि कृत्वा सुमेरोः
क्रान्तं येन क्षयिततमसा मध्यमं धाम विष्णोः।
सोऽयं चन्द्रः पतति गगनाद् अल्पशेषैर् मयूखैर्
अत्यारूढिर् भवति महताम् अप्यपभ्रंशनिष्ठा।।

'Moreover, the early dawn impurples the dew-drops upon the jujubes : the the peacock, shaking off sleep, quits the darbha-grass-thatch of the cottage : and yonder the antelope, rising hastily from the border of the altar impressed by his hoofs, afterwards raises himself on high, stretching his limbs. Moreover, after planting his foot on the head of Sumeru, lord of mountains, the Moon, by whom, dispersing the darkness, the central palace of Viṣṇu has been invaded, even he, descends from the sky with diminished beams. The highest ascent of the great terminates in a fall.'

आअरिदंत्ति।
आचरितम् इति।[1]

शिष्य : यावद् उपस्थितां होमवेलां[2] गुरवे निवेदयामि। [इति निष्क्रान्तः]

अनसूया : पडिबुद्धाबि किं करिस्सं। ण मे उइदेसुबि णिअ-
अनसूया : प्रतिबुद्धापि किं करिष्यामि। न मे उचितेष्वपि निज-
करणिज्जेसु हत्थपाआ पसरन्ति। कामो दाणिं सकामो होदु। जेण
करणीयेषु हस्तपादाः प्रसरन्ति। काम इदानीं सकामो भवतु। येन
असच्चसन्धे जणे सुद्धहिअआ सही पदं कारिदा। अहवा दुव्वाससाबो
असत्यसन्धे जने शुद्धहृदया सखी पदं कारिता।[3] अथवा दुर्वासःशाप

1. 'It is not unknown to this person [myself], however withdrawn (she may be) from worldly concerns, that an indignity has been wrought towards Śakuntalā by that king.' *Evaṁ nāma* is the reading of the Mackenzie MS., supported by K. *Na etat na viditam* is given on the authority of K. *Imassa* is inserted from the old MS. [E. I. H., 1060] : Śaṅkara has *amuṣya janasya*. The other Devanāgarī MSS. read *yadyapi nāma viṣaya-parānmukhasyāpi janasya etan na viditaṁ tathāpi tena,* etc. The margin of the Bengālī MS., as well as that of Chēzy, has a not referring *viṣaya-parān-mukhasya janasya* to Kaṇva; but a comparison of other passages shews that be *ayaṁ jana,* the person speaking is commonly intended. *Anāryam, i.e., Śakuntalā-vismaraṇa-rūpam,* 'consisting of the forgetting of Śakuntalā :' Ś. and Ch.

2. 'The time for (making) the burnt-offering :' *see* page 146, note 2.

3. 'Although wide-awake, what shall I do ? My hands and feet do not move-freely in their own usual occupations. Let Love now be possessed of his wish [enjoy his triumph], by whom our innocent-minded friends has been made to place confidence in that perfidious man.' *Uciteṣu karaṇīyeṣu,* Such as 'gathering flowers, etc. :' Ś. *Sakāmo=kṛtārthī,* 'one who has attained his end :' Ś. Compare *bhavatu pañca-vāṇaḥ kṛtī* : Vikram., Act 2. *Asatya-sandhe=asatya-pratijñe* : Ś.=*mithyā-pratijñe* : Ch.: *lit.,* 'one who is not true to his contract [*sandhi*].' *Śuddha-hṛdaya* is the reading of two Devanāgarī MSS., and of the Bengālī. *Padam=sthānam,* 'a place :' Ś.=*vyavasāya* or *vyavasiti,* 'industry,' 'appication,' 'business :' Ch. and Amara-koṣa, p. 317, 1.

एसो विआरेदि। अणहा कहं सो राएसी तारिसाणि मन्तिअ
एष विकारयति।[1] अन्यथा कथं स राजर्षिस् तादृशानि मन्त्रयित्वा
एत्तिअस्स कालस्स लेहमत्तम्पि ण विसज्जेदि। ता इदो अहिणा-
एतावतः कालस्य लेखमात्रमपि न विसर्जयति। तस्माद् इतोऽभिज्ञा-
णं अङ्गुलीअअं से विसज्जेम। दुक्खसीले तबस्सिजणे को अब्भत्थी-
नम् अङ्गुलीयकम् अस्य विसर्जयावः। दुःखसीले तपस्विजने कोऽभ्यर्थ्य-
अदु। णं सहीगामी दोसोत्ति ववसिदाबि ण पारेमि पवासपडिणि-
ताम्।। ननु सखीगामी दोष इति व्यवसितापि न पारयामि प्रवासप्रतिनि-
उत्तस्स तादकस्सबस्स दुस्सन्तपरिणीदं आबणसत्तं सउन्दलं णिवे-
वृत्तस्य तातकाश्यपस्य दुष्यन्तपरिणीताम् आपन्नसत्त्वां शकुन्तलां निवे-
दिदुं। इत्थंगए अन्हेहिं किं करणिज्जं।
दयितुं। इत्थंगतेऽस्माभिः। किं करणीयम्।[2]

4. Hence, *padaṁ kṛ* in the causal must mean 'to cause to have dealings or transactions with,' 'to cause to apply one's self,' 'to cause to take up a station;' whence may easily flow the interpretation, 'made to trust.' Compare a similar phrase in Kumāra-sam., vi, 14, where also the commentators explain *padam* by *vyavasāya*.

1. 'Or rather, it is the curse of Durvāsas that has caused the change.' *Athavā* : *see* p. 24, line 10; page 30, note 3. *Vikārayati* : *see* p. 128, note 4.

2. 'Among ascetics inured-to-hardships, who is to be solicited (to carry the ring to the king) ? Assuredly, even though I were convinced that blame was attributable to Śakuntalā, I should not have the power to make known to Father Kāśyapa (just) returned from his pilgrimage, that Śakuntalā is married to Duṣyanta, and is pregnant. Such being the case, what is to be done by us ?' *Duḥkha-śīle* : so read all the Devanāgarī; the oldest Bengālī, supported by Ch. as *nirduḥkha-śītale. Sakhī-gāmī* : see p. 42, note 2. *Vyavasitā*, pass. part. of *vy-ava-so,* 'to determine,' 'resolve,' 'strive;' also 'to be persuaded,' 'convinced,' as in Rāmāy. ii, 12, 61, *satīm tvām vyavasyāmi. Pārayāmi* is either the causal form of *prī* meaning 'to accomplish,' 'fulful,' and thence 'to be able,' or is a nominal from *pāra,* 'the other side,' 'the end.' *Ittham-gate, i.e., evaṁprāpte karmaṇi.*

प्रियंवदा : (प्रविश्य सहर्षं) सहि। तुवर तुवर सउन्दलाए पत्थाणकोदुअं

प्रियंवदा : (प्रविश्य सहर्षं) सखि।। त्वरय त्वरय शकुन्तलाया: प्रस्थानकौतुकं

णिव्वत्तिदुं।

निर्वर्तयितुम्।[1]

अनसूया : सहि। कहं एदं।

अनसूया : सखि। कथम् एतत्।

प्रियंवदा : सुणाहि दाणिं। सुहसइदं पुच्छिदुं सउन्दलासआसं गदम्हि।

प्रियंवदा : शृणु इदानीं। सुखशयितं प्रष्टुं[2] शकुन्तलासकाशं गतास्मि।

अनसूयाः तदो तदो।

अनसूया : ततस् ततः।

प्रियंवदा : दाव एणं लज्जावणदमुहिं परिस्सजिअ सअं तादक-

प्रियंवदा : तावद् एनां लज्जावनतमुखीं परिष्वज्य स्वयं तातका-

स्सबेण एव्वं अहिणन्दिदं। दिट्ठिआ। धूमाउलिददिट्ठिणोबि जअमा-

श्यपेन एवम् अभिनन्दितम्। दिष्ट्या। धूमाकुलितदृष्टेरपि यजमा-

णस्स पाअए एव्व आहुदी पडिदा। वच्छे। सुसिस्सपरिदिणा विअ

नस्य पावके एव आहुतिः पतिता।[3] वत्से। सुशिष्यपरिदत्ता इव

1. 'Hasten to celebrate [complete] the festivities at the departure of Śakuntalā.' *Prasthāna-kautakam=prayāṇa-maṅgalam,* 'festive solemnities which take place at the departure of a member of the family.'

2. 'To inquire (whether she had had) a comfortable sleep. *Pucchidum* for *praṣṭum,* so reads my own Mumbai MS., supported by a parallel passage in Mālavikāgn., 44, 7, *suhaṁ pucchidum āgatā.* The other Devanāgarī have *suha-saida-pucchiā* for *sukha-śayita-pracchikā,* which is given as another reading in the Mālavikāgnimitra. Dr. Boehtlingk remarks that the agent may be used with the sense of a fut. part. active and refers to Pāṇini, iii, 3, 10.

3. 'By father Kaṇva [see p. 22, note 1] having of his own accord embraced her whilst her face was bowed down with shame, she

विज्जा असोअणिज्जा संवुत्ता। अज्ज एव इसिपडिरक्खिदं तुमं भत्तुणो
विद्या अशोचनीया संवृत्ता। अद्य एव ऋषिप्रतिरक्षितां त्वां भर्तुः
सआसं विसज्जेमित्ति।
सकाशं विसर्जयामीति।[1]

अनसूया : अह केण सूइदो तादकस्सबस्स वुत्तन्तो।

अनसूया : अथ केन सूचितम् तातकाश्यपस्य वृत्तान्तः।

प्रियंवदा : अग्गिसरणं पविट्ठस्स सरीरं विणा छन्दोमईए वांआए।

प्रियंवदा : अग्निशरणं प्रविष्टस्य शरीरं विना छन्दोमय्या वाचया।[2]

was thus congratulated [congratulation was made] "Hail (to thee) ! the oblation of the sacrificing priest, although his sight was obscured by the smoke, fell directly into the fire :"' see note 2 below, and p. 94, note 1. *Dhūmākulita* : *Cf.* p. 66, 1. 3. *Yajamānasya* : see p. 94, note 1.

1. 'My child, as knowldege delivered over to a good student (is not to be deplored; so has it) come to pass that thou art not to be sorrowed for. This very day I dismiss thee protected by [under the excort of some] Ṛṣis to the presence of (thy) husband.' Compare Manu, ii., 114, 'Learning having approached a Brāhmaṇa said to him, "I am thy divine treasure, deliver me not to a scorner, but communicate me to that student who will be a careful guardian of the treasure."' The Bengālī and K. insert *me* before *aśochanīyā*, and read *parigṛhītām* for *pratirakṣitām*.

2. 'By an incorporeal [without body, without visible speaker] metrical speech (addressed to him from heaven), when he had entered the fire sanctuary. *Śarīraṁ vinā, i.e., ākāśe sarasvatyā niveditaḥ*, 'he was informed by Sarasvatī (by a voice) in the sky :' Ś. : see p. 96, note 3. *Agni-śaraṇam=agnyāgāraṁ*, 'the place where the sacred fire was kept;'=*yajña-śālā*, 'hall of sacrifice :' Schol. Chēzy. Fire was an important object of veneration with the ancient Hindūs, as with the ancient Persians. Perhaps the chief worship recommended in the Vedas is that of Fire and the Sun. Bhāhmaṇas when they married and became householders, unless they intented giving up their saceredotal office, kindled with two pieces of the hard Śami, Araṇi, Khadira wood, or with a piece of the Śami and Aśvattha wood [see page 23, note 1], a sacred fire [*homāgni, gṛhyāgni, hutāgni*] which

अनसूया : (सविस्सयं) कहेहि।

अनसूया : (सविस्मयं) कथय।

प्रियंवदा : (संस्कृतम् आश्रित्य।)

they deposited in a cavity or hearth called Kuṇḍa or Vitāṇa, in some hallowed part of the house; or, like the Persians, in some sacred building proper for the purpose [called *agnyāgāra,* Manu, iv., 58, *homa-śālā, agni-gṛha*], and which they carefully kept lighted throughout their lives, using it first for their nuptial ceremony [Manu, ii, 231; iii, 171; Sir W. Jones, vol. iii, 127], and for the regular morning and evening oblations to Agni [*homa, hotra*], performed by dropping clarified butter, etc. into the flame, with prayers and invocations [Manu, xi, 41; iii, 81, 84, 85. *See* also p. 131, note 2 of this book]; for the performance of solemn sacrifices [Manu, ii, 143]; for the *Śrāddha* or obsequies to departed parents and ancestors [Manu, iii., 212, *et seq. See* also page 111, note 1 of this book]; and finally, for the funeral pile. The perpetual maintenance of this sacred fire was called *agni-hotra, agnyādhāna, agni-rakṣaṇa;* and the consecration of it, *agnyādheya* [Manu, ii, 143]; and the Brāhmaṇa or householder who maintained it, *agni-hotrin, āhitāgni, agnyāhita, sāgnika.* At Benares even to this day, according to Sir W. Jones, many *agni-hotras* are continually blazing. Sometimes the householder did not himself attend to the sacred fire, but engaged an officiating priest [*ṛtvij, yajamāna, agnīdhra* : *see* p. 94, note 1; p. 95, note 2]. The Brāhmaṇa who did not maintain a fire was called *anāhitāgni* [Manu, xi, 38]. According to Manu, iii, 212 (with commentary) there were three periods when he was necessarily without it, *viz.,* just before his investiture, before his marriage after the completion of his studentship, and at the death of his wife; but he usual daily oblation was then to be placed in the hand of a holy Brāhmaṇa, who is said to be one form of firm [see p. 74, note 3; p. 50, note 2]. Sacred fire is sometimes considered to be of three kinds [*tretā,* 'the triad of fires'] : 1. Gārhapatya, nuptial or household; 2. Āhavanīya, sacrificial, taken from the preceding, and prepared for receiving oblations; 3. Dakṣiṇa, that palced towards the south, or ceremonial, taken from either of the former. See Prof. Wilson's Introduction to the Vikramorvaśīya, p. 8, and Manu, ii, 231. The man who maintained all these three was called *tretāgni.*

दुष्यन्तेनाहितं तेजो दधानां भूतये भुवः।
अवेहि तनयां ब्रह्मन् अग्निगर्भां शमीमिव[1] ।। 84 ।।

अनसूया : (प्रियंवदाम् आश्लिष्य) सहि। पिअं मे। पिअं मे। किन्दु

अनसूया : (प्रियंवदाम् आश्लिष्य) सखि। प्रियं मे। प्रियं मे। किन्तु

अज्ज एव्व सउन्दला णीअदित्ति उक्कण्ठासाहारणं परितोसं अणुहोमि।

अद्य एव शकुन्तला नीयते इति उत्कण्ठासाधारणं परितोषम् अनुभवामि।[2]

प्रियंवदा : सहि। वअं दाव उक्कण्ठं विणोदइस्सामो। मा तबस्सिणी

प्रियंवदा : सखि। आवां तावद् उत्कण्ठां विनोदयिष्यावः। सा तपस्विनी

णिव्वुदा होदु।

निर्वृता भवतु।[3]

1. '[*Having recourse to Sanskṛt.*] Know that (thy adopted) daughter, O Brāhmaṇa, has conceived a glorious-germ [seed] implanted [lodged, deposited] by Duṣyanta for the welfare of the earth, as the Śamī-tree is pregnant with fire.' *Śamī*, 'a thorny kind of acacia :' [see the last note, and p. 23, note 2.] The legend is that the goddess Pārvatī being one day under the influence of strong passion, reposed on a trunk of this tree, whereby an intense heat was generated in the pith or interior of the wood, which ever after broke into a sacred flame on the slilghtest attrition. *Ahita=arpita. Teja=śukra* : Ch. *Cf.* Raghu-v., ii, 75; Megh., verse 45. 'By this it was indicated that Śakuntalā would have a son in glory equal to Agni :' Ś.

2. 'O friend, how pleased I am ! but when I think that this very day Śakuntalā is being conveyed away (to her husband's house), I feel a satisfaction mingled [associated] with regret.' *Iti*, 'so thinking :' *see* page 138, note 2. *Utkaṇṭhā-sādhāraṇa, lit.*, 'in common with regret or sorrow.' 'I am partly glad, partly sorry :' Ś.

3. '(Only) let this (our) poor-sister be made happy.' *Tapasvin*, 'a devotee,' also denotes a person in a pitiable state, a poor wretch. *Nirvṛta=susthita-cittā* : Ś.

Verse 84. *Śloka* or *Anuṣṭubh*. *See* Verses 5, 6, 11, 12, 26, 47, 50, 51, 53, 73, 76.

अनसूया : तेण हि एदस्सिं चूदसाहावलम्बिदे णारिएरसमुग्गए
अनसूया : तेन हि एतस्मिन् चूतशाखावलम्बिते नारिकेरसमुद्गके
एतणिमित्तं एव्व कालन्तरक्खमा णिक्खित्ता मए केसरमालिआ।
एतन्निमित्तम् एव कालान्तरक्षमा निक्षिप्ता मया केशरमालिका।
ता इमं हत्थसलिहिदं करेहि। जाव अहम्पि से मिअलोअणं
तद् इमां हस्तसन्निहितां कुरु। यावद् अहम् अपि अस्या मृगरोचनां
तित्थमित्तिअं दुव्वाकिसलआणित्ति मङ्गलसमालम्भणाणि विरएमि।
तीर्थमृत्तिकां दूर्वांकिसलयानीति[1] मङ्गलसभालम्भनानि विरचयामि।[2]
प्रियंवदा। तह करीअदु।
प्रियंवदा। तथा क्रियताम्।

1. 'Therefore in this cocoa-nut box, suspended on a bough of the Mango, a Keśara-garland, capable of (keeping fresh for) the intervening period, was with this very object deposited by me. Therefore make it rest on (thy) hand [taken it down with thy hand].' *Nārikera* or *nārikela*, 'the cocoanut,' 'the fruit of the cocoanut tree.' *Cūta* or *Āmra*, the Mango-tree [*Mangifera Indica*]. *Kālāntara-kṣama=virala-kāla-sthāyinī* : S. *Keśara-mālikā*, a wreath made of the flowers of the Bakula :'see p. 26, note 1. This was probably a *maṅgala-puṣpa-mayī sraj*, or garland made of auspicious flowers, to be suspended round the neck of Śakuntalā, such as that described in Raghuvaṁśa, vi, 84. Śaṅkara and the Bengālī read *keśara-guṇḍāḥ* or *keśara-cūrnāḥ*, and Śaṅkara observes that the fragrant dust of this plant is much used by women in making unguents [*udvartanām*].

2. 'Whilst I also will compound auspicious unguents composed of *Mṛga-rocanā*, holy earth, (and) Dūrbā sprouts.' *Mṛga-rocanā* is said to be either the concrete bile of a deer or an exudation from his head, used as a medicine, a yellow dye or a perfume : *see* Wilson, under *Gorocanā*. The latter word is the reading of the Bengālī MSS. *Tīrtha-mṛttikā* is earth brought from *tīrthas* or holy bathing-places : *see* p. 17, note 1. *Dūrbā*, 'bent-grass' [*Agrostis Linearis, Panicum Dactylon*], a kind of sacred grass, not quite so sacred as *darbha*, but possessing many virtues, and used for the *argha* : *see* p. 36, note 2. Sir W. Jones says of it. 'Its flowers in their perfect state, are among the loveliest objects in the vegetable world, and appear, through a lens, like minute rubies and emeralds. It is the sweetest and most

[अनसूया निष्क्रान्ता। प्रियंवदा। नाट्येन सुमनसो गृह्णाति]।

नेपथ्ये : गौतमि। आदिश्यन्तां शार्ङ्गरवमिश्राः शकुन्तलानयनाय।[1]

प्रियंवदा : (कर्णं दत्त्वा) अणसूए। तुवर तुवर। एदे खु हत्थि-

प्रियंवदा : (कर्णं दत्त्वा) अनसूये। त्वरय त्वरय। एते खलु हस्ति-

णाउरगामिणो इसीओ सद्दाबीअन्ति।

नापुरगामिन ऋषयः शब्दाय्यन्ते।[2]

अनसूया : प्रविश्य समालम्भनहस्ता। सहि। एहि। गच्छम्ह।

अनसूया : प्रविश्य समालम्भनहस्ता।। सखि। एहि। गच्छाव:।

।। इति परिक्रामतः।।

प्रियंवदा : (विलोक्य) एसा सुज्जोदए एव्व सिहामज्जिदा पडिच्छिदणी

प्रियंवदा : (विलोक्य) एषा सूर्योदये एव शिखामार्जिता प्रतिष्ठितनी

वारहत्थाहिं सोत्थिवाअणकाहिं ताबसीहिं अहिणन्दीअमाणा सउन्दला

वारहस्ताभिः स्वस्तिवाचनिकाभिस् तापसीभिर् अभिनन्द्यमाना शकुन्तला

nutritious pasture for cattle, and its usefulness, added to its beauty, induced the Hindūs to believe that it was the mansion of a benevolent nymph.' The Atharva-Veda celebrates it thus : 'May Dūbrā, which rose from the water of life, which has a hundred roots and a hundred stems, efface a hundred of my sins, and prolong my existence on earth for a hundred years.' *Samālambhana* is the act of smearing the body with coloured perfumes, such as saffron, sandal etc.; the plural is here used for the unguents themselves, which are said to be *maṅgala*, 'conducive to good fortune.' The Bengālī have *samālambhanam*.

1. '*Śārṅgarava* and the (other) good-people :' *see* page 7, note 1. The Bengālī have *Śārṅgarava-śāradvata-miśrāḥ*. According to Ś. and Ch. these were the names of two *śiṣyāḥ*, 'religious students,' pupils of Kaṇva.

2. 'Truly these *Ṛṣi* who are to go to Hastināpur are being called.' *Śabdāyyante* (so written by Ch.)=*āhūyante* : Ś. and Ch. It is the passive form of the nominal *śabdāyate* : Śaṅkara has *śabdāyante*, which could only mean 'they sound,' 'make a noise;' Pāṇini, iii., 1, 17, *Hastināpura*, [*lit.*, 'the city of elephants'] was the ancient Delhi, situated on the Gaṅgā, and the residence of Duṣyanta.

चिट्ठइ। उबसप्पन्ह णं।। इत्युपसर्पतः।।

तिष्ठति।[1] उपसर्पाव एनां।। इत्युपसर्पतः।।

[ततः प्रविशति यथोद्दिष्टव्यापारा आसनस्था शकुन्तला]

तापसीनामन्यतमा [शकुन्तलां प्रति] जादे। भत्तुणो बहुमाणसूअअं महादेईसद्दं लहेहि।

तापसीनामन्यतमा [शकुन्तलां प्रति] जाते। भर्तुर् बहुमानसूचकं महादेवीशब्दं लभस्व।[2]

द्वितीया : वच्छे। वीरप्पसविणी होहि।

द्वितीया : वत्से। वीरप्रसविनी भव।

तृतीया : वच्छे। भत्तुणो बहुमदा होहि।

तृतीया : वत्से। भर्तुर् बहुमता भव।

1. 'There stands Śakuntalā at earliest sunrise, with her locks combed-and-washed, in the act of being congratulated by the holy-women, (having) consecrated wild-rice in their hands, (and) invoking-blessing-with-their-offerings.' *Śikhā-mārjitā, lit.*, 'having her top-knot combed and cleansed,' a compound similar to *śirah-snāta*, 'having the head bathed.' The Bengālī MSS. have *kṛta-majjanā. Svasti-vācanikābhiḥ* is here an epithet of the women who make the *svasti-vācanam, i.e.* (according to K.) 'a gift of flowers, sweet-meats [*prahelaka*], fruit, or any eatables presented with good wishes and prayers for the blessing of some deity.' It is especially the blessing which is coupled with the gift. In the present case the hallowed rice which they held in their hands, might have constituted the offering which accompanied the *svati-vācanam.* In the Vikramorvaśīya the Vidūṣaka is propitiated by a *svasti-vācanam* (or-*nakam*), consisting of a *modaka-śarāva*, 'dish of sweetmeats.' Birthday-gifts, wedding-presents, Christmas-boxes, etc., with their accompanying compliments, are the *svasti-vācanaka* of our day. The words *vāyana* and *vāyanaka* seem to have a similar signification, though without any necessary implication of *good-wishes Nīvāra*, 'wild-rice,' Manu, vi, 16.

2. 'My child, take the title of "Great Queen" indicative of the high esteem of (thy) husband.' *Jātā*, 'a child,' is used affectionately in addressing any young female. *Mahā-devī*, 'cheif queen :' compare p. 123, note 1.

[इत्याशिषो दत्त्वा गौतमीवर्जं निष्क्रान्ताः]।

सख्यौ : (उपसृत्य) सहि। सुहमज्जणं दे होदु।

सख्यौ : (उपसृत्य) सखि। सुखमार्जनं ते भवतु।[1]

शकुन्तला : साअदं मे सहीणं। इदो णिसीदह।

शकुन्तला : स्वागतं मे सखीभ्यां। इतो निषीदतम्।

उभे : (मङ्गलपात्राण्यादाय। उपविश्य) हला। सज्जा होहि। जाव मङ्गलसमालम्भणं विरएम।

उभे : (मङ्गलपात्राण्यादाय।[2] उपविश्य) हला। सज्जा भव। यावन् मङ्गलसमालम्भनं विरचयावः।

शकुन्तला : एदम्पि बहुमन्तव्वं। दुल्लहं दाणिं मे महीमण्डणं भविस्सदि। (इति वाष्पं विसृजति)

शकुन्तला : एतदपि बहुमन्तव्यं। दुर्लभम् इदानीं मे सखीमण्डनं भविष्यति। (इति वाष्पं विसृजति[3])

उभे : सहि। उइदं ण दे मङ्गलकाले रोइदुं।। इत्यश्रूणि प्रमृज्य नाट्येन प्रसाधयतः।

उभे : सखि। उचितं न ते मङ्गलकाले रोदितुं।। इत्यश्रूणि प्रमृज्य नाट्येन प्रसाधयतः।

प्रियंवदा : आहरणोइदं रूबं अस्समसुलहेहिं पसाहणेहिं विप्पआरीअदि।

प्रियंवदा : आभरणोचितं रूपम् आश्रमसुलभैः प्रसाधनैर् विप्रकार्यते।[4]

---

1. 'May it be to thee an auspicious ablution !' *i.e.*, May it bring thee good fortune ! may it be an omen of happiness to thee !

2. 'Taking up the propitiatory-vessels,' *i.e.*, the vessels containing the flowers, unguents, etc., intended to propitiate Fortune in favour of Śakuntalā. So read all the Devanāgarī MSS., excepting one (Colebrooke's), which has *patrāṇi.*

3. 'This (friendly service of yours) too ought to be highly valued (by me). The being attired by (you) my friends, will now be a rare-occurrence. [*So she sheds tears.*]' *Visṛjati* is the reading of my own Devanāgarī MS. : the others have *viharati.*

4. '(Thy) person worthy of (the costliest) ornaments is

[प्रविश्योपायनहस्ताव् ऋषिकुमारकौ]

उभौ : इदम् अलङ्करणम्। अलङ्क्रियताम् अत्रभवती।

[सर्वा विलोक्य विस्मिताः]

गौतमी : वच्छ णारअ। कुदो एदं।

गौतमी : वत्स नारद। कुत एतत्।

प्रथम : तातकाश्यप्रभावात्।

गौतमी : किं माणसो सिद्धी।

गौतमी : किं मानसी सिद्धिः।[1]

द्वितीय : न खलु। श्रूयतां। तत्रभवता वयम् आज्ञप्ताः। शकुन्तलाहेतोर् वनस्पतिभ्यः कुसुमान्याहरतेति।[2] तत इदानीं–

क्षौमं केनचिद् इन्दुपाण्डु तरुणा माङ्गल्यम् आविष्कृतं
निष्ठ्यूतश् चरणोपभोगसुलभो लाक्षारसः केनचित्।
अन्येभ्यो वनदेवताकरतलैर् आपर्वभागोत्थितैर्
दत्तान्याभरणानि तत्किसलयोद्भेदप्रतिद्वन्द्विभिः[3] ।। 85 ।।

disfigured by decorations easily procured in a hermitage,' *i.e.*, Thy beauty which deserves to be set off by golden ornaments, etc., is impaired by such decorations as sprouts of *Dūrbā-grass*, etc. : Ś. *Viprakāryate* : K. has *vikāryate*, the Bengālī *vipralabhyate* and *vipratāryate*.

1. 'Was it a mental creation ?' *i.e.*, Were these ornaments created by the power of his mind ? Kāṭav. has *sṛṣṭiḥ* for *siddhiḥ*. Compare p. 79, note 1.

2. 'Bring hither flowers for Śakuntalā from the trees of the forest.'

3. 'By a certain tree a fine-linen-robe white-as-the-moon indicative-of-good-fortune was made to appear [produced]; by another, juice-of-lac, ready for the use of [the dyeing of] the feet was distilled [exuded]; from others, ornaments were presented by the hands [palms] of wood-nymphs raised (so as to be visible) as

---

Verse 85. *Śārdūla-vikrīḍita* (variety of *Atidhṛti*). *See* Verses 14, 30, 36, 39 40, 63, 79.

प्रियंवदा : [शकुन्तलां विलोक्य] हला। इमाए अब्भुबबत्तीए सूइदा

प्रियंवदा : [शकुन्तलां विलोक्य] हला। अनया अभ्युपपत्त्या सूचिता

दे भत्तुणो गेहे अणुहोदव्वा राअलच्छित्ति।

ते भर्तुर् गृहेऽनुभवितव्या राजलक्ष्मीः[1]।

[शकुन्तला व्रीडां रूपयति]

far as the wrist, emulating the first sprouting of the young-shoots of those (trees).' *Kṣauma=vālkala-vastra-bheda* : Ch. *Kṣaumaṁ māṅgalyam=dukūlaṁ maṅgalārham* : Ś. *Māṅgalya* may mean 'with words of good omen,' 'with blessings and prayers for good fortune [*kalyāṇa vākyaiḥ*] such as "May she be the beloved wife of her lord," etc. :' Ś. *Indu-pāṇḍu=candra-dhavalam. Āviṣkṛtam=udbhāvitam* : K. :=*dānāya prakāśitam* : Ś. *Niṣṭhyūtaḥ=udgīrṇah. Caraṇopabhoga-sulabho* : some of the Bengālī have *caraṇoparāga-subhago;* the oldest have *upabhoga. Sulabha* is here equivalent to *kṣama* or *yogya,* 'adapted.' Compare kumāra-s, v. 69. *Lākṣā=alakta* or *alaktaka,* 'lac,' 'a red dye,' prepared from an insect, analogous to the cochineal insect. This minute red insect is found in great numbers in the Palāśa, Indian fig-tree, and some other trees. It punctures the bark, whence exudes a resinous milky juice, with which it surrounds itself in a kind of nest, and which when dry may be broken off, and used for various purposes. This hardened and reddened substance is variously called gum-lac, shell-lac, stick-lac, etc. *Āparva,* etc.=*parva-bhāga-paryantam udgataiḥ. Parva-bhāga=maṇi-bandha,* 'the wrist :' K. *Ā,* 'as far as,' generally requires the ablat c. of a word not in composition, as *āmanibhandhāt pāṇiḥ,* 'the hand as far as [from] the wrist.' It may sometimes have the sense of 'from,' as in *ādarśanāt,* 'from the first sight.' *Tat-kisalaya,* etc. : the Bengālī and Ś. read *naḥ,* 'to us,' for *tat,* and *kiśalaya-cchāya-parispardhibhiḥ,* 'rivalling the hue of young shoots.' According to Kavikaṇṭhahāra, quoted by Ś., ornaments are divided into four kinds :— 1. *Āvedhya,* as ear-rings, etc.; 2. *Bandhanīya* or *Vedhaya,* as flowers, etc.; 3. *Kṣepya* or *Prakṣepya,* as anklets, foot-ornaments, etc.; 4. *Āropya,* as necklaces, garlands, etc.

1. 'By this favour, royal fortune is indicated as (ever) to be enjoyed by thee in the house of thy husband.' *Abhyupapattyā=vṛkṣānugraheṇa,* 'by the favour or the sylvan deities.'

प्रथम : गौतम। एह्येहि। अभिषेकोत्तीर्णाय[1] काश्यपाय वनस्पतिसेवां निवेदयावः।

द्वितीय : तथा।

[इति निष्क्रान्तौ]

सख्यौः अए अणुबहुत्तभूसणो अअं जणो। चित्तकम्मपरिअएण अङ्गेसु

सख्यौः अये अनुपभुक्तभूषणोऽयं जनः। चित्रकर्मपरिचयेन अङ्गेषु

दे आहरणविणिओअं करेन्ह।

ते आभरणविनियोगं कुर्वः।[2]

शकुन्तला : जाणे वो णेउणं (उभे नाट्येनालङ्कुरुतः)।

शकुन्तला : जाने वां नैपुणं (उभे नाट्येनालङ्कुरुतः)।

[ततः प्रविशति स्नानोत्तीर्णः काश्यपः]

काश्यप :

यास्यत्यद्य शकुन्तलेति हृदयं संस्पृष्टम् उत्कण्ठया
कण्ठः स्तम्भितवाष्पवृत्तिकलुषश् चिन्ताजडं दर्शनम्।
वैक्लव्यं मम तावद् ईदृशमपि स्नेहाद् अरण्यौकसः
पीड्यन्ते गृहिणः कथं नु तनयाविश्लेषदुःखैर् नवैः[3] ।। 86 ।।

1. 'Returned [come up] from bathing.' *Uttṛī* is 'to come out of the water,' 'to come to land.' So *jalād uttīrya* : Mahābh. 3, 211.

2. 'We [these persons] are unused to ornaments. By our acquaintance with the art of painting we will make the arrangement of the ornaments on thy limbs.' *Aṇubahutta* for *anupabhukta* is the reading of my own MS. and the Mackenzie, supported by K. *Citra-karma,* etc., 'by our knowledge of painting,' *i.e.,* We will decorate thee in the manner we have seen in paintings. [*Citra-likhane yathābharaṇa-prayogo dṛṣṭo' sti tenaiva prakāreṇa* : Ś.]

3. ' "This very day will Śakuntalā depart," at such (a thought), my heart is smitten with melancholy [grief for her loss] : my voice [throat] is agitated by suppressing the flow of tears : my sight is paralysed by anxious thought. So great indeed through affection (is) the mental-agitation even of me a hermit. How (much more) then, are heads-of-families afflicted by new pangs at separation

---

Verse 86. *Śārdūla-vikrīḍita* (variety of *Atidhṛti*). *See* Verses 14, 30, 36, 39, 40, 63, 79, 85.

[इति परिक्रामति]

सख्यौ : हला सउन्दले। अवसिदमण्डणासि। परिधेहि सम्पदं
सख्यौ : हला शकुन्तले। अवसितमण्डनासि। परिधत्स्व साम्प्रतं
खोमजुअलं।
क्षौमयुगलम्।[1]

[शकुन्तलोत्थाय परिधित्ते]

गौतमो : जादे। एसो दे आणन्दपरिवाहिणा चक्खुणा परिस्स जन्तो
गौतमी : जाते। एष ते आनन्दपरिवाहिणा चक्षुषा परिष्वजमान

from their daughters !' *Iti* : *see* page 138, note 2. *Saṁspṛṣṭam*, etc. : one MS. reads *spṛṣṭam samut-kaṇṭhayā* [E. I. H., 1060]. *Kaṇṭhaḥ*, etc. : the Bengālī have *antar-vāṣpa-bharoparodhi gaditam*, 'My voice is obstructed by the weight [*ādhikyena* : Ś.] of suppressed tear.' *Vāṣpa, i.e., āsruṇaḥ pūrvāvasthā*, 'the first stage or state of a tear,' 'the hot moisture that overspreads the eye, before the teardrop is formed :' K. *Darśanam=nayanam*, 'eye-sight.' *Jaḍam=viṣayā-grāhakam*, 'having no perception of external objects :' or=*kartavyāpari-chedakam*, but in this case *darśanam=jñānam* : Ś. The effect of deep thought and abstraction of mind is to paralyse for the moment the organs of vision. Śaṅkara quotes an aphorism of Bharata, *Nidrā-nāśaśca cintā ca bhrāntiścotsuka-cetasām*. *Nu* is used *prāsne* 'in asking a question :' Ś. *Araṇyaukas=vāna-prastha* or *araṇya-vāsin*, 'one whose dwelling [*okas*] is in the woods,' 'a hermit :' *see vanaukas*. *Gṛhim=gṛhastha*, 'a house holder,' 'the father of a family.' The Brāhmaṇa was required to divine his life into four stages or orders [*āśrama*]. In the first, he was a *Brahmacārī*, or 'student of religion,' under a preceptor [see p. 94, note 1]; in the second, a *Gṛhasthaḥ*, or 'householder,' living with his wife and children; in the third, a *Vānaprasthaḥ* [*vaikhānasaḥ*] or 'anchorite,' living in the woods apart from his children, and sometimes also from his wife; in the fourth, a *Bhikṣuḥ*, or 'religious mendicant,' wandering from house to house, and subsisting on alms.

1. 'Thy decoration [toilet] is completed. Now do thou put on the pair of linen vestments.' A Hindū woman's dress generally consisted of two pieces : one covered the breast and shoulders, the other was a long robe enveloping the person. *Avasita-maṇḍana=niṣpanna-prasādhanā*.

विअ गुरू उबट्ठिदो। आआरं दाव पडिबज्जस्स।

इव गुरुर् उपस्थितः। आचारं तावत् प्रतिपद्यस्व।[1]

शकुन्तला : (सव्रीडं) ताद। वन्दामि।

शकुन्तला : (सव्रीडं) तात। वन्दे।

काश्यप : वत्से।

ययातेर् इव शर्मिष्ठा भर्तुर् बहुमता भव।
सुतं त्वमपि सम्राजं सेव पुरुम् अवाप्नुहि[2] ।। 87 ।।

गौतमी : भअवं। वरोक्खु एसो। ण आसिसा।

गौतमी : भगवन्। वरो खलु एषः। न आशीः।[3]

1. 'Here close-at-hand-stands thy spiritual-father as if (already) embracing thee [about to embrace thee], with an eye overflowing with joy. Perform now the customary-salutation.' *Ānanda*, etc. : the Bengālī have *ānandavāṣpa-parivāhiṇā* : Compare page 89, line 5. *Ācāra*, 'good-manners,' 'the usual complimentary greeting.' *Paḍibajjassa* for *pratipadyasva* is the reading of my own MS. and Mackenzie : Compare p. 133, line 5. The very same expression occurs in the 2nd. Act of the Vikramorvaśīya.

2. 'Daughter, be thou highly honoured of thy husband, as was Śarmiṣṭhā of Yayāti. Do thou also obtain a son, a sovereign monarch, as she (obtained) Puru.' Śarmiṣṭhā, according to K., was the daughter of Vṛṣa-parvan, king of the Asuras or demons, and wife of Yayātī, son of Nahuṣa, one of the princes of the Lunar race, and ancestor of Duṣyanta : see p. 15, note 2. The Sāhityadarpaṇa (p. 190) adduces this verse as an example of *āśīrvāda*, 'benediction,' but reads (as also do the Bengālī) *patyur* for *bhartur*, and *putram* for *sutam*. According to Amara-Sinha (viii., 3, a *ṣamrāj* is a sovereign prince, who has performed a *Rājasūya* sacrifice, and exercises despotic sway over others.

3. 'This is actually a boon (conferred), not a (mere) benediction.' '*Santuṣṭa-devādīnam avaśyam-bhāvi vacanaṁ varaḥ, āśistu kadācit phala-dāyinī vāk.*' 'A *vara* is the promise of a propitiated deity, etc., which must necessarily come to pass; an *āśis* is a benediction which occasionally bears fruit [comes true] :' Ch. Ś.

Verse 87. *Śloka* or *Anuṣṭubh*. *See* Verses, 5, 6, 11, 12, 26, 47, 50, 51, 53, 73, 76, 84.

काश्यप : वत्से। इत: सद्यो हुताग्नीन् प्रदक्षिणीकुरुष्व।[1]

[सर्वे परिक्रामन्ति]

काश्यप : (ऋक्छन्दसा आशास्ते)

अमी वेदिं परित: क्लृप्तधिष्ण्या:
समिद्वन्त: प्रान्तसंस्तीर्णदर्भा:।
अपघ्नन्तो दुरितं हव्यगन्धैर्
वैतानास् त्वां वह्नय: पावयन्तु[2] ।। 88 ।।

1. 'My child, this way ! do thou at once circumambulate the sacrificial fires :' See page 146, note 2. *Sadyo-hutāgnīm-kṛta-homāgnīm* : Ś. The Taylor and my own MS. has *sadyohutān*. *Sadyo* may, however, be separated from the next word, and translated 'at once,' 'immediately.' The rite of circumambulation is performed by slowly walking round any object, keeping the right side towards it.

2. [Pronounces a blessing in the metre of the *Ṛk*, *i.e.*, according to the usual metre of the *Ṛgveda*.] Let these fires taken-from-the-sacred hearth [*vaitānās*] whose places are fixed round the altar, fed with (consecrated) wood, having darbha [*kuśa*] grass strewed around the margin, destroying sin by the perfume of the oblation, purify thee.' The Ṛgveda is the most celebrated of the four most ancient sacred books of the Hindūs. It consists of metrical hymns or prayers termed *sūktas* or *mantras*, each stanza of which is called a *ṛc* or *ṛk*, addressed cheifly to the gods of the elements, Fire, Air, etc., and ascribed to different holy authors, styled *Ṛṣis*. *Asya vṛttasya vedoktāśīrvāda-sadṛ-satvam agni-prayuktatvādi bodhavyam*, 'It is to be understood that there is a similarity between the metre of this verse

---

Verse 88. *Triṣṭuk Catuṣ-padā*, a form of *Vaidika* metre, consisting of four times eleven syllables, the first and third half-lines resembling the *Vātormī*, and the second and fourth, the *Śālinī* variety of *Triṣṭubh*. In the second, however, the first syllable is short.

◡ — — — ◡ ◡ — — ◡ — — || ◡ — — — — ◡ — — ◡ — —
◡ — — — ◡ ◡ — — ◡ — — || — — — — — ◡ — — ◡ — —

In the Ṛgveda, i, 59, 5, the first *pāda* is exactly like the first in the above scheme, but the other *pādas* are arranged differently, as far at least as the seventh syllable. Kālidāsa, accustomed to the strictness of the later Sanskṛt metres, seems here to have endeavoured to imitate the *Vaidika* rhythm, in which greater liberty was allowed. Thus, he produced a verse too irregular to come under any of the later metres, but rather too regular for a Vaidika hymn.

प्रतिष्ठस्वेदानीं (सदृष्टिक्षेपं) क्व ते शार्ङ्गरवमिश्राः।

शिष्य : (प्रविश्य) भगवन्।[1] इमे स्मः।

काश्यप : भगिन्यास् ते मार्गम् आदेशय।[2]

शार्ङ्गरव : इत इतो भवती (सर्वे परिक्रामन्ति)

काश्यप : भो भोः सन्निहिताम् तपोवनतरवः।

पातुं न प्रथमं व्यवस्यति जलं युष्मास्वपीतेषु या
नादत्ते प्रियमण्डनापि भवतां स्नेहेन या पल्लवम्।
आद्ये वः कुसुमप्रसूतिसमये यस्या भवत्युत्सवः
सेयं याति शकुन्तला पतिगृहं सर्वैर् अनुज्ञायताम्[3] ।। 89 ।।

and that of the benedictions uttered in the Vedas addressed to fire, etc. :' K. It is certain that the verse itself does not occur in the Ṛgveda, but the metre [see p. 158] resembles that which commonly prevails there. Doubtless Kālidāsa intended it as an imitation of the sacred style of poetry. That it is addressed to Agni constitutes another point of resemblance. *Vaitānās* : *see* p. 146, note 2; p. 96, note 2. *Klṛpta-dhiṣṇyāḥ=racitādhiṣṭhānāḥ. Prānta-saṁstīrṇa-darbhāḥ, i.e., pārśweṣu catasṛṣu dikṣu saṅkīrṇā darbhā yeṣām*. At a sacrifice, the fires, severally termed *Āhavanīya, Māñjalīya, Gārhapatya,* and *Agnīdhrīya,* were lighted at the four cardinal points, east, west, north, and south, and *Kuśa*-grass [see p. 19, note 1] was scattered round each fire. See Wilson's translation of the Ṛgveda, p. 3, note 1; and compare Ṛgveda, vii., 13, 'Thou, four-eyed Agni, blazest as the protector of the worshippers,' etc. *Pālayantu=rakṣantu* is the reading of all the Bengālī MSS., supported by Kāṭavema, Śaṅkara, and Candraśekhara, but the Devanāgarī MSS. all have *pāvayantu*.

1. Śaṅkara quotes a verse of Bharata, *Devāśca, munayaścaiva, liṅginaḥ, sādhanāśca* [*sādhakāśca* : Ch.] *ye, bhagavanniti te vācyāḥ sarvaiḥ strī-punnapuṁsakaiḥ,* 'Both Gods, and also Munis, Liṅgis, and Sādhanās (? *sādhavas,* 'saints :' see Viṣṇu-Pur., p. 300) are to be addressed as 'Bhagavān,' by all women, men and eunuchs.'

2. Compare in the 2nd. Act of the Vikramorvaśīya, *bhavān pramada-vana-mārgam ādeśayatu*.

3. 'Listen ! listen ! ye neighbouring trees of the penance-grove. She who never attempts to drink water first, when you have not

---

Verse 89. *Śārdūla-vikrīḍita* (variety of Atidhṛti). *See* Verses 14, 30, 36, 39, 50, 63, 79, 85, 86.

[कोकिलरवं सूचयित्वा[1]]

अनुमतगमना शकुन्तला
तरुभिर् इयं वनवासबन्धुभिः।
परभृतविरुतं कलं यथा
प्रतिवचनीकृतम् एभिर् ईदृशम्[2] ।। 90 ।।

drunk, and who, although fond of ornaments, never plunks a blossom, out of affection for you, whose greatest-holiday [highest-joy] is at the season of the first appearance of your bloom, even that same Śakuntalā now departs to the house of her husband. Let her be affectionately-dismissed by (you) all.' *Bhoḥ* is a vocative particle, generally joined with *śrūyatām*, 'Listen !' *Vyavasyati*, 'makes effort,' may also mean 'resolves upon,' 'make up her mind,' 'thinks,' 'it never enters into her head.' *Apīteṣu* : the Bengālī have *asikteṣu*, *i.e.*, 'as long as you remain unwatered.' The Devanāgarī reading is supported by K., who includes *pīta* among the passive participles, like *gata, sthita, ārūḍha*, etc. [Pāṇini, iii, 4, 72] which may have an active signification. *Vismṛta* may included in the same list : see p. 28, 1. 4. *Priyamaṇḍanā* : *Priya* with the sense' forth of' may stand at the beginning or end of a compound. Compare *jala-priya*, 'fond of water.' So *philo* in words like *philosophia, philoxenos* [*priyātithi*], etc.

1. 'Acting as if he heard the note of a cuckoo,' *lit.*, 'Showing the note of a cuckoo,' Compare *nimittam sūcayitvā* : Vikram., Act 2.

2. 'This Śakuntalā is permitted to depart by the trees, the foresters'-kinsfolk; since a song to this effect, warbled by the cuckoo, was employed as an answer by them.' *Vana-vāsa-bandhubhiḥ*= *aranya-vāsa-snigdhaiḥ*, 'beloved by foresters.' It may be translated 'her sylvan relatives.' *Para-bhṛta* [=*pika*] *lit.*, 'nourished by a stranger.' The Indian Cuckoo is supposed to leave her eggs in the nest of the crow to be hatched. This bird must have resembled the nightingale rather than the bird known as the cuckoo in Europe. One of its names was *Vasanta-dūta*, 'messenger of spring.' Its song had none of the monotony which characterises the note of the cuckoo, but was as sweet [*madhura* : Ṛtu-s.] and varied as that of the nightingale with us. 'The beauty of cuckoo is their song :' Hitop.,

---

Verse 90. *Aparavaktrā*, containing eleven syllables to the first half-line, and twelve to the second, each whole line being alike.

⏑ ⏑ ⏑ ⏑ ⏑ ⏑ — ⏑ — ⏑ — || ⏑ ⏑ ⏑ ⏑ — ⏑ ⏑ — ⏑ — ⏑ —

आकाशे।

रम्यान्तरः कमलिनीहरितैः सरोभिश्
छायाद्रुमैर् नियमितार्कमयूखतापः।
भूयात् कुशेशयरजोमृदुरेणुर् अस्याः
शान्तानुकूलपवनश्च शिवश्च पन्थाः[1] ।। 91 ।।

[सर्वे सविस्मयम् आकर्णयन्ति]

गौतमी : जादे। णादिजणसिणिद्धाहिं अणुणादगमणासि तबोवण-

गौतमी : जाते। ज्ञातिजनस्निग्धाभिर् अनुज्ञातगमनासि तपोवन-

1. 839. 'On a journey [*yātrāyām*] the note of a cuckoo is indicative of good-fortune [*śubha-sūcakaḥ*]. The answer of the trees was effected by the song of the cuckoo [*pika-raveṇaiva sampannam*]. Next the answer of the sylvan deities is given (by a voice in the air) :' Ś.

1. 'May her path be pleasantly-diversified [pleasant at intervals] by lakes (that are) verdant with-lotus-beds, (my it have) the heat of the sun's rays moderated by shady trees, (may) its dust be soft with the [as the] pollen from the lotuses and (may it be cheered by) gentle favourable breezes and (be altogether) prosperous.' *Ramyāntaraḥ=manohara-madhyaḥ* : Ś. :=*manojña-madhyaḥ* : Ch., 'having its middle space delightful,' 'pleasant throughout the intervening distance,' and epithet of *panthāt*. *Chāyā-drumaiḥ= chāyā-pradhānair-vṛkṣaiḥ*, 'trees chiefly abounding in shade :' K. : =*chāyā-lakṣita-drumaiḥ*, 'trees characterised by shade :' Ch. It is a compound similar to *śāka-pārthiva* and *abhijñāna-śakuntalā* : *see* p. 3, note 3. *Chāyā-taruḥ*, 'a large tree, one that gives shade,' is found in Wilson. Compare Hitop., line 1717. 'That is called a *chāyā-taru*, 'shade-tree' whose under-part *[talam]* excessively cool shade *[atyanta-śitala-chāyā*] does not quit either in the forenoon or afternoon :' Ś. and Ch. *Niyamita=apanīta. Kuśeśaya=śatapatra*, 'a lotus.' *Śānta=śānta-vega, manda* : K. =*pātaccarādi-śūnya*, 'free from robbers, etc. :' Ś. and Ch. The compound may therefore be translated 'free from molestation and having favourable breezes.' *Śivaśca bhūyāt panthāḥ* : This seems to have been a phrase commonly used as a parting benediction, like the English 'A pleasant journey to you !' Compare *Panthānas te santu śivāḥ* : Hitop., 1. 1442, Sāhit.-darp., p. 344, Mudrā-r., p. 30, 1. 17, and further on in this act.

Verse 91. *Vasanta-tilakā* (variety of *Śakkarī*). *See* Verses 8, 27, 31, 43, 46, 64, 74, 80, 82, 83.

देवदाहिं। पणम भअवदीणं।
देवताभिः। प्रणम भगवतीभ्यः।[1]

शकुन्तला : (सप्रणामं परिक्रम्य जनान्तिकं) हला पिअंवदे। णं
शकुन्तला : (सप्रणामं परिक्रम्य जनान्तिकं) हला प्रियंवदे। ननु
अज्जउत्तदंसणुस्सुआएबि अस्समं परिच्चअन्तीए दुक्खेण मे चलणा पुरदो
आर्य्यपुत्रदर्शनोत्सुकाया अपि आश्रमं परित्यजन्त्या दुःखेन[2] मे चरणौ पुरतो
पवट्टन्ति।
प्रवर्तेते।

प्रियंवदा : ण केवलं तबोवणविरहकादरा सही एव्व। तुए उब-
प्रियंवदा : न केवलं तपोवनविरहकातरा सखी एव। त्वया उप-
ट्ठिदविओअस्स तबोवणस्सबि दाव समवत्था दीसइ।
स्थितवियोगस्य तपोवनस्यापि तावत् समवस्था दृश्यते।[3]

उग्गलिअदब्भकवला मिआ परिच्चत्तणच्चणा मोरा।
उद्गलितदर्भकवला मृगाः परित्यक्तनर्तना मयूराः।
ओसरिअपण्डुपत्ता मुअन्ति अंसू विअ लदाओ।। 92।।
अपसृतपाण्डुपत्रा मुञ्चन्ति अश्रूणि इव लताः[4] ।। 92।।

1. 'Dear to thee as (thy own) kinsfolk.' Compare *vana-vāsa-bandhubhiḥ* in verse 90. My own Mumbai MS. *ṇṇādi* (supported by the Kolkata edition), the others all *ṇādi* for *jñāti*. There is no doubt about the doubling of the *ṇ* when initial, as Vararūci, iii., 44, gives *viṇṇāṇa* for *vijñāna*. As to *bhaavadīnam* : see p. 128, note 1.

2. My own MS. (supported by K.) has *duḥkhena*, the others *duḥkha-duḥkhena*.

3. 'One may observe the same (troubled) condition [the same condition is observed] of the penance-grove, as the (time of) separation from thee approaches.' *Samavasthā* is equivalent to *samāvasthā*, as in Raghuvaṁśa, viii, 41. The Taylor MS. reads *samāvatthā*.

4. 'The deer let fall the mouthfuls of darbha-grass, the peacocks

---

Verse 92. *Āryā or Gāthā. See* Verse 2.

—⏑⏑|⏑—⏑|⏑⏑—‖⏑—⏑|——|⏑—⏑| —— |—
—⏑⏑|⏑—⏑| —— ‖⏑—⏑|——| ⏑ |⏑⏑—|—

शकुन्तला : (स्मृत्वा) ताद। लदाबहिणिअं वणजोसिणिं दाव
शकुन्तला : (स्मृत्वा) तात। लताभगिनीं वनज्योत्स्नां तावद्
आमन्तइस्सं।
आमन्त्रयिष्ये।[1]

काश्यपः : अवैमि ते तस्यां सोदर्यस्नेहं। इयं तावद् दक्षिणेन।[2]

शकुन्तला : (लताम् उपेत्य) वणजोसिणि चूदसङ्गदाबि मं पच्चा-
शकुन्तला : (लताम् उपेत्य) वनज्योत्स्ने। चूतसङ्गतापि मां प्रत्या-
लिङ्ग इदोगदाहिं साहाबाहाहिं। अज्जप्पहुदि दूरपरिवत्तिणी दे खु
लिङ्ग इतोगताभिः शाबाबाहाभिः।[3] अद्य प्रभृति दूरपरिवर्तिनी ते खलु

cease (thier) dancing, the creepers as they cast [in casting] their pale leaves, appear to shed tears [as it were shed tears].' *Udgalita* : so read all the Devanāgarī and K.; the root *gal*, 'to drop,' is not given in the dictionaries in conjunction with the preposition *ut*, but as one sense of this root is 'to swallow' [whence *gala*, 'the throat'], *udgalita* may possibly be equivalent to *udgīrṇa*, 'ejected from the throat or mouth,' which is the reading of the Bengālī MSS. *Mṛgāḥ* : all the Devanāgarī read *miīo* for *mṛgyaḥ*, and in the next line *assūṇi* for *aśrūṇi*, apparently in violation of the metre. Dr. Boehtlingk has suggested *miā* and *aṁsū*, the latter is a legitimate acc. pl. from *aṁsu*, the masculine Prākṛt equivalent of the neuter *aśru* : *see* Vararuci, iv, 15. *Parityakta-nartanā* : The dancing of the Indian peacock, especially at the approach of rain, in which it is said to take especial delight, is frequently alluded to in Hindū poetry. Compare Megh., verses 46 and 78; Ṛtusaṁhāra, ii, 6. Bhartṛ-h., i., 43. *Osaria* for *apasṛta* : compare p. 5, 1. 9, and Lassen's Instit. Prāk., p. 363. Raghuvaṁśa, xiv, 69, contains a sentiment precisely parallel to the above, *Nṛtyaṁ mayūrāḥ kusumāni vṛkṣā darbhān upāttān vijahur hariṇyaḥ*, etc.

1. 'Father, I will just bid farewell to (my) tendril-sister, the Light of the Grove,' *i.e.*, to the Nava-Mālikā, or young jasmine-creeper, mentioned in page 28, line 4, with note 1.

2. 'I know thy sisterly affection for it. Here it is now to the right.' *Sodarya*, 'of whole blood.' 'born from the same womb' [*udara*] : compare p. 22, l. 13.

3. 'O Light of the grove, though united with Mango-tree, embrace me with (thy) arms-of-branches turned in this direction.'

भविस्सं।

भविष्यामि।

काश्यपः :

सङ्कल्पितं प्रथममेव मया तवार्थे
भर्तारम् आत्मसदृशं सुकृतैर् गता त्वम्।
चूतेन संश्रितवती नवमालिकेयम्
अस्याम् अहं त्वयि च सम्प्रति वीतचिन्तः[1] ।। 93 ।।

इतः पन्थानं प्रतिपद्यस्व।

शकुन्तला : (सख्यौ प्रति) हला। एसा दुवेणं वो हत्थे णिक्खेबो।

शकुन्तला : (सख्यौ प्रति) हला। एषा द्वयोर् वां हस्ते निक्षेपः।[2]

Cūta-saṅgatā : see p. 28, note 1. *Itogatābhiḥ*, etc. is the reading of all the Devanāgarī MSS. (supported by K.) excepting one, which has *idogadehiṁ sāhā-bāhūhim* for *itogataiḥ śākhā-bāhubhiḥ*. The feminine noun *bāhā* is more appropriately joined with *śākhām* but *bāhu* is admissible : compare p. 25, l. 6. The Bengālī have *śākhāmayair bāhubhiḥ*, 'with arms consisting of branches.'

1. 'Thou by (thy) merits hast obtained [hast gone to] a husband suited-to-thyself, just as originally determined upon by me on thy account : this young Mālikā (creeper) has united itself with the Mango-tree : now (therefore) I am free from solicitude about it and about thee. Set out on thy journey hence.' *Saṅkalpitam*, etc. : see p. 49, l. 4; and p. 133, l. 12 with note 2. *Tavāthe=tava kṛte* : K. *Ātma-sadṛśam=tvat-samam* : K. *Rūpa-kulā-dinā sva-sadṛśam*, 'resembling thyself in beauty, family, etc. :' Ś. : *see* p. 31, note 1. *Gatā=prāptā* : K. : see p. 159, note 3 at end. *Saṁśritavatī=saṅgatavatī* : K: My own has. *saṁskṛtavatī*, and the Colebrooke *sammitavatī*. *Vīta-cintaḥ=tyakta-varānusandhānaḥ*, 'ceased from searching after a husband :' Ś. *Pratipadyasva* : *see* p. 133, note 1.

1. 'This (creeper) is (committed by me) as a pledge [deposit] into the hand of you two.' *Nikṣepa=sthāpya* : Ś. *Yathā sthāpyo rakṣyate tatheyam*.

Verse 93. *Vasanta-tilakā* (variety of *Śakkarī*). *See* Verses 8, 27, 31, 43, 46, 64, 74, 80, 82, 83, 91.

सख्यौ : अअं जणो कस्स हत्थे समप्पिदो (इति वाष्पं विहरतः)

सख्यौ : अयं जनः कस्य हस्ते समर्पितः[1] (इति वाष्पं विहरतः)[2]।

काश्यपः : अनसूये। अलं रुदित्वा। ननु भवतीभ्यामेव स्थिरीकर्तव्या शकुन्तला।[3]

[सर्वे परिक्रामन्ति]

शकुन्तला : तादा एसा उडजपज्जन्तचारिणी गब्भमन्थरा

शकुन्तला : तात। एषा उटजपर्यन्तचारिणी गर्भमन्थरा

मिअबहू जदा अणघप्पसवा होइ। तदा मे कम्पि पिअणिवेदइत्तअं

मृगवधूर् यदा अनघप्रसवा भवति। तदा मे कमपि प्रियनिवेदयितारं

विसज्जइस्सह।

विसर्जयिष्यथ।[4]

काश्यपः : नेदं विस्मरिष्यामः।

शकुन्तला : (गतिभङ्गं रूपयित्वा) को णुक्खु एसो णिवसणे मे

शकुन्तला : (गतिभङ्गं रूपयित्वा) को नु खलु एष निवसने मे

सज्जइ (इति परावर्तते)।

सज्जति (इति परावर्तते)।

काश्यपः : वत्से।

1. *Ayaṁ janaḥ, i.e., asmad-rūpaḥ* : Ś. Ch. 'Into whose hands are *we* committed (by thee) ?'

2. '*Vi-hṛ* in the sense of 'to shed,' is not noticed by Wilson or Westergaard.

3. 'Enough of weeping ! [see p. 48, note 3] Surely Śakuntalā should be cheered [rendered firm, supported] by you indeed ?' *i.e.,* You are the very persons who should rather support and comfort your friend. *Sthirī-kartavyā=tapovana-viraha-kheda-rahitā vidheyā* : Ś.

4. 'When this doe [female deer] grazing in the neighbourhood of the hut, slow by (the weight of) her young, has happily brought forth; then you will send some one to announce [as an announcer of] the agreeable news to me.' *Anagha-prasavā=vyasana-rahita-prasūtiḥ,* 'bringing forth without any mishap :' K. *Priya, i.e., priya-vārtā* : Ś.

यस्य त्वया व्रणविरोपणम् इङ्गुदीनां
तैलं न्यषिच्यत मुखे कुशसूचिविद्धे।
श्यामाकमुष्टिपरिवर्धितको जहाति
सोऽयं न पुत्रकृतकः पदवीं मृगस्[1] ते।। 94।।

शकुन्तला : वच्छ। किं सहवासपरिच्चाइणिं मं अणुसरसि।
शकुन्तला : वत्स। किं सहवासपरित्यागिनीं माम् अनुसरसि।
अचिरप्पसूदाए जणणीए विणा विवड्ढिदो एव्व। दाणिम्पि मए वि-
अचिरप्रसूतया जनन्या विना विवर्धित एव।[2] इदानीमपि मया वि-

1. 'That same fawn, thy adopted child, tenderly reared with handfuls of Śyāmāka-grains, on whose mouth, when pricked by the sharp-points of the *kuśa*-grass, sore-healing oil of Iṅgudī-plants was sprinkled by thee, will not forsake thy footsteps [path].' *Vraṇa-viropaṇa=kṣata-prarohaka* : Ś. *lit.*, 'That which cause a scar to cicatrize.' See *ropaṇa* : Wilson. *Iṅgudīnām* : *see* p. 18, note 1. *Kuśa-sūci* : *see* p. 57, note 3. *Parivardhitaka=anukampayā vardhitaḥ*, 'compassionately reared :' K.=*atiśayena poṣitaḥ*, 'exessively nourished :' Ś. Ch. The affix *ka* sometimes gives the sense of compassionating [*anukampāyām*]. So *putrakaḥ=anukampitaḥ putraḥ* according to Pāṇini v., 3, 76. The preposition *pari* may give the sense of *atiśayena* noticed by the other scholiasts. *Śyāmāka=vrīhi-viśeṣa*, 'a kind of rice:' Ś. It is rather the grain of a kind of Panic grass, [*Panicum frumentaceum* or colonum] eaten by the Hindūs. *Muṣṭi*, 'a handful,' is the first measure of capacity, equivalent to 1/8th of a *kuñji*, 1/12th of a *kuḍava*, 1/48th of a *prastha*. *Putra-kṛtaka=kṛtrima-putra*, 'a factitious or adopted son :' Ś. Ch. Kāṭavema explains this compound by refering to Pāṇini, ii. 1, 59, so that *putra-kṛta*, 'made into a son' *i.e.*, *aputra*, 'not really a son'] is like *śreṇi-kṛta*, 'made into a line,' and *Pūga-kṛta*, 'made into a heap.'

2. 'Why dost thou follow me, an abandoner of (my) companions ? Thou indeed wast reared (by me) without (thy) mother [when deprived of thy mother] shortly after she had brought thee forth.' *Saha-vāsa, lit.*, 'one who lives with another,' The Bengālī have *acira-prasūtoparatayā=prasavāvya-vahita-kāla-mṛtayā*, 'that died directly after bringing thee forth.'

Verse 94. *Vasanta-tilakā* (variety of *Śakkarī*). *See* Verses 8, 27, 31, 43, 46, 64, 74, 80, 82, 83, 91, 93.

रहिदं तुमं तादो चिन्तइस्सदि। णिवत्तेहि दाव (इति रुदन्ती
रहितं त्वां तातश् चिन्तयिष्यति। निवर्तस्व तावत् (इति रुदन्ती
प्रस्थिता)।
प्रस्थिता)।

काश्यपः :

उत्पक्ष्मणोर् नयनयोर् उपरुद्धवृत्तिं
वाष्पं कुरु स्थिरतया विरतानुबन्धम्।
अस्मिन्न् अलक्षितनतोन्नतभूमिभागे
मार्गे पदानि खलु ते विषमीभवन्ति[1] ।। 95 ।।

शार्ङ्गरवः : भगवन्। ओदकान्तात् स्निग्धो जनोऽनुगन्तव्य इति श्रूयते। तद् इदं सरस्तीरम्। अत्र सन्दिश्य प्रतिगन्तुम् अर्हसि।[2]

1. 'By-a-vigorous-effort [by firmness] make the tears cease to hang [cling] in (thy) upturned-eyelashed eyes, obstructing (their) free-action [impeding our business]. In this path (of life) in which the undulations of ground [the depressed and elevated portions of ground] are not discernible, thy footsteps must certainly be uneven.' *Utpakṣmaṇor* : see page 130, note 1 in middle. *Uparuddha-vṛttim=pratiruddhaa-vyāpāram,* 'impeding the functions or proper action of the organs of vision :' Ch. *Uparuddhā antaritā vṛttir vyāpāro yena* : K. In p. 155, l. 13, *vṛtti* is applied to the course of a tear; but if so translated here, the other epithet, *viratānubandham,* would be superfluous. It is not necessary, however, to connect it with *nayanayor,* as the passage might be rendered 'make the tears that impede our business cease to cling in (thy) upturned-eyelashed-eyes.' *Vāṣpa* is the hot moisture that precedes the formation of tears :' *see* p. 155, note 3. It does not seem to be used in the plural. *Cf. muñcato vāṣpam uṣṇam* : Megh., verse 12. *Viratānubandha* : my own MS. has *vihatānubandha* : *Anubandha, lit.,* 'binding after,' 'following after;' hence 'cleaving,' 'adhering.' The Beṅgāli MSS. have *śithilānu-bandham=sāntārambham* [sic ?] : Ś. *Viṣamībhavanti= skhalitāni syuḥ,* 'are liable to trip or stumble :' Ś. and Ch. Compare page 137, line 4.

2. ' "A friend is [friends are] to be escorted as far as the water's

---

Verse 95. *Vasanta-tilakā* (variety of *Śakkarī*). *See* Verses 8, 27, 31, 43, 46, 64, 74, 80, 82, 83, 91, 93, 94.

काश्यपः : तेन हीमां क्षीरवृक्षच्छायाम्[1] आश्रयामः।

[सर्वे परिक्रम्य स्थिताः]

काश्यपः : (आत्मगतं) किं नु खलु तत्रभवतो दुष्यन्तस्य युक्तरूपम् अस्माभिः सन्देष्टव्यं।[2] (इति चिन्तयति)

शकुन्तला : (जनान्तिकं) हला। पेक्ख। णलिणीपत्तन्तरिदं पिअ-

शकुन्तला : (जनान्तिक) हला। प्रेक्षस्व। नलिनोपत्रान्तरितं प्रिय-

सहअरं अदेक्खन्ती आदुरा चक्कवाई आरडदि। दुक्करं अहं करेमित्ति।

सहचरम् अपश्यन्ती आतुरा चक्रवाकी आरटति। दुष्करम् अहं करोमीति।[3]

brink :" such is the sacred precept. This, then, is the margin of lake. Here having given (us) directions, be pleased to return.' *Odakāntāt=ā + udakāntāt=ājalāntāt* : see page 153, note 4 at end. *Odakāntād* is found in all the Devanāgarī : my own has *odakāntaṁ. Snigdha-janaḥ* may be either 'a friend,' or 'friends :' Compare p. 126, note 4. *Śrūyate, lit.*, 'it is heard,' *i.e.*, it is enjoined is *śruti*, 'scripture,' 'holy writ.'

1. *Kṣira-vṛkṣa, lit.*, 'milk-tree,' a kind of fig-tree, not the Vaṭa or Banyan-tree *[Ficus Indica]*, nor the Pippala *[Ficus religiosa]*, but the glomerous fig-tree *[Ficus glomerata]*, which yields a resinous milky juice from its bark [see page 153, note 4 in middle] and is large enough to afford abandant shade.

2. 'What message is to be sent by us (that will be) most appropriate for his majesty Duṣyanta ?' *Yukta-rūpam* : *Cf.* page 88, note 3; and page 16, line 1.

3. 'Friends, see ! the poor female-Cakravāka not perceiving her dear mate hid by the lotus-leaves, calls to (him) thus : "Hard (is the lot) I suffer :"' See page 129, note 1, and compare in Vikram., Act IV, *Sarasinalinī-patreṇāpi tvaṁ dvṛta-vigrahāṁ nanu sahacarīṁ dūre matvā virauṣi samutsukaḥ,* 'Thou indeed [*i.e.*, the male cakravāka] art sorrowfully crying to thy mate thinking her to be far away, although her body is only concealed from thee by a lotus-leaf.' A few lines before this passage, the cry is compared to the sound *ka ka*. Whether this may have anything to do with the somewhat harsh phrase *dukkaram karemi,* here employed as the cry of bird, need not be discsussed. All the Devanāgarī concur in this reading Kāṭavema, however, has *duṣkaram khalu aham tarkayāni*. The root *kri* sometimes

अनसूया : सहि। मा एव्वं मन्तेहि।

अनसूया : सखि। मा एवं मन्त्रयस्व।

एसाबि पिएण विणा गमेइ रअणिं विसाअदीहअरं।

एषापि प्रियेण विना गमयति रजनीं विषाददीर्घतराम्।

गरुअम्पि विरहदुक्खं आसाबन्धो सहाबेदि।। 96।।

गुर्वपि विरहदुःक्खम् आशाबन्धः साहयति[1] ।। 96 ।।

काश्यपः : । शार्ङ्गरव । त्वया मद्वचनात् स **राजा** :शकुन्तलां पुरस्कृत्य[2] वक्तव्यः।

शार्ङ्गरव : । आज्ञापयतु भवान्।

काश्यपः

has the sense of task, 'think', 'imagine' [cf. page 10 note 1] indeed there are few senses which this root 'of all work' may not have when conjoined with nouns; and *duṣkaram kṛ* is not more harsh than *śokam kṛ* 'to make or suffer sorrow.' Śaṅkara has *duṣkaram ayam cakravākaḥ karoti.* Instead of *pia* tree of the MSS have *bi api.*'This verse indicates that Śakuntalā foresees she is about to experience similar sorrow, in having to endure separation from Duṣyanta in consequence of the curse' [*śāpa-tirohita-Duṣyantam alapsyamānā*] : K.

1. 'Speak not so. Even she [the female cakravāka], without her beloved, passes away the night made too long by sorrow. Expectation (of meeting again) makes the pain of separation, however severe, supportable.' *Gamayati, lit.*, 'causes to go,' *i.e.*, brings to an end. The Prākṛt *visāa* may stand either for *viśāda*, 'sorrow,' 'melancholy,' or for *viśaya*, 'sleeping and watching alternately.' Śaṅkara explains the phrase by *visūraṇa-dīrghām, kheda-dirghām, duḥkha-dustarām. Āśā-bandha*, 'hope,' *i.e.*, *Prātar māṁ saṅgamayiṣyati*, 'in the morning he will be united to me.' Śaṅkara observes that this verse afford an example of the *Āśvāsa alaṅkāra*. Kāṭavema refers to a parallel passage in the Megha-dūta, verse 12, *Āśā-bandhaḥ kusumasadṛśaḥ* [sic] *prāyaśo hyaṅganānām sadyaḥ-pāti hṛdayam praṇayi viprayoge ruṇaddhi.*

2. 'Having placed in front,' *i.e.*, 'having introduced,' 'having presented.'

Verse 96. *Āryā* or *Gāthā*. *See* Verse 2.

— — | ◡ ◡ — | ◡ ◡ — ‖ ◡ — ◡ | ◡ ◡ — | ◡ — ◡ | — ◡ ◡ | —

◡ ◡ — | ◡ ◡ ◡ ◡ | — — ‖ — — | — — | ◡ | — — | ◡

अस्मान् साधु विचिन्त्य संयमधनान् उच्चैः कुलं चात्मनस्
त्वय्यस्याः कथमप्यबान्धवकृतां स्नेहप्रवृत्तिं च ताम्।
सामान्यप्रतिपत्तिपूर्वकम् इयं दारेषु दृश्या त्वया
भाग्यायत्तम् अतः परं न खलु तद् वाच्यं वधूबन्धुभिः[1] ।। 97 ।।

शार्ङ्गरवः : गृहीतः सन्देशः।

काश्यपः : वत्से। त्वम् इदानीम् अनुशासनीयासि। वनौकसोऽपि सन्तो लौकिकज्ञा[2] वयम्।

1. 'Having well considered us as rich in devotion, and the exalted family of thyself, and that (free) flow of affection of this (maiden) towards thee [*or* the spontaneous flow of affection springing up in you for her] not in any manner brought about by relatives; she is to be regarded by thee, as (one) amongst (thy) wives, after raising her to an equality of rank [*or* with equal respect]. Beyond this is dependent on destiny, nor indeed ought that to be called in question by a wife's relations.' *Saṁyamadhanān*, 'This implies that they they were worthy of respect :' K. *Uccaiḥ-kulam*, etc. 'This implies that he would act with justice :' K. : *see* page 15, note 2. *Kathamapi=durgraheṇa* : Ś. and Ch. *Cf.* page 130, line 2. *Abāndhavakṛtām* : see page 126, note 3. *Sneha-pravṛttim=prema-ceṣṭām* : Ch. *Sāmānya-pratipatti-pūrvakam=sādhāraṇa-gaurava-purahsaram*, 'preceded by equal respect.' *Yādṛśena gauraveṇa aparā vadhūr ālokyate tādṛśeṇa iyam* etc. : Ś. *Pratipatti* is either 'the act of preferring to rank,' or 'the respect paid to rank.' *Pūrva* or *pūrvaka* at the end of a compound often simply denotes the manner in which anything is done, translateable by 'with' or 'after.' Compare page 116, note 1. *Dāreṣu* : *dāra-śabda pun-liṅgaḥ kalatra-vācako nitya-bahu-vacanāntaḥ*, 'the word *dāra*, meaning a wife, is of the masculine gender, and always has a plural termination :' Ś. *Dārāḥ*, therefore may be either wives or wife. *Atahparam*, etc., 'Here he tells the reason why he does not demand higher rank or greater honour for Śakuntalā :' Ś. In the first line, my own MS. read *asmān sādhu samīkṣya saṁyamaparān*. All marriages in the East are arranged by the relatives of the parties.

2. 'Acquainted with worldly affairs,' 'know the ways of the world' [=*lokavyavahāra-jñāḥ* : Ś.]

Verse 97. *Śārdūla-vikrīḍita* (variety of *Atidhṛti*). *See* Verses 14, 30, 36, 39, 40, 63, 79, 85, 86, 89.

शाङ्गरवः : न खलु धीमतां कश्चिद् अविषयो नाम।[1]

काश्यपः : सा त्वम् इतः पतिकुलं प्राप्य–

शुश्रूषस्व गुरून् कुरु प्रियसखीवृत्तिं सपत्नीजने
भर्तुर् विप्रकृतापि रोषणतया मास्म प्रतीपं गमः।
भूयिष्ठं भव दक्षिणा परिजने भाग्येष्वनुत्सेकिनी
यान्त्येवं गृहिणीपदं युवतयो वामाः कुलस्याधयः[2] ।। 98 ।।

कथं वा गौतमी मन्यते।

गौतमी : **एत्तिओ बहूजणस्स उबदेसो। जादे। एदंक्खु सव्वं**

गौतमी : एतावान् वधूजनस्य उपदेशः। जाते। एतत् खलु सर्व्वम्

1. 'There is no subject out of the reach [*agocaraḥ* : Ś.] of the intelligent.' [Wise men are conversant with all subjects.]

2. 'Pay respectful attention to (thy) superiors. Act the part of a dear friend towards (thy) fellow-wives [rival wives]. Even though wronged [treated harshly] by thy husband, do not out of anger show [go to] a refractory-spirit. Be ever courteous towards (thy) attendants; not puffed up [arrogant] in prosperity—in this manner, young-women attain the station [title] of housewife [matron]. Those of an opposite character are house-banes [banes of the family].' The Sāhityadarpaṇa adduces this as an example of the figure Upadiṣṭam, which is defined as *manohāri vākyaṁ śāstranusārataḥ* [p. 182]. Śaṅkara quotes the following aphorism : *Parisaṅgṛhya śāstrārthaṁ yad vākyam abhidhīyate vidvan monoharam jñeyam upadiṣṭam tad eva tu. Gurūn=svaśurādīn,* 'father-in-law,' etc. : A Guru is not only a father or a father-in-law, but also a preceptor, and in fact any male relation entitled to *gaurava,* 'respect.' *Śuśruṣasva= ārādhya. Vṛttim* : some of the Bengālī and the Sāhit.-darp., supported by Ś., read *vṛttam=caritram,* 'action,' 'deed,' 'behaviour,' 'demeanour.' *Viprakṛta=pīḍitā* : Ch.=*Kṛta-vipriyā,* offended :' Ś. *Pratīpam=prātikūlyam. Bhuyiṣṭam=atiśayena. Dakṣiṇā=sa-sneha. Bhāgyeṣu* : the Bengālī and Ś. have *bhogeṣu=sukheṣu,* 'in enjoyments,' 'in pleasures,' in which case *anutsekinī* will mean 'not given to excess.' The latter word is literally 'spouting up' like a fountain. Compare *anutseko lakṣmyām* : Bhart.-h., ii., 54. *Padam=śabdam,* ' title :' Ś.=*vyasāyam* or *pratiṣṭām* : Ch. *Vāmāḥ=tad-viparīta-kāriṇyaḥ* : Ś.=*tad-viruddhāḥ* : Ch.

Verse 98. *Śārdūla-vikrīḍita* (variety of *Atidhṛti*). *See* Verses 14, 30, 36, 39, 50, 63, 79, 85, 86, 89, 97.

ओधारेहि।
अवधारय।[1]

काश्यपः : वत्से। परिष्वजस्व मां सखीजनं च।

शकुन्तला : ताद। इदो एष्व किं पिअंवदामिस्साओ सहीओ
शकुन्तला : तात। इत एव किं प्रियंवदामिश्राः[2] सख्यो
णिवत्तिस्सन्ति।
निवर्तिष्यन्ते।

काश्यपः : वत्से। इमे अपि प्रदेये।[3] न युक्तम् अनयोस् तत्र गन्तुं। त्वया सह गौतमी यास्यति।

शकुन्तला : (पितरम् आश्लिष्य) कहं दाणिं तादस्स अङ्कादो
शकुन्तला : (पितरम् आश्लिष्य) कथम् इदानीं तातस्य अङ्कात्
परिब्भट्ठा मलअतरुम्मूलिआ चन्दणलदा विअ देसन्तरे जीविअं धारइस्सं।
परिभ्रष्या मलयतटोन्मूलिता चन्दनलता इव देशान्तरे जीवितं धारयिष्यामि।[4]

1. 'Lay to heart,' 'treasure up in the heart,' 'ponder well.'

2. *See* page 150, note 1. My own MS. and two others insert *kim.*

3. 'Are to be given away in marriage.' Compare page 48, line 7, note 4. *Ime api* : Dual terminations do not coalesce with following vowels : Laghukaum., No. 58; Pāṇini, I, i. ii.

4. 'How now, removed from my foster-father's side, like a tendril of the sandal-tree uprooted from the slopes of Malaya, shall I support life in a strange place ?' Candana [σανταλου], the Sirium myrtifolium, 'a large kind of myrtle with pointed leaves,' the wood of which affords many highly esteemed perfumes, unguents, etc., and is celebrated for its delicious scent. It is found chiefly on the slopes [*taṭa, upatyakā* : Ragh., iv., 46, 48] of the Malaya mountains, which are thence called *candanācala,* the tree being sometimes called *Malaya-ja,* 'Malaya-born., Evequent allusion is made to this tree being infested by snakes : see Ragh., iv, 48; Hitop., line 1582. *Tara,* of which the Sanskṛt equivalent is probably *taṭa* is the reading of all the Devanāgarī MSS. It is synonymous with *utsaṅga,* 'the slope of a hill,' so that *Malayasya utsaṅgāt* exactly answers to *tāṭasya-aṅkāt* [*aṅka=utsaṅga* : Amarakoṣa, iv, 1, 4.] *Ḍ* and *r* are certainly inter-

काश्यपः :। वत्से। किम् एवं कातरासि।

अभिजनवतो भर्तुः श्लाघ्ये स्थिता गृहिणीपदे
विभवगुरुभिः कृत्यैस् तस्य प्रतिक्षणम् आकुला।
तनयम् अचिरात् प्राचीवार्कं प्रसूय च पावनं
मम विरहजां न त्वं वत्से शुचं गणयिष्यसि[1] ।। 99 ।।

[शकुन्तला पितुः पादयोः पतति]

काश्यपः :। यद् इच्छामि ते। तद् अस्तु।

शकुन्तला : (सख्याव् उपेत्य) हला। दुवेबि मं समं एव्व परि-

शकुन्तला : (सख्याव् उपेत्य) हला। द्वे अपि मां समम् एव परि-

स्सजह।

ष्वजेथाम्।

सख्यौ : (तथा कृत्वा) सहि। जइ णाम सो राआ पच्चहिणाण-

सख्यौ : (तथा कृत्वा) सखि। यदि नाम स **राजा** प्रत्यभिज्ञान

मन्थरो भवे तदो मे इमं अत्तणामहेअङ्किअं अङ्गुलीअअं दंसेहि।

मन्थरो भवेत् ततो अस्मै इदम् आत्मनामधेयाङ्कितम्[2] अङ्गुलीयकं दर्शय।

changeable in Sanskṛt and Prākṛt, and the substitution of *d* for *ṭ* is usual. *L*, however, is the more common substitute, and, I confess that my first idea was that *Malaya-tara* was for *mayala-tala=Malayasya upatyakā* : Ragh., vi, 46.

1. 'Stationed in the honourable post of wife to a nobly-born husband; (and) incessantly [every moment] distracted with his affairs important from his dignity; having very shortly given birth to a pure son, like as the Eastern-quarter (gives birth to) the Sun, thou wilt not take account, O daughter, of the sorrow produced by separation from me.' *Abhijanavato=kulīnasya* : *see* p. 15, note 2. *Ākulā=vyagrā*, 'perplexed,' 'intently occupied :' Ś. *=sa-sambhramā*, 'bewildered :' K. *Acirāt=gamanāvyavahita-samaye*, 'immediately on thy arrival.' *Prācī iva*, etc.*=yathā pūrva-dik pavitra-janakaṁ sūryam* : Ś.

2. *See* page 53, notes 1 and 2; page 138, line 12, note 2.

Verse 99. *Hariṇī* (variety of *Atyaṣṭi*). *See* Verse 66.

शकुन्तला : इमिणा सन्देहेण वो आकम्पिदन्हि।

शकुन्तला : अनेन सन्देहेन वाम् आकम्पितास्मि।

सख्यौ : मा भाआहि। अदिसिणेहो पाबसङ्की।

सख्यौ : मा बिभीहि। अतिस्नेहः[1] पापशङ्की।

शार्ङ्गरव : युगान्तरम्[2] आरूढः सविता। त्वरताम् अत्रभवती।

शकुन्तला : (आश्रमाभिमुखी स्थित्वा) ताद। कदा णु भूओ तबोवणं

शकुन्तला : (आश्रमाभिमुखी स्थित्वा) तात। कदा न भूयम् तपोवनं

पेक्खिस्सं।

प्रेक्षिष्ये।

काश्यपः : श्रूयताम्।

भूत्वा चिराय चतुरन्तमहीसपत्नी
दौष्यन्तिम् अप्रतिरथं तनयं निवेश्य।
भर्त्रा तदर्पितकुटुम्बभरेण सार्द्धं
शान्ते करिष्यसि पदं पुनर् आश्रमेऽस्मिन्[3] ।। 100 ।।

1. 'Excessive affection is apt to suspect evil.' *Ati-snehaḥ*, so reads the Taylor MS. and my own, supported by Kātavema. Śaṅkara observes, *tathā coktaṁ kirāte. Prema paśyat bhayāni apade' pi*, and so it is said m̀ the Kirātārjunīya, 'Affection sees causes of alarm [*or* dangers], although without foundation.'

2. 'The sun has ascended to another division (of the sky).' The Mackenzie MS. has *yugāntam adhirūḍhaḥ;* the Kolkata edition *dūram adhirūḍhaḥ,* Chézy *gaganāntaram adhiruḍhāḥ*. According to Candra-śekhara, *yuga* is by some considered equivalent to *prahara*, 'a divison of the day, comprising one-eighth of the sun's diurnal revolution, or three hours;' by others, *hasta-catuṣṭayam*, 'a space of four cubits.' Dr. Boehtlingk considers *yugāntara* to be the second half of the are described by the sun in the heavens, and translates, 'The Sun has already entered the afternoon-quarter of the heavens.'

3. 'Having become for a long time the fellow-wife of the Earth bounded by the four cardinal-points, having settled-in-marriage

---

Verse 100. *Vasanta-tilakā* (variety of *Śakkarī*). *See* Verses 8, 27, 31, 43, 46, 64, 74, 80, 82, 83, 91, 93, 94, 95.

गौतमी : जादे। परिहीअदि गमणवेला। णिवत्तेहि पिदरं। अहवा।

गौतमी : जाते। परिहीयते गमनवेला। निवर्तय पितरम्। अथवा।

चिरेणबि पुणो पुणो एसा एव्वं मन्तइस्सदि। णिवत्तदु भवं।

चिरेणापि पुनः पुनर् एषा एवं मन्त्रयिष्यते। निवर्ततां भवान्।[1]

काश्यपः : वत्से। उपरुध्यते तपोनुष्ठानम्[2]।

शकुन्तला : (भूयः पितरम् आश्लिष्य) तबच्चरणपीडिदं तादसरीरं।

शकुन्तला : (भूयः पितरम् आश्लिष्य) तपश्चरणपीडितं तातशरीरम्।

thy matchless-warrior son Dauṣyanti; in-company-with thy husband, who shall have (first) transferred the cares of government [the burthen of family-cares] to him, thou shalt again set foot in this tranquil hermitage.' *Catur-anta-mahī* seem to be equivalent to *catur-dig-anta-mahī, i.e.,* 'the earth as far as the four quarters,' 'the entire earth.' The Bengālī have a parallel phrase *sadig-anta-mahī.* Kāṭavema explains it by *catvāraḥ antāḥ yasyāḥ sā*. Compare p. 123, 1. 5. *Dauṣyanti* is a regular, though not very common form of patronymic, derived from Duṣyanta, as Dākṣi, 'a descendant of Dakṣa,' from Dakṣa; Aindri from Indra, etc. See Laghu-kaum., No. 1072. *Apratiratham=asat-paripanthinam,* 'having no antagonist'= *apratirathikam* : K., *ratha* being put for *rathika* or *rathin,* 'a warrior who fights from a chariot,' *Niveśya = vivāhya,* 'having caused to marry :' K. *Niviś* has this sense in Mahābh. i. 7138. *Tad* refers to *Dauṣyanti. Arpita,* etc. Compare in Vikram., Act 5. *aham api sūnau vinyasya rājyam.* Also Manu, vi., 2, 3, 'When the Father of a family perceives his own wrinkles and grey hair, committing the care of his wife to his sons, or accompanied by her, let him repair to the woods,' *i.e.,* Let him enter upon the third quarter of his life, that of a hermit : see p. 155, note 3 at end. *Śānte* : compare p. 21, 1. 1. *Padam* : compare page 143, note 3 at end.

1. 'Allow the Father to return; or rather, (since) even for a long time she will go on again in this manner; let your reverence return,' *i.e.,* Return at once yourself, without asking her permission. To depart without asking leave, is contrary to all Hindū ideas of politeness. *Athavā* : see p. 30, note 3.

2. 'The prosecution of (my) devotions is interrupted (by this detention.)' Compare in Vikram., Act 5, *Uparudhyate me āśrama-vāsa-dharmaḥ.*

ता मा अदिमेत्तं मम किदे उक्कण्ठ।

तन् मा अतिमात्रं मम कृते उत्कण्ठस्व।[1]

काश्यपः : (सनि:श्वासं)

शमम् एष्यति मम शोकः कथं नु वत्से त्वया रचितपूर्वम्।

उटजद्वारविरूढं नीवारबलिं विलोकयतः[1] ।। 101 ।।

1. 'Therefore do not beyond measure sorrow on my account.' *Ukkaṇṭha* for Sanskṛt *utkaṇṭhasva* is the reading of my own MS. *Mā ukkaṇṭhidum* seems questionable. Kāṭavema has *Bhūyo'. pi tapaścaraṇapīḍitaṁ tātasya śarīraṁ atimātram mama kṛte utkaṇṭhitaṁ bhaviṣyati.*

2. 'How, my child, will by grief of me, looking at the oblation of rice grains formerly offered by thee, germinating at the door of the cottage, ever be assuaged [over go to assuagement] ?' *Carita*, so reads the Colebrooke MS.; the others have *racita-pūrvam=purā-vihitam* : Ś. *Carita* is supported by *caru*, 'an oblation of rice.' The *bali*, or *gṛhabali* is a perticular kind of offering, identical with the *bhūta-yajña, i.e.*, a sacrifice for all creatures, but especially in honour of those demigods and spiritual being called *gṛha-devatāḥ*, 'household deities,' which are supposed to hover round and protect household [Manu, iii, 80], to whom some particular part of the house is sacred. This offering was made by throwing up into the air [Manu, iii., 90] in some part of the house generally at the door [Manu, iii, 88] the remains of the morning and evening meal of rice or grain; uttering at the same time a *mantra* or prayer to some of the inferior deities, according to the place in which it was made [Manu, iii, 87, etc.] whether to Indra with his followers the Maruts, or to Kuvera with his followers the Guhyakas, Kinnaras, Yakṣas, etc., or to the spirits of trees, waters, etc. [Manu, iii, 88, 89]. According to Colebrooke it might be presented with the following Paurāṇika prayer, 'May gods, men, cattle, birds, demigods, benevolent genii, serpents, demons, departed spirits, blood-thirsty savages, trees, and all who desire food gives by me—may reptiles, insects, flies, and all hungry beings or spirits concerned in this rite, obtain

Verse 101. *Āryā or Gāthā*. (*See* Verse 2.)

⏑⏑—|⏑⏑⏑⏑|——||⏑—⏑| —— |⏑—⏑|⏑⏑—|—
⏑⏑—| —⏑⏑ |——|| —— |⏑⏑—| ⏑ |—⏑⏑|—

गच्छ। शिवास्![1] ते पन्थानः सन्तु।

contentment from this food left them by me !' It was sometimes offered by the women of the house, who might assist in any sacrifice, provided they abstained from repeating the *mantras* [Manu, iii, 121], and as the offering was intended for all creatures, even the animals were supposed to have their share in it. [Manu, iii, 92] In point of fact the crows, dogs, insects, etc. in the neighbourhood of the house were the real consumers of it [whence *balipuṣṭa, bali-bhuj, gṛha-bali-bhuj,* as names of a crow, crane, sparrow, etc. : compare Hitop., 1. 1076] and such of the grains as escaped being devoured by them would be likely to germinate about the threshold. This *bali* formed one of the five great sacrifices or religious rites, sometimes called sacraments, which the householder who maintained a perpetual fire [see p. 146, note 2] and devoted himself to the priesthood had daily to perform [Manu, iii, 67, vi, 21] : *viz.*—1. *Brahma-yajña,* in honour of the *Ṛṣis,* the authors of the Vedas, and therefore performed by the study of the Vedas and holy writ in general [Manu, vi, 147]. 2. *Deva-yajña,* in honour of the superior gods, performed by oblations to Fire himself, or through Fire to the other gods [see p. 146, note 2, and Manu, iii, 84, 85]. 3. *Pitṛ-yajña,* in honour of the progenitors of mankind [Manu, iii., 194], and especially deceased ancestors, performed by pouring out water with *tila,* etc. [Manu, iii., 202]. The solemn celebration of this offering at stated periods was called *Śrāddha* : see p. 110, note 1. 4. *Manuṣya-yajña* or *Nṛ-yajña,* in honour of men, performed by offering water, food, a seat, etc., to a guest : *see* p. 36 note 3; and Manu, iii, 99, etc. 5. *Bhūta-yajña,* or Bali, in honour or all creatures of every description but particularly of those not provided for by the other four sacrifices. It might have reference, however, to the deities and beings honoured in the other sacraments. That it had especial reference, however, to the *Gṛha-devatāḥ* is indicated in Manu, iii, 117, with commentary, and in the Mrcchhakaṭika, where Cārudatta, after fulfilling the *Deva-kārya,* or second of the above rites [compare p. 138, 1. 16] is described as offering the *bali* to the hosehold gods arround the threshold. His speech as he offers it, corresponds remarkably with that of Kāśyapa. *Yāsāṁ baliḥ sapadi mud-gṛha-dehalīnām, haṁsaiśca sārasa-ganaiśca vilupta-pūrvaḥ, tāsveva samprati virūḍha-triṇāṅkurāsu, vījāñjaliḥ patati kīṭa-mukhāvalīḍhaḥ.*

1. *See* page 161, note 1 at end.

[निष्क्रान्ता शकुन्तला सहयायिनश्च]

सख्यौ : (शकुन्तलां विलोक्य) हद्धी हद्धी। अन्तलिहिदा सउन्दला
सख्यौ : (शकुन्तलां विलोक्य) हा धिक् हा धिक्। अन्तर्हिता[1] शकुन्तला
वणराईए।

वनराज्या।

काश्यपः : (सनिःश्वासं) अनसूये। गतवती वां सहधर्मचारिणी। निगृह्य शोकम् अनुगच्छतं मां प्रस्थितम्।

उभे : ताद। सउन्दलाविरहिदं सुणं विअ तबोवणं कहं पविसामो।

उभे : तात। शकुन्तलाविरहितं शून्यमिव तपोवनं कथं प्रविशावः।

काश्यपः : स्नेहप्रवृत्तिर् एवंदर्शिनी[2] (सविमर्शं परिक्रम्य) हन्त[3] भोः। शकुन्तलां पतिकुलं विसृज्य लब्धम् इदानीं स्वास्थ्यं।[4] कुतः।

अर्थो हि कन्या परकीय एव
ताम् अद्य सम्प्रेष्य परिग्रहीतुः।
जातो ममायं विशदः प्रकामं
प्रत्यर्पितन्यास इवान्तरात्मा[5] ।। 102 ।।

।। इति निष्क्रान्ताः सर्वे ।।

।। चतुर्थोऽङ्कः ।।

1. So read all the Devanāgarī for *antarihidā* : *Cf.* page 138, 1. 7.

2. 'The course of affection views it thus,' The Bengālī have *sñea-vṛttir,* and one [E.I.H. 1050] *evaṁ śaṁsinī* for *evaṁ darśinī. Yasmin viṣaye sneho bhavati tad-asānnidhyāt etādṛśa eva kramo bhavati* : Ś.

3. *Hanta* : here an exclamation of joy [*harṣe* : Ś.]

4. 'My natural serenity of mind,' 'my natural good spirits.' A load of anxiety is taken off my mind.

5. 'Verily a girl is another's property. Heaving to-day sent her to her husband, this my conscience has become quite clear, as if (after) restoring a deposit,' *Kanyā-rūpo'rthaḥ,* etc., 'the property consisting of a girl belongs to another : Ś. Ch. *parigrahītuḥ=pariṇethu.*

Verse 102. *Indravajrā* (variety of *Triṣṭubh*) containing eleven syllables to the half-line, each half-line being alike.

— — ◡ — — ◡ ◡ ◡ — ◡ — — ||

Hence *parigraha,* 'a wife :' see p. 123, l. 4. The ceremonies of marriage are described by Colebrooke in the Asiatic Researches, vol. vii, p. 288-311, thus :—The bridegroom goes in procession to the house of the bride's father. The bride is given to him by her father, and their hands, on which turmeric has been previously rubbed, are bound together with *kuśa*-grass. The bridegroom next makes oblations to the sacred household fire, and the bridegroom drops rice into it. The bridegroom solemnly takes her hand in marriage [whence he is called *pāṇi-grahītā,* and marriage *pāṇi-grahaṇa*], and leads her round the sacred fire [whence he is called *pariṇetā*]. The bride steps seven times, and the marriage is then irrevocable. *Viśadaḥ=prasannaḥ,* 'serence,' tranquil :' K.=*sustha* : Ś. Compare *manasaḥ prasādaḥ* : Vikram., Act 5. *Prakāmam=atyartham* : *see* p. 108, note 1. The Bengālī reading of the last two lines is *jāto' smi samyag viśadāntarātmā, cirasya nikṣepam ivārpayitvā.*

ACT - V

।।अथ पञ्चमोऽङ्कः।।

[ततः प्रविशत्यासनस्थो[1] राजा विदूषकश्च]

विदूषक : (कर्णं दत्त्वा)भो भो वअस्स। सङ्गीदसालन्तरे अवधाणं

विदूषक : (कर्णं दत्त्वा) भो भो वयस्य। सङ्गीतशालान्तरे अवधानं

देहि। कलविसुद्धाए मीदीए सरसञ्जोओ सुणीअदि। जाणे। तत्तहोदी

देहि। कलविशुद्धायां गीत्यां स्वरसंयोगः श्रूयते।[2] जाने। तत्रभवतो

हंसबदिआ वणपरिअअं करेदित्ति।

हंसपदिका वर्णपरिचयं करोतीति।[3]

1. In the Bengālī MSS. the speech of the Chamberlain commences the Act.

2. 'Trun (thy) attention to the interior of the music-hall. In a soft and clear song harmonious sounds are heard [the union of notes is heard].' *Īśvarāṇāṁ yatra nṛtyādikaṁ bhavati sā saṅgīta-śālā,* 'A music-saloon is a place where dancing, etc., is performed before princes :' Ś. *Avadhānam* : Kāṭavema has *avadhāraṇam. Gītyām= dhruvāyām* : K. The Prākṛt *gīdie* may stand for the instrumental, genitive, or locative cases. *Svara-saṁyoga* : Kāṭavema has *svara-yoga.* Both expressions occur in the Mṛcchakaṭika [p. 33, 1. 2; p. 94, 1. 1; p. 222, 1. 5; p. 339, 1. 9], and in the Mālavikāgnimitra [p. 67, 1. 6 with note].

3. 'Is practising singing,' *lit.*, 'Is making acquaintance with the *varṇas.' Paricaya=abhyāsa* : Ch. *Varṇa,* 'the order or arrangement of a song.' It may also mean 'a musical mode.' These modes are numerous, personified either as male [Rāga,] or female [Rāginī.] According to Ś. and Ch., the *varṇas* intended here are of four kinds, the first two corresponding with the division of the *bhāvas,* or 'affection.j' *Gītiṣu catvāra varṇā bhavanti yad āha Bharataḥ; Śthāyī tathaiva sañcārī tathā Rohāvarohiṇau. Varṇāś catvāra evate kathitās sarva-gītiṣu.*

राजा : तूष्णीं भव। यावद् आकर्णयामि।

।। आकाशे गीयते।।

अहिणवमहुलोलुबो तुमं

अभिनवमधुलोलुपस् त्वं

तह परिचुम्बिअ चुअमञ्जरिं।

तथा परिचुम्ब्य चूतमञ्जरीम्।

कमलवसइमेत्तणिव्वुदो

कमलवसतिमात्रनिर्वृतो

महुअर विन्हरिदोसि णं कहं।। 103।।

मधुकर विस्मृतोऽसि एनां कथम्[1] ।। 103।।

राजा : अहो रागपरिवाहिणी गीतिः।[2]

1. 'O Bee, how (can it be) that thou, eagerly-longing for fresh honey, after having so kissed the mango-blossom, shouldst (now) be forgetful of it, being altogether satisfied with (thy) dwelling in the lotus !' *Cūta-mañjarī=āmra-kalikā* : Ś. Compare in Vikram., Act 2, *Īṣad-baddha-rajaḥ-kaṇāgra-kapiśa cūte navā mañjarī. Kamala-vasati=kamalāvasthiti* : Ś. The fondness of the bee (which in Sanskṛt is masculine) for the lotus is so great that he will remain for a long time in the interior of the flower. Compare *Na paṅkajaṁ tad yad alina-ṣaṭpadam,* 'That is not a lotus which has no bee clinging to it;' Bhaṭṭ-Kāvya, ii, 19; also *Guñjad-dvirepho' yam ambuja-sthaḥ,* 'the murmuring bee remaining in the lotus :' Ṛtu-s., vi, 15; and *Idam ruṇaddhi mām padmam antaḥ-kvaṇita-ṣāṭpadam* : Vikram., Act 4. *Madhu-kara* : *see* p. 32, note 3. *Vismṛto* : *see* p. 159, note 3. in Prākṛt, two forms *mar* and *sumar* are used for *smṛ* : the first becomes *mhar* after a preposition [as in *vimhao* for *vismayaḥ* : Varar., iii, 32], but *vimarido* would be equally correct according to Varar., iii, 56. Kāṭavema observes that under the figure of a bee, Haṁsapadikā covertly reproves the king for having forgotten her. Śaṅkara and Candra-śekhara call this verse a *Pracchādaka,* and quotes the following from Kavi-kaṇṭhahāra : *Anyāsasaktaṁ patiṁ matvā prema-viccheda-manyunā vīṇa-purahsaraṁ gānaṁ striyāḥ pracchādako mataḥ.*

2. 'Oh, what an impassioned strain !' *lit.*, a song overflowing with affection or a passion. *Rāga-parivāhiṇī=anurāga-niṣyandinī* : Ś.=*kāma-sampūrṇā* : K. Compare p. 88, note 2.

Verse 103. *Aparavaktrā. See* Verse 90.

विदूषकः : किं दाव गीदीए अवगदो अक्खरत्थो।

विदूषकः : किं तावद् गीत्या अवगतोऽक्षरार्थः।[1]

राजा :(स्मितं कृत्वा) सकृत् कृतप्रणयोऽयं जनः। तद् अस्या देवीं वसुमतीम् अन्तरेण महद् उपालम्भनं गतोऽस्मि।[2] सखे माठव्य। मद्वचनाद् उच्यतां हंसपदिका। निपुणम् उपालब्धोऽस्मीति।

विदूषकः : जं भवं आणबेदि (उत्थाय) भो वअस्स। गहीदस्स ताए

विदूषकः : यद् भवान् आज्ञापयति (उत्थाय) भो वयस्य। गृहीतस्य तया

परकीएहिं हत्थेहिं सिहण्डए ताडीअमाणस्स अचछ्राए वीदराअस्स विअ

परकीयैर् हस्तैः शिखण्डके ताड्यमानस्य अप्सरसा वीतरागस्य इव

णत्थि दाणिं मे मोक्खो।

नास्ति इदानीं मे मोक्षः।[3]

1. 'The meaning of the word,' *lit.*, of the letters or syllables.

2. 'This person [*i.e.*, I] once made love (to her); therefore I am incurring her severe censure on account of the queen Vasumatī,' *Kṛta-praṇayo=kṛta-premā. Ayam jana, i.e., mad-rūpaḥ,* 'consisting of me :' Ś. Compare page 143, note 1. *Vasumatī* is a name for the earth : compare p. 123, note 1. *Antareṇa* : see page 81, note 2. After *kṛta-praṇayo' yaṁ janaḥ,* the Kolkata. edit. adds *ityakṣarārthaḥ,* 'such is the meaning of the words.'

3. 'There is not now any liberation for me (suffered to be) seized by her with the hands of others by-the-hair-on-the-crown-of-my-head (and) beaten, any more than for a sage-with-suppressed-passions (if taken unawares) by a lovely-nymph.' Śukhaṇḍin is lock of hair left on the crown of the head at tonsurca. This was the only portion of hair suffered to remain on the head of a *Brāhmaṇa,* but in the case of the military class, three or five locks called *kāka-pakṣāḥ* were left on each side. The two ceremonies of tonsure are included by Manu among the twelve *saṁskāras* or rites which every Brāhmaṇa had to undergo. The first, or *cūḍā-karaṇa* took place from one to three years old, generally after teething [Manu, ii, 35]; the second or final tonsure *keśānta* in the sixteenth year from conception [ii. 65]. *Mokṣa* has here a double sense—1. 'Liberation of the body from danger;' 2. 'Liberation of the soul from further transmigration :' *see* p. 183, note 3. The last was the great object of sages and devotees in their bodily mortifications, but was often obstructed by the seductive artifices of Indra's nymphs : *see* p. 45, note 1.

राजा : गच्छ। नागरिकवृत्त्या[1] सञ्ज्ञापयैनाम्।

विदूषकः : का गई (इति निष्क्रान्तः)।

विदूषकः : का गतिः[2] (इति निष्क्रान्तः)।

राजा : (आत्मगतं) किं नु खलु गीतार्थम् आकर्ण्येष्टजनविरहाद् ऋतेऽपि बलवद् उत्कण्ठितोऽस्मि। अथवा।

रम्याणि वीक्ष्य मधुरांश्च निशम्य शब्दान्
पर्युत्सुकीभवति यत् सुखितोऽपि जन्तुः।
तच् चेतसा स्मरति नूनम् अबोधपूर्वं
भावस्थिराणि जननान्तरसौहृदानि[3] ।। 104 ।।

इति पर्याकुलस् तिष्ठति।

[ततः प्रविशति कञ्चुकी]

[4]**कञ्चुकी :** अहो नु खल्वीदृशीम् अवस्थां प्रतिपन्नोऽस्मि।

1. 'In the courtly (fashionable) style.' *Pravīṇasya ṛtyā* : K. *Nāgarika* here means more than 'polite.' It implies 'insincerity,' as when a man shews exaggerated attention to his first mistress, while he is courting some one else.

2. *See* page 62, line 8, with p. 63 note 1.

3. 'When a being (in other respects) happy becomes conscious-of-an ardent-longing on seeing charming objects and hearing sweet sounds, then in all probability, without being aware of it, he remembers with his mind the friendships of former births, firmly-rooted in his heart.' *Ramyāṇi, i.e., vastūni* : Ś. Kāṭavema has *rūpāṇi* for *ramyāṇi* and *sthitāni* for *sthirāṇi*. *Abodha-pūrvam,* 'without any previous intimation or suggestion,' 'unconsciously.' Compare the similar expressions, *amati-pūrvam abuddhi-pūrvam,* 'without any previous idea.' The doctrine of transmigration is an essantial dogma of the Hindū religion. Dim recollection of occurrences in a former, life are supposed occasionally to cross the mind, and the present condition of every person is supposed to derive its character of happiness or misery, elevation or degradation from the virtues or vices of a previous state of being. The consequences of actions in a former birth are called *vipāka*.

4. The Kañcukī or chamberlain was the attendant on the women's apartments. Śaṅkara and Candra-śekhara quote the following from Bharata : *Antaḥpura-caro vṛddho vipro guṇa-*

Verse 104. *Vasanta-tilakā* (variety of *Śakkarī*). *See* Verses 8, 27, 31, 43, 46, 64, 74, 80, 82, 83, 91, 93, 94, 95, 100.

आचार इत्यवहितेन मया गृहीता
या वेत्रयष्टिर् अवरोधगृहेषु राज्ञः।
काले गते बहुतिथे मम सैव जाता
प्रस्थानविक्लवगतेर् अवलम्बनार्थम्[1] ।। 105 ।।

भोः। कामं धर्मकार्थम् अनतिपात्यं देवस्य। तथापीदानीमेव धर्मासनाद् उत्थितस्य पुनर् उपरोधकारि कण्वशिष्यागमनम् अस्मै नोत्सहे निवेदितुम्। अथवा। अविश्रामोऽयं लोकतन्त्राधिकारः।[2] कुतः।

भानुः सकृद्युक्ततुरङ्ग एव
रात्रिन्दिवं गन्धवहः प्रयाति।

gaṇānvitaḥ sarva-kāryārtha-kuśalaḥ kaṅkhukiti abhidhīyate. Jarā-vaiklavya-yuktena viśed gātreṇa kañcukī; 'The character styled *kañcuki* is an attendant in the inner apartments, an oldman, *brāhmaṇa,* endowed wih numerous good qualities, and a clever man of business. The Kañcukī should enter with a body decrepit and tottering from age.' Compare this scene, and the speeches of the Chamberlain, with the opening scene of the 3rd. Act of the Vikramorvaśīya.

1. 'The wand [staff of office] which was assumed by me, having to watch over the royal female apartments, thinking "It is a matter of form, much time having elapsed since then, that same (wand) has become (indispensable, or a useful crutch) for the support of me whose step falters in walking.' *Vetra-yaṣṭi,* properly 'a cane-stick,' used as a badge of officê, like the gold stick or black rod in European courts. *Avahitena, lit.,* 'attentive,' 'careful,' 'watchful,' *i.e.,* 'appointed to a careful superintendence or watch.' So read all the Devanāgarī; the Beṅgāli, with Śaṅkara, have *adhikṛtena, i.e.,* 'by me set over,' etc. *Avarodha-gṛheṣu* : *see* p. 21, note 4. *Bahutithe=bhu-śaṅkhye* : Chēzy. Kāṭavema observes that *bahu* is here treated as a numeral, *titha* being a kind of ordinal afix. See Carey and Forster's Grammar, and Wilson's Dictionary. The latter translates *bahutitha* by "manieth.

2. 'But (why should I hesitate?) this office of supporting the world does not (admit of) repose.' *Athavā* : *see* p. 30, note 3. *Loka-tantra;* root *tantr* or *tatri,* 'to support or maintain a family :' see further on, note 2, p. 185.

Verse 105. *Vasanta-tilakā* (variety of *Śakkarī*). *See* Verses 8, 27, 31, 43, 46, 64, 74, 80, 82, 83, 91, 93, 94, 95, 100, 104.

शेषः सदैवाहितभूमिभारः

षष्ठांशवृत्तेर् अपि धर्म एषः[1] ।। 106 ।।

यावन् नियोगम् अनुतिष्ठामि [परिक्रम्यावलोक्य च] एष देवः।

प्रजाः प्रजाः स्वा इव तन्त्रयित्वा

निषेवते श्रान्तमना विविक्तम्।

यूथानि सञ्चार्य रविप्रतप्तः

शीतं दिवा स्थानमिव द्विपेन्द्रः[2] ।। 107 ।।

1. 'Because the Sun having but once (and once) only yoked his steeds travels onwards; night and day the wind (also travels); Śeṣa has the burden of the earth always resting (on his head). This also in the duty of him whose subsistence is on the sixth part (of the produce of the soil).' *Kutas* : *see* p. 54, note 4. *Bhānuḥ*, 'the Sun :' see p. 140, note 3. 'In other chariots the horses are yoked again after an interval of rest, but the horses of the Sun are allowed no repose :' Ś. *Sūrya evambhūtaḥ saṁprayāti* : Ś. *Gandhavahaḥ, lit.*, 'the scent-bearer'= *vāyuḥ* : Ś. *Śeṣa = Ananta*, 'a mythological serpent, the personfication of eternity [*anantatā*] and king of the Nāgas or snakes who inhabit the lowermost of the seven Pātālas or infernal regions. His body formed the couch of Viṣṇu, reposing on the waters of Chaos, whilst his thousand heads were the god's canopy. He is also said to uphold the world on one of his heads. He has become incarnate at various times, especially in the god Balarāma, the elder brother of Kṛṣṇa. *Āhita* : *see* p. 148, note 1. *Ṣaṣṭhānśa-vṛtter* : *see* p. 83, note 2.

2. 'Having supported his subjects as his own children, wearied in mind he seeks seclusion, as the chief of the elephants scorched by the sun, after conducting the herds to their pastures, in the (heat of the) day (seeks) a cool spot.' *Tantrayitvā* [*see* p. 184, note 1] so read all the Bengālī, supported by K.; two of the Devanāgari, *śāntvayitvā*; the Mackenzie, *harṣayitvā*. *Śrāntaḥ-manāḥ* is the reading of the Mackenzie, supported by K.; the other Devanāgarī, *śānta-manāḥ*, 'composed in mind.' *Sañcārya, lit.*, 'having cause to move about or graze :'=*bhramayitvā* : Ś. *Viviktam=vijana-pradeśam. Divā=madhyāhne*, 'in the middle of the day :' Chēzy. *Dvipendraḥ= hasti-rājah=yūtha-nāthaḥ*, 'a large elephant, the leader of a wild herd.'

Verse 106. *Indravajrā* (variety of *Triṣṭubh*). *See* Verse 102.

Verse 107. *Upajāti* or *Akhyānakī* (variety of *Triṣṭubh*). *See* Verse 41.

(उपगम्य) जयतु जयतु देवः। एते खलु हिमवतो गिरेर् उपत्यकारण्यवासिनः काश्यपसन्देशम् आदाय सस्त्रीकाम् तपस्विनः सम्प्राप्ताः। श्रुत्वा देवः प्रमाणम्।[1]

राजा : (सादरं) किं काश्यपसन्देशहारिणः।

कञ्चुकी : अथ[2] किम्।

राजा : तेन हि मद्वचनाद् विज्ञाप्यताम् उपाध्यायः सोमरातः। अमून् आश्रमवासिनः श्रौतेन विधिना[3] सत्कृत्य सवयमेव प्रवेशयितुम् अर्हतीति। अहमप्यत्र तपस्विदर्शनोचिते प्रदेशे स्थितः प्रतिपालयामि।

कञ्चुकी : यद् आज्ञापयति देवः (इति निष्क्रान्तः)

राजा : (उत्थाय) वेत्रवति। अग्निशरणमार्गम्[4] आदेशय।

प्रतीहारो : इदो इदो देवा।

प्रतीहारी : इत इतो देवः।

राजा : (परिक्रामति। अधिकारखेदं निरूप्य) सर्वः प्रार्थितम् अर्थम् अधिगम्य सुखी सम्पद्यते जन्तुः। राज्ञां तु चरितार्थता दुःखोत्तरैव।[5]

औत्सुक्यमात्रम् अवसादयति प्रतिष्ठा
क्लिश्नाति लब्धपरिपालनवृत्तिर् एव।
नातिश्रमापनयनाय न च श्रमाय
राज्यं स्वहस्तधृतदण्डम् इवातपत्रम्[6] ।। 108 ।।

1. 'Having heard, your majesty must decide (what is to be done).' Kāṭavema supplies *yat kartavyam. Pramānam : see* page 31, note 1 at the end.

2. *Atha kiṁ svīkāre* : S. : see p. 46, note 2.

3. 'In the form enjoined by the scriptures.' *Śruti-bodhitena prakārena* : Ś.

4. *Agni-śaraṇa* : *see* p. 146, note 2. *Mārgam* : see page 159, note 2.

5. 'The attainment of the object (of their ambition) is followed by pain.' *Caritārthatā=rājya-prāptiḥ,* 'the attainment of the throne :' Ś. *Duḥkhottarā=kheda-saṁvalitā,* 'encompassed with trouble :' Ś.

6. 'The-attainment-of-the-object-of-ambition satisfies anxious longing merely : the very business of guarding what has been obtained, harasses. Royalty [the office of king] like a parasol, the

---

Verse 108. *Vasanta-tilakā* (variety of *Śakkarī*). *See* Verses 8, 27, 31, 43, 46, 64, 74, 80, 82, 83, 91, 93, 94, 95, 100, 104, 105.

नेपथ्ये

वैतालिकौ :[1] विजयतां देवः।

handle of which is held in the hand, is not for the removal of great fatigue without leading to fatigue.' *Autsukyam=utkaṇṭhā,* 'longing,' 'eager desire :' such as *kadā rājā bhaviṣ-yāmītyādi,* 'when shall I become king ? etc. :' *tam eva duḥkha-dāyinī pratiṣṭhā avasādayati,* 'that (desire) certainly the harassing attainment-of-the-highest-rank allays :' Ch. Śaṅkara reads *pratiṣṭhām,* and places it in opposition to *autsukya-mātram,* making *rājyam* the nominative case to *avasādayati.* The Bengālī MS. [E.I.H. 1060] gives *pratiṣṭhām* in the margin, and this reading is certainly supported by the parallel passage (*sādayantī pratiṣṭhām,* etc.) in the beginning of Act 3 of the Vikramorvaśīya. Candraśekhara also notices this reading, but adopts the one in the text and censures the interpretation of Śaṅkara. *Pratiṣṭhā* may, without doubt, have the sense I have given, which agrees with the *prārthitārthādhigamaḥ* and *caritārthatā* of the preceding lines. *Atiśrama* may either refer to the trouble which the king has undergone in arriving at the object of his ambition, or to the troubles of is subjects which it is his office to remove. In the latter case *na ca śramāya* will mean 'without leading to personal trouble or weariness.' The Indian *cattar,* or parasol, from the shelter it affords has been chosen as one of the insignia of royalty. It is very heavy, and being fixed on a long pole greatly fatigues the person holding it. It is always borne by a servant; but here the king is figuratively made to bear it himself, so that he cannot give shelter to himself and others, without undergoing great personal fatigue. *Na ca śramāya :* is found in all the Devanāgarī MSS.; the Bengālī have *yathā śramāya, i.e.,* 'Royalty does not so much lead to the removal of fatigue.' According to Kāṭavema, who repeats the first negative before *na ca śramāya,* the two negatives are here employed affirmatively, *i.e.,* to affirm that royalty does lead to personal fatigue. 'It is not for the removal of great fatigue and not not for fatigue.' Compare the note on this use of the negatives, p. 24, note 2.

1. *Vaitālika=vandin,* 'a herald :' Ch.=*stuti-pāthaka,* 'a panegyrist :' Ś. He was a kind of herald or crier, whose duty was to announce in measured verse, the fixed periods into which the king's day was divided. The strain which he poured forth usually contained

प्रथमः :

स्वसुखनिरभिलाषः खिद्यसे लोकहेतोः
प्रतिदिनम् अथवा ते वृत्तिर् एवंविधैव।
अनुभवति हि मूर्ध्ना पादपस् तीव्रम् उष्णं
शमयति परितापं छायया संश्रितानाम्[1] ।। 109 ।।

द्वितीयः :

नियमयसि विमार्गप्रस्थितान् आत्तदण्डः।
प्रशमयसि विवादं कल्पसे रक्षणाय।

allusions to incidental circumstances. In the Vikramorvaśīya and Ratnāvali, onlly one Vaitālika appears, but here and in the Mālavikāgnimitra there are two. In the Vikramorvaśīya [Act 2] he announces the sixth hour or watch of the day, about two or three o'clock, at which period alone the king is allowed to amuse himself. Professor Wilson observes that the royal station was no sinecure. From the Daśakumāra it appears that the day and night were each divided into eight portions of one hour and a half, reckoned from sunrise, and thus distributed :—Day—1. The king being dressed, is to audit accounts; 2. He is to pronounce judgment in appeals; 3. He is to breakfast; He is to receive and make presents; 5. He is to discuss political questions with his ministers; 6. He is to amuse himself; 7. He is to review his troops; 8. He is to hold a military council.—Night—1. He is to receive the reports of his spies and envoys; 2. He is to sup or dine; 3. He is to retire to rest, after the perusal of some sacred work; 4 and 5. He is to sleep; 6. He is to rise and purify himself; 7. He is to hold a private consultation with his ministers, and instruct his officers; 8. He is to attend upon the *Purohita* or family priest, for the performance of religious ceremonies. See Wilson's Hindū Theatre, vol. i, p. 209.

1. 'Indifferent to thine own case, thou endurest toil every day for the sake of (thy) people. But thy regular-business is of this very kind. For the tree suffers intense heat with its head (while) it allays by (its) shade the heat of those seeking (its) shelter.' *Athavā* : *see* p. 30, note 3. *Vṛttir* : some of the Bengālī, supported by K. and Ś., have *sṛṣtir*.

Verses 109. *Mālinī* or *Māninī* (variety of *Ati-Śakkarī*.) *See* Verses 10, 19, 20, 38, 55.

अतनुषु विभवेषु ज्ञातय: सन्तु नाम
त्वयि तु परिसमाप्तं बन्धुकृत्यं प्रजानाम्[1] ।। 110 ।।

राजा : एते क्लान्तमनस: पुनर् नवीकृता: स्म: (इति परिक्रामति)।

प्रतीहारी : अहिणवसम्मज्जणससिरीओ सणिहिदहोमधेणू अस्मि-
प्रतीहारी : अभिनवसम्मार्जनसश्रीक: सन्निहितहोमधेनुर् अग्नि-
सरणालिन्दो। आरुहदु देवो।
शरणालिन्द:।[2] आरोहतु देव:।

1. 'Having assumed the mace [sceptre] thou restrainest those who advance on the wrong road [set out on bad courses]; thou composest differences; thou art adequate to the protection (of thy people). Let kinsmen make their appearance forsooth in affluent circumstances [when there is abundant property] but in thee the whole duty of a kinsman is comprehended towards thy subjects' *Ātta-daṇḍa=gṛhīta-daṇḍa. Daṇḍa,* 'a magistrate's staff,' taken as a symbol of punishment, and justice. It is sometimes 'the sceptre of a king.' Hence *daṇḍa-dhara, daṇḍin,* 'Staff-bearer,' etc., are names for Yama, the god of justice and lord of punishment. *Vimārga* : some have *kumārga,* 'bad ways.' *Kalpase=sampadyase* : K. Manu furnishes several examples of *klṛp* in the sense of 'to be sufficient,' 'to be fit :' ii, 151; ii, 266; vi, 20. Also Raghu-v, viii., 40. *Atanuṣu vibhaveṣu= utsaveṣu,* 'at times of festivity.' *Kukṣimbharibhis taiḥ kiṁ prayojanam,* 'What is the use of these parasitical gluttons as relations ?' : K. The Kolkata edition and Ś. have *saṁvibhaktāḥ* for *santu nāma.* The meaning may certainly be 'Let kinsmen make their appearance [*i.e.,* start up they will on all sides] when there is plenty of property to divide.' Kāṭavema refers to a verse towards the end of Act vi of this play, *yena yena viyujyante prajāḥ,* etc., 'Let it be publicly announced that of whatever dear kinsman his subjects are deprived, Duṣyanta will be (in the place of) that (kinsman) to them, the wicked excepted.'

2. 'The terrace of the fire-sanctuary, with the cow (that yields the ghee) for the oblations close by, is beautiful after its recent purification.' *Sa-śrika, lit.,* 'possessed of the goddess of beauty;' a bold metaphor, occurring elsewhere in Kālidāsa. *Homa-dhenu, Agni-śaraṇa* : *see* p. 18, note 3.

Verses 110. *Mālinī* or *Māninī* (variety of *Ati-Śakkarī*). *See* Verses 10, 19, 20, 38, 55.

राजा : (आरुह्य परिजनांसावलम्बी तिष्ठति) वेत्रवति। किमुद्दिश्य भगवता काश्यपेन मत्सकाशम् ऋषयः प्रेरिताः स्युः।

किं तावद् व्रतिनाम् उपोढतपसां विघ्नैस् तपो दूषितं
धर्मारण्यचरेषु केनचिद् उत प्राणिष्वसच्चेष्टितम्।
आहोस्वित् प्रसवो ममापचरितैर् विष्टम्भितो वीरुधाम्
इत्यारूढबहुप्रतर्कम् अपरिच्छेदाकुलं मे मनः[1] ।। 111 ।

प्रतीहारी : सुअरिदणन्दिणो इसीओ देवं सभाजइदुं आअदेत्ति

प्रतीहारी : सुचरितनन्दिन ऋषयो देवं सभाजयितुम्[2] आगता इति **तक्केमि।**

तर्कयामि।

[ततः प्रविशन्ति गौतमीसहिताः शकुन्तलां पुरस्कृत्य मुनयः। पुरश्चैषां कञ्चुकी पुरोहितश्च]

कञ्चुकीः : इत इतो भवन्तः।

शार्ङ्गरवः : शारद्वत।

महाभागः कामं नरपतिर् अभिन्नस्थितिर् असौ
न कश्चिद् वर्णानाम् अपथम् अपकृष्टोऽपि भजते।
तथापीदं शश्वत् परिचितविविक्तेन मनसा
जनाकीर्णं मन्ये हुतवहपरीतं गृहम्[3] इव ।। 112 ।।

1. 'Has the devotion [penance] of the ascetics who have just commenced (their) penitential rites been frustrated by impediments ? or else has any harm been inflicted by any one on the animals grazing in the sacred grove ? Or is it that the flowering of the creeping plants has been checked [stopped, stunted] through my misdeeds; thus my mind, in which so many doubtful-conjectures have arisen, is perplexed with an inability to decide.' *Upoḍha=samprāpta* : K. *Vighnais* : see p. 40, note 5. *Dharmāraṇya-careṣu prāṇiṣu* : Compare 12, 1. 8. *Āhosvit*, a particle of doubt. *Prasava, i.e., puṣpa-phalādi*, 'the flowers, fruit, etc.' : K. *Apacaritaiḥ=durācāraiḥ.*

2. 'To pay homage to.' *Sabhāj* is one of the few dissyllabic roots.

3. 'Granted that this king eminet-in-virtues [of high parts] swerves not from rectitude; (and that) none of the classes, (not)

Verse 111. Śārdūla-vikrīḍita (variety of *Atidhṛti*). *See* Verses 14, 30, 36, 39, 50, 63, 79, 85, 86, 89, 97, 98.

Verse 112. *Śikhariṇī* (variety of *Atyaṣṭi*). *See* Verses 9, 24, 44, 62.

शारद्वतः : स्थाने भवान् पुरप्रवेशाद् इत्थम्भूतः संवृत्तः।। अहमपि-

अभ्यक्तमिव स्नातः शुचिर् अशुचिमिव प्रबुद्ध इव सुप्तम्।
बद्धमिव स्वैरगतिर् जनम् इह सुखसङ्गिनम् अवैमि[1] ।। 113 ।।

शकुन्तला : (निमित्तं सूचयित्वा) अम्महे किं मे वामेदरं णअणं विप्फरदि।

शकुन्तला : (निमित्तं सूचयित्वा)[2] अहो किं मे वामेतरं नयनं विस्फुरति।

गौतमी : जादे। पडिहदं अमङ्गलं। सुहाइं दे भत्तुकुलदेवदाओ वितरन्दु।

गौतमी : जाते। प्रतिहतम् अमङ्गलम्। शुभानि ते भर्तृकुलदेवता वितरन्तु।

(इति परिक्रामति)

(इति परिक्रामति)

even the lowest, addicts itself to evil courses; nevertheless with my mind perpetually fimiliarized to seclusion I regard this thronged (palace) as a house enveloped in flames.' *Kāmam* occurs frequently in this sense : compare p. 24, note 2; p. 105, note 1. *Abhinna-sthitiḥ=avihata-maryādaḥ* : K.=*sa-maryādaḥ* : Ś. *Asau* : so reads the Mackenzie MS. and Bengāli; the others have *aho. Varṇānām, i.e., brāhmaṇādīṇām. Apakṛṣṭo' pi, i.e.,* The classes or castes were originally four in number :—1. Brāhmaṇas or priests; 2. Kṣatriyas or soldiers; 3. Vaiśyas or merchants and husbandmen; 4. Śūdra or slaves : *see* page 84, note 1. *Apatha,* ' wrong road,' 'a bad road;' a common metaphor like *amārga, unmārga, vimārga,* to express wicked courses. *Idaṁ janākīrṇam, i.e., idaṁ puro-varti nṛpāṅgaṇam,* 'this royal court before me eyes :' Ś. *janākīrṇam* may perhaps be used, as in line 2, Act 2 of Vikramorvaśīya, for a substantive meaning 'a crowded thoroughfare.' *Hutavaha-parītam=lagnāgnim* : Ś.

1. 'I also regard (these) people here devoted to pleasure, as one-who-has-performed-his-ablutions (regards) one-smeared (with oil), as the pure the impure; as the waking the sleeping; as he-whose-motion-is-free the bound.'

2. See p. 20, note 3. One MS. has *durnimittam* 'a bad omen.'

Verse 113. *Āryā* or *Gāthā*. *See* Verse 2.

— — |⏑ ⏑ —| — — ‖⏑ ⏑ ⏑ ⏑|⏑ ⏑ —|⏑ — ⏑|⏑ ⏑ —|—
— ⏑ ⏑| — — |⏑ ⏑ —‖⏑ ⏑ ⏑ ⏑|⏑ ⏑ —| ⏑ |⏑ ⏑ —|⏑

पुरोहित : (राजानं निर्दिश्य) भो भोस् तपस्विनः। असाव् अत्रभवान् वर्णाश्रमाणां रक्षिता[1] प्रागेव मुक्तासनो[2] वः प्रतिपालयति। पश्यतैनम्।

शार्ङ्गरवः : भो महाब्राह्मण। कामम् एतद् अभिनन्दनीयं। तथापि वयम् अत्र मध्यस्थाः।[3] कुतः।

भवन्ति नम्रास् तरवः फलागमैर्
नवाम्बुभिर् दूरविलम्बिनो घनाः।
अनुद्धताः सत्पुरुषाः समृद्धिभिः
स्वभाव एवैष परोपकारिणाम्[4] ।। 114 ।।

प्रतीहारी : देव। पसणमुहवणा दोसन्ति। जाणामि। विस्सद्धकब्जा

प्रतीहारी : देव। प्रसन्नमुखवर्णा दृश्यन्ते। जानामि। विश्रब्धकार्या

1. 'The protector of the (four) classes and (four) orders :' see p. 190, note 3. in middle, and p. 155, note 3 at end.

2. 'Having but just quitted the seat (of justice).' See p. 186, note 6 at end.

3. 'This is certainly a subject of rejoicing [to be rejoiced at]; nevertheless we here are indifferent parties [have nothing to do with it],' *i.e.*, 'Our merits and interests have nothing to do with his conduct.' 'This favour and pretection is onlywhat might be expected from his benevolent nature.' It is possible that by *vayaṁ madhyasthāḥ* may be meant, 'we are indifferent persons,' 'we have no suit to urge nor petition to present.'

4. 'Because trees become bent down by the growing-weight of fruit; clouds hang down the more (when charged) with fresh rain; good men are not made arrogant by abundant riches : this is the very nature of the benefactors of others.' *Kutas* : see p. 54, note 4. *Bhūri* : generally found in composition, but not always : see Mahābh., xii, 1410. Most of the Bengālī MSS. have *dūra.* This verse occurs in Bhartṛhari [ii, 62, edit. Bohlen], where *udgamaiḥ* is adopted for *āgamaiḥ,* and another reading *bhūmi* for *bhūri* is noticed. Oriental poets are fond of adducing trees and clouds as examples of disinterested liberality. 'The tree does not remove its shade from him who cuts it down :' Hitop., 1. 353.

Verse 114. *Vanśasthavila* (variety of *Jagatī*) *See* Verses 18, 22, 23, 67, 81.

इसीओ।

ऋषय :[1]

राजा : (शकुन्तलां दृष्ट्वा) अथात्रभवती।

का स्विद् अवगुण्ठनवती नातिपरिस्फुटशरीरलावण्या।[2]

मध्ये तपोधनानां किसलयम् इव पाण्डुपत्राणाम्।। 115।।

प्रतीहारी : देव। कुदूहलगब्भो पहिदो ण मे तक्को पसरदि। णं

प्रतीहारी : देव। कुतूहलगर्भः प्रहितो न मे तर्कः प्रसरति।[3] ननु

दंसणोआ दण से आकिदी लक्खीअदि।

दर्शनीया पुनर् अस्या आकृतिर् लक्ष्यते।

राजा : भवतु। अनिर्वर्णनीयं[4] परकलत्रम्।

शकुन्तला : (हस्तम् उरसि कृत्वा आत्मगतं) हिअअ। किं एव्वं

शकुन्तला : (हस्तम् उरसि कृत्वा आत्मगतं) हृदय। किम् एवं

वेबसि। अज्जउत्तस्स भावं ओधारिअ धीरं दाव होहि।

वेपसे। आर्यपुत्रस्य भावम् अवधार्य धीरं तावद् भव।[5]

1. 'The *Ṛṣis* appear to have serene complexions. (Hence) I conclude they have some business which may inspire confidence.' *Prasanna-mukhaḥ-varṇāḥ* : so read two of the Devanāgarī MSS. supported by a similar compound in Mālavikāgn., p. 55, l. 20. The Colebrooke has *maṇḍana* and my own *paṅkā* for *vaṇṇā*.

2. 'Who is this veiled-one, the loveliness of whose person is not fully displayed ?' *Svit* is a particle of question and doubt. *Avaguṇṭhana=mastakācadana-vastra* : Ch. The second half of this verse is clear.

3. 'The suspicion [conjecture] engendered by my curiosity does not seem appropriate.' The Mackenzie MS., supported by K., has *paḍihādi* for *pratibhāti* [in place of *pasaradi* for *prasarati*, the reading of the other Devanāgarī] and *paḍihado* for *pahido*. I have retained *pahido*, as it appears to make the best sense; but the Prākṛt seems here hardly to admit of literal Sanskṛt interpretation.

4. 'Ought not to be gazed at.' *Anirvarṇanīyam=adarśanīyam.*

5. 'Having reflected on [called to mind], the affection of thy

---

Verse 115. *Āryā* or *Gāthā*. *See* Verse 2.

—◡◡|◡—◡|◡◡—|| —◡◡ |—◡◡|◡—◡|——|—

—— |◡—◡| —— ||◡◡◡◡|◡◡—| ◡ |——|—

पुरोहित : (पुरो गत्वा) एते विधिवद् अर्चितास् तपस्विनः। कश्चिद् एषाम् उपाध्यायसन्देशः[1] । तं देवः श्रोतुम् अर्हति।

राजा : अवहितोऽस्मि।

ऋषयः : (हस्तान् उद्यम्य) विजयस्व राजन्।

राजा : सर्वान् अभिवादये।

ऋषय : इष्टेन युज्यस्व।

राजा : अपि निर्विघ्नतपसो[2] मुनयः।

ऋषय :

कुतो धर्मक्रियाविघ्नः सतां रक्षितरि त्वयि।
तमस् तपति घर्मांशौ कथम् आविर्भविष्यति[3] ।। 116 ।।

राजा :अर्थवान् खलु मे राजशब्दः।[4] अथ भगवाँल्लोकानुग्रहाय कुशली काश्यपः।[5]

lord, be firm.' *Bhāva=sneha* : compare p, 111, note 3. The Bengālī have *smṛtvā* for *avadhārya. Ārya-putra,* 'son of a venerable parent,' is the regular dramatic mode of addressing a husband.

1. 'Has a message from the preceptor.' A Bahuvrīhi agreeing with *kaścit.*

2. *See* page 35, note 3, and compare page 89, note 1.

3. 'Whence (can there be) obstruction to the religious rites of the good, thou being (their) defender ? How should darkness appear, the Sun emitting light [when the Sun shines] ?' *Tapati,* loc. case of the present part., here used absolutely. *Gharmāṁśau=sūrye* : Ś. The Dictionary gives *gharma-raśmi.*

4. 'My title of Rājā has indeed significancy.' The *Ṛṣis* had, in the preceding verse, compared the king to the Sun, and *rājan* is derived from *rāj,* 'to shine.' It is, however, probable that the play is on the words *rājan* and *rakṣitṛ.* Compare Manu, vii, 3. *Rakṣārtham asya sarvasya rājājam asṛjat prabhuḥ,* 'The Supreme Being created a king for the protection of this universe.' Dr. Boehtlingk remark that in these cases it little signifies whether the derivation be true of false. In Mahābh., xii, 1032, *rājan* is derived from the root *rañj,* to conciliate.'

5. 'Is his reverence Kāśyapa prosperous for the welfare of the

---

Verse 116. *Ślokā* or *Anuṣṭubh. See* Verses 5, 6, 11, 12, 26, 47, 50, 51, 53, 73, 76, 84, 87.

ऋषय : स्वाधीनकुशलाः सिद्धिमन्तः। स भवन्तम् अनामयप्रश्नपूर्वकम् इदम् आह।[1]

राजा : किम् आज्ञापयति भगवान्।

शार्ङ्गरवः : यन् मिथःसमयाद् इमां मदीयां दुहितरं भवान् उपायंस्त।[2] तन् मया प्रीतिमता युवयोर् अनुज्ञातम्। कुतः।

त्वम् अर्हतां प्राग्रसरः स्मृतोऽसि नः
शकुन्तला मूर्तीमती च सत्क्रिया।
समानयंस् तुल्यगुणं वधूवरं
चिरस्य वाच्यं न गतः प्रजापतिः[3] ।। 117 ।।

world ?' *Kuśalī* : see p. 35, note 3. *Bhagavāl*, etc : When the letter *l* is preceded by *t, d*, or *n* dental, is requires the assimilation of the letters to itself, and in the case of dental *n*, the mark called candravindu is written over, to show that the *l* substituted for it has a nasal sound : Laghu-Kaum., No. 79.

1. 'Saints [*lit.*, men endowed with or capable of perfection : Viṣ. Pur., p. 45] have prosperity in their power. He with inquiries about your safety says this to your highness.' It will be readily remarked that the character of these *Ṛsis* is evidently that of plain, honest independent men. *Anāmaya* : *see* Manu, ii., 127, 'Let a man ask a Brāhmaṇa, on meeting him, as to his *kuśalam;* a Kṣatriya, as to his *anāmayam;* a Vaiśya, as to his *kṣemam;* and a Śūdra, as to his *ārogyam.*' The king was of course a Kṣatriya : see page 31, note 1.

2. The 3rd. sing. 3rd. pret. *ātm.* of *yam* with *upa* (meaning 'to marry') is either *upāyata* or *upāyansta* : Pāṇini, i, 2, 16. The Bengālī have the 2d. pret., *upayeme.*

3. 'Thou art esteemed by us the chief of the worthy, and Śakuntalā, incarnate virtue. Brahmā [the Lord of creatures] bringing together a bride and bridegroom of equal merit, has after a long time (now first) incurred no censure.' *Naḥ*, the Colebrooke MS. reads *yat. Vadhū-varam*, a Dvandva compound in the neuter gender. *Vācyaṁ na gataḥ* : whether Brahmā was famous for presiding over ill-assorted marriages, or whether there may be some allusion here to the bad character he obtained among the gods by his incestuous attempt on the virtue of his own daughter, is not clear.

Verse 117. *Vanśasthavila* (variety of *Jagatī*). *See* Verses 18, 22, 23, 67, 81, 114.

तद् इदानीम् आपन्नसत्त्वा प्रतिगृह्यतां सहधर्मचरणायेति।[1]

गौतमी : अज्ज। किम्पि वत्तुकामम्हि। ण मे वअणावसरो अत्थि।

गौतमी : आर्य। किमपि वक्तुकामास्मि। न मे वचनावसरोऽस्ति।

कहंत्ति।

कथमिति।

णाबेक्खिदो गुरुअणो इमिणा ण तुएबि पुच्छिदो बन्धू।

नापेक्षितो गुरुजनोऽनया न त्वयापि पृष्टो बन्धुः।

एक्कक्कं एव्व चरिए किं भणदु एक्क एक्कस्स।। 118।।

एकैकम् एवं चरिते किं भणतु एक एकस्य[2] ।। 118।।

शकुन्तला : (आत्मगतं) किं णुक्खु अज्जउत्तो भणादि।

शकुन्तला : (आत्मगतं) किं नु खलु आर्यपुत्रो भणति।

1. 'Therefore now let her, being quick with child, be received, for the joint discharge of religious-rites,' *i.e.*, those rites or *saṁskāras*, which were performed for the child before and after birth, probably by the parents con jointly [*saha*] : *see* Manu, ii, 27, etc.

2. 'Her elder-relatives were not referred to by her; nor by you was any kinsman asked; (the affair) having been transacted quite privately [*lit.*, one with the other, *i.e.*, in a private tēte-ā-tēte], what has each one to say to the other ?' *Guru-jana* : *see* p. 171, note 2 in middle. The Devanāgarī MSS. have *imāe* for *imiṇā*. The latter, which is the reading of the oldest Bengāli, I have retained on account of the metre. There is no reason why in Prākṛt *imiṇa* should not be used for the fem. instrum., since *imassim* is admissible for the fem. loc. : see p. 37, l. 1. *Ekaitam=anyonyam*, 'mutually :' Ś., Ch. *Bhaṇṇadu* is the reading of some of the Bengālī MSS. followed by the Kolkata edition; I have written *bhaṇṇadu* for *bhaṇādu*, on account of the metre, and on the authority of Lassen's Inst. Prak., p. 277. The Devanāgarī have *kiṁ bhaṇāmi;* which reading violates the metre and makes the construction of the sentence very obscure. They also read *ekkam ekkassa*. *Eka* may be for *eka-janaḥ*, applicable to either gender. The commentary of Candraśekhara is in favour of the above interpretation.

Verse 118. Āryā *or Gāthā*. (*See* Verse 2.)

— — | ⏑ — ⏑ | ⏑ ⏑ — || ⏑ ⏑ — | ⏑ ⏑ — | ⏑ — ⏑ | — — | —
— — | ⏑ — ⏑ | ⏑ ⏑ — || — — | ⏑ ⏑ — | ⏑ | — — | —

राजा : किम् इदम् उपन्यस्तम्।

शकुन्तला : (आत्मगतं) पावओक्खु एसो वअणोबणासो।

शकुन्तला : (आत्मगतं) पावकः खलु एष वचनोपन्यासः।[1]

शार्ङ्गरवः : कथम् इदं नाम। भवन्त एव सुतरां लोकवृत्तान्तनिष्णाताः।[2]

सतीमपि ज्ञातिकुलैकसंश्रयां
जनोऽन्यथा भर्तृमतीं विशङ्कते।
अतः समीपे परिणेतुर् इष्यते
तदप्रियापि प्रमदा स्वबन्धुभिः[3] ।। 119 ।।

राजा : किं चात्रभवती मया परिणीतपूर्वा।

शकुन्तला : (सविषादं आत्मगतं) हिअअ। सम्पदं दे आसङ्का।

शकुन्तला : (सविषादं आत्मगतं) हृदय। साम्प्रतं ते आशङ्का।

शार्ङ्गरवः : किं कृतकार्यद्वेषाद् धर्मं प्रति विमुखतोचिता राज्ञः।[4]

1. 'Truly, the import of this speech [that which is proposed by this speech] is (like) fire.' The Mackenzie MS. insert *eso* after *kkhu.*

2. 'Such-persons-as-your-majesty are certainly full well acquainted with the ways of the world.' *Loka-vṛttānta-niṣṇātāḥ=loka-vyavahāra-jñātāḥ* Ś. *Ni-ṣṇāta* (*=abhijña* : Ch.) *lit.*, 'bathed in;' hence 'conversant with.' The Sāhit.-darp. [p. 193] reads *bhavāṇ loka-vṛttānte niṣṇātaḥ.*

3. 'People suspect a married-women [woman who has a husband] residing wholly in her kinsmen's family although chaste, (to be) the reverse. Hence, a young woman is preferred by her own relatives (to be) near her husband, even though she be disliked by him.' *Jñāti,* etc.*=nija-gṛha-vāsinīm* : Ś. *Anyathā, i.e., vyabhicāriṇīm,* unchaste :' Ś. *Iṣyate=ākāsṅkṣyate* : Ś. *Tadapriyāpi* : the Bengālī, my own MS., and the Sāh.-darp. read *priyāpriyā vā,* 'liked or disliked :' but K. supports the other reading.

4. 'On account of dislike to a deed done, is opposition to justice becoming in a king ?' This is the reading of the oldest Bengālī, and I have adopted is as preferable to that of the Devanāgarī, *Kiṁ kṛta-kārya-dveṣo dharmaṁ prati vimukhatā kṛtāvajñā.* Dr. Boehtlingk has endeavoured to solve the difficulty by suggesting that *kritavajñā*

Verse 119. *Vaṁśasthavila* (variety of *Jagatī.*) *See* Verses 18, 22, 23, 67, 81, 114, 117.

राजा : कुतोऽयम् असत्कल्पनाप्रश्नः।[1]

शार्ङ्गरवः : मूर्च्छन्त्यमी विकाराः प्रायेणैश्वर्यमत्तेषु।[2]

राजा : विशेषेणाधिक्षिप्तोऽस्मि।[3]

गौतमी : जादे। मुहुत्तअं मा लज्ज। अबणइस्सं दाव दे ओउण्ठणं। तदो तुमं भट्टा अहिजाणिस्सदि (इति यथोक्तं करोति)

गौतमी : जाते। मुहूर्तं मा जलञ्जस्व। अपनेष्यामि तावत् ते अवगुण्ठनम्। ततस् त्वां भर्त्ता अभिज्ञास्यति (इति यथोक्तं करोति)

राजा : शकुन्तलां निर्वर्ण्य (आत्मगतं)

इदम् उपनतम् एवं रूपम् अक्लिष्टकान्ति
प्रथमपरिगृहीतं स्यान् न वेत्यव्यवस्यन्।
भ्रमर इव विभाते कुन्दम् अन्तस्तुषारं
न खलु च परिभोक्तुं नैव शक्नोमि हातुम्[4] ।। 120।।

should be struck out of the text, as being probably an interpolation from the margin. All the Devanāgarī, however, introduce it.

1. 'Whence is this inquiry (accompanied) by the fabrication of a falsehood ?' *Avidyamānārthasya kalpanayā kṛtaḥ prasnaḥ* : K.

2. 'These changes-of-purpose [fickleness of disposition] mostly take effect [wax strong] in those who are intoxicated with sovereign-power.' *Mūrchanti=vardhante* : Ś.=*vyāpnuvanti* : K. *Cf.* Ragh., xii, 57; vi, 9; x., 80. The root *mūrch* has generally the opposite sense, to 'lose strength,' 'grow weaker,' 'faint away.' It is applied to the thickening of darkness, in the Vikramorvaśiya, Act 3, *tamasāṁ niśi mūrchatām*.

3. 'I am especially aimed-at-by-this censure,' *i.e.,* I am the especial object of this censorious remark about 'persons intoxicated with power.'

4. 'Not settling-in-my-mind [not deciding or determining] whether this form of unblemished beauty thus presented (to me) [brought near to me] may or may not have been formerly married [by me]; verily I am neither able to enjoy nor to abandon (it), like a

---

Verse 120. *Mālinī* or *Māninī* (variety of *Ati-Śakkarī*). *See* Verses 10, 19, 20, 38, 55, 109, 110.

इति विचारयन् स्थितः।।

प्रतीहारी : अहो धम्मावेक्खिदा भट्टिणो। ईदिसं णाम सुहोबणदं रूबं प्रतीहारी : अहो धर्मावेक्षिता भर्तुः। ईदृशं नाम सुखोपनतं रूपं **देक्खिअ को अणो विआरेदि।** प्रेक्ष्य कोऽन्यो विचारयति।

शार्ङ्गरवः : भो राजन्। किमिति जोषम् आस्यते।[1]

राजा : भोस् तपोधनाः। चियन्नपि न खलु स्वीकरणम्[2] अत्रभवत्याः स्मरामि। तत् कथम् इमाम् अभिव्यक्तसत्त्वलक्षणां प्रत्यात्मानं क्षेत्रिणम् आशङ्कमानः प्रतिपत्स्ये।[3]

शकुन्तला : (अपवार्य) अज्जस्स परिणए एव्व सन्देहो। कुदो दाणिं शकुन्तला : (अपवार्य) आर्यस्य परिणये एव सन्देहः। कुत इदानीं **मे दूराहिरोहिणी आसा।** मे दूराधिरोहिणी आशा।

शार्ङ्गरवः : मा तावत्–

कृताभिमर्शाम् अनुमन्यमानः
सुतां त्वया नाम मुनिर् विमान्यः।

bee at the break of day, the jasmine-blossom filled with dew.' *Aklișța-kānti=anavadya-saundaryam* : K. *Parigṛhītam* : see p. 178, note 5. *Avyavasyan* [=*aniścinvan*] so reads Kāțavema; I have ventured to follow him, although nearly all the Devanāgarī MSS. have *vyavasyan*. Compare p. 144, 1. 8, note 2, and p. 159, 1. 6. If *vyavasyan* is retained, it must be translated 'deliberating,' 'striving to discover.'

1. 'Why do you sit [is it sat] so silent ?' *Kimartharh maunam kṛtam asti* Ś. *Kim tūșṇīm evāste* : Vikram., Act 4.

2. *Svīkaraṇam* [=*vivāham* : Ś.j] *lit.*, 'making one's own,' *i.e.*, 'taking in marriage.'

3. 'How, then, shall I act towards her, bearing evident signs of pregnancy, doubting myself to be her husband.' *Katham pratipatsye* may mean 'how shall I make any reply ?' referring to *kiṁ joșam āsyate* in the previous speech; or, 'how shall I receive her ?' see p. 133, note 1.

मुष्टं प्रतिग्राहयता स्वम् अर्थं
पात्रीकृतो दस्युर् इवासि येन[1] ।। 121 ।।

शारद्वतः : शार्ङ्गरव। विरम त्वम् इदानीं। शकुन्तले। वक्तव्यम् उक्तम् अस्माभिः। सोऽयम् अत्रभवान् एवम् आह। दीयताम् अस्मै प्रत्ययप्रतिवचनम्।

शकुन्तला : (अपवार्य) इमं अवत्थन्तरं गदे तारिसे अणुराए किं वा
शकुन्तला : (अपवार्य) इदम् अवस्थान्तरं गते तादृशेऽनुरागे किं वा
सुमराबिदेण। अत्ता दाणिं मे सोअणीओत्ति[2] ववसिदं (प्रकाशं) अज्जउत्त
(स्मारितेन) आत्मा इदानीं में शोचनीय इति व्यवसितम्।। प्रकाशम्।। आर्यपुत्र।।
इत्यर्द्धोक्ते।। संसइदे दाणिं परिणए ण एसो समुदाआरो। पोरव।
इत्यर्द्धोक्ते।। संशयिते इदानीं परिणये न एष समुदाचारः।[3] पौरव।
ण जुत्तं णाम दे तह पुरा अस्समपदे सहावुत्ताणहिअअं इमं जणं
न युक्तं नाम ते तथा पुरा आश्रमपदे स्वभावोत्तानहृदयम् इमं जनं

1. 'It the Sage after-consenting to his daughter, who had been seduced [carnally-embraced] by thee, to be (thus) insulted forsooth? (he) by whom allowing his stolen property [*i.e.*, Śakuntalā] to be kept [taken], thou hast been made as it were a justified revisher [robber].' *Kṛtābhimarśām=kṛta-saṁsparśām=kṛta-saṅgrahaṇām* : K. The first sense of *abhi-mriś* is 'to touch,' 'to handle.' Here as in *parā-mṛś* [Bhaṭṭi, xvii, 38] there is an implication of carnal connexion. *Muṣṭam* : the Taylor MS. has *iṣṭam*, and Bengālī *duṣṭam*. It must be borne in mind that Śakuntalā was married to Duṣyanta according to the Gāndharva form [p. 126, note 3] during the absense of her foster-father : *see* pp. 132, 133 with notes. *Pratigrāhayatā* : the causal may sometimes give the sense of 'allowing,' or 'permitting,' as in *nāśayati*, 'he suffers to perish.' *Pātrīkṛto*, a very noticeable phrase, is a Cvī compound, formed from *pātram*, a neuter noun meaning 'a receptacle,' applied to express any deserving or worthy person : see Manu, iv, 227.

2. Kāṭavema, Śaṅkara, and the old Bengālī MS. interpret *soanīo* by *śocanīya*, 'to be sorrowed for;' but Candra-śekhara has *śodhanīya*, and is followed by Chēzy and the Kolkata adition. The meaning will then be 'I mayself am now to be cleared [justified] by myself.' All the MSS., except one, insert *me*.

3. 'Now that my marriage is called-in-question, this is not the

---

Verse 121. *Upajāti* or *Ākhyānakī* (variety of *Triṣṭubh*). *See* Verse 41, 107.

समअपुव्वं पतारिअ ईदिसेहिं अक्खरेहिं पच्चाचक्खिदुं।

समयपूर्वं प्रतार्य ईदृशैर् अक्षरैः प्रत्याचष्टुम्।[1]

राजा : (कर्णौ पिधाय) शान्तम्। पापम्।[2]

व्यपदेशम् आविलयितुं किम् ईहसे जनम् इमं च पातयितुम्।

कूलङ्कषेव सिन्धुः प्रसन्नम् अम्भस् तटतरुं च[3]।। 122।।

शकुन्तला : होदु। जइ परमत्थदो परपरिग्गहसङ्किणा तुए एव्वं पउत्तं।

शकुन्तला : भवतु। यदि परमार्थतः परपरिग्रहशङ्किना त्वया एवं प्रवृत्तम्।

ता अहिणाणेण इमिणा तुह आसङ्कं अबणइस्सं।

तद् अभिज्ञानेन अनेन तव आशङ्काम् अपनेष्यामि।

(proper) form-of-address :' see p. 193, note 5. All the MSS. agree in reading *samudāro* for *samudācāro;* otherwise it might be suspected that *samudāhāro* was the correct word, to which *samudācāro* must be here equivalent.

1. 'It is not becoming in thee, having a while since in the hermitage seduced, after-a-formal-agreement, this person [myself] naturally open hearted, to repudiate her with such words.' *Uttāna,* 'shallow,' 'unreserved,' is the opposite of *gambhīra,* 'deep,' 'reserved :' see p. 39, note 1. *Samaya-pūrvam* : compare, p. 195, 1. 4; and p. 171, 1. 1 of the notes.

2. 'Peace ! a sin !' *i.e.,* 'Silence ! let me not listen to such sinful words;' or, if no stop is placed after *śāntam,* 'May the sin be palliated !' This seems to be the usual formula in the plays for averting the ill effects of blasphemous, malevolent, or lying words. Sometimes the stage-direction *karṇau pidhāya* is omitted : compare Acts vii, 57; Mṛch., 36, 1. 5; p. 230, 1. 6; p. 306, 1. 9; p. 329, 1. 1. Mālavik., p. 69, 1. 10. Mudr., p. 24, 1. 5.

3. 'Why seekest thou to sully the royal-title [race, family] and to ruin the person [myself]; as a stream that-carries-away-its-own-banks (disturbs) the clear water (and overturns) the tree on its margin ?' *Vyapadeśam, i.e., kūlam nāma vā,* 'either family or name :' Ch. *Vyapdiśyate anena iti vyapadeśaḥ kūlam* : Ś. *Āvilayitum* : infin. of a nom. verb from *āvila,* 'turbid.' *Sindhuh,* 'a river;' in Sanskṛt always feminine.

Verse 122. *Āryā* or *Gāthā.* (*See* Verse 2.)

⏑⏑—|⏑—⏑|⏑⏑—‖⏑—⏑|—⏑⏑|⏑—⏑|⏑⏑|—

—— |⏑—⏑| —— ‖⏑——⏑| —— | ⏑ |⏑⏑—|⏑

राजा : उदारः कल्पः।

शकुन्तला : (मुद्रास्थानं परामृश्य) हद्धी हद्धी। अङ्गुलीअअसुणा

शकुन्तला : मुद्रास्थानं परामृश्य।। हाधिक् हाधिक् अङ्गुलीयकशून्या

मे अङ्गुली (इति सविषादं गौतमीम् अवेक्षते)।

मे अङ्गुलिः (इति सविषादं गौतमीम् अवेक्षते)।

गौतमी : णूणं दे सक्कावदारब्भन्तरे सचीतित्थसलिलं वन्दमाणाए

गौतमी : नूनं ते शक्रावताराभ्यन्तरे शचीतीर्थसलिलं वन्दमानायाः

पब्भट्टं अङ्गुलीअअं।

प्रभ्रष्टम् अङ्गुलीयकम्।[1]

राजा : (सस्मितं) इदं तत् प्रत्युत्पन्नमति स्त्रैणमिति यद् उच्यते।[2]

शकुन्तला : एत्थ दाव विहिणा दंसिदं पहुत्तणं। अबरं दे कहिस्सं।

शकुन्तला : अत्र तावद् दर्शितं प्रभुत्वं।[3] अपरं ते कथयिष्यामि।

राजा : श्रोतव्यम् इदानीं संवृत्तम्।[4]

1. 'In all probability the ring slipped from (the finger of) thee as thou wert offering homage to the water as Śacī's holy-pool, within Śakrāvatāra.' Śakra is a name of Indra, and Śakrāvatāra some sacred place of pilgrimage where he descended upon earth. Śacī is his wife, to whom there was probably a *tīrtha,* or holy bathing-place [*see* p. 17, note 1], consecrated at this place, where Śakuntalā had performed her ablutions.

2. 'This is that which is said [thus is proved The truth of the proverb] "Woman-kind is ready-witted."' *Straiṇam=strī-jātiḥ,* 'the female sex :' K. The Bengālī have *idaṁ tat pratyutpanna-matitvaṁ strīṇām* : compare Hitop., 1. 2320, where *pratyutpanna-matiḥ* is the name given to the ready-witted fish. See also Hitop., line 2338, 'The food of women is said to be two-fold, their wit four-fold, their cunning six-fold, and their passion eight-fold.'

3. 'Here, however, sovereignty has been shown by destiny.' A similar sentiment occurs further on in this play, and at the beginning of the 4th Act of the Vikramorvaśīya, *bhavitavyatā atra balavatī.* 'Here destiny has shown its power.'

4. Dr. Boehtlingk considers that *śrotavyam* is here taken as a substantive, and construes, 'The moment-for-hearing (what else

शकुन्तला : णं एक्कदिअहे णोमालिआमण्डबे णलिणीपत्तभाअणगअं

शकुन्तला : ननु एकदिवसे नवमालिकामण्डपे[1] नलिनीपत्रभाजनगतम्

उअअं तुह हत्थे सणिहिदं आसि।

उदकं तव हस्ते सन्निहितम् आसीत्।

राजा : शृणुमस् तावत्।

शकुन्तला : तक्खणं सो मे पुत्तकिदओ दीहापङ्गो णाम मिअपो-

शकुन्तला : तत्क्षणं स मे पुत्रकृतको दीर्घापाङ्गो[2] नाम मृगपो-

दओ उबट्ठिदो। तुए अअं दाव पढमं पिअउत्ति अणुअम्पिणा उब-

तक उपस्थितः। त्वया अयं तावत् प्रथमं पिबतु इति अनुकम्पिना उप-

च्छन्दिदो उअएण। ण उण दे अपरिचआदो हत्थब्भासं उबगदो।

च्छन्दित[3] उदकेन। न पुनस् से अपरिचयाद् हस्ताभ्यासम् उपगतः।

पच्छा तस्सिं एव्व मए गहिदे सलिले णेण किदो पणओ। तदा

पश्चात् तस्मिन्न् एव मया गृहीते सलिलेऽनेन कृतः प्रणयः।[4] तदा

तुमं इत्थं पहसिदोसि। सव्वो सगन्धेसु विस्ससदि। दुवेबि एत्थ

त्वम् इत्थं प्रहसितोऽसि। सर्वः सगन्धेषु[5] विश्वसिति। द्वावपि अत्र

you have to say) has now arrived :' compare page 110, line 7. As the passive participle is often used substantively the translation may be 'What took place is now to be heard.'

1. 'Lying in a lotus-leaf-cup.' As to *gatam* : see p. 38, note 1. As to *sannihitam* : *see* p. 149, l. 6, with note.

2. 'Having eyes with long outer corners.' This was the fawn mentioned p. 166, l. 3.

3. *Upacchanditaḥ=jala-pānāya preritaḥ*, 'was coaxed to drink the water :' Ś.=*pralobhitaḥ*, 'enticed,' 'coaxed :' Chēzy. According to Pāṇini, I, 3, 47, the meaning of the root *chand* or *chadi* (10th conj.) with *upa* is 'to conciliate privately by flattering or coaxing language.' It occurs in Ragh., v, 58 where stenzler has translated it by *'obsecro,'* 'supplicate,' 'beg.'

4. *Praṇayaḥ* is here, 'trust,' 'confidence' (=*viśvāsaḥ* : Ś.)

5. 'In relatives.' *Sagandha=sadṛśa=sannihita*. *Gandha=sambandha* : Ś.

आरणआत्ति ।1

आरण्यकाविति ।

राजा : एवमादिभिर् आत्मकार्यनिवर्तिनीनाम् अनृतमयवाङ्मधुभिर् आकृष्यन्ते विषयिण: ।[2]

गौतमी : महाभाअ। ण अरुहसि एव्वं मन्तिदुं। तबोवणसंवड्ढिदो

गौतमी : महाभाग। न अर्हसि एवं मन्त्रयितुम्। तपोवनसंवर्धितो-

अणभिणो अअं जणो कइदवस्स।

ऽनभिज्ञोऽयं जन: कैतवस्य।

राजा : तापसवृद्धे ।[3]

स्त्रीणाम् अशिक्षितपटुत्वम् अमानुषीषु
सन्दृश्यते किमुत या: प्रतिबोधवत्य: ।
प्राग् अन्तरिक्षगमनात् स्वम् अपत्यजातम्
अन्यैर् द्विजै: परभृता: खलु पोषयन्ति[4] ।। 123 ।।

1. So reads my own MS. Kāṭavema has *ārannaa* [Lass. Inst. Prāk., p. 187], and interprets it by *āraṇyakau.* Some read *āraṇṇao* which seems to be an error *aranṇaāo* nom. pl. fem. The femine is admissible on the principle of the superiority of the human species over animals.

2. 'By such false honied words as these are voluptuaries allured by (women) repenting of their own deeds.' The Taylor and my own MS. have *nirvartinīnām.* The Mackenzie has *yoṣitāṁ madhura-grīrbhiḥ* for *anṛtamaya-vānmadhubhiḥ.*

3. According to Pāṇini, ii, 2, 38, *tāpasa-vṛddhā* is a legitimate compound, although *vṛddha-tāpasī* would be more usual.

4. 'The untaught cunning is observed of females (even) in-these-that-are-not-of-the-human-race [*i.e.,* even in animals]; how much more (of those) who are endowed with reason [*i.e.,* of women]. the female cuckoos, as-is-well-known [*khalu*] allow their own offspring to be reared by other birds, before soaring in the sky.' *Amānuṣīṣu; i.e., mānuṣa-jāti-vyatiriktāsu tiryag-jātiṣu* : K. *Pratibodhavatyaḥ=jñāninyaḥ=caitanya-bhājaḥ* : Ś. The most obvious sense of this word, if the context would allow it, would be, 'those women who have received instruction.' *Pra-bhṛtāḥ* : see p. 160, note 2.

Verse 123. *Vasanta-tilakā* (variety of *Śakkarī*). *See* Verses 8, 27, 31, 43, 46, 64, 74, 80, 82, 83, 91, 93, 94, 95, 100, 104, 105, 108.

शकुन्तला : (सरोषं) अणज्ज। अत्तणो हिअआणुमाणेण पेक्खसि।

शकुन्तला : (सरोषम्) अनार्य। आत्मनो हृदयानुमानेन प्रेक्षसे।

को दाणिं अणो धम्मकञ्चुअप्पवेसिणो तिणच्छणकूबोबमस्सः तव अणुकिदं

क इदानीम् अन्यो धमकञ्चुकप्रवेशिनस् तृणच्छन्नकूपोपमस्य तव अनुकृतं

पडिबदिस्सदि।

प्रतिपत्स्यते।[1]

राजा : (आत्मगतं)सन्दिग्धबुद्धिं मां कुर्वन्न् अकैतव इवास्याः कोपो लक्ष्यते।

तथा ह्यनया–

मय्येव विस्मरणदारुणचित्तवृत्तौ
वृत्तं रहःप्रणयम् अप्रतिपद्यमाने।
भेदाद् भ्रुवोः कुटिलयोर् अतिलोहिताक्ष्या
भग्नं शरासनम् इवातिरुषा स्मरस्य[2] ।। 124 ।।

(प्रकाशम्) भद्रे। प्रथितं दुष्यन्तस्य चरितम्। तथापीदं न लक्षये।

1. 'What other (person) now would act like [in imitation of] thee, that putting on the garb of virtue resemblest a grass-concealed well ?' *Prati-patsyate* : *see* p. 133, 1. 4, with note 1.

2. 'For (when) I, whose state of feeling was dreadfully-severe from the absence of (all) recollection, (persisted in) not admitting that affection had privately existed (between us); it (seemed) as if (the god) *Smara's* bow was snapped asunder by that very-red-eyed one with excessive anger, on the parting of her curved eyebrows.' The double-entendre in the word *Smara,* which means 'recollection' as well as 'the god of Love,' is noticeable. See the notes on Kāmadeva, p. 98, note 2, and p. 100, note 1. The figure by which the eyebrows of a beautiful woman are compared to Cupid's bow is common, and the glances from the eye are by a similar metaphor often likened to arrows discharged from it. Śakuntalā is said to break the bow by the parting of her eyebrows, which were contracted in anger, Possibly one effect of anger might be to wrinkle the brow, which would appear to separate the eyebrows.

Verse 124. *Vasanta-tilakā* (variety of *Śakkarī*). *See* Verses 8, 27, 31, 43, 46, 64, 74, 80, 82, 83, 91, 93, 94, 95, 100, 104, 105, 108, 123.

शकुन्तला : सुट्ठु दाव अत्त सच्छन्दचारिणी किदम्हि। जा अहं इमस्स
शकुन्तला : सुष्ठु तावद् अत्र स्वच्छन्दचारिणी।[1] कृतास्मि। या अहम् अस्य
पुरुवंसप्पच्चवएण मुहमहुणो हिअअट्ठिअविसस्स हत्थब्भासं उबगदा (इति
पुरुवंशप्रत्ययेन मुखमधोर् हृदयस्थितविषस्य हस्ताभ्यासम् उपगता (इति
पटान्तेन मुखम् आवृत्य रोदिति)।
पटान्तेन मुखम् आवृत्य रोदिति)।

शार्ङ्गरवः : इत्थम् आत्मकृतम् अप्रतिहतं चापलं दहति।[2]
अतः परीक्ष्य कर्तव्यं विशेषात् सङ्गतं रहः।
अज्ञातहृदयेष्वेवं वैरीभवति सौहृदम्[3] ।। 125 ।।

राजा : अयि भोः। किम् अत्रभवतीप्रत्ययाद् एवास्मान् सम्भृतदोषैर् अधिक्षिपथ।[4]

1. Literally, 'a wilful, self-willed woman,' 'one who acts on the impulse of the moment.' It may have this sense here, but Śaṅkara interprets it by *gaṇikā*, 'a wanton, unchaste woman.'

2. 'Thus a self-committed hasty-action, when not counteracted leads-to-keen-remorse [burns].' Most of the Devanāgarī MSS. have *parihatam* for *apratihatam;* the Mackenzie has *pratihatam;* the oldest Bengālī *apratihatam. Cāpalam* is 'any action proceeding from thoughtlessness or over-precipitation.' *Dahati* : the Hindūs connect a burning or smarting sensation with the idea of remorse of conscience : compare the equivalent expressions *manas-tāpa, paścāt-tāpa, anutāpa*, etc.

3. 'Therefore an union, expecially (when) in private, ought to be formed with-great-circumspection [after having made proper inquiry or experiment, *i.e.*, after investigating each other's character and circumstances]. Thus (is it that) between those who know not (each other's) hearts, friendship becomes enmity.' *Parīkṣya* : the Bengālī have *samīkṣya. Saṅgatam raha=rahasi saṅgamaḥ* : K.

4. 'Do you reproach us with accumulated accusations [faults] ?' Most of the Devanāgarī MSS. have *saṁyuta-doṣākṣareṇa kṣiṇutha*. The above is the reading of the oldest Bengālī, supported by Kāṭavema, who has *sambhṛta-doṣa karṣaṇena*.

Verse 125. *Śloka* or *Anuṣṭubh. See* Verses 5, 6, 11, 12, 26, 47, 50, 51, 53, 73, 76, 84, 87.

शार्ङ्गरवः : (सासूयम्[1]) श्रुतं भवद्भिर् अधरोत्तरम्।[2]

आजन्मनः शाठ्यम् अशिक्षितो यस्
तस्याप्रमाणं वचनं जनस्य।
परातिसन्धानम् अधीयते यैर्
विद्येति ते सन्तु किलाप्तवाचः[3] ।। 126।।

राजा : भोः सत्यवादिन्। अभ्युपगतं तावद् अस्माभिर् एवं। किं पुनर् इमाम् अतिसन्धाय लभ्यते।

शार्ङ्गरवः : विनिपातः।[4]

राजा : विनिपातः पौरवैः प्रार्थ्यत इति न श्रद्धेयम् एतत्।

शारद्वत : शार्ङ्गरव। किम् उत्तरेण। अनुष्ठितो गुरोः सन्देशः। प्रतिनिवर्तामहे वयम्। (राजानं प्रति)

1. 'Scornfully,' 'sarcastically;' *lit.*, 'with detraction.'

2. *Adharottaram=nikṛṣṭa-prādhānyam,* 'ascendancy of the base,' 'placing that at the top which ought to be at the bottom :' Ch. In Manu, viii, 53, the word occurs in the sense of 'confused and contradictory statement :' and again in vii, 21, it is applied to express the confusion of ranks [*adharam=śūdrādi; uttaram=pradhānam* : Schol.] which would ensue, if justice were not duly administered by the king. It may be translated here 'perversion of the truth,' 'confusion of principles,' 'inversion of the proper order of things,' and probably refers to the proverbial sentiment expressed in the succeeding verse.

3. 'The declaration of that person who from birth is untrained to guile (is) without authority. Let those persons, forsooth, by whom the deceiving of other is studied, calling it a science, be (alone considered) worthy of belief.' *Ājanmanaḥ* : *see* p. 153, note 4 at end. *Apramāṇam=ayathārtham* : Ś. *Atisandhānam* : compare p. 98, 1. 6. *Āpta-vācaḥ=yathārtha-vacanāḥ* : Ś.=*pramāna-vācaḥ* : K.

4. *Vinipāta=pratyavāya* : K.=*naraka-gamana* : Ś. 'ruin,' 'destruction.'

Verse 126. *Upajāti* or *Ākhyānakī* (variety of *Triṣṭubh1*). *See* Verses 41, 107, 121.

तद् एषा भवतः कान्ता त्यज वैनां गृहाण वा।
उपपन्ना हि दारेषु प्रभुता सर्वतोमुखी[1] ।। 127 ।।

गौतमी। गच्छाग्रतः।

[इति प्रस्थिताः]

शकुन्तला : कहं इमिणा किदवेण विप्पलद्धम्हि। तुम्हेबि मं परिदेविणिं
शकुन्तला : कथम् अनेन कितवेन विप्रलब्धास्मि। यूयमपि मां परिदेविनीं
परिच्चअह (इत्यनुप्रतिष्ठते)।
परित्यजथ (इत्यनुप्रतिष्ठते)।

गौतमी : (स्थित्वा) वच्छ सङ्गरव। अणुगच्छदि इअंक्खु णो
गौतमी : (स्थित्वा) वत्स शार्ङ्गरव। अनुगच्छति इयं खलु नः
करुणपरिदेविणी सउन्दला। पच्चादेसपरुसे भत्तुणि किं वा मे पुत्तिआ
करुणपरिदेविनी शकुन्तला। प्रत्यादेशपरुषे भर्तरि किं वा मे पुत्री
करिस्सदि।
करिष्यति।

शार्ङ्गरवः : सरोषं निवृत्य।। किं पुरोभागिनि स्वातन्त्र्यम् अवलम्बसे[2] ।। शकुन्तला भीता वेपते।।

1. 'She is, then, your wife : either abandon her or take her : for the authority over wives is admitted to be unlimited [reaching everywhere, unbounded].' *Kāntā* : the Bengālī MSS. have *patnī Sarvato-mukhī=sarva-karaṇa-samarthā,* 'omnipotent,' 'able to do everything :' Ch.=*sarva-prakāreṇa,* 'of every kind :' Ś. The literal meaning of the word is 'looking or facing in every direction.'

2. 'O naughty one, dost thou affect independence [art thou deter-mined to have thy own way] ?' *Puro-bhāgini=duṣṭe* : K.=*doṣaika-darśini=doṣaika-dṛk* : Ś. Ch. The first sense of *puro-bhāgin* is 'one who takes the first share or more than his proper share,' *i.e.,* 'a forward, grasping character.' In this sense it occurs at the end of 3rd Act of Vikram., *mā māṁ purobhāgīi'ti samarthayasi.* It next passes into the sense of 'a malevolent, censorious, calumniating person:' see Amarakoṣa. Lastly, as here, it seems to be used generally for 'a

Verse 127. *Śloka* or *Anuṣṭubh. See* Verses 5, 6, 11, 12, 26, 47, 50, 51, 53, 76, 84, 87, 125.

शार्ङ्गरवः : शकुन्तले!

यदि यथा वदति क्षितिपस् तथा
त्वम् असि किं पितुर् उत्कुलया त्वया।
अथ तु वेत्सि शुचि व्रतम् आत्मनः
पतिकुले तव दास्यमपि क्षमम्[1] ।। 128 ।।

तिष्ठ। साधयामो वयं।[2]

राजा : भोस् तपस्विन्। किम् अत्रभवतीं विप्रलभसे। कुतः।

कुमुदान्येव शशाङ्कः सविता बोधयति पङ्कजान्येव।
वशिनां हि परपरिग्रहसंश्लेषपराङ्मुखी वृत्तिः[3] ।। 129 ।।

wilful, pervers, wicked person.' Most of the Devanāgarī, unsupported by the Scholiasts, have *purobhāge. Svātantryam:* compare Manu ix, 3, *na strī svātantryam arhati;* and see p. 49, note 1.

1. 'If thou art so, as the king asserts, what (connection will remain) to the father with thee fallen from thy family [an outcast from thy family, degenerated]? But if thou art conscious that thy own marriage-vow [conduct] is free-from-taint [pure, inviolate], even slavery will be supportable in thy husband's household.' *Kiṁ pitur* : some of the Bengālī MSS. have *kiṁ punar utkulayā, i.e., Kula-vyavahārātikrameṇa vidyamānayā* : Ś. *Vratam = caritram,* 'conduct:' K. = *pati-vratam* : Ś.

2. 'We must set off on our return,' *lit.*, We must finish our business.

3. 'The moon awakes [expands] the night-lotuses only, the sun the day-lotuses only: for the character [feelings] of those who control their passions recoils [turns away with abhorrence] from embracing the wife of another.' *Kumuda* is a kind of lotus, which blossoms in the night [see p. 120, note 2] the *paṅkaja,* or mud-born lotus [Nelumbium speciosum] opens its petals only in the day. *Bodhayati = prakāsayati. Parigraha* : see p. 178, note 5.

Verse 128. *Druta-Vilambita* (variety of *Jagatī*). *See* Verses 45, 72.

Verse 129. *Āryā* or *Gāthā*. *See* Verse 2.

⏑⏑—| —⏑⏑ | —— ‖⏑⏑—|—⏑⏑|⏑—⏑|——|—
⏑⏑—|⏑⏑⏑⏑|—⏑⏑‖ —— |⏑⏑—| ⏑ |——|—

शार्ङ्गरवः : यदा तु पूर्ववृत्तम् अन्यसङ्गाद्[1] विस्मृतो भवान्। तदा कथम् अधर्मभीरुः।

राजा : भवन्तम् एवात्र गुरुलाघवं[2] पृच्छामि।

मूढः स्याम् अहम् एषा वा वदेन् मिथ्येति संशये।[3]
दारत्यागी भवाम्याहो परस्त्रीस्पर्शपांशुलः।। 130।।

पुरोहित : (विचार्य) यदि तावद् एवं क्रियताम्।

राजा : अनुशास्तु मां भवान्।

पुरोहित : अत्रभवती तावद् आप्रसवाद् अस्मद्गृहे तिष्ठतु। कुत इदम् उच्यत इति चेत्। त्वं साधुभिर् उद्दिष्टः। प्रथममेव चक्रवर्तिनं पुत्रं जनयिष्यसीति।[4] स चेन् मुनिदौहित्रस् तल्लक्षणोपपन्नो भविष्यति। अभिनन्द्य शुद्धान्तम् एनां प्रवेशयिष्यसि।[5] विपर्यये तु पितुर् अस्याः समीपनयनम् अवस्थितमेव।

1. *Anya-saṅgāt, i.e., anyasyāḥ kāntāyāḥ saṅgāt,* 'on account of union with another wife.' As to *vismṛta* : *see* p. 159, note 3 at end.

2. *Guru-lāghava* is properly a kind of abstract noun formed from the Dvandva *guru-laghu,* the *vṛddhi* taking place in the second member of the compound instead of the first. The sense will then be, 'I ask your reverence as to the greater and the less [*i.e.* the heavier and the lighter] sin.' This is addressed to the *Brāhmaṇa* who acts as the *Purohita* or family priest, whose duty it would be to advise the king as to which was the greater or less sinful course. This sense of *guru-lāghava* is supported by two other passages : Mahābh., xii, 1273; and Episode of Yajñ., 6. The more obvious sense of the compound would be, 'the alleviation [solution] of a grave matter.'

3. 'In a doubt as to whether I may be infatuated or she may speak falsely, shall I become a repudiator of my wife, or defiled by contact with another's wife?' *Āho* : see p. 48, note 1 at end.

4. 'A son who has the mark of the *cakra* or discus in his hand.' When the lines of the right hand formed themselves into a circle, this was the mark of a future hero and emperor. *Cakra-vartin* is generally explained to mean, 'an emperor whose dominion extends to the horizon [*cakra*] or from sea to sea.'

5. 'If the Muni's daughter's-son shall be endowed with this

Verse 130. *Śloka* or *Anuṣṭubh. See* Verses 5, 6, 11, 12, 26, 47, 50, 51, 53, 73, 76, 84, 87, 125, 127.

राजा : यथा गुरुभ्यो रोचते।

पुरोहितः : वत्से। अनुगच्छ माम्।

शकुन्तला : भअवदि वसुहे। देहि मे विवरं।

शकुन्तला : भगवति वसुधे। देहि मे विवरम्।[1]

[इति रुदन्ती प्रस्थिता। निष्क्रान्ता सह पुरोधसा सह तपस्विभिश्च। **राजा** :शापव्यवहितस्मृतिः शकुन्तलागतमेव चिन्तयति]

नेपथ्ये : आश्चर्यम्।

राजा : (आकर्ण्य) किं नु खलु स्यात्।

पुरोहितः : (प्रविश्य सविस्मयं) देव। अद्भुतं खलु संवृत्तम्।

राजा : किमेवम्।

पुरोहितः : देव। परावृत्तेषु कण्वशिष्येषु–

सा निन्दन्ती स्वानि भाग्यानि बाला
बाहूत्क्षेपं क्रन्दितुं च प्रवृत्ता।[2]

राजा : किं च।

पुरोहितः :

mark [those marks], having congratulated her thou shalt introduce her to the female-apartments.' *Dauhitra*, from *duhitṛ*, is like *pautra*, 'a son's from *putra*. *Śuddhānta* : *see* p. 21, note 14.

1. 'Grant me admission or entrance,' 'Open to receive me' *i.e.*, Let me remain no longer in the land of the living. *Maṁ praveśaya dvidhā bhava*, 'Cleave in two to let me enter:' Ś. The Bengālī MSS. have *antaram=avakāśam* instead of *vivaram*.

2. 'That young-creature upbraiding her own fortunes, throwing up her arms, and beginning to weep'—or, 'and beginning to weep with repeated uplifting of her arms.'—*Bāhūtkṣepam* [so read all the MSS.]; this is an instance of an adverbial indeclinable participle of repetition compounded with a noun. *Bhujoccālanaṁ yathā bhavati evaṁ kranditum pravṛttā: Ś.* It is equivalent to *bāhū utkṣipya*, repetition of the action being perhaps implied. Examples of this participle are numerous in Bhaṭṭi, as in ii, 11, *Latānupātaṁ kusumāni agṛhṇāt, silopavesam āsta*, etc.

स्त्रीसंस्थानं चाप्सरस्तीर्थम् आराद्
उत्क्षिप्यैनां ज्योतिर् एकं जगाम[1] ।। 131 ।।

[सर्वे विस्मयं रूपयन्ति]

राजा : भगवन्। प्रागपि सोऽस्माभिर् अर्थः प्रत्यादिष्ट एव। किं वृथा तर्केणान्विष्यते। विश्राम्यतु भवान्।

पुरोहित : [विलोक्य] विजयस्व [इति निष्क्रान्तः]।

राजा : वेत्रवति। पर्याकुलोऽस्मि। शयनभूमिमार्गम् आदेशय।

प्रतीहारो। इदो इदो देवो [इति प्रस्थिता]।

प्रतीहारी : इत इतो देवः [इति प्रस्थिता]।

राजा :

कामं प्रत्यादिष्टां स्मरामि न परिग्रहं मुनेस् तनयाम्।
बलवत् तु दूयमानं प्रत्याययतीव मां हृदयम्[2] ।। 132 ।।

।। इति निष्क्रान्ताः सर्वे ।।

।। पञ्चमोऽङ्कः ।।

1. 'A single flash-of-light in female shape having snatched her up near Apsarās-tīrtha went off (with her).' *Strī-saṁsthānam, i.e., striyā iva ākṛtir yasya* : Ś. *Tirtha* : *see* page 17, note 1. *Ārāt = antike = nikaṭe* : K., Ś. *Jyotir - tejas. Jagāma* : the Bengālī and the Mackenzie MSS. have *tirobhūt*, 'disappeared,' 'vanished.'

2. 'Granted, I remember not the repudiated Muni's daughter (to be my) wife; nevertheless (my) heart being powerfully agitated forces me as it were to believe (her).' *Kāmam = atyartham* : K. *Kāmam kāmānumatau* : Ś. Compare p. 24, 1. 10; p. 55, note 1. *Pratyāyayati, i.e., tatparigrahe* : Ś.

Verse 131. *Śālinī* (variety of *Triṣṭubh*), consisting of eleven syllables to the half-line, each half-line being alike.

— — — — | — ⌣ — — ⌣ — — ||

Verse 132. *Āryā or Gāthā*. (*See* Verse 2.)

— — — | — — | — — || ⌣ — ⌣ | ⌣ ⌣ — | ⌣ — ⌣ | — ⌣ ⌣ | —
⌣ ⌣ — | ⌣ — — ⌣ | — — || — — | ⌣ ⌣ — | ⌣ | — ⌣ ⌣ | —

।। अथ पञ्चमषष्ठाङ्कमध्ये प्रवेशकः[1] ।।

[ततः प्रविशति नागरिकः श्यालः पश्चाद्बद्धपुरुषम् आदाय रक्षिणौ[2] च]

रक्षिणौ : (ताडयित्वा) अले कुम्भिलआ। कहेहि। कहिं तुए एशे

रक्षिणौ : (ताडयित्वा) अरे कुम्भिलक।[3] कथय। कुत्र त्वया एतन्

1. *See* page 97, note 3.

2. 'Then enters the king's brother-in-law (as) superintendent of the city-police, and two policemen [guards] bringing a man (with his hands) bound behind.' *Nāgarika=nagarādhikārī,* 'superintendent of the city:' Ś. = *nagare niyuktaḥ* 'one set over the city:' K., and equivalent here to 'the chief of the police.' *Śyāla=rāṣṭriyaḥ* or *rāṣṭrīyaḥ* [Am.-koṣa, i, vii, 14]. The king's brother-in-law, who here acts as the superintendent of police, is a character not unfrequently introduced in the plays: compare Mṛcch., p. 244, 1. 4; p. 227, 1. 12; p. 230. 1. 1, in which passages he is called *rāja-śyālaḥ and rāṣṭriya-śyālaḥ*. Kāṭavema observes that the policemen and the fishermen in this scene speak the Māgadhī form of Prākṛt: see Lassen's Instit. Prāk., p. 391, but Śaṅkara affirms that the fisherman speaks the Śakāra or Śakārika dialect [*Caura-pātras tu Śakāra-nāmadheya śakārapräya-bhāṣaṇāt*] see Lass. Inst., Prāk., p. 422. Both Śaṅkara and Kāṭavema have omitted to make mention of the dialect spoken by the Śyāla or Nāgarika. According to Viśwanātha [Sāit. Darp., page 180, line 12] he ought to speak the Dākṣiṇātyā form of Prākṛt. In the Bengālī MSS., and some of the Devanāgarī, he is certainly made to speak a dialect, distinct from the other characters of this scene, but in the best MSS. pure Prākṛt forms are found in the speeches attributed to him. Indeed, as brother-in-law of the king, he must have been a Kṣatriya, or one of the military caste.

3. 'O thief!' *Kumbhila* or *kumbhilaka,* seems to be indentical with *kumbhīla, kumbhīlaka, kumbhīra, kumbhīraka,* etc., although the

मणिबन्धणुक्किणणामहेए लाअकीए अङ्गुलीअए शमाशादिए।
मणिबन्धनोत्कीर्णनामधेयं[1] राजकीयम् अङ्गुलीयकं समासादितं। भीतिनाटितकेन।।[2]

पुरुषः : (भीतिनाटितकेन) पशीदन्ते भावमिश्शे। अहके ण ईदिशकम्मकाली।

पुरुषः : (भीतिनाटितकेन) प्रसीदन्तु भावमिश्राः।[5] अहं न ईदृशकर्मकारी।

प्रथमः : किं खु शोहणे बम्हणेत्ति कलिअ रणा पडिग्गहे दिणे।

प्रथमः : किं खलु शोभनो ब्राह्मण इति कृत्वा राज्ञा प्रतिग्रहो दत्तः।[4]

पुरुषः : शुणुह दाणिं। अहके शक्कावदालब्भन्तलवाशी धीवले।

पुरुषः : शृणुत इदानीम्। अहं शक्रा[5]वताराभ्यन्तरवासी धीवरः।

meaning 'thief' is not given to the two latter words in the dictionary. Compare in the beginning of Act 5 of the Vikramorvaśīya, *maṇi-kumbhīraka,* 'gem-stealer, (applied to the bird who swallowed the crest-jewel); at the end of Act 2, *loptreṇa sūcitasya kumbhīrakasya;* and in Mālavik., *aho kumbhīlakaiḥ pariharaṇīyā candrikā.*

1. 'The setting of which is engraven with his name.' *Maṇi-bandhana* which usually signifies 'the wrist,' is here the place of the setting [technically, the collect, *nigīn dān*] of the jewel which formed the *mudrā* or seal of the ring, mentioned p. 52, note 2. *Maṇi khacyate yasmin iti maṇi-bandhana:* K. The name might have been engraven on the stone itself, or on the gold in which it was set. *Utkṛī* is used in the sense of 'excavating,' in Mahābh., i, 5813; and *samutkīrṇa* with the meaning 'perforated,' in Ragh., i, 4.

2. 'With a gesticulation of fear.' The *ka* added to *nāṭita* may possibly signify a poor, sorry, or ludicrous gesture. It is often pleonastic, but in the plays it will sometimes be found affixed to the passive participle, to which it gives the sense of a verbal noun. Thus *udbhrāntaka* and *apavāritaka* [Mṛcch., p. 171] for *udbhrānti* and *apavāraṇa.*

3. 'Your honour.' *Bhāva* = *mānya* : Ś., 'venerable,' 'respectable' [*see* Wilson], to which *miśra* may be added : see p. 6, note 2.

4. 'Was it forsooth a present given by the king (to thee) imagining (thee to be) an illustrious *Brāhmaṇa?' Pratigraha* [*see* p. 52, l. 3 with note] is especially 'a donation to a Brāhmaṇa at suitable periods.' *Kṛtvā* : *see* p. 171, note 1 in middle; and compare Mālavikāgn., 23, 9, *para-kāryam iti kṛtvā.* Also Mṛcch., 147, 5.

5. *Śakrāvatāra* : *see* page 202, line 7, note 1.

द्वितीयः : पाडच्चला। किं अम्हेहिं जादी पुच्छिदा।

द्वितीयः : पाटच्चल। किम् अस्माभिर् जातिं पृष्टः।[1]

श्यालः : सूअअ। कहेदु सत्वं अनुक्कमेण। मा णं अन्तरा पडि-

श्यालः : सूचक।[2] कथयतु सर्वम् अनुक्रमेण। मा एनं अन्तरा प्रति-

बन्धह।

बध्नीतं।

उभौ : जं आबुत्ते आणबेदि। कहेहि।

उभौ : यद् आबुत्त[3] आज्ञापयति। कथय।

पुरुषः : अहके जालुग्गालादीहिं मच्छबन्धणोबाएहिं कुडुम्बभलणं

पुरुषः : अहं जालोद्गारादिभिर् मत्स्यबन्धनोपायैः कुटुम्बभरणं करोमि।[4]

कलेमि।

श्यालः : (विहस्य) विसुद्धो दाणिं आजीवो।

श्यालः : (विहस्य) विशुद्ध इदानीम् आजीवः।[5]

1. Verbs of 'asking' in Sanskṛt govern a double accusative case, one of which is retained after the pass. participle.

2. *Sūcaka*, 'a spy,' 'an informer,' is the name of one of he *rakṣiṇah*, or policemen.

3. *Ābutta*, 'a sister's husband,' or 'brother-in-law,' according to Amara-k., vii, 12. In Mṛcch, p. 339, 1. 12, this word is applied as a title of respect by a son to his father; but Dr. Boehtlingk conjectures that this may be an error for *āvuka*, the regular theatrical term for 'father.'

4. 'I make the support of my family by nets, hooks, and the other contrivances for catching fish.' *Udgāla* or *udgāra* = *valiśa* or *vadiśa*, 'a fishhook : ' K.

5. This is spoken ironically, as according to Manu (x, 46-48), the *niṣāda*, or fisherman caste, was one of the lowest. 'Those who are considered as low-born shall subsist only by such employments as the twice-born despise. *Niṣādas* (must subsist) by catching fish, etc.' Any occupation which involved the sin of slaughtering

पुरुषः : भट्टा। मा एव्वं भण।

पुरुषः : भर्तः। मा एवं भण।

शहजे किल जे विणिन्दिए ण हु दे कम्म विवज्जणीअए।

सहजं किल यद् विनिन्दितं न खलु तत् कर्म्म विवर्जनीयम्।

पशुमालणकम्मदालुणे अणुकम्पामिदु एव्व शोत्तिए।। 133।।

पशुमारणकर्म्मदारुणो अनुकम्पामृदुर् एव श्रोत्रियः[1] ।। 133 ।।

(excepting in the case of sacrificing to the god Śiva) was considered despicable. Butchers and leather-sellers were as great, or even greater, objects of scorn.

1. 'That occupation in which one was born, as-the-saying-is (*kila*), though in-bad-repute, verily must not be abandoned. The same sacrificing-*Brāhmaṇa,* who is savage in the act of slaughtering animals, may be (of a disposition) tender with compassion.' *Sahajam=kula-kramānugatam,* 'inherited from one's forefathers.' Manu is very peremptory in restricting special occupations to the different castes, especially to the mixed and lowest castes, formed by intermarriage with the others. 'A man of the lowest class, who, through covetousness, lives by the acts of the highest, let the king strip of all his wealth and banish. His own office, though badly performed, is preferable to that of another, though well performed; for he who lives by the duties of another class, immediately falls from his own:' x, 96, 97. Hence, we find the employments of fishing, slaughtering animals for food, leather-selling, basket-making, burning the dead, etc., assigned to men born in certain impure castes, and confined perpetually to their descendants. To the higher and purer castes a greater variety of employment was allowed. Śaṅkara observes that the Brāhmaṇa is called *Ṣaṭ-karmā,* from the precept of Manu (i, 88), which enjoins upon him six occupations, *viz.,* reading, teaching, sacrificing, assisting others to sacrifice, giving, and receiving. Under certain circumstances he was allowed by Manu to engage even in trade, and other employments. The sacrifice of animals was enjoined only on the priests of the god Śiva. The Brāhmaṇa, in the worship of this god, might have to kill

Verse 133. *Vaitālīya,* containing twenty-one syllables to the line, each whole line being alike, the first and third half-lines ending at the tenth syllable. *See* Verse 52.

⏑⏑—⏑⏑—⏑—⏑—||⏑⏑——⏑⏑—⏑—⏑—

श्याल: : तदो तदो।

श्याल: : ततस् तत:।

पुरुष: : एक्कशिशं दिअशे खण्डशो लोहिअमच्छे मए कप्पिदे जाव।

पुरुष: : एकस्मिन् दिवसे खण्डशो रोहितमत्स्यो[1] मया कल्पितो यावत्।

तश्श उदलब्भन्तले एद लदणभाशुलं अङ्गुलीअअं देक्खिअं पच्छा अहके ।

तस्य उदराभ्यन्तरे एतद् रत्नभासुरम् अङ्गुलीयकं दृष्टम्। पश्चाद् अहम्

शे विक्कआअ दंशअन्ते गहिदे भावमिश्शेहिं। मालेह वा। मुञ्चेह वा। अअं

अस्य विक्रयाय दर्शयन् गृहीतो भावमिश्रै:। मारयत वा। मुञ्चत वा। अयम्

शे आअमघुत्तन्ते।

अस्य आगमवृत्तान्त:।

श्याल: : जाणुअ। विस्सगन्धी गोहादी मच्छबन्धो एव्व णिस्संसअं।

श्याल: : जानुक। विस्रगन्धिर् गोघाती मत्स्यबन्ध एव नि:संशयम्।[2]

animals; but this was as much a necessary part of his business, as killing fish, of the fisherman, and was no proof of any natural cruelty of disposition. Śaṅkara defines a *Śrotriya Brāhmaṇa* thus: *Janmanā Brāhmaṇo jñeyaḥ saṁskārair dvija ucyate vidyate vidyayā yāti vipratvam tribhiḥ śrotriya ucyate, i.e.,* 'Birth constitutes the title *Brāhmaṇa*, sacramental rites (especially that of investitutre with the sacred thread) the title Dvija, or twice-born; knowledge, the title Vipra; and all three Śrotriya.' The usual definition of this word is, a *Brāhmaṇa* conversant with *śruti*, or scripture.

1. The *Rohita* or *Rohi* fish [Cyprinus Rohita] *lit.*, Red-fish, is a kind of carp, found in lakes and ponds in the neighbourhood of the Ganges. It grows to the length of three feet, is very voracious, and its flesh, though coarse, is eaten. Its back is olive-coloured, its belly of a beautiful golden hue, its fins and eyes red.

2. 'O Jānuka, the villain stinking (as he does) of raw flesh (is) doubtless a fisherman.' *Jānuka* is the name of the other policeman, who is supposed to have detected the thief; *jānuka iti cora-jñātur apara-padāter nāma* : Ś. Some of the Bengālī MSS. have *jālua* for *jāluka. Visra-gandhi = āmiṣagandhi* : Ch. *Go-ghātī* : the killing of a cow [*go-hatyā*] is reckoned by the Hindūs a most heinous crime : compare Hitop., 1, 162. Hence *go-ghātī*, 'cow-killer,' is applied as a reproach-

अङ्गुलीअअदंसणं से विमरिसिदव्वं। राउलं एव्व गच्छामो।
अङ्गुलीयकदर्शनम् अस्य विमर्ष्टव्यम्।[1] राजकुलम् एव गच्छामः।
रक्षिणौ। तह। गच्छ अरे गण्ठिभेदअ।
रक्षिणौ। तथा। गच्छ अरे ग्रन्थिभेदक।[2]

[सर्वे परिक्रामन्ति]

श्यालः : सूचअ। इमं पुरदुवारे अप्पमत्ता पडिबालह। जाव
श्यालः : सूचक। इमं पुरद्वारेऽप्रमत्तौ प्रतिपालयतम्। यावद्
इमं अङ्गुलीअअं जहागमणं भट्टिणो णिवेदिअ वदो सामणं पडिच्छिअ
इदम् अङ्गुलीयकं यथागमनं भर्तुर् निवेद्य ततः शासनं प्रतीष्य
णिक्कमामि।
निष्क्रमामि।

उभौ : पविशदु आबुत्ते शामिपशादश्श।
उभौ : प्रविशतु आबुत्तः स्वामिप्रसादाय।

[निष्क्रान्तः श्यालः]

प्रथमः। जाणुअ। चिलाअदि खु आबुत्ते।
प्रथमः : जानुक। चिरायति खलु आबुत्तः।
द्वितीयः : णं अवशलोबशप्पणीआ लाआणो।
द्वितीयः : ननु अवसरोपसर्पणीया राजानः।
प्रथमः : जाणुअ। फुलन्ति मे हत्था इमश्श बज्झश्श शुमणो पिणद्धुं।।
प्रथमः : जानुक। स्फुरतो मे हस्तौ अस्य बध्यस्य सुमनः। पिनद्धुं[3]।।

ful epithet to any rogue or low person. Thus, in the Mṛcchakaṭi, p. 299, 1. 4; p. 317, 1. 2, the *Cāṇḍāla* is called *go-ha* or *go-ghna*.

1. '(But) the finding [seeing, showing] of the ring by him must be (more closely) inquired into.' *Vimarṣṭavyam=jijñāsitavyam* : Ś. The root *mṛś* with *vi* has usually the sense of 'to consider of,' 'investigate;' but if the root be *mṛj*, the sense would be 'must be pardoned,' 'overlooked.' Kāṭavema has *vimārṣṭavyam*, from *mṛj*.

2. 'Cut-pure,' *lit.*, 'knot-breaker' or 'knot-cutter.' The Hindūs generally carry their money tied up in a knot in one end of a cloth, which is bound round the waist.

3. 'My hands tingle [my fingers itch] to bind a flower (about

[इति पुरुषं निर्दिशति]

[इति पुरुषं निर्दिशति]

पुरुषः : ण अलुहदि भावे अकालणमालणे भविदुं।

पुरुषः : न अर्हति भावोऽकारणमारणो भवितुम्।

द्वितीयः (विलोक्य) एशे अन्हाणं शामी पत्तहत्थे लाअशाशणं

द्वितीयः : (विलोक्य) एष नौ स्वामी पत्रहस्तो राजशासनं

पडिच्छिअ इदोमुहे देक्खीअदि। गिद्धवली भविश्शशि। शुणो मुहं वा

प्रतीष्य इतोमुखो दृश्यते। गृध्रबलिर् भविष्यसि। शुनो मुखं वा

देक्खिश्शशि।

द्रक्ष्यसि।[2]

श्यालः : (प्रविश्य) सूअअ। मुञ्चेदु एसो जालोअजीवी। उबबणो

श्यालः : (प्रविश्य) सूचक। मुच्यताम् एष जालोपजीवः। उपपन्नः

the head) of this victim [criminal about to be executed].' All the Devanāgarī MSS. have *sumanaḥ pinaddhum,* excepting the Mackenzie, which has *sumahaṇam* for *śumaṇo.* The Bengālī have got rid of the difficulty by substituting *vyāpādayitum,* 'to kill.' It is clear from what follows that the two policemen expected that their master would return with the king's order for putting the fisherman to death. From the Mālati-Mādhava, and other plays, it is evident that a person about to be offered as a victim to Śiva or Durgā had a wreath of flowers bound round the head. It may reasonably be assumed that this was also the case with common criminals, previous to their axecution.

1. 'Thou wilt be food for [an offering to] the crows [vultures], or wilt see the face of a dog.' *Gṛdhraḥ-baliḥ* : *see* p. 176, note 2. *Śuno mukham* : so read all the Devanāgarī MSS., excepting the Mackenzie, which omits the clause entirely. Dr. Boehtlingk has adopted as an emendation, *śiśuṇo muham, i.e., śiśor* [not *śiśuṇo*] *mukham,* and translated 'or thou wilt see the face (thy) child (once more).' He has supported this interpretation by a reference to two other passages, one in the 7th Act of this play [*putra-mukha-darśanena*], anoter in Mṛcch., 303, 4. Doubtless *putra-mukhaṁ dṛś* is a common phrase, but the whole point of this passage seems to me to lie in the ludicrous substitution of *śunaḥ* for *putrasya.*

किल अअं अङ्गुलीअअस्स आअमो।

किल अयम् अङ्गुलीयकस्य आगमः।

सूचक : जह आबुत्ते भणादि।

सूचक : यथा आबुत्तो भणति।

द्वितीयः। एशे जमशदणं पविशिअ पडिणिवुत्ते (इति पुरुषं

द्वितीयः : एष यमसदनं[1] प्रविश्य प्रतिनिवृत्तः (इति पुरुषं

परिमुक्तबन्धनं करोति)।

परिमुक्तबन्धनं करोति)।

पुरुषः : (श्यालं प्रणम्य) भट्टा। अह कीलिशे मे आजीवे।

पुरुषः : (श्यालं प्रणम्य) भर्तुः। अथ कीदृशो मे आजीवः।[2]

श्यालः : एस भट्टिणा अङ्गुलअअमुल्लसस्मिदो पसादोबि दाबिदो।

श्यालः : एष भर्त्रा अङ्गुलीयकमूल्यसम्मितः प्रसादोऽपि[3] दापितः।

(इति पुरुषायार्थं प्रयच्छति)

(इति पुरुषायार्थं प्रयच्छति)

पुरुषः : (सप्रणामं प्रतिगृह्य) भट्टकेण अणुग्गहिदम्हि। सूचकः।

पुरुषः : (सप्रणामं प्रतिगृह्य) भर्त्रा अनुगृहीतोऽस्मि। सूचकः।

एशे णाम अणुग्गहिदे जे शूलादो अवदालिअ हत्थिक्कन्धे पडिट्ठा-

एष नाम अनुगृहीतो यः शूलाद् अवतार्य हस्तिस्कन्धे प्रतिष्ठा-

बिदे।

पितः।[4]

1. *Yama-sadana*, 'the abode of Yama,' *i.e.*, the infernal city, Yama-pur, whither the Hindūs believe a departed soul immediately repairs, and receives a just sentence for Yama, the Hindū Pluto or Minos. The name Yama, *i.e.*, Restrainer or Punisher [from *yam*, 'to restrain'] is given to him as judge of departed spirits and god of punishment.

2. This is said ironically, in reference to p. 215, line 16, note 6.

3. Properly 'a favour,' here 'a present,' 'a gift.'

4. 'This (fellow) forsooth (my well say he) has been favoured, who, after being made to descend from the stake, has been mounted on the withers of an elephant.' *Śūla*, 'a stake for impaling criminals.'

जानुकः : आबुत्त। पालिदोशिअं कहेदि तेण अङ्गुलीअएण भट्टिणो

जानुकः : आबुत्त। पारितोषिकं कथयति तेन अङ्गुलीयकेन भर्तुः

शम्मदेण होदध्वं।

सम्मतेन भवितव्यम्।[1]

श्यालः : ण तस्सं महारुहं रदणं भट्टिणो बहुमदंत्ति तक्केमि। तस्स

श्यालः : न तस्मिन् महार्हं रत्नं भर्तुर् बहुमतमिति तर्कयामि। तस्य

दंसणेण भट्टिणो अभिमदो जणो सुमरिदो। मुहुत्तअं पकिदिगम्भीरोबि

दर्शनेन भर्तुर् अभिमतो जनः स्मृतः। मुहूर्तं प्रकृतिगम्भीरोऽपि

पज्जुस्सुअमणो आसि।

पर्य्युत्सुकमनाः आसीत्।[2]

सूचकः : शेविदं णाम आबुत्तेण।

सूचकः : सेवितं नाम आबुत्तेन।

जानुकः : णं भणाहि। इमश्श कए मच्छिआभत्तुणोत्ति (इति पुरुषम्

जानुकः : ननु भण। अस्य कृते मत्स्यिकाभर्तुरिति।।[3] (इति पुरुषम्

The act of impaling was called *śūlāropaṇa* and one who deserved it *śūlya.* 'Mounting on an elephant,' denotes elevation to high dignity, elephants being used in triumphal processions.

1. This is the reading of Kāṭavema. Most of the Devanāgarī have *palidośaṁ kahehi* for *paritoṣaṁ kathaya.* Translate : 'The present proves [intimates] that this ring must be highly prized by the king.'

2. 'Though naturally reserved [unruffled, deep, profound] he became for a moment agitated in mind.' *Gambhīra* : see p. 39, note 1, and p. 201, note 1, at end. Kāṭavema reads : *pajjasu-ṇaaṇo* for *paryaśru-nayama.* All Asiatics are skilful in suppressing or concealing emotion.

3. So read most of the Devanāgarī MSS. *Matsyikā* is not given in the Dictionary. Dr. Boetlingk translates it by *fisc-brut*, 'the fry of fish,' and observes that it is also the name for a kind of fish called in German *scaar.* Had the word been *matsyika* or *mātsyika*, 'a fisherman,' there would have been no difficulty. May it not mean 'a fish-woman,' and the phrase be translated, 'this lord of a fish-woman,' 'this husband of a fish-woman ?' Kāṭavema and the Beṅgālī have *matsya-śatror*, 'enemy of fishes.'

असूयया पश्यति)।

असूयया पश्यति)।

पुरुषः : भट्टालके। इदो अद्धं तुम्हाणं शुमणोमुल्लं होदु।

पुरुषः : भट्टारकाः। इतोऽर्द्धं युष्माकं सुमनोमूल्यं भवतु।[1]

जानुकः : एत्तके जुज्जइ।

जानुकः : एतावद् युज्यते।

श्यालः : धीवर। महत्तरो तुमं पिअवअस्सको दाणिं मे संवुत्तो। कादम्बरीसक्खिअं अम्हाणं पढमसोहिदं इच्छीअदि। ता सोण्डिआपणं एव्व गच्छामो।

श्यालः : धीवर। महत्तरम् त्व प्रियवयस्य इदानीं मे संवृत्तः। कादम्बरीसाक्षिकम् अस्माकं प्रथमसौहृदम् इष्यते।[2] तत् शोण्डिकापणम् एव गच्छामः।

सर्वे : तह।

सर्वे : तथा।।

[इति निष्क्रान्ताः सर्वे]

[प्रवेशकः]

1. 'Let the half of this be the price of your flower (for binding about my head).' The fisherman is again ironical. The allusion of course is to the flower mentioned at p. 219, note 1. There is probably a double-entendre in *sumanaḥ,* which may signify 'good-will,' as well as 'flower.'

2. 'Our first friendship requires to be attested over (some) wine,' *i.e.,* We must pledge ourselves over our cups or in drinking each other's health. *Kādambarī,* 'an intoxicating liquor distilled from the Kadamba flower.' *Sākṣikam* : compare Mālavikāg., page 53, line 7; Raghuvaṁśa, xi, 48, and Hitopadeśa, line 842.

ACT - VI

।। अथ षष्ठोऽङ्कः ।।

।। ततः प्रविशत्याकाशयानेन सानुमती नामाप्सराः ।।

सानुमती। णिव्वत्तिदं मए पज्जाअणिव्वत्तणिज्जं अच्छरातित्थ-

सानुमती : निर्वर्तितं मया पर्यायनिर्वर्तनीयम् अप्सरस्तीर्थ-

सणिज्झं। जाव साहुजणस्स अभिसेअकालोत्ति सम्पदं इमस्स राएसिणो

सान्निध्यम्। यावत् साधुजनस्य अभिषेककाल इति साम्प्रतम् अस्य राजर्षेर्

उदन्तं पच्चक्खीकरिस्सं। णं मेणआसम्बन्धेण सरीरभूदा दाणिं मे

उदन्तं प्रत्यक्षीकरिष्यामि।[1] ननु मेनकासम्बन्धेन शरीरभृता इदानीं मे

सउन्दला। ताएअ दुहिदुणिमित्तं आदिट्ठपुव्वन्हि (समन्ताद् अवलोक्य)

शकुन्तला।[2] तया च दुहितृनिमित्तम् आदिष्टपूर्वास्मि (समन्ताद् अवलोक्य)

1. 'Attendance at Apsaras-tīrtha (which is wont) to be performed (by us) in regular-rotation has been performed by me. Now, whilst (it is) the bathing-time of the good people [*i.e.*, of Śakuntalā and the nymphs], I will with my own eyes ascertain the circumstances [news] of this Rājarṣi.' *Sānnidhyam, lit.*, 'proximity.' Here it denotes 'close attendance or waiting,' as in Hitop., line 1112, *anujīvinā sānnidhyam avaśyaṁ karaṇīyaṁ karaṇīyam*. In the interlude before the 4th Act of Vikram., *upasthāna* occurs with the same sense in a parallel pasage : *Apsaro-vyāpāra-paryāyeṇa sūryasya upasthāne vartamānayā priya-sakhyā vinā vasanta-samaya āgata iti balavad utkaṇṭhitā' smi,* 'I am mightily troubled that the spring season has arrived during the absence of my dear friends, who is in attendance upon Sūrya, according to the regular cycle of nymph's duty.'

2. 'Verily by (my) connexion with Menakā, Śakuntalā has now become part of myself,' *lit.*, 'my own body,' *i.e.*, 'part of my own flesh and blood,' 'indentified with myself.' As to the nymph Menakā, the mother of Śakuntalā, see p. 44, 1. 10 with note 2, and p. 45, note 1. *Śarīra-bhūta* : this is the same sort of compound as *pūga-kṛta* or *pūga-bhūta* : *see* Pāṇini, II, i, 59, and p. 168, note 1 at

किं णुक्खु उदुच्छवेबि णिरुच्छवारम्भं विअ एदं राअउलं
किं नु खलु ऋतूत्सवेऽपि[1] निरुत्सवारम्भम् इव एतद् राजकुलं
दीसइ। अत्थि मे विहवो पणिधाणेण सव्वं परिणादुं। किन्दु सहीए
दृश्यते। अस्ति मे विभवः प्रणिधानेन[2] सर्वं परिज्ञातुम्। किन्तु सख्या
आदरो मए माणइदव्वो। होदु। इमाणं एव्व उज्जाणपालिआणं
आदरो मया मानयितव्यः। भवतु। अनयोर् एव उद्यानपालिकयोम्
तिरक्खरिणीपरिच्छणा पस्सपरिवत्तिणी भविअ उबलम्भिस्सं। (इति
तिरस्करिणोपरिच्छन्ना पार्श्वपरिवर्तिनी भूत्वा उपलप्स्ये।। इति
नाट्येनावतीर्य स्थिता)
नाट्येनावतीर्य स्थिता।।

[ततः प्रविशति चूताङ्कुरम् अवलोकयन्ती चेटी। अपरा च पृष्ठतस् तस्याः]

end. Compare in Mālavikāg., 33, 12, *śarīram asi me,* 'thou art my body.'

1. *Ṛtūtsava, lit.,* 'the festival of the season,' *i.e.,* the *Vasantotsava,* or 'great vernal festival,' in celebration of the return of spring, and said to be in honour of the god Kṛṣṇa. Originally his son Kāmadeva, the god of Love, must have been the object of worship in this festival. It is identified with the Holi or Dolā-yātra, the Saturnalia, or rather, Carnival of the Hindūs, when people of all conditions take liberties with each other, especially by scattering red powder and coloured water on the clothes of persons passing in the street, as described in Ratnāvalī, pp. 5, 6, 7, where syringes and waterpipes are used by the crowd. Flowers and especially the opening blossoms of the Mango, would naturally be much used for decoration at this festival, and as offerings to the god of Love. It was formerly held on the full moon of the month Caitra, or about the beginning of April, but now on the full moon of Phālguna, or about of March. The other great Hindū festival, held in the autumn, about October, is called *Durgotsava* or *Durgā-pūjā,* being in honour of the goddess Durgā.

2. *Praṇidhāna,* 'profound meditation,' or that mental faculty by which divine beings were supposed to be able to ascertain future events. The verb *praṇidhā* is primarily 'to fix in;' hence 'to fix the mind on,' 'be intent on.' Compare in Vikram. [interlude before the 4th Act] *mayā praṇidhāna-sthitayā atyāhitam upalabdham.*

प्रथमा :

आअम्बहरिअपण्डुर वसन्तमासस्स जीअसव्वस्स।

आताम्रहरितपाण्डुर वसन्तमासस्य जीवसर्वस्व।

दिट्ठोसि चूदकोरअ उदुमङ्गलं तुमं पसाएमि।। 134।।

दृष्टोऽसि चूतकोरक ऋतुमङ्गलं त्वां प्रसादयामि[1] ।। 134।।

द्वितीया : परहुदिए किं एआइणी मन्तेसि।

द्वितीया : परभृतिके किम् एकाकिनी मन्त्रयसे।

प्रथमा : महुअरिए। चूदकलिअं देक्खिअ उम्मत्तिआ परहुदिआ होदि।

प्रथमा : मधुकरिके। चूतकलिकां दृष्ट्वा उन्मत्ता परभृतिका भवति।

द्वितीया : (सहर्षं त्वरया उपगम्य) कहं उबट्ठिदो महुमासो।

द्वितीया : (सहर्षं त्वरया उपगम्य) कथम् उपस्थितो मधुमासः।

1. 'O reddish pale-green-mango-blossom, the very essence of the life of the vernal month, thou art seen (by me, and) I bid thee hail, auspicious-her binger of the season.' *Ātāmra*, etc. This kind of Dvandva Bahuvrīhi compound, expressing varieties of colour is noticed by Pāṇini, II, i, 69. Compare *kṛṣṇa-śukla, lohita-śavala*, etc. *Ā*, prefixed, implies diminution, and is equivalent to *īṣat*. So *āpāṇḍu*, 'yellowish,' or 'slightly yellow :' Vikram., Act 2. *Jīva-sarva-sva, lit.*, 'whose whole substance is contituted of life :' see p. 33, note 2 in middle. Some MSS. have *jīva-sarva-svam,* agreeing with *tvām. Maṅgalam,* 'anything auspicious,' any symbol or sign of happiness;' in this latter sense it seems to be used here. The goddess Durgā is called in the same way *sarva-maṅgalā*, 'presiding over the happiness of the whole world.' *Ṛtu* is evidently here the season *par excelleñce*, the season of all others. *Prasādayāmi, lit.*, 'I ask thee to be favourable,' 'I entreat thee to be propitious.'

Verse 134. *Āryā* or *Gāthā*. (*See* Verse 2.)

— — | ⏑ ⏑ ⏑ ⏑ | — ⏑ ⏑ ‖ ⏑ — ⏑ | — — | ⏑ — ⏑ | — — | ⏑
— — | ⏑ — — — | — ⏑ ⏑ ‖ ⏑ ⏑ — | ⏑ — ⏑ | ⏑ | ⏑ — ⏑ | —

In the last half-line the syllables *mam* and *e* are considered short by a license peculiar to Prākṛt prosody.

प्रथमा : महुअरिए। तव दाणिं कालो एसो मदविब्भमगोदाणं।

प्रथमा : मधुकरिके। तव इदानीं काल एष मदविभ्रमगीतानाम्।

द्वितीया : सहि। अवलम्ब मं। जाव अग्गपादट्ठिआ भविअ चूदकलिअं

द्वितीया : सखि। अवलम्बस्व मां। यावद् अग्रपादस्थिता भूत्वा चूतकलिकां

गेण्हिअ कामदेवच्चणं करेमि।

गृहीत्वा कामदेवार्चनं करोमि।

प्रथमा : जइ ममबिक्खु ऋद्धं अच्चणफलस्स।

प्रथमा : यदि ममापि खलु अर्द्धम् अर्चनफलस्य।

द्वितीया : अकहिदेबि एदं सम्पज्जइ। जदो एक्कं एव्व णो जीविदं।

द्वितीया : अकथितेऽपि एतत् सम्पद्यते। यत एकम् एव नौ जीवितम्।

दुधाठिदं सरीरं।। सखीम् अवलम्ब्य स्थिता चूताङ्कुरं गृह्णाति।। अए।

द्विधास्थितं शरीरम्।। सखीम् अवलम्ब्य स्थिता चूताङ्कुरं गृह्णाति।। अये।

अप्पडिबुद्धोबि चूदप्पसवो एत्थ बन्धणभङ्गसुरभी होदि।

अप्रतिबुद्धोऽपि चूतप्रसवोऽत्र बन्धन[1]भङ्गसुरभिर् भवति।

[कपोतहस्तकं कृत्वा][2]

तुंसि मए चूदङ्कुर दिणो कामस्स गहिदधणुअस्स।

त्वमसि मया चूताङ्कुर दत्तः कामस्य गृहीतधनोः।

1. *Bandhana, i.e., prasava-bandhana,* 'the foot-stalk of the flower :' *see* p. 102, l. 6, note 3.

2. 'Having joined the hands together,' or 'having placed them one over another.' *Kapota* is properly 'a dove or pigeon;' but Kāṭavema informs us that it is also the name for a mode of joining the hands. Probably the hands and fingers were brought into a position bearing some fancied resemblance to a pigeon. Śaṅkara and Candraśekhara quote the following verse which seems to intimate that this position was significant of humble entreaty, respectful representation, or fear; *Sarva-pārśva-samāśleṣāt kapotaḥ sarva-śīrṣaka* [*sarpa-śīrṣaka* : Ś.], *Bhītau vijñāpane caiva vinaye ca prayujyate.*

पहिअजणजुवइलक्खो पञ्चब्भहिओ मरो होहि।। 135।।

पथिकजनयुवतिलक्ष्यः पञ्चाभ्यधिकः शरो भव[1]।। 135।।

[इति चूताङ्कुरं क्षिपति]

कञ्चुकी : [प्रविश्य पटाक्षेपेण[2] कुपितः] मा तावद् अनात्मज्ञे।[3] देवेन प्रतिषिद्धे वसन्तोत्सवे त्वम् आम्रकलिकाभङ्गं किम् आरभसे।

उभे : [भीते] पसीददु अज्जो। अग्गहीदत्थाओ वअं।

उभे : [भीते] प्रसीदतु आर्यः। अगृहीतार्थे आवाम्।

कञ्चुकी : न किल श्रुतं युवाभ्याम्। यद् वासन्तिकैम् तरुभिर् अपि देवस्य शासनं प्रमाणीकृतं तदाश्रयिभिः पत्रिभिश्च।[4] तथा हि–

चूतानां चिरनिर्गतापि कलिका बध्नाति न स्वं रजः
सन्नद्धं यदपि स्थितं कुरुवकं तत्कोरकावस्थया।
कण्ठेषु स्खलितं गतेऽपि शिशिरे पुंस्कोकिलानां रुतं
शङ्के संहरति स्मरोऽपि चकितम् तूणार्द्धकृष्टं शरम्[5]।। 136।।

1. 'O mango-sprout, thou art offered by me to Kāmadeva (now in the act of) taking-up-his-bow. Become the most excellent arrow of the five, having-for-thy-mark maidens whose lovers are journeying (to some distant land).' As to Kāma or Kāmadeva and the epithet *pañcābhyadhika* [=*śreṣṭha* : K.=*ṣaṣta* : Ś.] : *see* p. 98, note 2. *Pathika-jana-yuvati* : compare Meghadūta, verse 8, *pathika-vanitāh.* With reference to the offering of flowers to Kāmadeva, compare Ratnāvalī, pp. 14, 17.

2. 'With a hurried toss of the curtain :' see p. 142, note 1.

3. 'Do not so, thou thoughtless woman !' *Anātma-jña* [=*ātma-paricaya-rahita*] *lit.*, 'one who does not know his own nautre.' It denotes here, 'one who is thoughtless about orders.' As to the Kañcukī or chamberlain, *see* page 183, note 4.

4. 'When even by the vernal shrubs, and by the feathered tribes [birds] their inhabitants, the commands of the king are made the rule [obeyed].' *Pramāṇa* is 'a rule or standard of action,' and *pramāṇī-kṛ*, 'to receive as a rule,' 'to admit as authority :' compare p. 186, 1. 2.

5. 'The bud of the mangoes, though long since protruded, does

---

Verse 135. *Āryā* or *Gāthā*. (*See* Verse 2.)

— ⏑ ⏑ | — — | — ⏑ ⏑ || — — | — — | ⏑ ⏑ ⏑ ⏑ | ⏑ ⏑ — | ⏑

⏑ ⏑ ⏑ ⏑ | ⏑ ⏑ ⏑ ⏑ | — — || — — | ⏑ ⏑ — | ⏑ | — — | —

Verse 136. *Śārudūla-vikrīḍiṭa* (variety of *Atidhṛti*). *See* Verses 14, 30, 36, 39, 50, 63, 79, 85, 86, 89, 97, 98, 111.

उभे : णत्थि सन्देहो। महप्पहावो राएसी।

उभे : नास्ति सन्देहः। महाप्रभावो राजर्षिः।

प्रथमा : अज्ज। कति दिअहाइं अम्हाणं मित्तावसुणा रट्ठिएण

प्रथमा : आर्य। कति दिवसानि आवयोर् मित्रावसुना राष्ट्रियेण

भट्टिणो पाअमूलं पेसिदाणं। इत्थं च णो पमदवणस्स पालणकम्म

भर्तुः पादमूलं प्रेषितयोः।[1] इत्थं च नौ प्रमदवनस्य पालकर्म

not form [gahter] its own pallen [dust]. The Kuruvaka, although ready-to-flower [completely studded with buds] remains stationary in its budding state. The note [voice] falters in the throats of the male-cuckoos, though the colddews are passed. I suspect even *Smara*, being daunted, arrests [replaces] the shaft half-drawn from (his) quiver.' *Badhnāti* : *see* p. 29, note 1 in middle; and compare *īṣad-baddha-rajaḥ-kaṇāgra-kapiśā cūte navā mañjarī* : Vikram., Act 2. *Sannaddham=puṣpitum udyatam* : Ś=*vikāsonmukham* : K. : Compare p. 27, 1. 7, note 2. *Sthitam* : compare p. 1, 1. 2. *Kuruvaka* is either the crimson amaranth, or a purple species of Barleria. Sir W. Jones makes no mention of it. *Tat-korakāvasthayā=kalikā-daśāyā* : Ś., *i.e., na vikāsitam* : Ch. *Skhalitam=gadgaditam* : K. *Śiśira*, properly 'the dewy season,' or 'season of hoar-frost.' The Hindūs divide the year into six seasons of two months each, *viz.*—1. Spring, Vasanta, beginning about the middle of March, or according to some, February; 2. Summer, Grīṣma; 3. Rains, Varṣāḥ; 4. Autumn, Śarad; 5. Winter, Hemanta; 6. Dews, Śiśira. *Puṁskokila* : *see* p. 160, note 2. *Saṁharati* : compare p. 14, 1. 1. It is clear that *saṁ-hṛ* and *prati-saṁ-hṛ* may have the sense of 'replace,' in reference to a quiver, as in Mahābh., 3, 772, we have *saṁharasva punar vāṇam*. See also Ragh., iii, 64. *Smara* : *see* p. 205, note 2.

1. '(But) few days (have elapsed) to us sent to the feet of his majesty by Mitrā-vasu, the king's brother-in-law.' *Kati* like *kiyat* may be either interrogative or indefinite. So *kati padāni gatvā* : Ratnāvali, p. 14, 1. 6. After *divasāni*, Kāṭavema supplies *gatāni*, 'have passed.' The construction of the genitive case after *gata* expressing the lapse of time is not uncommon, Compare *aṣṭa pañcāśataṁ rātryaḥ śayānasya adya me gataḥ* : Mahābh., xiii., 7732. *Adya daśamo māsas tātasya uparatasya* : Mudr., 80, 11. *Māso jātasya* : Pāṇini, II, 2, 5. *Pāda-mūlaṁ, lit.*, 'the root of the feet,' 'the heel.' The phrase *pāda-mūlam*

समप्पिदं। ता आअन्तुअदाए अस्सुदपुव्वो अन्हेहिं एसो वुत्तन्तो।
समर्पितं। तद् आगन्तुकतया[1] अश्रुतपूर्व आवाभ्याम् एष वृत्तान्तः।

कञ्चुकी : भवतु। न पुनर् एवं प्रवर्तितव्यम्।

उभे : अज्ज। कोदूहलं णो। जइ इमिणा जणेण सोदव्वं कहेदु भअं।

उभे : आर्य। कौतूहलं नौ। यदि अनेन जनेन[2] श्रोतव्यं कथयतु

किणिमित्तं भट्टिणा वसन्तूसवो पडिसिद्धो।
भवान्। किन्निमित्तं भर्त्रा वसन्तोत्सवः प्रतिषिद्धः।

सानुमती : उस्सवप्पिआ खु मणुस्सा। गरुणा कारणेण होदव्वं।

सानुमती : उत्सवप्रियाः[3] खलु मनुष्याः। गुरुणा कारणेन भवितव्यम्।

कञ्चुकी : बहुलीभूतम्[4] एतत् किं न कथ्यते। किम् अत्रभवत्योः कर्णपथं नायातं शकुन्तलाप्रत्यादेशकौलीनम्।[5]

उभेः सुदं रट्ठिणो मुहादो जाव अङ्गुलीअअदंसणं।

उभे : श्रुतं राष्ट्रियस्य मुखाद् यावद् अङ्गुलीयकदर्शनम्।

preṣita, expressive of the most humble servitude, occurs elsewhere : see Mudr., p. 16, 1. 8; and p. 64, 1. 16. *Rāṣṭriyeṇa* : see p. 216 note 2. The king's brother-in-law probably acted as a kind of viceroy.

1. 'Since we are but just arrived,' or 'by reason of our being strangers.' See note on *baddha-pallavatayā*, p. 29, 1. 2.

2. 'By us :' see note to *ayaṁ janaḥ*, p. 142, l. 4, and compare p. 109, l. 4.

3. *Utsava-priyāḥ*, 'fond of festivals :' see p. 159, note 3 at end.

4. *Bahulī-bhūtam=sakala-viditam*, 'generally known,' 'notorious :' Ś.

5. 'Has not the scandal about the repudiation of Śakuntalā reached your ladyships' ears ?' *Karṇa-patha, lit.*, 'the path or range of the ears :' *see* p. 109, note 3; and compare *locana-patham yāntyā* : Ratnāvalī, 1. 2. *Kaulīna=loka-vāda*, 'report :' K.=*parīvāda* or *apavāda*, evil report :' Ch. It is certainly derived from *kula*, 'a family,' and may signify 'report relating to family or private matters,' 'family scandal.' It is so used in Vikramorvaśīya, Act 2, *etat kaulīnam vijṛmbhate.*

6. This must come from a Sanskṛt crude form *rāṣṭri* or from *rāṣṭrin*, neither of which are given in the Dictionary.

कञ्चुकी : तेन ह्यल्पं कथयितव्यम्। यदैव खलु स्वाङ्गुलीयकदर्शनाद् अनुस्मृतं देवेन सत्यम् ऊढपूर्वा मया तत्रभवती रहसि शकुन्तला मोहात् प्रत्यादिष्टेति तदा प्रभृत्येव पश्चात्तापम् उपगतो देवः। तथा हि

रम्यं द्वेष्टि यथा पुरा प्रकृतिभिर् न प्रत्यहं सेव्यते
शय्याप्रान्तविवर्तनैर् विगमयत्युन्निद्र एव क्षपाः।
दाक्षिण्येन ददाति वाचम् उचिताम् अन्तःपुरेभ्यो यदा
गोत्रेषु स्खलितम् तदा भवति च व्रीडाविलक्षश् चिरम्[1] ।। 137 ।।

सानुमती : पिअं मे।

सानुमती : प्रियं मे।

1. 'He abhors (everything) pleasurable. He is not as formerly respectfully-waited-on every day by (his) courtiers [counsellors, ministers]. He spends his nights, without even closing his eyes, in tossing [rolling] about on the edge of his couch. When, out of politeness, he addresses the usual-civil speeches to the women of the palace, then he blunders in (their) names and becomes for a long while disconcerted [abashed] with shame.' *Ramyam, i.e., srak-candana-vanitādi*, 'garlands, sandal, women, etc. :' K.; in fact, 'the pleasures of sense.' *Prakṛtibhiḥ=sacivaiḥ* : Ch.=*siṣṭaiḥ* : Ś. *Ucitām=arhām=tatkāla-yogyām* : K. : *see* p. 143, 1. 5. *Antaḥpurebhyo* : *see* p. 122, note 2. *Gotreṣu=nāmasu* : Ś., Ch.=*nāmadheyeṣu* : K. *Skhalitah=viparyastaḥ* : K., *i.e.*, 'by mistake he utters the name of Śakuntalā :' K., Ś. To indicate a lover's absence of mind or rather the one engrossing object of his thoughts, Hindū poets are fond of making him fall into the trap of calling others by the name of his mistress. Compare Kumāra-sam., iv., 8. See also Ragh., xix, 14—*Nāma vallabha-janasya te mayā prāpya bhāgyam api tasya kāṅkṣyate iti taṁ gotra-viskhalitam ūcur aṅganāḥ*, 'The women thus addressed him making mistakes in their names [calling them by the name of his beloved], Since I have received the name of thy beloved I desire also her lot :' also Praveśaka to Act 2 of Vikram., *yan-nimittaṁ bhartā utkaṇṭhitas tasyāḥ striyā nāmnā bhartrā devī ālapitā*. And another passage in the Viṣkambha at the opening of the next Act, *tayā puruṣottama iti vaktavye purūravasīti nirgatā vāṇī.*

Verse 137. *Śārdūla-vikrīḍita* (variety of *Atidhṛti*). *See* Verse 136.

कञ्चुकी : अस्मात् प्रभवतो वैमनस्याद्[1] उत्सवः प्रत्याख्यातः।

उभे : जुज्जइ।

उभे : युज्यते।

नेपथ्ये। एदु एदु भवं।

नेपथ्ये : एतु एतु भवान्।

कञ्चुकी (कर्णं दत्त्वा) अये। इत एवाभिवर्तते देवः। स्वकर्मानुष्ठीयताम्।

उभे : तह (इति निष्क्रान्ते)।

उभे : तथा (इति निष्क्रान्ते)।

[ततः प्रविशति पश्चात्तापसदृशवेशो राजा विदूषक प्रतीहारी च]

कञ्चुकी : [राजानम् अवलोक्य] अहो सर्वास्ववस्थासु रमणीयत्वम् आकृतिविशेषाणाम्। एवम् उत्सुकोऽपि प्रियदर्शनी देवः। तथा हि–

प्रत्यादिष्टविशेषमण्डनविधिर् वामप्रकोष्ठार्पितं
बिभ्रत् काञ्चनम् एकम् एव वलयं श्वासापरक्ताधरः।
चिन्ताजागरणप्रताम्रनयनम् तेजोगुणाद् आत्मनः
संस्कारोल्लिखितो महामणिर् इव क्षीणोऽपि नालक्ष्यते[2] ।। 138 ।।

1. 'In consequence of this mental derangement of his majesty.' *Vaimanasya,* abstract noun from *vimanas,* 'disordered in mind.' 'changed in mind,' 'absent in mind.' *Prabhavato* [=*rājñaḥ* : Chēzy : =*prabhoḥ* : K.] gen. case of *prabhavat,* 'rulling,' 'one who rules;' it seems to be used like *prabhu* and *prabhaviṣṇu* in addressing or speaking of kings. Compare *nāsti prabhavato' parādhaḥ* : Vikramorvaśīya, Act 2 at end.

2. 'Scorning distinguished [superior] forms of decoration; wearing but a single golden bracelet fastened [placed] on the left fore-arm; with lips bloodless from sighing; with eyes very red from sleeplessness (caused) by thought (upon Śakuntalā); through the excellence of his own (inherent) lustre, though he be attenuated he is not observed (to be so), like a magnificent gem (whose surface is) ground away by the polishing-stone.' *Pratyādiṣṭa-viśeṣa-maṇḍana-vidhir=nirākṛta-viśiṣṭālaṅkāra-vidhānaḥ* : Ś. Compare Megh., verse 92 and *prasādhana-vidheḥ prasādhana-viśeṣaḥ* : Vikram., Act 2. *Prakoṣṭha* [see page 51, note 3]=*kūrpara-maṇi-bandhana-madhyabhāga* : K.

Verse 138. *Śārdūla-vikrīḍita* (variety of *Atidhṛti*). *See* last verse.

सानुमती : (राजानं दृष्ट्वा) ठाणेक्खु पच्चादेसविमाणिदाबि इमस्स

सानुमती : (राजानं दृष्ट्वा) स्थाने खलु प्रत्यादेशविमानितापि अस्य

किदे सउन्दला किलम्मदि।

कृते शकुन्तला क्लाम्यति।

राजा : (ध्यानमन्दं परिक्रम्य)

प्रथमं सारङ्गाक्ष्या प्रियया प्रतिबोध्यमानमपि सुप्तम्।
अनुशयदुःखायेदं हतहृदयं सम्प्रति विबुद्धम्[1] ।। 139 ।।

सानुमती : णं ईदिसाणि तबस्सिणीए भाअहेआणि।

सानुमती : ननु ईदृशानि तपस्विन्या भागधेयानि।

विदूषक : (अपवार्य) लङ्घिदो एसो भूओबि सउन्दलावाहिणा।

विदूषक : (अपवार्य) लङ्घित एष भूयोऽपि शकुन्तलाव्याधिना।[2]

ण आणे। कहं चिकिच्छिदव्वो भविस्सदित्ति।

न जाने। कथं चिकित्सितव्यो भविष्यतीति।

Compare page 114, note 1. *Bibhrat=dadhat* : in the pres. part. of verbs of the 3rd. conj., the nom. case in identical with the crude. *Aparakta* is equivalent to *nīrakta, rakta-hīna,* 'bloodless,' 'pale.' The effect of long and deep sighs would be to draw the blood away from the lips. Compare Megh., verses 83, 89. *Cintā-jāgragaṇa, i.e., Śakuntalā-viṣayiṇyā cintayā* : Ś. *Guṇāt=utkarṣāt* : K. *Saṁskāro=śāṇa* : K.=*prastara-viśeṣa* : Wilson gives the sense 'polishing;' compare Hitopadeśa, line 15. *Sāṇollikhitaḥ=śāṇodghṛṣṭaḥ* : K. *Nālakṣyate* : *see* page 70, note 3 at end.

1. 'Previously this paralysed [blighted] heart slumbered even whilst-it-was being-roused-from-sleep by my fawn-eyed beloved. Now it is broad-awake to the anguish of remorse.' *Anuśaya-duḥkhāya=paścāttāpa-khedāya. Samprati, i.e., tad-virahe* : Ś. *Vibuddham= jāgṛtam* : Ś.

2. 'He is again attacked [seized, afflicted] by a Śakuntalā-fever,' *i.e.,* He is again love-sick for Śakuntalā. *Laṅghita* : *see* p. 95, note 5.

Verse 139. *Āryā* or *Gāthā*. (*See* Verse 2.)

◡◡— |——|——‖ ◡◡— |◡◡—|◡—◡|◡◡—|—
◡◡◡◡|——|——‖◡◡◡◡| —— | ◡ |◡◡—|—

कञ्चुकी : (उपगम्य) जयतु जयतु देव:। महाराज। प्रत्यवेक्षिता: प्रमदवनभूमय:। यथाकामम् अध्यास्तां विनोदस्थानानि महाराज:।

राजा : वेत्रवति। मद्वचनाद् अमात्यम् आर्यपिशुनं ब्रूहि। चिरप्रबोधान् न सम्भावितम् अस्माभिर् अद्य धर्मासनम् अध्यासितुम्। यत् प्रत्यवेक्षितं पौरकार्यम् आर्येण। तत् पत्रम् आरोप्य दीयताम् इति।[1]

प्रतीहारी : जं देवो आणबेदि (इति निष्क्रान्ता)।

प्रतीहारी : यद् देव आज्ञापयति (इति निष्क्रान्ता)।

राजा : वातायन। त्वम् अपि स्वं नियोगम् अशून्यं कुरु।[2]

कञ्चुकी : यद् आज्ञापयति देव: (इति निष्क्रान्त:)

विदूषक :। किदं भवदा णिम्मच्छिअं। सम्पदं सिसिरातबच्छेअ

विदूषक :। कृतं भवता निर्मक्षिकम्।[3] साम्प्रतं शिशिरातपच्छेदरमणीये

रमणीए इमस्सिं पमदवणुद्देसे अत्ताणं रमइस्ससि।

अस्मिन् प्रमदवनोद्देशे आत्मानं रमयिष्यसि।

राजा : वयस्य। रन्ध्रोपनिपातिनोऽनर्था[4] इति यद् उच्यते तद् अव्यभिचारि वच:। कुत:।

1. 'Having committed that to writing [to a letter], let it be sent to me;' or, 'having written that in a letter, let it be given (to some messenger.)' *Dīyatām=prahīyatām* : Ś.

2. *Sva-niyogam antaḥpurāvekṣā-rūpam,* 'thy stated business consisting of superintendece of the female apartments :' Ś. *Vātāyana* is the name of the Kañcukī : 186, note 1.

3. *See* page 75, line 10, note 5, *Makṣikāya api abhāvān nirjanam* : Ś.

4. 'Misfortunes rush in through the (first) hole (they can find)' *i.e.,* Misfortunes are continually on the watch for an opening or vulnerable point by which to assail us; they seize the first opportunity that offers for attacking us; they quickly succeed each other before we have time to stand on our guard. This must have been a common proverb, something like our 'Misfortunes never come alone.' The king observes that 'this which is a saying commonly current among men is quite consistent and true [*avyabhicāri*] in his own case,' and he then proceeds to explain why [*kutas : see* p. 54, note 4] in the subsequent verse. *Randhra= chidra* :

मुनिसुताप्रणयस्मृतिरोधिना
मम च मुक्तम् इदं तमसा मनः।
मनसिजेन सखे प्रहरिष्यता
धनुषि चूतशरश्च निवेशितः[1] ।। 140 ।।

विदूषकः : चिट्ठ दाव। जाव इमिणा दण्डकट्ठेण कन्दप्पवाणं[2]

विदूषकः : तिष्ठ तावत्। यावद् अनेन दण्डकाष्ठेन कन्दर्पवाणं

णासइस्सामि।। इति दण्डकाष्ठम् उद्यम्य चूताङ्कुरं पातयितुम् इच्छति।

नाशयिष्यामि।। इति दण्डकाष्ठम् उद्यम्य चूताङ्कुरं पातयितुम् इच्छति।

राजा : (सस्मितम्) भवतु। दृष्टं ब्रह्मवर्चसम्।[3] सखे। क्वोपविष्टः प्रियायाः किञ्चिद् अनुकारिणीषु लतासु दृष्टिं विलोभयामि।

K. *Upanipātino=samāpatanti* : K. *Anarthāḥ=āpadaḥ* : K. *Yad ucyate, i.e., lokena* : K. *avyabhicāri=aviparyāsi [i.e., nānyathā bhavati]* : K.= *avaśyaṁ-bhāvi* or *yathārtham* : Ś. Dr. Boehtlingk translates, 'The unfortunate fall into a hole [grave],' which seems to me only supportable by a reading *randhropari-pātino' narthā*, noticed by Kāṭavema, although not adopted by him. Compare Bhartṛhari, ii., 86. *Prāyo gacchati yatra bhāgya-rahitas tatraiva yānty āpadaḥ.*

1. 'No sooner is this my soul freed from the darkness that obstructed the remebrance of my love for the sage's daughter, than a mango-blossom-shaft, O my friend, is fixed on (his) bow by the Heart-born (god) now-about-to-shoot-at-me.' The occurrence of *ca* in each clause denotes immediate connexion or succession, expressed in English by 'so soon as,' 'immediately on,' 'scarcely—when,' etc. : compare Kumāra-sam., iii., 58. *Manasi-ja*, 'born in the mind or heart,' a name of the Hindū Cupid : *see* page 101, note 1. *Praharisyat*, 'about to strike,' part. of the 2d. future. *Cūta-śara* : *see* p. 98, note 2 in middle. The verse which follows this in the Bengālī and Mackenzie MSS. is probably spurious.

2. I have adopted *vāṇam* from the oldest Bengālī MSS. Śaṅkara and Candraśekhara have *vāṇān*. The Devanāgarī, *vvāhim* for *vyāāhim*. Kāṭavema reads *vvāham* for *vyādham*, 'a hunter,' 'shooter.' May not *vyādhi* like *vyādha* signify 'hunting,' 'shooting,' 'sport ?' in which case the Devanāgarī reading might be retained.

3. 'The mighty power of a *Brāhmaṇa* is seen (by me).' This is

Verse 140. *Druta-Vilambita* (variety of *Jagatī*). *See* Verses 45, 72, 128.

विदूषकः : णं आसणपरिआरिआ चदुरिआ भवदा सन्दिट्ठा। माहवी-

विदूषकः : ननु आसन्नपरिचारिका[1] चतुरिका भवता सन्दिष्टा। माधवी-

मण्डबे इमे वेलं आदिवाहिस्सं। तहिं मे चित्तफलअगदं सहत्थलिहिदं

मण्डपे इमां वेलाम् अतिवाहयिष्यामि।[2] तस्मिन् मे चित्रफलक[3]गतां स्वहस्तलिखितां

तत्तहोदीए सउन्दलाए पडिकिदिं आणेहित्ति।

तत्रभवत्याः शकुन्तलायाः प्रतिकृतिम् आनयेति।

राजा : ईदृशं हृदयविनोदस्थानम्। तत् तमेव मार्गम् आदेशय।

विदूषकः : इदो इदो भवं।

विदूषकः : इतो इतो भवान्।

[उभौ परिक्रामतः सानुमत्यनुगच्छति]

विदूषकः : एसो मणिसिलापट्टअसणाहो माहवीमण्डबो उबहार-

विदूषकः : एष मणिशिलापट्टकसानाथो[4] माधवीमण्डप उपहार-

रमणिज्जदाए णिस्संसअं साअदेण विअ णो पडिच्छदि। ता पविसिअ

रमणीयतया[5] निःसंशयं स्वागतेन इव नौ प्रतीच्छति। तत् प्रविश्य

णिसीददु भवं।

निषीदतु भवान्।[6]

said ironically in reference to the Vidūṣaka's ridiculous attempt to destroy the arrows of Kāmadeva.

1. Literally, 'a near attendant,' *i.e.*, 'an attendant about one's person.'

2. *Vaḥ* in the the caus. with *ati,* has the sense of 'to pass time.' Compare Ragh., xix, 47; ix, 70.

3. *Citra-phalaka,* 'a picture-tablet,' 'a tablet for painting.' The same expression occurs in Ratnāvalī, p. 21, 1. 8; and p. 22, 1. 1, and Vikram., Act 2. As to *gatām,* here meaning 'committed to,' *see* p. 203, note 1.

4. *Maṇi-śilāpaṭṭaka-sanātha,* 'furnished with a marble seat :' see p. 26, note 2.

5. 'With the agreeableness of its flowery offerings.' 'with its charming flowery gifts.' *Upahāra,* or according to the Scholiasts *upcāra=kusumadi-Vistār* : Ś Flowers were used as complimentary presents or offerings, expecially to the god of Love.

6. *Sa bhavān* is in all the MSS. except my own, which omits *sa.*

[उभौ प्रवेशं कृत्वोपविष्टौ]

सानुमती : लदासंस्सिदा देक्खिस्सं दाव महीए पडिकिदिं। तदो से
सानुमती : लतासंश्रिता द्रक्ष्यामि तावत् सख्याः प्रतिकृतिम्। ततो ऽस्या
भत्तुणो बहुमुहं अणुराअं णिवेदइस्सं।। इति तथा कृत्वा स्थिता।
भर्तुर् बहुमतम् अनुरागं निवेदयिष्यामि [इति तथा कृत्वा स्थिता]

राजा : सखे। सर्वम् इदानीं स्मरामि शकुन्तलायाः प्रथमवृत्तान्तम्। कथितवान् अस्मि भवते। स भवान् प्रत्यादेशवेलायां मत्समीपम् उपगतो नासीत्। पूर्वमपि न त्वया कदाचित् सङ्कीर्तितं तत्रभवत्या नाम। कच्चिद् अहमिव विस्मृतवान् असि त्वम्।

विदूषकः : ण विसुमरामि। किन्तु सव्वं कहिअ अवसाणे उण
विदूषकः : न विस्मरामि। किन्तु सर्वं कथयित्वा अवसाने पुनस्
तुए परिहासविअप्पओ एसो ण भूदत्थात्ति आचक्खिदं। मएबि मिप्पिण्ड-
त्वया परिहासविजल्प[1] एष न भूतार्थ इत्य आचक्षितम्। मयापि मृत्पिण्ड-
बुद्धिणा तह एव्व गहीदं। अहवा भविदव्वदा बलवदी।
बुद्धिना[2] तथा एव गृहीतम्। अथवा भवितव्यता बलवती। **सानुमती। एव्वं णेदं।**
न्वेतत्।

राजा : ध्यात्वा।। सखे। त्रायस्व माम्।

विदूषकः : भो। किं एदं। अणुबबणंक्खु ईदिसं तुइ। कदाचि
विदूषकः :। भोः। किम् एतत्। अनुपपन्नं खलु ईदृशं त्वयि। कदाचित्
मप्पुरिसा सोअपत्तप्पाणो ण होन्ति। णं पवादेबि णिक्कम्पा
सत्पुरुषा शोकपात्रात्मानो न भवन्ति।[3] ननु प्रवातेऽपि निष्कम्पा

Sa may be used to emphasize other pronouns, and *sa bhavān* is therefore equivalent to *ille tu, i.e.*, 'your honour, that same person to whom alone I mentioned the circumstances.'

1. *See* page 93, line 8. As to *bhūtārtha* : *see* page 4, line 4.

2. 'Whose brains [intellect] is like a lump of clay,' 'whose understanding is dense as a clod of earth.' Compare our expression 'clod-pated,' 'clod-poll,' 'blockhead,' etc. Some of the MSS. have *manda-buddhinā*. As to *bhavitavyatā balavatī, see* p. 202, note 3.

3. 'Have not hearts that give place to sorrow,' 'do not give

गिरीओ।

गिरयः।

राजा : वयस्य। निराकरणविक्लवायाः प्रियायाः समवस्थाम्[1] अनुस्मृत्य बलवद् अशरणोऽस्मि। सा हि–

इतः प्रत्यादेशात् स्वजनम् अनुगन्तुं व्यवसिता
मुहुस् तिष्ठेत्युच्चैर् वदति गुरुशिष्ये गुरुसमे।
पुनर्दृष्टिं वाष्पप्रकरकलुषाम् अर्पितवती
मयि क्रूरे यत् तत् सविषम् इव शल्यं दहति माम्[2] ।। 141 ।।

सानुमती : अम्हहे। ईदिसी सकज्जपरदा। इमस्स सन्दावेण अहं
सानुमती : अहो। ईदृशी स्वकार्यपरता।[3] अस्य सन्तापेन अहं
रमामि।
रमे।

themselves up to uncontrolled grief.' As to *pātra*, 'a receptacle :' *see* p. 200, note 1 at end. I have followed Kāṭavema's reading. That of the other Devanāgarī MSS., *soa-vattavvā*, is hardly intelligible.

1. *Samavasthā*, with the sense of *avasthā*, 'state,' 'condition,' occurs not unfrequently in the plays. Compare Mālavik., p. 66, I. 1; p. 68, 1. 15. See also p. 162, l. 12 of this play, where it has the sense of *samāvasthā*.

2. '(The thought) that after her repudiation from hence, (when) she attempted to follow her attendants, the *Guru's* pupil, (who claimed obedience) like-the-Guru-himself, repeatedly saying to her in a loud voice, "Stay," she cast on me inexorable [cruel, hard-hearted] a second look bedimmed with gushing tears; that (it is which) torments me like an envenomed shaft.' *Itaḥ, i.e., mattaḥ,* 'by me :' Ś. *Vyavasitā=yatnaṁ kṛta-vatī* : Ś. *Muhus tiṣṭha, etc.* : p. 209, 1. 6. *Guru-same, i.e., alaṅghyādeśatayā.*

3. 'Alas ! such is (the force of) avarsion to one's own action,' or 'such is the force of self-reproach for wrong committed by one's self.' *Paratā* may mean either 'addiction to,' or 'alienation from.' It seems here to have the latter sense. Some of the Bengālī MSS. have *a-kajja-paradā*. *Sva-kārya, i.e.,* 'relating to Śakuntalā :' Ś. Compare p, 204, 1. 3.

Verse 141. *Śikhariṇī* (variety of *Atyaṣṭi*) *See* Verses 9, 24, 4[illegible], 62, 112.

विदूषकः : भो। अत्थि मे तक्को। केणबि तत्तहोदी आआसचारिणा

विदूषक5 : भोः। अस्ति मे तर्कः। केनापि तत्रभवती आकाशचारिणा

णीदेत्ति।

नीतेति।

राजा : कः पतिदेवताम् अन्यः परिमार्ष्टुम् उत्सहेत।[1] मेनका किल सख्यास् ते जन्मप्रतिष्ठेति[2] श्रुतवान् अस्मि। तत्सहचारिणीभिः सखी ते हृतेति मे हृदयम् आशङ्कते।

सानुमती : सम्मोहोक्खु विम्हअणिज्जो ण पडिबोहो।

सानुमती : सम्मोहः खलु विस्मयनीयः न प्रतिबोधः।[3]

विदूषकः :जइ एव्वं। अत्थिक्खु समाअमो कालेण तत्तहोदीए।

विदूषकः :। यदि एवं। अस्ति खलु समागमः कालेन तत्रभवत्या।

राजा : कथमिव।

विदूषकः : णक्खु मादापिदरा भत्तुविओअदुक्खिदं दुहिदरं देक्खिदुं

विदूषकः : न खलु मातापितरौ भर्तृवियोगदुःखितां दुहितरं द्रष्टुं

1. 'Who else could presume [would have the power] to-lay-a-finger-on [touch, bear off] the idol or (her) husband ?' *Kaḥ anya* : compare p. 205, 1. 4. *Pati-devatā*, 'the goddess of her husband,' or as we should say, 'a wife idolized by her husband.' This I take to be the sense of this expression, which is found in all the Devanāgarī MSS. The Bengālī have *pati-vartām*, 'a wife devoted to her husband.' *pari-mārṣṭum* [so read all the Devanāgarī] must come from *pari-mṛj*, to which Westergard gives but one meaning, 'abstergere.' Doubtless, it may be used like *pari-mris*, 'to lay hands on,' 'lay hold of :' *cf.* p. 199, note 7. One MS. [E.I.H. 1060] has *parā-marṣṭum*.

2. *Janma-pratiṣṭhā=janma-sthānam*, 'place of birth :'=*mātā*, 'mother :' Schol., Chēzy. *Janma-pratiṣṭhā=jananī* : Ś. Duṣyanta speaks of Śakuntalā to the Vidūṣaka as, 'thy friend.' So, the Yakṣa speaks of his wife to the Cloud, in Meghadūta, verses 87, 93.

3. 'Truly the state-of-mental-delusion [delirium, hallucination] is to be wondered at, not the recovery-from-it [the awakening from it].' According to Śaṅkara, *sammoha* is equivalent to 'forgetfulness,' and *pratibodha* to 'recollection.'

पारेन्ति।

पारयत:।[1]

राजा : वयस्य।

स्वप्नो नु माया नु मतिभ्रमो नु
क्लिष्टं नु तावत्फलम् एव पुण्यम्।
असन्निवृत्त्यै तद् अतीतम् एव
मनोरथानाम् अतटप्रपात:[2] ।। 142 ।।

1. This is either the causal form of the root *prī,* or a nominal verb from *pāra,* 'the other side;' meaning first 'to traverse,' 'get through,' 'bring to an end;' and secondly in Prākṛt and more modern Sanskṛt, 'to be able.' In the latter sense, which is the one required here, it is much used int he Bengālī dialect. Compare in Greek, πέρα, πέραδ, πεπαω, πεπαινω.

2. 'Was it a dream ? or an illusion-of-magic ? or a mental-delusion ? or (the result of my) good-works so far indeed rewarded (and then) marrred ? It has certainly passed away, never to returnT: (and so has become) the steep precipice of my heart's-fondest-hopes.' Such is the reading of all the Devanāgarī MSS., and doubtless the true one. In the third and fourth half-lines. I have adopted *eva* and *prapātaḥ* [in place of *ete* and *prapātāḥ*] from the Mackenzie, the former supported by Kāṭavema. *Māyā, i.e., indra-jālādi-kriyā* : Ś. Bhrama : one so affected imagines that to be present which does not really exist [*asad api sākṣāt-karoti* : Ś. Ch.] *Puṇyam, i.e., svakīyam sukṛtam* : K. *Tāvat phalam eva, i.e., darśana-phalam eva* : K. *darsana-mātra-phalam* : Ch., 'fruitful so far only as the sight of Śakuntalā :' K. *Kliṣṭam* [*cf.* p. 198, l. 9] : the best explanation of this idea will be found in p. 80 1. 6, with note 2, and in note 2 in this page. *Asannivṛttyai* : compare Raghu-v., viii, 48, *para-lokam asannivṛttaye gatāsi,* 'thou art gone to the other world never to return.' Śaṅkara thus explains the second half of the verse : 'As a man after ascending the peak of a mountain falls headlong, so my hopes after ascending to the sight of Śakuntalā are precipitated.' As to *taṭa, see* p. 172, note 1. Amara [ii, 3, 4] gives *ataṭa* as a synonym of *prapāta* and *bhṛgu*, each of these words signifying 'a precipice,'

Verse 142. *Upajāti* or *Ākhyānakī* (variety of *Triṣṭubh*). *See* Verses 41, 107, 121. 126.

विदूषकः : मा एव्वं। णं अङ्गुलीअअं एव्व णिदंसणं। अवस्सम्भाविणो

विदूषकः : मा एवम्। ननु अङ्गुलीयकम् एव निदर्शनम्। अवश्यम्भाविनो-

अचिन्तणिज्जो समाअमो होदित्ति।[1]

ऽचिन्तनीयः समागमो भवतीति।

राजा : [अङ्गुलीयकं विलोक्य] अये। इदं तावद् असुलभस्थानभ्रंशि शोचनीयम्।

तव सुचरितम् अङ्गुलीय नूनं

प्रतनु ममेव विभाव्यते फलेन।

अरुणनखमनोरमासु तस्याश्

च्युतमसि लब्धपदं यद् अङ्गुलीषु[2] ।। 143 ।।

सानुमती : जइ अणहत्थगदं भवे। सच्चं एव्व सोअणिज्जं भवे।

सानुमती : यदि अन्यहस्तगतं भवेत्। सत्यम् एव शोचनीयं भवेत्।

विदूषकः : भो। इअं णाम मुद्दा केण उद्देसेण तत्तहोदीए हत्थसंसग्गं

विदूषकः : भोः। इयं नाम मुद्रा केन उद्देशेन तत्रभवत्या हस्तसंसर्गं

पाविदा।

प्रापिता।

but there is no reason why *atața* should not be used as an epithet of *prapāta,* to denote a very precipitous declivity. The Bengālī MSS. read *Kḷriptaṁ nu tāvat phalam eva puṇyaiḥ asannivṛttau tad* [*asannivṛtyaitad*] *atīva manye manorathānām atața-prapātam.*

1. 'Is not the very ring a proof that there may be an unexpected meeting with that which must necessarily come ?' *Nanu* is often=the Latin *nonne.*

2. 'Verily, O ring, the-merit-of-thy-good-works like mine is judged [proved] to be insignificant [slender] by the reward [result]; since after-gaining-a-station on the charming-rosy-nailed fingers of that-lady thou hast fallen (from it).' The doctrine of laying up a store of merit by good deeds performed in the present and former births is an essential part of the Hindū creed : see the last verse, and compare p. 183, note 3. *Aruṇa-nakha* : see p. 124, note 2 at end. *Aruṇa* may imply 'ruddy as the dawn :' see page 140, note 3.

Verse 143. *Puṣpitāgrā,* in which each whole line is alike. *See* Verses 32, 37.

सानुमती : ममबि कोदूहलेण आआरिदो एसो।

सानुमती : ममापि कौतूहलेन आकारित एषः।[1]

राजा : श्रूयताम्। तदा स्वनगराय प्रस्थितं मां प्रिया सवाष्पम् आह। कियच्चिरेणार्यपुत्रः प्रतिपत्तिं[2] दास्यतीति।

विदूषकः : तदो तदो।

विदूषकः : ततस् ततः।

राजा : पश्चाद् इमां मुद्रां तदङ्गुलौ निवेशयता मया प्रत्यभिहिता।

एकैकम् अत्र दिवसे दिवसे मदीयं
नामाक्षरं गणय गच्छसि यावद् अन्तम्।
तावत् प्रिये मदवरोधगृहप्रवेशं
नेता जनस् तव समीपम् उपैष्यतीति[3] ।। 144 ।।

तच्च दारुणात्मना मया मोहान् नानुष्ठितम्।

सानुमती : रमणीओक्खु अवही विहिणा विसंवादिदो।

सानुमती : रमणीयः खलु अवधिर् विधिना विसंवादितः[4]।

1. 'By my curiosity also he (would be) incited (to ask the reason).' *Kautūhala=śravaṇotkaṇṭā*, 'desire of hearing :' Ś. *Ākārita=āhata, prerita* : Compare *taṁ vara-dānāya ākārayāmāsa* : Rāmāyaṇa, ii, 13, 2. Śaṅkara reads *vādita*, 'made to speak,' in place of *ākārita*. The Bengālī MSS. have *vyāpārita*.

2. Compare page 170, line 3, with note 1 in middle.

3. 'Count [spell] hereon [*i.e.*, on this ring] one by one each day the letters of my name until thou reachest the end. So soon, O loved one, (as thou hast spelt the whole name) a messenger will come into thy presence who-will-conduct thee to the entrance of my private-apartments.' *Nāmākṣaram* : compare p. 53, 1. 2. *Gacchasi* : so reads the Taylor MS. and my own, supported by the Kolkata edition; the others, *gaccati*. *Netā* : the noun of agency has sometimes the sense of a future participle, and my govern the case of the ver. So *vaktā vākyam*, 'one who is about to speak a speech :' Draup., 32. Indeed the nom. case of this form of noun is never distinguishable from the 3d pers. of the 1st fut.

4. 'Verily (this) charming period (of expectation) was by Destiny made (to pass away) without-the-appointment-being-kept,'

Verse 144. *Vasanta-tilakā* (variety of *Śakkarī*). *See* verses 8, 27, 31, 43, 46, 64, 74, 80, 82, 83, 91, 93, 94, 95, 100, 104, 105, 108, 123, 124.

विदूषकः : कहं धीवरकप्पिअस्स लोहिअमच्छस्स उदलब्भन्तले
विदूषकः : कथं धीवरकल्पितस्य रोहितमत्स्यस्य उदराभ्यन्तरे
आसि।
आसीत्[1]।

राजा : शचीतीर्थं वन्दमानायाः सख्यास् ते हस्ताद् गङ्गास्रोतसि परिभ्रष्टम्।[2]

विदूषकः : जुज्जइ।

विदूषकः : युज्यते।

सानुमती : अदो एव्व तवस्सिणीए सउन्दलाए अधम्मभीरुणो इमस्स
सानुमती : अत एव तपस्विन्याः शकुन्तलाया अधर्म्मभीरोर् अस्य
राएसिणो परिणए सन्देहो आसि। अहवा। ईदिसो अणुराओ अहिणाणं
राजर्षेः परिणये सन्देह आसीत्। अथवा। ईदृशोऽनुरागोऽभिज्ञानम्
अवेक्खदि। कहं विअ एदं।
अपेक्षते। कथम् इव एतत्।

राजा : उपालप्स्ये तावद् इदम् अङ्गुलीयकम्।

विदूषकः : (आत्मगतं) महीदो णेण पन्था उन्मत्तआणं।

विदूषकः : (आत्मगतम्) गृहीतोऽनेन पन्था उन्मत्तानाम्।

राजा :

कथं नु तं बन्धुरकोमलाङ्गुलिं
करं विहायासि निमग्नम् अम्भसि।
अथवा। अचेतनं नाम गुणं न लक्षयेन्
मयैव कस्माद् अवधीरिता प्रिया[3] ।। 145 ।।

or 'Destiny caused that the delightful appointment-of-a-period (for the reunion of these lovers) should fail of being kept.' *Visamvad* is 'to fail in keeping a promise or agreement.' Cf. *phale visamvadati* : Vikram., Act 2.

1. The Vidūṣaka designedly uses the dialect of the fisherman : see page 217, line 1 and 3; page 213, note 2.

2. Compare page 202, line 7-9, note 1.

3. 'How (couldest) thou (allow thyself) to be immersed in the water, having abandoned that hand with (its) slender delicate fingers ? But (where is the wonder ? for) an inanimate-object may

---

Verse 145. *Vaṁśasthavila* (variety of *Jagatī*) *See* Verses 18, 22, 23, 67, 81, 114, 117.

विदूषकः : (आत्मगतं) कहं बुभुक्खाए खादिदष्वोम्हि।

विदूषकः : (आत्मगतं) कथं बुभुक्षया खादितव्योऽस्मि।[1]

राजा : अकारणपरित्यक्ते। अनुशयतप्तहृदयम् तावद् अनुकम्प्यताम् अयं जनः पुनर्दर्शनेन।

[प्रविश्य पटाक्षेपेण चित्रफलकहस्ता]

चतुरिका : इअं चित्तगदा भट्टिणी (इति चित्रफलकं दर्शयति)।

चतुरिका: इयं चित्रगता भर्त्री (इति चित्रफलकं दर्शयति)।

विदूषकः : साहुवअस्स। महुरावत्थाणदंसणिज्जो भावाणुप्पवेसो। खलदि

विदूषकः : साधु वयस्य। मधुरावस्थानदर्शनीयो भावानुप्रवेशः। स्खलति

विअ मे दिट्ठी णिणुणअप्पदेसेसु।

इव मे दृष्टिर् निम्नोन्नतप्रदेशेषु।[2]

सानुमती : अम्मो एसा राएसिणो णिउणदा। जाणे। सही अग्गदो मे

सानुमती : अहो एषा राजर्षेर् निपुणता। जाने। सखी अग्रतो मे

वट्टदित्ति।

वर्तत इति।

राजा :

यद् यत् साधु न चित्रे स्यात् क्रियते तत् तद् अन्यथा।
तथापि तस्या लावण्यं रेखया किञ्चिद् अन्वितम्[3] ।। 146 ।।

well not distinguish excellence. How (was it that) even by me (my) beloved was rejected ?' *Bandhura=unnatānata,* 'undulating :' Schol., Chēzy :=*ramya,* 'beautiful :' Ch. *Athavā* : *see* p. 30, note 3.

1. 'Why am I to be devoured by hunger (while he is apostrophizing his ring) ?' A very characteristic remark : *see* p. 59, note 1 in middle.

2. 'The imitation of nature is charming by (reason of) the sweet position [disposition, arrangement, posture, attitude, of the figure or figures]. My sight stumbles as it were amidst the depressions and prominences;' *i.e.,* The relief or appearance of projection and depression in the picture is so well managed that my eye is deceived, and seems to follow the inequalities of surface.

3. 'Whatever is not well (executed) in the picture [whatever

Verse 146. *Śloka* or *Anuṣṭubh. See* Verses 5, 6, 11, 12, 26, 47, 50, 51, 53, 73, 76, 84, 87, 125, 130.

सानुमती : सरिसं एव्वं पच्छादाबगरुणो सिणेहस्स अणवलेबस्सअ।

सानुमती : सदृशम् एवं पश्चात्तापगुरोः स्नेहस्य अनवलेपस्य च।

विदूषकः : भो। दाणिं तिणि तत्तहोदीओ दीसन्ति। सव्वाओअ

विदूषकः : भोः। इदानीं तिस्रम् तत्रभवत्यो दृश्यन्ते। सर्वाश्च

दंसणीआओ। कदमा एत्थ तत्तहोदी सउन्दला।

दर्शनीयाः। कतमा अत्र तत्रभवती शकुन्तला।

सानुमती : अणभिणोक्खु ईदिसस्स रूबस्स मोहदिट्ठी अअं जणो।

सानुमती : अनभिज्ञः खलु ईदृशस्य रूपस्य मोघ[1]दृष्टिर् अयं जनः।

राजा : त्वं तावत् कतमां तर्कयसि।

विदूषकः : तक्केमि। जा एसा सिढिलकेसबन्धणुव्वन्तकुसुमेण केसन्तेण

विदूषकः :। तर्कयामि। या एषा शिथिलकेशबन्धनोद्वान्तकुसुमेन केशान्तेन

उब्भिणस्सेअविन्दुणा वअणेण विसेसदो ओसरिआहिं बाहाहिं अवसेअ-

उद्भिन्नस्वेदविन्दुना वदनेन विशेषतोऽपसृताभ्यां बाहुभ्याम् अवसेक-

सिणिद्धतरुणपल्लवस्स चूतअपाअबस्स पासे इसिपरिस्सन्ता विअ

स्निग्धतरुणपल्लवस्य चूतपादपस्य पार्श्वे ईषत्परिश्रान्ता इव

आलिहिदा। एसा सउन्दला। इदराओ सहीओत्ति।

आलिखिता। एषा शकुन्तला। इतरे सख्याविति।[2]

falls short of perfect beauty], all that is wrongly (pourtrayed). Nevertheless her loveliness is in some measure possessed by the drawing,' *i.e.*, The artist has to some extant made a likeness though very inferior to the original. *Rekhā=lekhana*, 'a sketch,' 'delineation :' K. The Bengālī have *lekhayā*. The Dictionary gives *citra-lekhā* only.

1. Compare page 76, line 9, note 2; Bhaṭṭi-kāvya, v, 19.

2. 'I imagine that she who is delineated as if a little fatigued at the side of the mango-tree, the tender shoots of which are glistening after her watering (of them), with arms extended in a peculiar manner, with a face having drops of perspiration breaking out (upon it), with locks of hair the flowers of which have escaped through the slackened hair-band-this (I imagine) is Śakuntalā, the other two (are her) female friends.' *Udvānta, lit.*, 'vomited up;' here 'dropped off,' 'fallen down.' *Udbhinna-sveda-vindunā* : compare p. 70, note 3 : hence in line 11 of that page, *sveda-leśair abhinnam* is a

राजा : निपुणो भवान्। अस्त्यत्र मे भावचिह्नम्।

स्विन्नाङ्गुलिविनिवेशो रेखाप्रान्तेषु दृश्यते मलिनः।

अश्रु च कपोलपतितं दृश्यम् इदं वर्णिकोच्छ्रासात्[1] ।। 147 ।।

चतुरिके। अर्द्धलिखितम् एतद् विनोदस्थानम्।[2] तस्माद् गच्छ। वर्तिकां तावद् आनय।

चतुरिका : अज्जमाठव्व। अवलम्ब चित्तफलअं। जाव आअच्छामि।

चतुरिका : आर्यमाठव्य। अवलम्बस्व चित्रफलकम्। यावद् आगच्छामि।

राजा : अहम् एवैतद् अवलम्बे (इति यथोक्तं करोति)

[निष्क्रान्ता चेटी]

राजा :अहं हि

साक्षात् प्रियाम् उपगताम् अपहाय पूर्वं

better reading than *kleśa-leśair*. *Viśeṣato apasṛtābhyām* : it appears from a subsequent passage that she is represented in the act of warding off the bee mentioned in the 1st Act, p. 32, 1. 2. *Itare*, nom. dual feminine.

1. 'Here is a sign of my passion : the soiled impression of (my) perspiring fingers is observed on the edges of the picture, and a tear here [this tear] fallen from (my) cheek is perceptible from the obliteration [effacement, disappearance, cessation] of the colour.' However offensive to our notions of good taste, it is certain that in Hindū erotic poetry, perspiration is considered to be one of the signs of passionate love. *Varṇikā* [=*varṇa*] is the reading of Kāṭavema, supported by most of the Bengālī MSS., which have *varṇakā*. The other Devanāgarī have *vartikā*, which may possibly, like *varti*, mean 'collyrium,' 'pigment.' *Ucchvāsa*, lit., 'breathing-time;' hence, 'cessation.' *Kapola-patitam* might be rendered 'fallen on the cheek,' [*i.e.*, of the portrait] as well as 'from my cheek.' Compare Vikram., Act 2, *aṅguli-svedana me lupyante'kṣrāṇi*.

2. Literally, 'pleasure-ground,' *i.e.*, landscape; '*lieu de la scēne :*' Chēzy.

Verse 147. *Āryā* or *Gāthā*. (*See* Verse 2.)

—◡◡| ◡—◡ |◡◡—‖—◡◡|——| ◡ | —— |—

—— |◡◡◡◡| —— ‖ —— |——|◡—◡|—◡◡|—

चित्रार्पितां मुहुर् इमां बहु मन्यमानः।
स्रोतोवहां पथि निकामजलाम् अतीत्य
जातः सखे प्रणयवान् मृगतृष्णिकायाम्[1] ।। 148 ।।

विदूषक : (आत्मगतं) एसो अत्तभवं णदिं अदिक्कमिअ मिअतिण्हिआए सङ्कन्तो (प्रकाशं) भो। अबरं किं एत्थ लिहिदव्वं।

विदूषक : (आत्मगतम्) एषोऽत्रभवान् नदीम् अतिक्रम्य मृगतृष्णया सङ्क्रान्तः (प्रकाशम्) भोः। अपरं किम् अत्र लिखितव्यम्।

सानुमती : जो जो पदेसो सहीए मे अहिरूबो। तं तं आलिहिदुकामो भवे।

सानुमती : यो यः प्रदेशः सख्या मेऽभिरूपः। तं तम् आलिखितुकामो भवेत्।

राजा : श्रूयताम्।

कार्या सैकतलीनहंसमिथुना स्रोतोवहा मालिनी
पादास् ताम् अभितो निषणहरिणा गौरीगुरोः पावनाः।
शाखालम्बितवल्कलस्य च तरोर् निर्मातुम् इच्छाम्यधः

1. '(While) again and again making much of her (image) committed to a picture, having previously repudiated my beloved when she came into my presence, I have become, O friend, (as it were) possessed of a longing for the waters-of-the mirage, after passing by a river in-my-road having-plenty-of-water;' *i.e.*, I am like one who prefers the shadow to the substance, the semblance to the reality. *Citrārpitām=citra-gatām* : *see* p. 235, note 3. *Srotovahā* : Beautiful women are often compared by Hindū poets to rivers, which in Sanskṛt are always feminine. *Nikāma-jalām*, 'yielding abundance of water, as much as can be desired :' as to *nikāma* in this sense, see p. 187, note 1 in middle. *Mṛga-tṛṣṇikā*, lit., 'thirst of deer,' 'a vapour floating over waste places, which appears at a distance like water, and deceives men and animals.'

2. 'The river Mālinī ought to be drawn [made] with a pair of swans [flamingoes] resting on a sandbank; (and) on both sides of it

---

Verse 148. *Vasanta-tilakā* (variety of *Śakkarī*). *See* Verses 8, 27, 31, 43, 46, 64, 74, 80, 82, 83, 91, 93, 94, 95, 100, 104, 105, 108, 123, 124, 144.

Verse 149. *Śārdūla-vikrīḍita* (variety of *Atidhṛti*). *See* Verses 14, 30, 36, 39, 50, 63, 79, 85, 86, 97, 98, 111, 137, 138.

शृङ्गे कृष्णमृगस्य वामनयनं कण्डूयमानां मृगीम्[2] ।। 149 ।।

विदूषकः : (आत्मगतं) जह अहं देक्खामि। पूरिदव्वं णेण चित्तफलअं

विदूषकः : (आत्मगतम्) यथा अहं पश्यामि। पूरयितव्यम् अनेन चित्रफलकं

लम्बकुच्चाणं ताबसाणं कदम्बेहिं।

लम्बकूर्चानां तापसानां कदम्बैः[1]।

राजा : वयस्य। अन्यच्च शकुन्तलायाः प्रसाधनम् अभिप्रेतम्[2] अत्र विस्मृतम् अस्माभिः।

विदूषकः : किं विअ।

विदूषकः : किम् इव।

सानुमती : वणवासस्स सोउमारस्सअ जं सरिसं भविस्सदि।

सानुमती : वनवासस्य सौकुमारस्य च यत् सदृशं भविष्यति।

the sacred hills-contiguous to Himālaya [Gaurī's father,] with-some-deer-reaclining (on them); and I wish under a tree, on-whose-boughs-some-bark-garments-are-suspended, to form a doe rubbing (her) left eye on the horn of a black antelope.' *Haṁsa*, 'a kind of wild-goose of a white colour, with golden wings; something between a swan and a flamingo.' It serves the god Brahmā as a vehicle, and hence the *haṁsa-nāda* or 'cry' of this bird has a sacred character, just as the cry of the swan, with the Greeks : the voice of a beautiful woman is even compared to it : Bhaṭṭi-kāvya, v. 18. *Mālinī* : compare p. 102, 1. 4; p. 16, 1. 6. *Pādāḥ=pratyanta-parvatāḥ* : Ś.=*paryanta-parvatāḥ* : K. *Gaurī-guroḥ=Himālayasya* : Ś. *Himāla*, the god of the great snowy range was the father of the goddess Gaurī, the wife of Śiva, whence she is called Pārvatī, Himavatsutā, Himajā, etc. *Śākhā*—etc. : compare p. 18, note 1 at end; p. 24, note 1.

1. 'With multitudes of long-bearded monks.' *Lamba, lit.*, 'hanging down;' *kūrcca=śmaśru* : Ś. The Mackenzie reads *Lamba-kucchāṇaṁ paḍikamma kuvvāṇeṇa tābasaṇiṁ ṇiareṇa.*

2. Chēzy considers that *abhipretam* must here be taken in the sense of 'going before all other,' 'having the preference,' *i.e.*, the favourite ornament. There seems to me no reason why this word should not retain its regular meaning, and the passage be translated, 'there is another of Śakuntalā's ornaments intended (to be drawn) on this picture (but) forgotten by me.'

राजा :

कृतं न कर्णार्पितबन्धनं सखे
शिरीषम् आगण्डविलम्बिकेशरम्।
न वा शरच्चन्द्रमरीचिकोमलं
मृणालसूत्रं रचितं स्तनान्तरे[1] ।। 150 ।।

विदूषकः : भो। किं णु तत्तहोदी रत्तकुवलअपल्लवसोहिणा
विदूषकः : भोः। किं नु तत्रभवती रक्तकुवलयपल्लवशोभिना
अग्गहत्थेण मुहं आवारिअ चइदचइदा विअ ठिदा (सावधानं निरूप्य।
अग्रहस्तेन मुखम् आवार्य चकितचकिता इव स्थिता (सावधानं निरूप्य।
दृष्ट्वा) आ। एसो दासीएपुत्तो कुसुमरसपाडच्चरो तत्तहोदीए वअणं
दृष्ट्वा) आः। एष दास्याःपुत्रः कुसुमरसपाटच्चरस् तत्रभवत्या वदनम्
अहिलङ्घदि महुअरो।
अभिलङ्घति मधुकरः।[2]

राजा : ननु वार्यताम् एष धृष्टः।

विदूषकः : भवं एव्व अविणीदाणं सासिदा इमस्स वारणे पहवि-
विदूषकः : भवान् एव अविनीतानां शासिता अस्य वारणे प्रभवि-
स्सदि।
ष्यति।

राजा : युज्यते। अयि भोः कुसुमलताप्रियातिथे। किम् अत्र परिपतनखेदम् अनुभवसि।

1. 'A śirīṣa-blossom, with its stalk fastened in her ear, (and) its-filaments-hanging-down-to-her-cheek has not been drawn [made], O friend, Nor has a necklace-of-lotus-fibres, soft-as-the-rays-of-the autumnal-moon, been formed in the midst of her bosom.' *Bandhana=prasava-bandhana=vṛnta* : Ś. Ch. Compare p. 102, note 3, and p. 226, note 1. *Śirīṣa* : *see* p. 5, note 4, and p. 52, note 3. The blossom of a plant is always neuter in Sanskṛt.

2. With regard to this passage and what follows, compare pp., 32, 33, 34. As to *rakta-kuvalaya*, etc. : see p. 25, note 1. As to *dāsyāḥ-putra, see* p. 61, note 3.

Verse 150. *Vanśasthavila* (variety of *Jagatī*). *See* Verses 18, 22, 23, 67, 81, 114, 117, 119, 145.

एषा कुसुमनिषण्णा तृषितापि सती भवन्तम् अनुरक्ता।
प्रतिपालयति मधुकरी न खलु मधु विना त्वया पिवति[1] ।। 151 ।।

सानुमती : अज्ज अभिजादंक्खु एसो वारिदो।

सानुमती : अद्य अभिजातं खलु एष वारितः।[2]

विदूषकः : पडिसिद्धाबि वामा एसा जादी।

विदूषकः : प्रतिषिद्धापि वामा एषा जातिः।[3]

राजा : एवं भो न मे शासने तिष्ठसि। श्रूयतां तर्हि सम्प्रति।

अक्लिष्टबालतरुपल्लवलोभनीयं
पीतं मया सदयम् एव रतोत्सवेषु।
बिम्बाधरं स्पृशसि चेद् भ्रमर प्रियायास्
त्वां कारयामि कमलोदरबन्धनस्थम्[4] ।। 152 ।।

1. 'Wherefore dost thou undergo the fatigue of hovering round about ? There [*eṣā*] resting-on-a-flower the-devotedly-attached female-bee, although being thirsty, waits for the thee; nor indeed without thee will she sip (its) nectar.' *Paripatana,* 'flying round about,' the first sense of *pat* is 'to fly.'

2. 'For-once-now this (bee) is warned-off [kept off] quite in a courteous manner.' The meaning is somewhat obscure, but there seems to be a satirical allusion to the king's polite address to the bee, followed as it is by a threat.

3. 'This race (of animals), however (it may be driven off, is perverse.' The Bengālī MSS. and Kāṭavema have *pratiṣiddha-vāmā*. *Vāmā* in its first sense means 'left,' 'not right;' hence anything 'turned from the right,' 'reverse,' 'perverse,' 'refractory.'

4. 'If, O bee, thou touchest the bimba-lip of (my) beloved charming as the uninjured blossom of a young tree, that very (lip which has been) tenderly drunk by me in love's banquets, (then) I will make thee imprisoned in the hollow of a lotus.' Compare verse 77, p. 127, note 1. *Bimbādharam* : 'lip like the *bimba,' i.e.,* of a bright red colour, like the gourd of the Bimba or Momordica monadelpha, a cucurbitaceous plant. So *Bimbādharālaktakaḥ* : Mālavik., p. 30, 1;

Verse 151. *Āryā* or *Gāthā*. (*See* Verse 2.)

—— |◡◡◡◡| —— ‖ ◡◡— |◡◡—|◡—◡|◡◡—|—
—◡◡| ◡—◡ |◡◡—‖◡◡◡◡|◡◡—| ◡ |—◡◡|—

Verse 152. *Vasanta-tilakā* (variety of *Śakkarī*). *See* Verses 8, 27, 31, 43, 46, 64, 74, 80, 82, 83, 91, 93, 94, 95, 100, 104, 105, 108, 123, 124, 144, 148.

विदूषकः : एव्वंति एहदण्डस्स किं ण भाइस्सदि (प्रहस्य। आत्मगतं)

विदूषकः : एवंतीक्ष्णदण्डस्य किं न भेष्यति[1] (प्रहस्य। आत्मगतम्)

एसो दाव उम्मत्तो। अहम्पि एदस्स सङ्गेण ईदिसवअणो विअ संवुत्तो।

एष तावद् उन्मत्तः। अहमपि एतस्य सङ्गेन ईदृशवचन इव संवृत्तः।

(प्रकाशं) भो। चित्तंक्खु एदं।

(प्रकाशम्) भोः। चित्रं खलु एतत्।

राजा : कथं चित्रम्।

सानुमती : अहम्पि दाणिं अणवगदत्था। किं उण जहलिहिदाणुभावी

सानुमती : अहमपि इदानीम् अनवगतार्था। किं पुनर् यथालिखितानुभावी

एमो।

एषः।[2]

राजा : वयस्य। किम् इदम् अनुष्ठितं पौरोभाग्यम्।[3]

दर्शनसुखम् अनुभवतः साक्षाद् इव तन्मयेन हृदयेन।
स्मृतिकारिणा त्वया मे पुनरपि चित्रीकृता कान्ता[4] ।। 153 ।।

Ragh., xiii, 16. Compare our expression, 'cheery-lip.' *Kamalodara*—etc. : see p. 181, note 1. *Bandhana* seems here to mean 'the place of imprisonment.'

1. 'How should he not stand in awe of one who has (threatened him with) so severe a punishment ?' *Tīkṣṇa-daṇḍa*, 'severe in punishing,' 'a strict disciplinarian.' The Prākṛt equivalent of *tīkṣṇa* is *tiṇha*, according to Vararuci, iii, 33, although most of the MSS. have *tikkhaṇa*. The root *bhī* in Sanskṛt is usually joined with an able. case, but the gen. is admissible. Kāṭavema, however, observes that this construction is peculiar to Prākṛt. Compare *dākṣiṇya-paścāttāpasya bibhemi* : Vikram., end of Act 2.

2. 'Even I now did not understand the thing : how much less should he perceive that it was painted ?' *Anavagatārthā* : so reads the Mackenzie MS., supported by Kāṭavema; the others, *avagatārthā*.

3. 'Why has this ill-natured-act been perpetrated (by you) ?' As to *paurobhāgyam* : *see* p. 208, note 2. Kāṭavema observes, *purobhāgī=doṣaika-darśī=duṣṭaḥ, tasya karma paurobhāggam*, and refers to Pāṇini, V, 1, 124.

4. 'My beloved in once more transformed into a picture by thee

---

Verse 153. *Āryā* or *Gāthā*. (*See* Verse 2.)

—⏑⏑|⏑⏑⏑⏑|⏑⏑—‖ —— |⏑⏑—|⏑—⏑|⏑⏑—|⏑
⏑⏑—|⏑—⏑|——‖⏑⏑⏑⏑| ——| ⏑ |——|—

[इति वाष्पं विहरति]

सानुमती : पुव्वाबरविरोही अपुव्वो एसो विरहमग्गो।

सानुमती : पूर्वापरविरोधी अपूर्व एष विरहमार्ग[1]:।

राजा : वयस्य। कथम् एवम् अविश्रान्तदु:खम् अनुभवामि।

प्रजागरात् खिलीभूतस् तस्या: स्वप्ने समागम:।
वाष्पम् तु न ददात्येनां द्रष्टुं चित्रगताम् अपि[2] ।। 154 ।।

सानुमती : सव्वहा पमज्जिइं तुए पच्चादेमदुक्खं सउन्दलाए।

सानुमती : सर्वथा प्रमार्जितं[3] त्वया प्रत्यादेशदु:खं शकुन्तलाया:।

reviving the recollection of me enjoying the bliss of beholding her just-as-if (she were) present before my eyes, having my (whole) soul wrapped-up-in-her.' *Tan-mayena=Śakuntalā-mayena* : Ś., *lit.*, 'with a heart made of Śakuntalā,' *i.e.*, wholly absorbed by her. As to *viharati* in the line following this verse : see p. 165, note 2.

1. 'The demeanour of (one in a state of) separation, opposing first one thing and then another, is singular [unexampled, without a precedent].' *Pūrvā-para-virodhī* may mean 'setting itself against everything from first to last,' or 'from first to last untoward.' Lovers, when separated from each other, were supposed to find comfort and amusement in various trifling employments expressive of their passion [*see* Megha-dūta, verse 86]; but here was the case of one whom nothing could divert.

2. '(The hope of) meeting her in sleep is rendered vain through (my) wakefulness. Moreover the (blinding) tears (that fill my eyes) will not permit me to behold her even represented-in-a-picture.' As to *vāṣpa, see* p. 155, note 3 in middle. *Khilībhūta=durlabha* : Ś. In Hindū poetry dreams and pictures are te regular standing artifices of Lovers for tricking themselves into fictitious unions with their mistresses; just as sleeplessness and tears are the regular standing impediments to such devices.Compare Megh., 104, *Tvān ālikhya aśrais tāvan muhur upacitair dṛṣṭir ālupyate me krūras tasminnapi na sahate saṅgamaṁ nau kṛtāntaḥ*. See also Megh., 89. And Vikram., Act 2, *Katham upālabhe nidrāṁ svapne samāgama-kāriṇīm; na ca suvadanām ālekhye' pi priyāṁ samavāpya tāṁ mama nayanayor udvāṣpatvaṁ ṣakhe na bhaviṣyati.*

3. 'Atoned for,' *lit.*, 'wiped clean,' 'wiped out.'

Verse 154. *Śloka* or *Anuṣṭubh. See* Verses 5, 6, 11, 12, 26, 47, 50, 51, 53, 73, 76, 84, 87, 125, 127, 146.

चतुरिका : (प्रविश्य) जेदु जेदु भट्टा । वट्टिआकरण्डअं मेण्हिअ इदोमुहं
चतुरिका : (प्रविश्य) जयतु जयतु भर्ता। वर्तिकाकरण्डकं[1] गृहीत्वा इतोमुखं
पत्थिदन्हि।
प्रस्थितास्मि।

राजा : किं च।

चतुरिका : सो मे हत्थादो अन्तरा तरलिआदुदिआए देवीए वसुमदीए
चतुरिका : स मे हस्ताद् अन्तरा[2] तरलिकाद्वितीयया देवया वसुमत्या
अहं एव्व अज्जउत्तस्स उबणइस्संत्ति सबलक्कारं गहिदो। विदूषक :।
अहम् एव आर्यपुत्रस्य उपनेष्यामि इति सबलात्कारं गृहीतः। **विदूषक** :।
दिट्ठिआ तुमं मुक्का।
दिष्ट्या त्वं मुक्ता।

चतुरिका : जाव देवीए विडबलग्गं उत्तरीअं तरलिआ मोचेदि। ताव
चतुरिका : यावद् देव्या विटपलग्नम् उत्तरीयं तरलिका मोचयति। तावन्
मए णिव्वाहिदो अत्ता।
मया निर्वाहित आत्मा।[3]

राजा : वयस्य। उपस्थिता देवी बहुमानगर्विता[4] च। भवान् इमां प्रतिकृतिं रक्षतु।

विदूषकः : अत्ताणंत्ति भणाहि (चिचफलकम् आदायोत्थाय च)।
विदूषकः : आत्मानमिति भण। चित्रफलकम् आदायोत्थाय च।।

1. 'Box of colours :' see page 245, note 1.

2. 'On the way,' 'midway.' The same expression occurs in p. 253, 1. 11. See also Mālavik. 8, 18. As to Vasumatī, see p. 182, note 2.

3. 'I took myself off,' 'I made my escape,' *lit.* 'By me my own person was carried off.' The Prākṛt is responsible for this idiom and construction. *Nirvāhita* is the reading of most of the Devanāgarī MSS. and there seems no reason why it should not stand with the sense 'carried away,' 'borne off.' Kāṭavema has *nirvāsita,* 'expelled.' Some of the Bengālī, *ṇihṇavida* for *nihnuta,* 'concealed.' Śaṅkara has *nirgato.*

4. 'Rendered insolent by my great attention to her.'

जइ भवं अन्तेउरकालकूडादो मुञ्चीअदि। तदो मं मेहप्पडिच्छन्दे पासादे
यदि भवान् अन्तःपुरकालकूटद्[1] मुच्यते।। ततो मां मेघप्रतिच्छन्दे प्रासादे
सहाबेहि (इति दुतपदं निष्क्रान्तः)
शब्दय[2] (इति द्रुतपदं निष्क्रान्तः)

सानुमती : अणसङ्कन्तहिअओबि पढमसम्भावणं अबेक्खदि।
सानुमती : अन्यसङ्क्रान्तहृदयेऽपि[3] प्रथमसम्भावनाम् अपेक्षते।
अदिसिढिलसोहदो दाणिं एसो।
अतिशिथिलसौहृद इदानीम् एषः।

प्रतीहारी : (प्रविश्य पत्रहस्ता) जेदु जेदु देवो।

प्रतीहारी : (प्रविश्य पत्रहस्ता) जयतु जयतु देवः।

राजा : वेत्रवति। न खल्वन्तरा दृष्टा त्वया देवी।

प्रतीहारी : अहइं। पत्तहत्थं मं देक्खिअ पडिणिउत्ता।

प्रतीहारी : अथ किम्। पत्रहस्तां मां दृष्ट्वा प्रतिनिवृत्ता।

राजा : कार्यज्ञा कार्योपरोधं मे परिहरति।

प्रतीहारी : देव। अमच्चो विणबेदि। अत्थजादस्स गणणाबहुलदाए
प्रतीहारी : देव। अमात्यो विज्ञापयति। अर्थजातस्य गणनाबहुलतया
एक्कं एव्व पोरकव्जं अबेक्खिदं। तं देवो पत्तारूढं पच्चक्खीकरेदुत्ति।
एकम् एव पौरकार्यम् अपेक्षितम्।[4] तद् देवः पत्रारूढं प्रत्यक्षीकरोत्विति।

1. 'From the bane of the inner apartments.' *kāla-kūṭa :* At the churning of the ocean, after the deluge, by the gods and demons, for the recovery or production of fourteen sacred things, a deadly poison called *kāla-kūṭa* or Halā-hala was generated, so virulent that it would have destroyed the world, had not the god Śiva swallowed it. Its only effect was to leave a black mark on his throat, whence his name *nīla-kaṇṭha*. Kāṭavema has *kalahādo* for *kalahāt*, 'strife,' and Śaṅkara, *kūṭāt*, snare.'

2. 'Call me in the palace (named) Megha-particchanda.' *Śabha* may form either a nominal or a verb of the 10th class : compare p. 150, note 2.

3. 'Although his heart [affection] is transferred to another.' Compare in Vikram., Act 3, *'Anya-saṅkrānta-premāṇo nāgarā adhikaṁ dakṣiṇā bhavanti*.

4. 'By reason of the length of the calculation of the various-items-of-revenue, only one case among the citizens has been

राजा : इतः पत्रिकां दर्शय।

।। प्रतीहार्युपनयति।।

राजा :(अनुवाच्य) कथम्। समुद्रव्यवहारी सार्थवाहो धनमित्रो नाम नौव्यसने विपन्नः। अनपत्यश्च किल तरस्वी। राजगामी तस्यार्थसञ्चय इत्येतद् अमात्येन लिखितम्। कष्टं खल्वनपत्यता। बहुधनत्वाद् बहुपत्नीकेन तत्रभवता भवितव्यं। विचार्यतां। यदि काचिद् आपन्नसत्त्वा तस्य भार्यासु स्यात्।

प्रतीहारी : देव। दाणिं एव्व साकेदअस्स सेट्ठिणो दुहिआ णिव्वुत्तपुंस-

प्रतीहारी : देव। इदानीम् एव साकेतकस्य श्रेष्ठिनो दुहिता निर्वृत्तपुंस-

वणा जाआ से सुणीअदि।

वना जाया अस्यस श्रूयते।[1]

राजा : ननु गर्भः[2] पित्र्यं रिक्थम् अर्हति। गच्छ। एवम् अमात्यं ब्रूहि।

प्रतीहारी : जं देवो आणबेदि [इति प्रस्थिता]।

प्रतीहारी : यद् देव आज्ञापयति [इति प्रस्थिता]।

राजा : एहि तावत्।

प्रतीहारी : इअम्हि।

प्रतीहारी : इयमस्मि।

brought under consideration.' *Artha-jātasya,* etc. : some of the Bengālī have *rāja-kāryasya bahulatayā. Bahulatayā* : compare *pallavatayā* : p. 28, note 1.

1. 'It is reported that his wife, the daughter of the foreman of a guild belonging to Ayodhyā, has even now just completed the ceremony (performed) at the quickening (of the unborn child).' *Sāketakasya* : Sāketa is a name of Ayodhyā, 'the invincible city,' the ancient capital of Rāmacandra and founded by Ikṣvāku, the first of the monarchs of the solar dynasty [see p. 15, note 2]. It was situated on the river Sarayu in the North of India, and is now called Oude. *Śreṣṭhin,* 'the head of a guild or corporation practising the same trade.' *Puṁsavana,* 'the rite performed on the quickening of the foetus,' is the second of the twelve purificatory ceremonies enjoined by Manu on the three superior classes [ii, 27, etc.]. It comes next in order to the *garbhādhāna* or 'ceremony on conception :' compare p. 196, 1. 1, note 1.

2. *Garbha=garbha-sthaḥ putraḥ,* 'the child in the womb :' K.

राजा : किम् अनेन सन्ततिर् अस्ति नास्तीति।

येन येन वियुज्यन्ते प्रजाः स्निग्धेन बन्धुना।

स स पापाद् ऋते तासां दुष्यन्त इति घुष्यताम्[1] ।। 155 ।।

प्रतीहारी : एव्वं णाम घोसइदव्वं (निष्क्रम्य पुनः प्रविश्य) काले

प्रतीहारी : एवं नाम घोषयितव्यं (निष्क्रम्य पुनः प्रविश्य) काले

पवुट्ठं विअ अहिणन्दिदं देवस्स सासणं।

प्रवृष्टम् इव अभिनन्दितं[2] देवस्य शासनम्।

राजा : (दीर्घम् उष्णं च निःश्वस्य) एव भोः सन्ततिच्छेदनिरवलम्बानां कुलानां मूलपुरुषावसाने सम्पदः परम् उपतिष्ठन्ति।[3] ममाप्यन्ते। पुरुवंशश्रीर् अकाल इवोप्तवीजा भूर् एवंवृत्ता।

प्रतीहारी : पडिहदं अमङ्गलं।

प्रतीहारी : प्रतिहतम् अमङ्गलम्।[4]

राजा : धिङ् माम् उपस्थितश्रेयोवमानिनम्।

सानुमती : असंसअं सहिं एव्वं हिअए करिअ णिन्दिदो णेण अप्पा।

सानुमती : असंशयं सखीम् एव हृदये कृत्वा निन्दितोऽनेन आत्मा।

राजा :

संरोपितेऽप्यात्मनि धर्मपत्नी

त्यक्ता मया नाम कुलप्रतिष्ठा।

1. *See* the translation of this verse, page 189, note 1 at end.

2. 'Like grateful-rain at the right season.' *Pravṛṣṭam- prahṛṣṭa-varṣaṇam* : Schol., Chēzy. Some of the Bengālī MSS. have *paviṭṭham* for *praviṣṭam*.

3. 'The goods of families who are bereft of support through the failure of lineal descendants, pass over to a stranger at the decease of the representative-of-the-original-stock.' *Mūla-puruṣa*, 'the man who represents the original progenitor from whom, in a direct line, the family is descended,' 'the eldest surviving son,' *lit.*, 'the stock-man.'

4. 'The misfortune be averted !' compare page 191, line 9.

Verse 155. Śloka or *Anuṣṭubh*. *See* verse 154.

कल्पिष्यमाणा महते फलाय।

वसुन्धरा काल इवोप्तवीजा[1] ।। 156 ।।

सानुमती : अपरिच्छिण्णा दाणिं दे मन्ददी भविस्सदि।

सानुमती : अपरिच्छिन्ना इदानीं ते सन्ततिर् भविष्यति।

चतुरिका : (जनान्तिकं) अए। इमिणा सत्थवाहवुत्तन्तेण विउणुव्वेओ

चतुरिका : (जनान्तिकम्) अये। अनेन सार्थवाहवृत्तान्तेन विगुणोद्वेगो

भट्ठा। णं अस्सासिदुं सेहप्पडिच्छन्दादो अज्जं माठव्वं गेण्हिअ

भर्ता। एनम् आश्वासयितुं मेघप्रतिच्छन्दाद् आर्यं माठव्यं गृहीत्वा

आअच्छेहि।

आगच्छ।

प्रतीहारी : सुट्ठु भणासि (इति निष्क्रान्ता)

प्रतीहारी : सुष्ठु भणसि (इति निष्क्रान्ता)।

राजा : अहो दुष्यन्तस्य संशयाम् आरूढाः पिण्डभाजः। कुतः।

अस्मात् परं वत यथाश्रुतिसम्भृतानि

को नः कुले निवपनानि नियच्छतीति।

नूनं प्रसूतिविकलेन मया प्रसिक्तं

धौताश्रुशेषम् उदकं पितरः पिवन्ति[2] ।। 157 ।।

।। इति मोहम् उपागतः।।

1. 'Although myself was implanted (in her womb), verily (my) lawful wife, the glory of (my) family, was repudiated by me, like the earth sown with seed at the right-season, about to become adequate to the production of mighty fruit.' *Sanropite ātmani= svasmin upte sati* : K., *lit.*, 'myself being sown,' she being sown with myself,' *i.e.*, 'she bearing my second self in her womb.' According to the Hindū notion, a child is reproduction of one's self. *Ātmaiva patnyā jāyate* : K. *Kula-pratiṣṭhā* : *see* p. 123, note 1. *Kalpiṣyamāṇā* : see p. 189, note 1 in middle. *Vasundharā* : compare p. 182, note 2.

1. 'Woe is me ! the ancestors of Duṣyanta are brought to a critical situation; because—Thinking to themselves, Who, alas ! after this

Verse 156. *Upajāti* or *Ākhyānakī* (variety of *Triṣṭubh*). *See* Verses 41, 107, 121, 126, 142.

Verse 157. *Vasanta-tilakā* (variety of *Śakkarī*). *See* Verses 8, 27, 31, 43, 46, 64, 74, 80, 82, 83, 91, 93, 94, 95, 100, 104, 105, 108, 123, 124, 144, 148, 152.

चतुरिका : (ससम्भ्रमम् अवलोक्य) समस्ससदु समस्ससदु भट्टा।

चतुरिका : (ससम्भ्रमम् अवलोक्य) समाश्वसितु समाश्वसितु भर्ता।

सानुमती : हद्धी हद्धी। सदिक्खु दीबे ववधाणदोसेण एसो

सानुमती : हा धिक् हा धिक्। सति खलु दीपे व्यवधानदोषेण एषो

अन्धआरदोसं अणुहोदि। अहं दाणिं एव्व णिव्वुदं करेमि।

अन्धकारदोषम् अनुभवति।[1] अहम् इदानीम् एव निर्वृतं करोमि।

अहवा। सुदं मए सउन्दलं समस्सासअन्तीए महेन्दजणणीए मुहादो।

अथवा। श्रुतं मया शकुन्तलां समाश्वासयन्त्या महेन्द्रजनन्या मुखात्।

जणभाओसुआ देवा एव्व तह अणुचिट्ठिस्सन्ति जह अइरेण धम्म-

यज्ञभागोत्सुका[2] देवा एव तथा अनुष्ठास्यन्ति यथा अचिरेण धर्म-

(man), in our family, will offer (us) the oblations prepared according to scriptural-precept ? in all probability,' etc. : see page 111, note 1. *Piṇḍa-bhājaḥ=pitaraḥ* : Ś., *lit.*, 'partakers of oblations to the dead,' *i.e.*, the manes of deceased ancestors for whom the *Śrāddha* was performed. *Kutaḥ* : *see* p. 54, note 4. *Asmāt, i.e., Duṣyantāt* : Ś. *Dhautāśru-śeṣa* : compare the analogous compounds *tvag-asthi-śeṣa*, 'having nothing left but skin and bone;' *nāma-śeṣa*, 'having nothing surviving but a name.' The Bengālī MSS. read *dhautāsru-sekam*. The duty of performing the *Śrāddha* devolved on the eldest son or on the nearest surviving relative. If no one survived to celebrate this rite, the manes of deceased progenitors sank from their celestial aboade to the lower regions. Compare Ragh. I, 66, 67.

1. 'A light being really (near at hand) this-man by reason [fault] of the screen (which covers it) experiences (all the) ill-effects of darkness.' Dr. Boehtlingk proposes to interpret *andhaāra-dosam* by *andhakāra-doṣām*, 'dark night,' or 'the darkness of night,' but this seems hardly a legitimate compound, nor does the sense require it.

2. 'Longing for their portions of the sacrifice.' *Jaṇṇa* is the Prākṛt equivalent for *yajña* by Var., iii., 44. Great sacrifices were performed by kings in celebration of auspicious events, especially after marriage, in the hope of securing issue, and Indra with the inferior gods were invited to partake of portions set apart for them. These sacrifices were accompanied by largesses to the *Brāhmaṇas*, and

पदिणिं भट्टा अहिणन्दिस्सदित्ति। ता जुत्तं एदं कालं[1] पडिपालिदुं।
पत्नीं भर्ता अभिनन्दिष्यतीति। तस्माद् युक्तम् एतं कालं प्रतिपालयितुम्।
जाव इमिणा वुत्तन्तेण पिअसहिं समस्सासेमि (इत्युद्घान्तकेन
यावद् अनेन वृत्तान्तेन प्रियसखीं समाश्वासयामि (इत्युद्भ्रान्त[2]केन
निष्क्रान्ता)।
निष्क्रान्ता)।

नेपथ्ये : अब्बन्हणं अब्बन्हणं।

नेपथ्ये : अब्रह्मण्यम् अब्रह्मण्यम्।[3]

राजा : (प्रत्यागतप्राणः।[4] कर्णं दत्त्वा) अये। माठव्यस्येवार्त्तस्वरः। कः कोऽत्र भोः।

प्रतीहारी : (प्रविश्य) परित्ताअदु देवो संसअगदं वअस्सं।

प्रतीहारी : (प्रविश्य) परित्रायतां देवः संशयगतं[5] वयस्यम्।

festivities, in which the gods were supposed to be eager to participate. Compare Rāmāyaṇa I, xiii, 6, 8. The mother of Indra was Aditi, who was the wife of Kaśyapa [see page 22, note 4]. It appears from Act 7 of the present play that Śakuntalā was at this time enjoying an asylum with the illustrious pair Kaśyapa and Aditi in some sacred retreat, where they were engaged in acts of mortification and penance.

1. 'Therefore it is proper to wait for this period.' This is the reading of Kāṭavema. Some of the Devanāgarī have *tā ṇa juttaṁ kālam*, etc., for *tasmān na yuktaṁ kālam*, etc.

2. *See* page 214, note 2 : *i.e., udbhramaneṇa ākāśaṁ pratyudgamena* : K.

3. *Abrahmaṇyam*, ('Help ! to the rescue !') according to Amara I, vii, 14, is *abadhyoktau, i.e.*, implies an assertion that the thing in question is not to be killed. *Abadhyo'ham ityarthaḥ* : Ś., 'the meaning is that, as a Brāhmaṇ, my person is sacred and inviolable.' Compare in the Uttara-Rāmacaritra, p. 30 : 'Then by a *Brāhmaṇa*, having placed his dead son at the royal gate, a cry of "Abrahmaṇya" was set up, accompanied by a smiting on the breast.'

4. So reads my own MS. One Devanāgarī has *pratyāgataḥ*, the others simply *karṇaṁ dattvā*. The Bengālī *pratyāgata-cetanaḥ*.

5. 'Fallen into danger,' 'placed in jeopardy.' As to *gata*, *see* p. 38, note 1.

राजा : केनात्तगन्धो[1] माणवकः।

प्रतीहारी : अदिट्ठरूबेण केणबि सत्तेण अदिक्कमिअ मेहप्पडिच्छन्दस्स पासादस्स अम्मभूमिं आरोबिदो।

प्रतीहारी : अदृष्टरूपेण केनापि सत्त्वेन अतिक्रम्य मेघप्रतिच्छन्दस्य प्रासादस्य अग्रभूमिम् आरोपितः।[2]

राजा : (उत्थाय) मा तावत् ममापि सत्त्वैर् अभिभूयन्ते गृहाः।[3] अथवा।

अहन्यहन्यात्मन एव तावज्
ज्ञातुं प्रमादस्खलितं न शक्यम्।
प्रजासु कः केन पथा प्रयाती-
त्यशेषतो वेदितुम् अस्ति शक्तिः[4] ।। 158 ।।

1. *Ātta-gandha=ātta-garva*, 'humbled,' having the pride taken down,' 'insulted.' Compare in the Mahābh., *rājyam ātta-lakṣmi*, 'a kingdom stripped of its wealth.' The Mackenzie has *ārta-kaṇṭha*, 'throattled.'

2. 'By some demon of invisile form, having seized [over-powered] him, he has been mounted on a pinnacle of the palace (called) Megha-pratichchanda.' *Sattva=bhūta*, 'a goblin' or 'evil spirit.'

3. *Gṛha*, 'a house,' or 'a wife,' is masc. in the plur. : Am.-ko., ii, 5. The Sāh.-Darp. [p. 190] inserts *nāma*, 'forsooth,' after *mamāpi*.

4. 'Even one's own false-steps (proceeding from) heedlessness (occurring) day by day cannot be altogether ascertained. Is there (then) the power to know in every case by what road each of my subjects is walking ?' *lit.*, 'by what road who among my subjects,' etc. *Tāvat=sākalyena* : K. *Pramāda-skhalitam*, 'tripping,' 'stumbling,' 'blundering,' from carelessness. *Aśeṣato=sākalyena* : K. According to Kāṭavema, this last clause presents an example of *kāku* which is defined as 'a change in the tone of the voice,' 'giving emphasis.' Thus, 'Is there the power ?' becomes equivalent to 'There certainly is not the power :' *see* Sāh.-darp., p. 24.

Verse 158. *Upajāti* or *Ākhyānakī* (variety of Triṣṭubh). *See* verse 41, 107, 121, 126, 142, 156.

नेपथ्ये : भो वअस्स। अविहा अविहा।

नेपथ्ये : भो वयस्य। अविधा अविधा।[1]

राजा :। गतिभेदेन[2] परिक्रामन्।। सखे। न भेतव्यं न भेतव्यम्।

नेपथ्ये : (पुनस् तदेव पठित्वा) कहं ण भाइस्सं। एस मं कोबि

नेपथ्ये : (पुनस् तदेव पठित्वा) कथं न भेष्यामि। एष मां कोऽपि

पच्चावणदसिरोहरं इक्खुं विअ तिण्हभङ्गं करेदि।

पश्चादवनतशिरोधरम्[3] इक्षुम् इव तीक्ष्णभङ्गं करोति।

राजा :(सदृष्टिक्षेपं) धनुम् तावत्।

यवनी : (प्रविश्य शार्ङ्गहस्ता) भट्टा। एदं हत्थावाबसहिदं सरासणं।

यवनी :[4] (प्रविश्य शार्ङ्गहस्ता[4]) भर्तः। एतद् हस्तावापसहितं[5] शरासनम्।

[**राजा** :सशरं धनुर् आदत्ते]

नेपथ्ये :

एष त्वाम् अभिनवकण्ठशोणितार्थी।
शार्दूलः पशुम् इव हन्मि चेष्टमानम्।

1. *Avidhā ityākrośe.* The interjection *avidhā* is used in calling for assistance : K. Translate, 'Help ! help !' The word is not given in the Dictionary, nor in any mention of it made in the grammars. Two of the MSS. have *aviha* for *avidha;* the Mackenzie, *aviddho;* my own *avidū. Aviha* and *avihā* seem to be interchangeable. *Avihā* occurs in Mālavik., p. 12, 1. 22; p. 24, 1. 7; p. 56, 1. 8. Dr. Boehtlingk suggests that *avida* in Mṛcch., 213, 6; 312, 9. may be for *aviha* or *avihā.*

2. *Gati-bhedana,* 'with long strides.' *Tvarita-gamanena ityarthaḥ* : K.

3. A Bahuvrīhi compound agreeing with *mām.* Some MSS. have *pratyavanata.*

4. As to *Yavanī* and *Śārnya-hastā, see* page 63, note 1.

5. *Hastāvāpa=jyāghāta-vāraṇa* : K.=*aṅguli-trāṇa,* 'a guard to protect the hand or fore-arm from the bow-string,' 'an arm-guard,' 'a finger-guard;' from *hasta,* 'a hand,' or 'the lower arm,' *āvāpa,* 'a band' or 'bracelet :' compare p. 114, note 1. The Bengālī have *hastāvāra.*

आर्त्तानां भयम् अपनेतुम् आत्तधन्वा
दुष्यन्तस् तव शरणं भवत्विदानीम्[1] ।। 159 ।।

राजा : (सरोषं) कथं माम् एवोद्दिशति। तिष्ठ कुणपाशन। त्वम् इदानीं न भविष्यसि (शार्ङ्गम् आरोप्य) वेत्रवति। सोपानमार्गम् आदेशय।

प्रतीहारी : इदो इदो देवो।

प्रतीहारी : इत इतो देवः।

[सर्वे सत्वरम् उपसर्पन्ति]

राजा : [समन्ताद् विलोक्य] शून्यं खल्विदम्।

नेपथ्ये : अविहा अविहा। अहं अत्तभवन्तं पेक्खामि। तुमं मं ण पेक्खसि। विडालग्गहिदो मूसओ विअ णिरासोम्हि जीविदे संवुत्तो।

नेपथ्ये : अविधा[2] अविधा। अहम् अत्रभवन्तं प्रेक्षे। त्वं मां न प्रेक्षसे। विडालगृहीतो मूषक इव निराशोऽस्मि जीविते संवृत्तः।

राजा : भोस् तिरस्करिणीगर्वित।[3] मदीयम् अस्त्रं त्वां द्रक्ष्यति। एष तम् इषुं सन्धत्ते।

1. 'Here, thirsting for (thy) fresh throat-blood, will I slay thee struggling, as a tiger (slays) a beast. Let Duṣyanta now, who grasps his bow to remove the fear of the oppressed, be thy refuge [protector]. *Ārttānām,* etc. : compare page 15, line 2. *Ātta-dhanvā* : compare page 226, line 17.

2. *See* page 260, note 1. My own MS. has *avihā* in this place.

3. 'Priding thyself on the power of rendering thyself invisible.' *Tiraskariṇi* is properly a veil to cover the head, used by celestial beings to render themselves invisible : compare p. 224, 1. 8. It is here the science or art, peculiar to such beings, of so concealing themselves. This interpretation is supported by the gloss of Raṅganātha on *tiraskaraṇī-pracchannā* in Act 2 of Vikr.; *tiraskaraṇi=antardhāna-vidyā*. It answers to the *śikhā-bandhanī vidyā,* 'art of tying [covering] the top-knot,' called *aparājitā* in a preceding page.

Verse 159. *Praharṣiṇī* (variety of *Atijagatī*), containing thirteen syllables to the half-line, each half-line being alike.

— — — | ◡ ◡ ◡ ◡ — ◡ — ◡ — — ||

यो हनिष्यति बध्यं त्वां रक्ष्यं रक्षति च द्विजम्।
हंसो हि क्षीरम् आदत्ते तन्मिश्रा वर्जयत्यप:[1] ।। 160 ।।

(इत्यस्त्रं सन्धत्ते)

[तत: प्रविशति विदूषकम् उत्सृज्य मातलि:]

मातलि: ।[2]

कृता: शरव्यं हरिणा तवासुरा:
शरासनं तेषु विकृष्यताम् इदम्।
प्रसादसौम्यानि सतां सुहृज्जने
पतन्ति चक्षूंषि न दारुणा: शरा:[3] ।। 161 ।।

1. 'He it is fits the arrow (to the bow) who will slay thee worthy-of-death, and save a *Brāhmaṇa* worthy-of-preservation. For the flamingo extracts [takes] the milk (and) leaves behind the water that is mixed with it.' The Hindūs imagine that the Haṁsa or flamingo [see page 246, note 2] has the power of separating milk from water. Compare Mahābh., Śakuntalopākhyāna, vii, 88, *Prājñas tu jalpatāṁ puṁsāṁ śrutvā vācaḥ śubhāśubhāḥ, Guṇavad vākyam ādatte, haṁsaḥ kṣīram ivāmbhasaḥ*. Bhartṛhari [II. 15] has the following sentiment—'Brahmā [whose vehicle is the flamingo] when very angry with this bird, can destroy his nest among the lotuses, but cannot deprive him of that celebrated and inestimable faculty which he possesses, of separating milk from water.' The reference is probably to the milky juice of the water-lily, which would be its natural food, and to which allusion is often made by the Hindū poets. As to *rakṣati*, see p. 84, note 5.

2. *Mātali* is the charioteer of Indra. In the pictures which represent this god mounted on his other vehicle, an elephant (called Airāvata), Mātali is seen seated before him on the withers of the animal, acting as its driver. In the plays, however, [see page 11, note 1] Indra is generally borne in a chariot drawn by two horses [called Harī or *Harayaḥ*], which were guided by Mātali.

3. 'The demons are made by Indra thy mark : let this bow (of thine) be drawn against them. Not on a friendly-person are dreadful arrows directed [fall] by the good, [but rather] eyes soft-with-(looks of)-favour.' *Asurāḥ*, etc. : see page 86, note 1: page 86, note 2.

Verse 160. *Śloka* or *Anuṣṭubh*. *See* Verses 5, 6, 11, 12, 26, 47, 51, 53, 73, 76, 84, 87, 125, 127, 130, 146, 154, 155.

Verse 161. *Vaṁśasthavila* (variety of *Jagatī*). *see* Verses 18, 22, 23, 67, 81, 114, 117, 119, 145, 150.

राजा : [अस्त्रम् उपसंहरन्] अये मातलिः। स्वागतं महेन्द्रसारथे।

विदूषकः : [प्रविश्य] अहं जेण इट्ठिपसुमारं मारिदो सो इमिणा साअदेण अहिणन्दीअदि।

विदूषक : (प्रविश्य) अहं येन इष्टिपशुमारं मारितः सो ऽनेन स्वागतेन अभिनन्द्यते।[1]

मातलिः : (सस्मितम्) आयुष्मन्। श्रूयतां। यदर्थम्[2] अस्मि हरिणा भवत्सकाशं प्रेषितः।

राजा : अवहितोऽस्मि।

मातलिः : अस्ति कालनेमिप्रसूतिर्[3] दुर्जयो नाम दानवगणः।

राजा : अस्ति श्रुतपूर्वं मया नारदात्।[4]

मातलिः–

सख्युस् ते स किल शतक्रतोर् अजय्यस्
तस्य त्वं रणशिरसि स्मृतो निहन्ता।
उच्छेतुं प्रभवति येन् न सप्तसप्तिम्
तन् नैशं तिमिरम् अपाकरोति चन्द्रः[5] ।। 162 ।।

1. 'He by whom I was being slaughtered like a sacrificial victim, is greeted with a welcome by this man!' *Iṣṭi-paśu-māraṁ māritaḥ = iṣṭipaśur iva māritaḥ* : K. This kind of adverbial compound is noticed in Pāṇini, III, 4, 45, 46. So *aj-nāśaṁ naṣṭaḥ* is equivalent to *aja iva naṣṭah,* and *ghṛta-nidhāyaṁ nihitaḥ* to *ghṛta iva nihitaḥ.*

2. The Mackenzie MSS. has *yadartham,* supported by some of the Beṅgālī.

3. *Kālanemi,* son of the demon Hiraṇyakaśipu, was a Daitya or Asura [see p. 86, note 1] with a hundred arms and as many heads. These Daityas were sometimes called Dānavas, from their mother Danu, who as well as Diti was one of the wives of Kaśyapa and daughters of Dakṣa. The Rākṣasas, or cannibal demons who, for the sake of human flesh, waged perpetual war with men, as the Daityas did with the gods, were related to the Daityas.

4. *Nārada* is a celebrated divine sage or *Ṛṣi,* usually reckoned among the ten *Prajāpatis* or *Brahmādikas* first created by Brahmā and called his sons. He acts as a kind of messenger of the gods : *see* the end of Act V. of the Vikramorvaśīya.

5. 'Verily that (troop of demons) is not to be subdued by thy

Verse 162. *Praharṣiṇī* (variety of *Atijagatī*). *See* verse 159.

स भवान् आत्तशस्त्र[1] एवम् इदानीं तम् ऐन्द्ररथम् आरुह्य विजयाय प्रतिष्ठताम्।

राजा : अनुगृहीतोऽहम् अनया मघवतः सम्भावनया। अथ माठव्यं प्रति भवता किम् एवं प्रयुक्तम्।

मातलिः : तदपि कथ्यते। किञ्चिन्निमित्तादपि मनःसन्तापाद् आयुष्मान् मया विक्लवो दृष्टः। पश्चात् कोपयितुम् आयुष्मन्तं तथा कृतवान् अस्मि। कुतः।

ज्वलति चलितेन्धनोऽग्निर् विप्रकृतः पन्नगः फणं कुरुते।
प्रायः स्वं महिमानं क्षोभात् प्रतिपद्यते हि जनः[2] ।। 163 ।।

राजा : (जनान्तिकम्) वयस्य। अनतिक्रमणीया दिवस्पतेर्[3] आज्ञा। तद् अत्र परिगतार्थं कृत्वा[4] मद्वचनाद् अमात्यपिशुनं ब्रूहि।

friend Indra : thou, at the head of the fight, art appointed [termed, called] its destroyer. That noctural darkness which the sun has no power to remove, the moon dispels.' *Śata-kratuḥ,* 'the lord of a hundred sacrifices;' another of Indra's thousand names. He is so called because the rank which he occupies is unattainable excepting through a hundred *aśva-medhas,* or 'horse-sacrifice :' see page 86, note 1. *Sapta-saptiḥ,* 'drawn by seven steeds :' see page 12, note 1. *Candraḥ* : the appositeness of this comparison depends on the fact that Duṣyanta's pedigree was traceable to the moon : see page 15, note 2; page 112, note 2.

1. Compare *ātta-daṇḍa* : p. 188, 1. 7, and *ātta-dhanvā* : p. 261, 1. 1.

2. 'Fire blazes up when the fuel is stirred; the snake when irritated expands its hood; verily a man generally regains his own high-spiritedness [greatness, courage] through being roused-to-action [shaken, excited].' *Phaṇaṁ kurute, lit.,* 'makes a hood;' *phaṇa,* 'the expanded hood of the cobra.' *Kṣobhāt* : Kāṭavema has *kopāt.* My own MS. and the Mackenzie have *jantuḥ* for *hi janaḥ.* Most of the Beṅgālī MSS. read *tejasvī saṅkṣobhāt prāyaḥ pratipadyate tejaḥ.*

3. Indra, as the Hindū Jove, is lord of the atmosphere and winds : see page 86, note 1.

4. 'Having made acquainted with the circumstance :' *Piśuna [Informer] is the name of the minister :* compare p. 233, 1. 3.

Verse 163. *Āryā* or *Gāthā.* (*See* Verse 2.)

⏑⏑⏑⏑|⏑—⏑|——‖—⏑⏑| —— |⏑—⏑|—⏑⏑|—
—— |—⏑⏑|——‖ —— |⏑⏑—| ⏑ |—⏑⏑|—

त्वन्मतिः केवला तावत् परिपालयितुं प्रजाः।
अधिज्यम् इदम् अन्यस्मिन् कर्मणि व्यापृतं धनुः[1] ।। 164 ।।

इति ।।

विदूषकः : जं भवं आणबेदि (इति निष्क्रान्तः)।

विदूषकः : यद् भवान् आज्ञापयति (इति निष्क्रान्तः)।

मातलिः : आयुष्मान् रथम् आरोहतु।

[राजा रथारोहणं नाटयति]।

[इति निष्क्रान्ताः सर्वे]

[षष्ठोऽङ्कः]

1. 'Let the-powers-of-thy mind be wholly and solely (exerted) to protect-by-good-government (my) subjects. This (my) braced [strung] bow is (for a time) occupied in a different employment.' *Tāvat* : compare p. 259, 1. 7. The root *pāl,* 'to protect,' in reference to a king or his officers, implies protection by a just administration of the laws. *Samyak pāl* occurs frequently in the sense of 'to govern justly,' *Adhi-jyam* : *see* page 9, note 2; and compare page 68, line 1; page 86, line 7.

Verse 164. *Śloka* or *Anuṣṭubh. See* Verses 5, 6, 11, 12, 26, 47, 50, 51, 53, 73, 76, 84, 87, 125, 127, 146, 154, 155, 160.

ACT - VII

।। अथ सप्तमोऽङ्कः ।।

[ततः प्रविशत्याकाशयानेन रथाधिरूढो **राजा** :मातलिश्च]

राजा : मातले। अनुष्ठितनिदेशोऽपि मघवतः सत्क्रियाविशेषाद् अनुपयुक्तम् इवात्मानं समर्थये।[1]

मातलिः : (सस्मितं) आयुष्मन्।[2] उभयम् अप्यपरितोषं समर्थये।

प्रथमोपकृतं मरुत्वतः प्रतिपत्त्या लघु मन्यते भवान्।

गणयत्यवदानतोषितो भवतः सोऽपि न सत्क्रियागुणान्[3] ।। 165 ।।

राजा : मातले। मा मैवम्। स खलु मनोरथानाम् अप्यभूमिर् विसर्जनावसरम-

1. 'Although I have executed (his) commission, after-such-a-distinguished reception (on the part) of Indra, I consider myself as unworthy (of so much honour).' *Satkriyā-viśeṣād* : compare p. 41, 1. 11; p. 132, l. 18. The ablative may imply 'in consequence of,' 'after.' *Anupayuktam, i.e., tādṛk-satkriyāyā ayogyam* : Schol., Chézy. *Samarthaye = avagacchāmi.*

2. Compare page 9, line 3, note 2.

3. 'Your highness makes light of the prior benefit (conferred by you) on Indra, (compared) with the (subsequent) mark-of-distinction (conferred by him on you). He too (Indra) takes no account of the distinguished honours (bestowed) on your highness, being-filled-with-admiration at your heroic-achievement.' *Prathamo-pakṛtam, i.e., rākṣasa-jaya-rūpaṁ pūrvopakāram* : K. *Pratipattyā = sambhāvanayā. Avadān = pauruṣam,* 'a deed of heroism :' K. The Celebrooke MS. has *toṣito* instead of *vismito. Satkriyā-guṇān = sambhāvanā-viśeṣān;* K. *Guṇa* appears to be used at the end of a compound with the sense of *viśeṣa* : compare line 2 of verse 168. The following is the Beṅgālī reading : *Upakṛtya hares tathā bhavān laghu satkāram avekṣya manyate : Ganayaty avadāna-sammitāṁ bhavataḥ so'pi na satkṛyām imām.*

Verse 165. *Vaitālīya. See* Verses 52, 133.

त्कार:।[1] मम हिदिवौकसां समक्षम् अर्द्धासनोपवेशितस्य
अन्तर्गतप्रार्थनम् अन्तिकस्थं
जयन्तम् उद्वीक्ष्य कृतस्मितेन।
आमृष्टवक्षोहरिचन्दनाङ्का
मन्दारमाला हरिणा पिनद्धा[2] ।। 166 ।।

मातलिः : किमिव नामायुष्मान् अमरेश्वरान् नार्हति। पश्य।
सुरसखस्य हरेर् उभयैः कृतं
त्रिदिवम् उद्धृतदानवकण्टकम्।

1. 'That honorary-distinction on the occasion of (his) dismissing (me) was certainly beyond the compass [reach, place] of my hopes.' *i.e.*, exceeded all my expectation. *Abhūmiḥ* = *asthānam*, 'want of place' = *aviṣaya*, 'beyond the reach :' K. The expression occurs again in this act, and in Mālavik., p. 35, line 4, *Abhūmir iyaṁ mālavikāyāḥ*.

2. 'For a garland of Mandāra (flowers), marked with yellow-sandal from (its) rubbing on (his) breast, was fastened (round the neck) of the me; made to sit on half his throne, before the eyes of the gods, by Indra, smiling and looking up at (his son) Jayanta (who was) standing by and inwardly longing (for the same honours).' *Āmṛṣṭa*, etc.; The breast of Indra was dyed yellow with a fragrant kind of sandal-wood called Haricandana [comapre Kumāra-sam., V, 69], and the garland, from coming in contact with it, became tinged with the same colour. Wreaths and garlands of flowers were much used by the Hindūs as marks of honorary distinction, as well as for ornaments on festive occasions, and to adorn sacrificial victims : compare page 219, line 1, note 1. They were suspended round the neck [see page 149, note 1], or placed on the head. Mandāra is one of the five everblooming trees of Svarga, or Indra's heaven. Another of these trees is said to be the Hari-candana mentioned above, and another the Santāna; but the two most celebrated are the Pārijāta and the Kalpadruma, or tree granting all desires. Jayanta is the son of Indra by his favourite wife Paulomī or Śaci.

Verse 166. *Upajāti* or *Ākhyānakī* (variety of *Triṣṭubh*). *See* Verses 41, 107, 121, 126, 142, 156, 158.

तव शरैर् अधुना नतपर्वभिः
पुरुषकेशरिणश्च पुरा नखैः[1] ।। 167 ।।

राजा : अत्र खलु शतक्रतोर् एव महिमा स्तुत्यः।
सिध्यन्ति कर्मसु महत्स्वपि यन् नियोज्याः
सम्भावनागुणम् अवेहि तम् ईश्वराणाम्।
किं वाभविष्यद् अरुणस् तमसां विभेत्ता
तं चेत् सहस्रकिरणो धुरि नाकरिष्यत्[2] ।। 168 ।।

1. 'The heaven of Indra, friend of the gods, has been made free from the plague of the Dānavas by two (means) : now by thy flat-jointed arrows : and formerly by the claws of the Man-lion.' *Sura-sakha* : *see* p. 86, note 1. *Tridiva* = *Svarga* : each of the superior Hindū gods has a heaven, paradise, or elysium of his own. That of Brahmā is called Brahma-loka, situated on the summit of Mount Meru; that of Viṣṇu, Vaikuṇṭha, on the Himālayas; that of Śiva and Kuvera, Kailāsa, also on the Himālayas; that of Indra, Svarga or Nandana. The latter, though properly on one of the points of Mount Meru, below Brahmā's paradise, is sometimes identified with the sphere of the sky or heaven in general. *Uddhṛta*, etc., *lit.*, 'having the thorns of Dānavas extracted.' *Kaṇṭaka*, 'a thorn,' is often used for a pestilent or noxious person or thing. *Dānava* : *see* p. 263, note 3. *Nata-parvabhiḥ* = *nimna-parvabhiḥ; Natāni anunnatāni parvāṇi yeṣām* : K. Compare *nata-nāsikaḥ*, 'flat-nosed.' Also in Rāmāy., I. i, 64, *śareṇ-ānata-parvaṇā [bibheda sapta-tālān]* which should be resolved into *śareṇa-ānata-parvaṇā*, not *anata*, etc. *Puruṣa-keśariṇ* = *nara-siṁha*, 'the man-lion,' *i.e.*, Viṣṇu; for in this monstrous shape of a creature half-man, half-lion, which was his fourth *avatār* or incarnation, Viṣṇu delivered the three worlds, or earth, Pātāla, and heaven, from the tyranny of an insolent demon called Hiraṇyakaśipu, who had usurped the sovereignty of Indra : see Viṣṇu-Purāṇa, p. 126.

2. 'Verily, when servants [delegates] succeed in mighty enterprises, understand thou that (there has been) peculiar condescension [distinguished capacity] on-the-part-of (their) masters. How indeed could Aruṇa be the disperser of the-shades-

Verse 167. *Druta-Vilambita* (variety of *Jagatī*). *See* Verses 45, 72, 128. 140.

Verse 168. *Vasanta-tilakā* (variety of *Śakkarī*). *See* Verses 8, 27, 31, 43, 46, 64, 74, 80, 82, 83, 91, 93, 94, 95, 100, 104, 105, 108, 123, 144, 148, 152, 157.

मातलिः : सदृशम् एवैतत् (स्तोकम् अन्तरम् अतीत्य) आयुष्मन्। इतः। पश्य नाकपृष्ठगतस्य सौभाग्यम् आत्मयशसः।

विच्छित्तिशेषैः सुरसुन्दरीणां
वर्णैर् अमी कल्पलतांशुकेषु।
सञ्चिन्त्य गीतिक्षमम् अर्थबन्धं
दिवौकसस् त्वच्चरितं लिखन्ति[1] ।। 169 ।।

of-night, if the thousand-rayed-one did not place him in front (of his car)?' *Niyojyāḥ = sevakāḥ* : Ś. *Sambhāvanā-guṇam=satkāra-viśeṣam* : K. : *see* p. 266, note 1. *Sambhāvanā* may mean fitness,' 'capability,' as well as honour.' The condescension consisted in placing Duṣyanta in front of the battle, just as the Sun places the Dawn in front of his chariot. *Sahasra-kiraṇa* is one of the innumerable names for the Sun. As to Aruṇa, 'the Dawn :' see page 140, note 3. *Dhuri= rathāgre* : Ś.*=agre, purobhāge* : K.

1. 'Behold the sublimity [beauty, auspiciousness] of (thy) own fame that has reached to the vault of heaven. With the tints remaining from the colours [used in the toilet] of the heavenly fair-ones, these inhabitants of the sky are painting [tracing] thy exploits on vestments [tapestry, leaves] of the Kalpa-tree, thinking of verses suitable for singing.' *Vicchitti-raṅga, rāga* : Ś., Ch. *Vicchitti-śeṣaiḥ=viśiṣṭair varṇaiḥ* : K., *i.e., kusuma-kasturikā-candanādibhiḥ,* 'with flowers, musk, sandae, and other cosmetics.' The first sense of the word is 'excision,' 'cutting off;' it rarely has the sense required here, of 'rouge,' 'paint.' Compare *bhakti-cheda,* 'the coloured streak (marking Vaiṣṇava) devotion :' Megh., verse 20. *Sura-sundarīṇām=divya-strīṇām. Kalpa-latāṁśukeṣu=kalpa-latā-vastreṣu* : Ś., Ch. The first sense of *aṁśuka* is 'cloth,' 'tapestry;' it is said to bear the meaning 'leaf,' and may be so used here : in which case the idea may be that the gods are writing Duṣyanta's memoirs on the leaves of the Kalpa-tree. Kāṭavema's gloss is not quite clear, *kalpa-latāsu aṁśukābharanādi [na] vidyante iti prasiddha;* but it seems likely, especially if reference is made to page 153, note 4, of this book, that he intends to imply that the Kalpa-tree, which was a tree yielding everything [see p. 267, note 1], produced the vestments or tapestry on which they might be supposed to design the adventures of Duṣyanta. *Gīti-*

Verse 169. *Upajāti* or *Ākhyānakī* (variety of *Triṣṭubh*). *See* Verse 41, 107, 121, 126, 142, 156, 158, 166.

राजा : मातले। असुरसम्प्रहारोत्सुकेन पूर्वेद्युर् दिवम् अधिरोहता न लक्षितः स्वर्गमार्गः। कतरस्मिन् मरुतां पथि वर्तामहे।[1]

kṣamam=gāna-yogyam is the reading of Kāṭavema and the Beṅgālī; most of the Devanāgarī MSS. have *gīta-kṣamam* : compare p. 29, note 1 at end. *Artha-bandham=padam,* 'a verse,' 'word.' *Artho badhyate anena iti artha-bandhaḥ padam* : K. Compare in Act 2 of Vikram. : *Tulyānurāgapiśunaṁ lalitārtha-bandhaṁ patre niveśitam udāharaṇaṁ priyāyāh,* etc.

1. 'In which course [path, orbit] of the (seven) winds are we now moving?' The Hindūs divide the heavens into seven Mārgas or Pathas, *i.e.,* paths, courses, orbits (like the stories of the Mussalmān creed) assigning a particular *vāyu* or wind to each. Compare Viṣṇu-Purāṇa, p. 212 [Wilson]. The first of these seven *vāyu-mārgas* or *vāyu-pathas* is identical with the *bhuvar-loka,* or atmosphereic region, extending from the *bhūr-loka,* or terrestrial region [comprising the earth, and the *adho-loka,* called Pātāla] upwards to the sun. The wind assigned to this marg is called *āvaha,* and its office is to bear along the atmosphere, clouds, meterors, lightning, etc. The other six make up the *svar-loka* or heavenly region with which *Svarga* is often identified [compare p. 268, note 1] in the following order :—The 2nd Mārga is that of the sun, and its wind, called *pravaha* or *pravāha* causes the sun to revolve; 3rd. that of the moon, its wind *saṁvaha* or *saṁvāha* impels the moon; 4th. That of the *nakṣatra,* or lunar constellations, its wind, *udvaha,* causes the revolution of these asterisms; 5th. that of the *graha,* or planets, its wind *vivāha* bears along the seven planets; 6th. that of the *saptarṣi,* or seven stars of the Great Bear, its wind *parivaha* bears along these luminaries, as well as the *svar-gaṅgā,* or heavenly Ganges [*saptarṣicakram svar-gaṅgāṁ ṣaṣṭhaḥ parivahas tathā* : not as Dr. Boehtlingk suggests *saptarṣi-cakraṁ svarga-gaḥ,* etc.]: it appears from the next verse that this was the Mārga in which Indra's car was at the moment moving; 7th. that of *dhruva,* or the polar-star, the pivot or axis of the whole planetary system, to which, according to the Viṣṇu-Purāṇa [pp. 230, 240, Wilson], 'all the celestial luminaries are bound by aerial cords, and are made to travel in their proper orbits, being kept in their places by their respective bands of air.' According to the Brahmāṇḍa-Purāṇa, from which, as quoted by Kāṭavema, the above account is taken, the wind of the 7th Mārga, causing the revolution of the polar-star, is *parāvāha* [? *parāvaha*]. Obs. *katara* is sometimes used for *katama.* All the Devanāgarī MSS. read *katarasmin* for *katamasmin.*

मातलिः—

त्रिस्रोतसं वहति यो गगनप्रतिष्ठां
ज्योतींषि वर्तयति च प्रविभक्तरश्मिः।
तस्य द्वितीयहरिविक्रमनिस्तमस्कं
वयोर् इमं परिवहस्य वदन्ति मार्गम्[1] ।। 170 ।।

1. 'They call this road, freed-from-all-impurities-by-the-second-stride-of-Viṣṇu, (the road) of that wind *Parivaha*, which bears along the triple-flowing-river [Ganges] located in heaven, and causes the stars [of the Great Bear] to revolve, duly-distributing-their-rays.' See the last note. *Tri-srotas=svar-gaṅgā=mandākinī* : K. The Ganges was supposed to take its rise in the toe of Viṣṇu [whence one of its names, *Viṣṇu-padī*]; thence it flowed through the heavenly sphere, being borne along by the wind Parivaha and identified with the Mandākinī, or Milky way : its second course is through the earth; but the weight of its descent was borne by Śiva's head, whence after wandering among the tresses of his hair, it descended through a chasm in the Himālayas : its third course is through Pātāla, or the lower regions, the residence of the Daityas and Nāgas, and not to be confounded with *Naraka*, 'hell,' 'the place of punishment.' *Gagana-pratiṣṭhām=ākāśa-sthām* : Ś., Ch.; were it not for this interpretation I should translate 'the glory of the skies:' compare p. 256, 1. 2. There is doubtless a double-entendre. *Jyotīṁṣi*, etc., *i.e., saptarṣīṇām dhiṣṇyāni* : K. *Pravibhaktaraṣmiḥ, i.e., asaṅkīrṇa-raśmayaḥ tejāṁsi yasmin karmaṇi tat tathoktam* : K. *Vartayati= sañcārayati* : K. *Dvitīya*, etc., *i.e., dvitīyena harer viṣṇor vikrameṇa pāda-nyāsena nirdoṣam;* K. *Tasya vāyor*, etc., *i.e., tasya parīvāhākhyasya vāyor mārgaṁ panthānam imam gṛhṇanti āmananti. Parivāho* [sic] *nāma svar-gaṅgāṁ saptarṣi-maṇḍalaṁ pravartayati ṣaṣṭho vāyuskandho yathoktaṁ brahmāṇḍa-purāṇe* : K. The story of Viṣṇu's second stride was this— An Asura or Daitya [see p. 86, note 1] named Bali or Mahābali, a descendant of Hiraṇyakaśipu had, by his devotions, gained the dominion of Heaven, Earth, and Pātāla. Viṣṇu undertook to trick him out of his power, and assuming the form of a Vāmana, or dwarf [his 5th *avatāra*] he appeared before the giant, and begged, as a boon, as much land as he could pace in three steps. This was

Verse 170. *Vasanta-tilakā* (variety of *Śakkarī*). *See* Verses 8, 27, 31, 43, 46, 64, 74, 80, 82, 83, 91, 93, 94, 95, 100, 104, 105, 108, 123, 124, 144, 148, 152, 157, 168.

राजा : मातले। अतः खलु सवाह्यान्तःकरणो ममान्तरात्मा प्रसीदति[1] [रथाङ्गम् अवलोक्य] मेघपदवीम् अवतीर्णौ स्वः।[2]

granted, and the god immediately expanded himself till he filled the world, deprived Bali at the first step, of earth; at the second, of heaven; but, in consideration of some merit, left Pātāla stil under his rule. Another account makes him comprehend earth in his first step, the region of the air in his second, and heaven in his third. Hence, *tri-vikrama, tri-pāda,* as names of Viṣṇu. The Beṅgālī MSS. have in place of *tasya dvitīya,* etc.; *tasya vyapeta-rajasaḥ pravahasya vāyor mārgo dvitīya-hari-vikrama-pūta eṣaḥ.*

1. 'Hence, indeed, do-I-feel-a-delightful-repose in all my senses [organs] external and internal,' *lit.*, 'Hence, my inner soul along with my external organs feels (a pleasurable) repose.' Compare in Vikram. end of Act IV, *tvad-darśanena prasanno me savāhyāntarātmā, i.e.,* 'body and soul,' 'my external and internal being,' 'my outer and inner man.' And again, *Urvaśī-gātra-sparśād iva nirvṛtaṁ me sa-hṛdayaṁ śarīram.* The organs of sense [*indriya*] according to the Sāṅkhya system are divided into two classes, external, *vāhyendriya;* and internal, *antarindriya.* The external are of two kinds : the five 'organs of perception,' *jñānendriya, viz.*, the ear, eye, skin, tongue, and nose; and the five 'organs of action,' *karmendriya, viz.*, the throat, hand, foot, organ of excretion, and that of generation. The internal organs are three, *viz., manas,* 'the mind,' or organ of thought; *buddhi,* 'the reason,' or organ of apprehension; *ahaṅkāra,* 'individuality,' or 'selfconsciousness.' *Citta,* 'the heart,' or organ of feeling is sometimes added. Amara [I, 4, 17] divides the *indriya* into two grand classes— 1. *karmendriyāṇi;* and 2. *buddhīndriyāṇi* or *dhīndriyāṇi,* 'intellectual organs;' the latter comprises the *jñānendriyāṇi* with *manas* : this seems to be the popular division. Compare Vikram., Act iii, *Bhavitavyatānuvidhayīni buddhīndriyāṇi.*

2. 'We have descended to the path of the clouds,' *i.e.,* to the atmospheric region between the sun and the earth, the Mārga of the clouds and of the *Āvaha* wind : *see* p. 270, note 1. The chariot must, therefore, have traversed with the speed of lightning, the four intervening Mārgas of the planets, lunar constellations, moon, and sun. If the Bengālī reading, *pravahasya,* be adopted in the last verse, the transition would merely be from one Mārga to the next.

मातलिः : कथम् अवगम्यते।

राजा :

अयम् अरविवरेभ्यश् चातकैर् निष्पतद्भिर्
हरिभिर् अचिरभासां तेजसा चानुलिप्तैः।
गतम् उपरि घनानां वारिगर्भोदराणां
पिशुनयति रथस् ते शीकरक्लिन्ननेमिः[1] ।। 171 ।।

मातलिः : क्षणाद् आयुष्मान् स्वाधिकारभूमौ वर्तिष्यते।

राजा : (अधोऽवलोक्य) वेगावतरणाद् आश्चर्यदर्शनः संलक्ष्यते मनुष्यलोकः। तथा हि–

शैलानाम् अवरोहतीव शिखराद् उन्मज्जतां मेदिनी
पर्णाभ्यन्तरलीनतां विजहति स्कन्धोदयात् पादपाः।
सन्तानात् तनुभावनष्टसलिला व्यक्तिं भजन्त्यापगाः
केनाप्युत्क्षिपतेव पश्य भुवनं मत्पार्श्वम् आनीयते[2] ।। 172 ।।

1. Here [*ayam*] by the *cātakas* flying forth through the interstices of the spokes, and by the horses glistening with the flash of the lightnings, thy chariot, the rings [circumferences] of whose wheels are bedewed with mist, betrays (our) progress over clouds whose bellies are pregnant with rain.' *Ara=nemyavaṣṭambhaḥ* : the Beṅgālī MSS. and the Mackenzie read *aga*, 'a mountain.' *Ara-vivarebhyaḥ cakrāvayavānāṁ vivarebhyo antarāla-pradeśebhyaḥ* : K. *Niṣpatadbhiḥ = nirgacchadbhiḥ* : K. : see p. 249, note 1, at end. The *Cātaka* is a kind of cuckoo [Cuculus Melano-leucus]. The Hindūs suppose that it drinks only the water of the clouds, and their poets usually introduce allusions to this bird in connexion with cloudy or rainy weather : see Megh., verses 9, 23, 113; Ragh., xvii, 60. So *Triṣākulaiś cātaka-pakṣiṇāṁ kulaiḥ prayācitāḥ valāhakāḥ* : Ṛtu-s., ii, 3. *Haribhir=aśvaiḥ*, especially Indra's horses : see p. 12, note 1, and compare Ragh., iii, 43. *Acira-bhāsām=vidyutām* : Ś. *Gatam*, etc. *Teṣām meghānām uparī ūrdhva-bhāge gataṁ gamanam* : K. *Piśunayati = sūcayati* : K.

2. 'The earth descends as it were from the summit of the upward-rising [emergent] mountains. The trees, from the elevation

---

Verse 171. *Mālinī* or *Māninī* (variety of Ati-*Śakkarī*). *See* Verses 10, 19, 20, 38, 55, 109, 110, 120.

Verse 172. *Śārdūla-vikrīḍita* (varaiety of *Atidhṛti*). *See* Verses 14, 30, 36, 39, 50, 63, 79, 85, 86, 89, 97, 98, 111, 137, 138, 149.

मातलिः : साधु दृष्टम्।। सबहुमानं विलोक्य।। अहो उदाररमणीया पृथिवी।

राजा : मातले। कतमोऽयं पूर्वापरसमुद्रावगाढः कनकरसनिस्यन्दी सान्ध्य इव मेघपरिघः सानुमान् आलोक्यते।[1]

मातलिः : आयुष्मन्। एष खलु हेमकूटो[2] नाम किम्पुरुषपर्वतस् तपसां सिद्धिक्षेत्रम्। पश्य।

[coming-into-view, rising, appearing] of (their) trunks, lose their state of being enveloped [concealed, wrapped] in their foliage. The rivers whose-waters-were-lost-in-narrowness, become visible [acquire manifestation] from the expansion (of their waters). Behold! the earth is being brought up to my side [near me], as if by some one flinging it upwards.' In the same way to a voyager in a balloon at a very great height, the surface of the earth would seem flat, the trees would be compressed within their foliage like mushrooms, and the rivers shrivel into threads or tiny rivulets; but, on descending, the mountains would appear to stand out, and the earth to recede from them, the trees would exhibit their elevation, and the rivers their breadth of water. *Unmajjatām=udgacchatām* : K. *Avarohati=adho-gacchati* : K. *Parṇābhyantara,* etc. : The Colebroke MS. and my own have *parṇa-svāntara;* the Taylor, *parṇeṣvantara;* the Mackenzie, *parṇa-prastara;* Kāṭavema, *parnāntara-vilīnam. Skandhodayāt=kroḍāvirbhāvāt* : K. *Santānat=jala-vistārāt* : K. : the other Devanāgarī have *santānais. Tanubhāva,* etc., *Tanubhāvena sūkṣmatvena adṛṣṭam salilaṁ yāsām* : K. *Vyaktiṁ bhajanti, i.e., vyakt bhavanti* : K.

1. 'What mountain younder is seen, bathing itself in the eastern and western ocean, pouring down a golden stream like a bar [bank, gate] of evening clouds?' *Parigha* occurs in p. 86, 1. 5, with the sense of 'the bar of a gate,' but it may also denote the gate itself. *Sānumān,* lit., 'possessed of table-land,' 'a mountain having extensive level ground on its summit.'

2. *Hema-kūṭa,* 'golden-peaked,' a sacred range of mountains lying among the Himālaya chain, and apparently identical with, or immediately adjacent to Kailāsa, the paradise of Kuvera, the god of wealth, as it is here described as the mountain of the Kiṁpuruṣas, or servants of Kuvera. They are a dwarfish kind of monster, with the body of a man and the head of a horse, and are otherwise called Kinnara : *aśva-mukha, turaṅga-mukha.* This mountain is also here described as 'the scene [place, field] of the

स्वायम्भुवान् मरीचेर् यः प्रबभूव प्रजापतिः।
सुरासुरगुरुः सोऽत्र सपत्नीकस् तपस्यति[1] ।। 173 ।।

राजा : तेन ह्यनतिक्रमणीयानि[2] श्रेयांसि। प्रदक्षिणीकृत्य भगवन्तं गन्तुम् इच्छामि।

मातलिः : प्रथमः कल्पः।[3]

perfect fulfilment of penance.' The Mackenzie MS. has *tapasvinām* for *tapasām*.

1. 'That Prajāpati [Kaśyapa], who sprang from Marīci, the Self-existent's-son [*i.e.*, from Marīci, son of Brahmā], (and who is) the father of the gods and demons, practices penance here along with his wife (Aditi).' An account of Kaśyapa, who, as son of Marīci, is called Mārīca, is given in page 22, note 4, and p. 86, note 1. He is here said to be one of the Prajāpatis, or fathers of all created things, who were Brahmā's sons, created by him to supply the universe with inhabitants, and who, after fulfiling their mission, retired from the world to practise penance and prepare for death. The Vāyu-purāṇa certainly reckons Kaśyapa, with his father-in-law Dakṣa and other sages, among the Prajāpatis, but he does not belong to the seven original Prajāpatis of whom his father Marīci is one, nor to the ten enumerated by Manu [I, 35]. Of the thirteen daughters of Dakṣa married to Kaśyapa, the eldest, and his favourite wife, was the Aditi introduced here, from whom were born the gods and particularly the twelve Ādityas, the several representatives of the sun in the twelve months of the year. From Diti, Danu, and others of the remaining twelve, came the Asuras or demons; and, from Vinatā, Aruṇa 'the Dawn,' [*see* p. 140, note 3] and Garuḍa, 'the vehicle of Viṣṇu and king of birds.' *Svāyambhuvāt = Brahma-sunoḥ* : K. *Surāsuraguruḥ* : as to *guruḥ*, see p. 171, note 2, in middle, and p. 91, note 1, correcting the typographical error in the second line of the last note, 'venerable *hermit*' being a misprint for 'venerable *parent*.' *Sa-patnīkas, i.e., patnyā adityā saha* : compare such compounds as *sa-strīka, sa-śrīka*, etc.

2. Compare page 68, line 11; page 91, line 1. *Śreyāṁsi = śubhāni, kaśyapa-darśana-namaskārādīni*, 'lucky occasions,' 'opportunities for obtaining blessings, such as visiting and paying homage to Kaśyapa.' As to *pradakṣinī-kṛtya, see* page 158, note 1.

3. 'A noble resolve,' 'a prime idea,' 'a first-rate conception :' compare p. 202, 1, 1. *Prathamaḥ=mukhyaḥ pakṣaḥ* : K.

Verse 173. Śloka or *Anuṣṭubh. See* Verses 5, 6, 11, 12, 26, 47, 50, 51, 53, 73, 76, 84, 87, 125, 146, 154, 155, 160, 164.

[नाट्येनावतीर्णौ]

राजा :(सविस्मयम्)

उपोढशब्दा न रथाङ्गनेमयः
प्रवर्तमानं न च दृश्यते रजः।
अभूतलस्पर्शतया निरुन्धतस्
तवावतीर्णाऽपि रथो न लक्ष्यते[1] ।। 174 ।।

मातलिः : एतावान् एव शतक्रतोर् आयुष्मतश्च विशेषः।

राजा : मातले। कतमस्मिन् प्रदेशे मारीचाश्रमः।

मातलिः : (हस्तेन दर्शयन्)

वल्मीकार्द्धनिमग्नमूर्त्तिर् उरसा सन्दष्टसर्पत्वचा
कण्ठे जीर्णलताप्रतानवलयेनात्यर्थसम्पीडितः।
अंसव्यापि शकुन्तनीडनिचितं बिभ्रज् जटामण्डलं
यत्र स्थाणुर् इवाचलो मुनिर असाव् अभ्यर्कबिम्बं स्थितः[2] ।। 175 ।।

1. 'The circumferences of the chariot-wheels cause no sound, and no dust is seen rising-in-advance (of us); the chariot of thee reining-in (thy steeds), although it has descended (to the earth), is not observed (to have done so) by-reason-of-its-not-touching the surface of the ground.' *Upoḍha-śabdāḥ=prāpta-dhvanayaḥ* : K. Compare *upoḍha-rāga* : Vikram., Act 2. *Pravartamānam* may mean 'rising in front of us :' compare p. 10, 1. 3. *Nirundhataḥ=nigṛhṇataḥ* : K. *Na lakṣyate* : *see* p. 70, note 3 at end. In the First Act of Vikramorvaśīya, when the car of Purūravas touches the ground, the direction is *rathāvatāra-kṣobhaṁ nāṭayantī*, 'acting the concussion (caused) by the descent of the chariot.' Such, Mātali remarks, is the difference between the car of Indra and that of mortal heroes.

2. 'Where stands you sage, towards [facing] the sun's orb, immovable as the trunk-of-a *tree*, (his) body half-buried in an ant-hill, with (his) breast closely-encircled by a snake's-skin, round the throat excessively pinched by a necklace (formed) of the tendril of a withered creeper, wearing a circular-mass-of-matted-hair

Verse 174. *Vaṁśasthavila* (variety of *Jagatī*.) *See* Verses 18, 22, 23, 67, 81, 114, 117, 119, 145, 150, 161.

Verse 175. *Śārdūla-vikrīḍita* (variety of *Atidhṛti*). *See* Verses 14, 30, 36, 39, 50, 63, 79, 85, 86, 89, 97, 98, 111, 137, 138, 149, 172.

राजा : नमस् ते कष्टतपसे।[1]

मातलिः : (संयतप्रग्रहं रथं कृत्वा) महाराज। एताव् अदितिपरिवर्धितमन्दारवृक्षं[2] प्रजापतेर् आश्रमं प्रविष्टौ स्वः।

enveloping (his) shoulders (and) filled with bird's-nests.' *Valmīkārddha*, etc.; so read K. and the Mackenzie MS. : the other Devanāgarī, *valmīkāgra. Valmīka [=kṛmi-kṛta-mṛttikācaya]* is the mound of earth thrown up by the large ants of India. These hillocks sometimes rise, in Bengal, to the height of eight or ten feet, and are held sacred : *see* Manu, iv, 46, 2238. Such was the immovable impassiveness of this ascetic, that the ants had thrown up their mound as high as his waist, without being distrubed, and the birds had built their nests in his hair. *Sandaṣṭa-*, etc. = *āśliṣṭa-nirmokena* : compare p. 120, note 1. The serpent's skin was used by the ascetic in place of the regular Brāhmaṇical cord. This thread or cord, sometimes called the sacrificial cord *yajñopavīta*, might be made of various substances, such as cotton, hempen or woollen thread, according to the class of the wearer, and was worn over the left shoulder and under the right. The rite of investiture with this thread, which conferred the title *dvija* 'twice-born,' and corresponded in some respects with the Christian rite of baptism, was performed on youths of three classes, at ages varying from eight to sixteen, from eleven to twenty-two, and from twelve to twenty-four, respectively : *see* Manu, ii, 36, etc. *Latā-pratāna=latā-santāna*, 'the spreading part of a creeper.' *Jaṭā-maṇḍala* is the circle or bundle of matted entangled hair which ascetics allowed to grow on the crown of their heads, and which fell in long clotted tresses over the back and shoulders. *Jaṭā* is, especially, Śiva's hair so plaited and arranged, through which the Ganges meandered before its descent upon the earth. *Nicitam=pūritam;* K. *Sthāṇur=śākhā-hīnas taru-skandhaḥ. Abhyarkavimbam=sūrya-maṇḍalābhimukham* : K. the Mack. MS. has *adhyarka*, etc.

1. *Kaṣṭaṁ kṛcchraṁ tapo yasya sa tathoktaḥ* : K.

2. 'Possessed of the Mandāra-tree reared by Aditi.' This was one of the five trees of *Svarga* [see p. 267, note 2], and is probably the tree intended here, as, in verse 176, the Kalpa-tree also is said to have graced Kaśyapa's retreat, which the Scholiast thence imagines to have been located in part of Svarga. Mandāra, however, may stand for the 'coral tree,' and 'swallow-wort.'

राजा : स्वर्गाद् अधिकतरं निर्वृत्तिस्थानम्। अमृतह्रदम्[1] इवावगाढोऽस्मि।

मातलिः : (रथं स्थापयित्वा) अवतरत्वायुष्मान्।

राजा : (अवतीर्य) मातले। भवान् कथम् इदानीम्।[2]

मातलिः : संयन्त्रितो मया रथः। वयम् अप्यवतरामः (तथा कृत्वा) इत आयुष्मन्। (परिक्रम्य) दृश्यन्ताम् अत्रभवताम् ऋषीणां तपोवनभूमयः।

राजा : ननु विस्मयाद् अवलोकयामि।

प्राणानाम् अनिलेन वृत्तिर् उचिता सत्कल्पवृक्षे वने
तोये काञ्चनपद्मरेणुकपिशे धर्माभिषेकक्रिया।
ध्यानं रत्नशिलातलेषु विबुधस्त्रीसन्निधौ संयमो
यत् काङ्क्षन्ति तपोभिर् अन्यमुनयस् तस्मिंस् तपस्यन्त्यमी[3] ।। 176 ।।

1. *Amṛta*, 'the beverage of immortality,' 'the nectar' of the Hindū gods, supposed to be a liquid substance distilled by the moon, who is thence called *amṛta-sūḥ*, 'nectar-producer,' *amṛtādhāraḥ*, 'nectar-repository.'

2. *Avatariṣyati, iti śeṣaḥ* : Ś. : *i.e.*, Supply *avatariṣyati.*

3. '(The place) to which other sages aspire by (their) penances, (where there is) habitual [suitable, adequate] support of life by air in a grove in-which-the-kalpa-tree-is-found; (where there is) the performance of religious ablutions in water, brown with the dust of the golden lotus; (where there is) meditation (while seated) on jewelled slabs of marble, (and) restraint (of the passions) in the presence of celestial nymphs; in (such a place as) this these (sages) are performing penance.' *Prāṇānām vṛttiḥ=jīvanam* : K. The Hindūs imagine that supporting life upon air is a proof of the highest degree of spirituality to which a man can attain. *Sat-kalpa-vṛkṣe= vidyamāna-kalpa-drume* : K. : = *vidyamāna-kalpa-tarau* : Ś., Ch. The Colebroke MS. has *saṅkalpa-vṛkṣe* : this use of *sat* is noticeable. *Śilā-tala*, 'the surface of a stone slab or seat :' compare p. 76, l. 2. *Vibudha-strī = divyāṅganā* : K. *Saṁyamaḥ = niyatendriyatvam* : K. *Ebhiḥ sat-kalpa-vṛkṣatvādikair viśeṣair ayam pradeśaḥ svarga iti pratīyate*, 'By these attributes of the Kalpa-tree, etc, it is inferred that this place was part of *Svarga* :' K. As to the Kalpa-tree, see p. 267, note 2. *Yat, etc.*,

---

Verse 176. *Śārdūla-vikrīḍita* (variety of *Atidhṛti*). *See* Verses 14, 30, 36, 39, 50, 63, 79, 85, 86, 89, 97, 98, 111, 137, 138, 149, 172, 175.

मातलिः : उत्सर्पिणी खलु महतां प्रार्थना[1] (परिक्रम्य। आकाशे[2])। अये वृद्धशाकल्य। किम् अनुतिष्ठति भगवान् मारीचः। किं ब्रवीषि।[2] दाक्षायण्या पतिव्रताधर्मम् अधिकृत्य पृष्टम् तत् तस्यै महर्षिपत्नीसहितायै कथयतीति।[3]

राजा : (कर्णं दत्त्वा) अये। प्रतिपाल्यावसराः खलु मुनयः।[4]

मातलिः : (राजानम् अवलोक्य) अस्मिन्न् अशोकवृक्षमूले[5] तावद् आस्ताम्

i.e., Yat sthānam anye kāṅkṣanti tasmin svarga-pradeśe amī munayas tāni phalāni parihṛtya tapasyanti iti anena teṣāṁ mokṣārthitvaṁ gamyate : K.

1. 'Verily the aspirations [earnest desire, longing] of the great soar upwards [are continually mounting upwards].' *Utsarpiṇī=udgamana-śīlā=atiśayinī* : K.

2. As to *ākāśe* and *kiṁ bravīṣi* : *see* p. 95, note 3.

3. 'Being questioned by Dākṣāyiṇī [*i.e.*, his wife Aditi, the daughter of Dakṣa; see p. 275, note 1.] respecting the duties [duty] of a wife devoted to her husband, he is recounting them [it] to her, in company with the wives of the *maharṣis*.' *Dākṣāyaṇī* is a patronymic applicable to any of the daughters of Dasha. *Pativratā* : compare p. 237, l. 10. *Adhikṛtya* : *see* p. 5, note 3. *Maharṣi*, 'a great saint :' this order of saint or sage was one step in advance of the *Ṛṣi* or simple 'saint.' The classification of *Ṛṣis* varies, but the following seems to be the usual gradation :—2. *Ṛṣi*; 2. *Maharṣi*; 3. *Paramarṣi*; 4. *Devarṣi*; 5. *Brahmarṣi*. Amara mentions two other orders, *Kāṇḍarṣis* and *Śrutarṣis*. The *Rājarṣi* was a mixed order : see p. 83, note 2.

4. 'We must await the leisure of saints.' So reads the Mackenzie MS., supported, apparently, by K. *Munayaḥ* is of course the nominative, but such is the terseness of compounds like *pratipālyāvasarāḥ* that a literal English translation is impossible. The other Devanāgarī have *pratipālyāvasaraḥ khalu prastāvaḥ*.

5. The Aśoka [Jonesia Asoka] is one of the most beautiful of Indian trees. Sir W. Jones observes that 'the vegetable world scarce exhibits a richer sight than an Aśoka-tree in full bloom. It is about as high as an ordinary cherry-tree.' The flowers are very large, and 'beautifully diversified with tints of orange-scarlet, of pale yellow, and of bright orange, which form a variety of shades according to the age of the blossom.'

1. 'Opportune time' is one of the meanings given for *antara*. As

आयुष्मान्। यावत् त्वाम् इन्द्रगुरवे निवेदयितुम् अन्तरान्वेषी[1] भवामि।

राजा : यथा भवान् मन्यते (इति स्थित:)।

मातलि: : आयुष्मन्। साधयाम्यहं[2] (इति निष्क्रान्त:)।

राजा : (निमित्तं सूचयित्वा)

मनोरथाय नाशंसे किं बाहो स्पन्दसे वृथा।
पूर्वावधीरितं श्रेयो दु:खं हि परिवर्तते[3] ।। 177 ।।

नेपथ्ये : मा खु चाबलं करेहि। कहं गदो एव्व अत्तणो पकिदिं।

नेपथ्ये : मा खलु चापलं कुरु। कथं गत एव आत्मन: प्रकृतिम्।[4]

राजा : (कर्णं दत्त्वा) अभूमिर् इयम् अविनयस्य।[5] को नु खल्वेष निषिध्यते।। (शब्दानुसारेणावलोक्य। सस्मितम्) अये। को नु खल्वयम् अनुबध्यमानस् तपस्विनीभ्याम् अबालसत्त्वो बाल:।[6]

to *gurave,* compare, p. 171, note 2 in middle. Kaśyapa was the reputed father of Indra.

2. 'I go-to-do (what I proposed),' 'I will do (as I said) :' compare page 209, line 6, and page 17, line 5.

3. 'I expect not to (obtain my) desire; why, O arm, throbbest thou (thus) vainly? For happiness formerly scorned turns to misery.' Kāṭavema observes that *manorathāya* is here equivalent to *manorathaṁ prāptum,* and refers to Pāṇini's Sūtra ii, 3, 14. So *phalebhyo yāti = phalāni āhartuṁ yāti.* As to the throbbing of the arm, and *nimittaṁ sūcayitvā [=śakunaṁ nirūpya* : K.] *see* p. 20, notes 1 and p. 21 note 1. *Śreyo = śubham, i.e., Śakuntalā-rūpam,* 'consisting of Śakuntalā :' K. *Hi parivartate;* Kāṭavema has *viparivartate* and *sat parivartate.*

4. 'Act not so wildly [do not commit such a wild, wilful act, be not so wild in your behaviour]. What! has he gone already to his own nature?' Compare Ragh., iii, 42. *Prakṛti,* 'the state or character which is natural to one :' compare p. 72, note 2. *Gataḥ* : *see* p. 159, note 3 at end.

5. 'This is no place for petulance [insolence]:' compare p. 266, line 7.

6. 'Who is this child with unchild-like disposition [nature], closely attended by two female ascetics?' *Anubadhyamāna* : the

---

Verse 177. *Śloka* or *Anuṣṭubh. See* Verses 5, 6, 11, 12, 26, 47, 50, 51, 53, 73, 76, 84, 87, 125, 127, 146, 154, 155, 160, 164, 177

अर्द्धपीतस्तनं मातुर् आमर्दक्लिष्टकेशरम्।
प्रक्रीडितुं सिंहशिशुं बलात्कारेण कर्षति[1] ।। 178 ।।

[ततः प्रविशति यथानिर्दिष्टकर्मा तपस्विनीभ्यां बालः]

बालः : जिम्भ सिङ्घ। दन्ताइं दे गणइस्सं।

बालः : जृम्भस्व सिंह। दन्तास् ते गणयिष्यामि।

प्रथमा : अविणीद। किं णो अपच्चणिव्विसेसाणि सत्ताणि विप्प-

प्रथमा : अविनीत। किं नोऽपत्यनिर्विशेषाणि सत्त्वानि विप्र-

अरेसि। हनत वड्ढइ दे संरम्भो। ठाणेक्खु इसिजणेण सव्वदमणोत्ति

करोषि।[2] हन्त वर्धते ते संरम्भः। स्थाने खलु ऋषिजनेन सर्वदमन इति

किदणामहेओसि।

कृतनामधेयोऽसि।

राजा : किं नु खलु बालेऽस्मिन्न् औरस इव पुत्रे स्निह्यति मे मनः। नूनम् अनपत्यता मां वत्सलयति।[3]

द्वितीया : एसा खु केसरिणी तुमं लङ्घेदि। जइ से पुत्तअं ण मुञ्चेसि।

द्वितीया : एषा खलु केशरिणी त्वां लङ्घयति।[4] यदि अस्याः पुत्रकं न मुञ्चसि।

Mackenzie MS. has *anugamyamāna. Anubandha, lit.*, 'tying after,' 'following at the heels,' 'sticking closely to;' very forcibly expresses the close attendance of a nurse upon a child.

1. 'He forcibly drags to play (with him) a lion's cub that-has-but-half-sucked-its mother's dug, (and) whose-mane-is-disordered-by-rough-handling,' or 'he forcibly drags from its mother,' etc.

2. 'Why dost thou teaze the animals (cherished by us as if) not-differing-from-our-offspring?' *Sattvāni* : compare p. 55, note 2. *Nirviśeṣāṇi* : compare *suta-nirviśeṣaṁ nakulam*, 'the ichneumon dear to him as a son :' Hitop., 1, 2721 : and *mūṣika-nirviśeṣam* : Hitop., 1, 2395.

3. 'It must certainly be my childlessness that causes me to yearn (towards this child).' *Vatsala* or *vātsalya* is, properly, the yearning affection of a cow for its calf, or a parent for its offspring.

4. *Laṅghayati* = *ākramati* : K. Compare page 95, note 5.

Verse 178. *Śloka* or *Anuṣṭubh. See* Verses 5, 6, 11, 12, 26, 47, 50, 51, 53, 73, 76, 84, 87, 125, 127, 146, 154, 155, 160, 164, 177.

बालः : (सस्मितं) अम्हहे। बलिअंक्खु भीदोम्हि।। इत्यधरं
बालः : (सस्मितम्) अहो। बलीयः खलु भीतोऽस्मि।। इत्यधरं

दर्शयति।।
दर्शयति[1] ।।

राजा :

महतस् तेजसो बीजं बालोऽयं प्रतिभाति मे।
स्फुलिङ्गावस्थया वह्निर् एधापेक्ष इव स्थितः[2] ।। 179 ।।

प्रथमा : वच्छ। एदं बालमिइन्दअं मुञ्च। अबरं दे कीलणअं दाइस्सं।

प्रथमा : वत्स। एतं बालमृगन्द्रकं मुञ्च। अपरं ते क्रीडनकं दास्यामि।

बालः : कहिं। देहि णं (इति हस्तं प्रसारयति)।

बालः : कुत्र। देहि एनं (इति हस्तं प्रसारयति)।

राजा : कथं चक्रवर्तिलक्षणम्[3] अप्यनेन धार्यते। तथा ह्यस्य

प्रलोभ्यवस्तुप्रणयप्रसारितो
विभाति जालग्रथिताङ्गुलिः करः।

1. Kāṭavema quotes a passage from the Vasanta-rājīya to show that different movements of the lips, such as biting the lip, pouting the under-lip, etc., were significant of various emotions. The gloss is corrupt, but it appears that *adhara-darśana=adhara-prasāraṇa* is [*anādare*] a gesture of contempt. Compare Psalm xxii, 7 : 'All they that see me laugh me to scorn; they shoot out the lip,' etc.

2. 'This child appears to me (to possess) the gern [rudiment] of mighty energy [spirit, courage]. He stands like fire in a state of scintillation [in a sparkling state], waiting (only) for fuel (that it may blaze up).' *Edhāpekṣa=indhanāni kāṅkṣiṇī* : K. The Beṅgālī MSS. have *edhaḥ-kṣayah.*

3. 'The mark of an universal emperor :' see p. 16, note 1, and p. 210, note 4.

Verse 179. *Śloka* or *Anuṣṭubh. See* Verses 5, 6, 11, 12, 26, 47, 50, 51, 53, 76, 84, 87, 125, 127, 146, 154, 155, 160, 164, 177, 178.

अलक्ष्यपत्रान्तरम् इद्धरागया
नवोषसा भिन्नम् इवैकपङ्कजम्[1] ।। 180 ।।

1. 'His hand stretched forth to beg for a coveted object, having the fingers connected by a web, appears like [shines like] a single lotus-blossom, the spaces between whose petals is imperceptible, expanded by the early dawn, whose-glow-is-just-kindled.' *Praṇaya=prārthana* : Ś. *Jāla*, etc.; *Jāleṣu antareṣu grathitāḥ saṁhatāḥ aṅgulayo yasya* : K. For *grathitāṅguliḥ* Śaṅkara has *sanhatāṅguliḥ* = *sanśliṣṭāṅguliḥ*, and remarks that a hand whose fingers were thus united was indicative of great valour [*mahā-puruṣatvam*]. He adds *jāla-pāda-bhujāviti nara-nārāyaṇa-viśeṣaṇam uktam*, 'webbed-feet and webbed-hands are said to be characteristics of Nara and Nārāyaṇa.' Hindū poets reckon thirty-two marks of greatness, and he who possessed them all was said to be *dvā-triṁśallakṣaṇopetaḥ*. The child's fingers, being drawn together by this membrane or web, would bear some resemblance to an expanding lotus-flower, the fingers answering to the long petals, which would be only separated towards the top. This seems to be the sense : my first inclination was to translate, 'having the fingers regularly marked with reticulated lines,' or 'having the fingers drawn together into (the form of) a bud.' *Alakṣya* [= *adṛśya* : K.] : So read all the Devanāgarī MSS. excepting my own, which has *ālakṣya*, with the Beṅgālī; Śaṅkara, however, has *alakṣya*. *Patrāntaram* = *dala-vivaram;* K., Ś. *Iddha-rāgayā navoṣasā*, etc.; *Uṣas*, 'the dawn,' is usually neuter in classical Sanskṛt. In the Vedas, as here, it is feminine. Thus in Ṛg-veda i, 46, 1, *Eṣo uṣā apūrvyā vyucchati priyā divaḥ*. See also Ṛg-veda i, 48; 3, 5, 7, 8, 13, and i, 62, 8 and i, 92, 4, and i, 113, 4, etc. It is possible that the feminine noun *uṣā* may form its vowel cases from *uṣas*, as *jarā* from *jaras;* nom. *jarā, jarasau, jarasaḥ;* instr., *jarasā, jarābhyām, jarābhiḥ*, etc. : see Professor Wilson's Grammar, rule 129. The following is the corrupt gloss of Śaṅkara : *uṣaḥpratyuṣasi klīvaṁ pihaprasvāntu [? piḥprasvāntu* : Ch.*] yoṣatīti koṣaḥ*. Kāṭavema explains *navoṣasā* as a Bahuvrīhi, 'by he early-dawned one :' *Navam uṣo yasyā sā navoṣā prātaḥsandhyā tayā bhinnaṁ vikasitam*. As to *paṅkajam* : *see* p. 209, note 3.

Verse 180. *Vaṁśasthavila* (variety of *Jagatī*. *See* Verses 18, 22, 23, 67, 81, 114, 117, 119, 145, 150, 161, 174.

द्वितीया : सुव्वदे। ण सक्को एसो वाआमेत्तेण विरमाबिदुं। गच्छ। मम
द्वितीया : सुव्रते। न शक्य एष वाचामात्रेण विरमयितुम्। गच्छ। मदीये
केरए[1] उडए मक्कण्डेअस्स इसिकुमारअस्स वणचित्तिदो मित्तिआमोरओ
उटजे मार्कण्डेयस्य ऋषिकुमारस्य वर्णचित्रितो मृत्तिकामयूरस्
चिट्ठदि। तं से उबहर।
तिष्ठति। तम् अस्य उपहर।

प्रथमा : तह (इति निष्क्रान्ता)।
प्रथमा : तथा (इति निष्क्रान्ता)।

बालः : इमिणा एव्व दाव कीलिस्सं (इति तापसीं विलोक्य हसति)।
बालः : अनेन एव तावत् क्रीडयिष्यामि (इति तापसीं विलोक्य हसति)।

राजा : स्पृहयामि खलु दुर्ललितायास्मै।[2]

आलक्ष्यदन्तमुकुलान् अनिमित्तहासैर्
अव्यक्तवर्णरमणीयवचःप्रवृत्तीन्।

1. This pleonastic word, according to Lassen [Instit. Prāk., p. 118] is derived from the Sanskṛt *kṛte,* and is equivalent to *pertinens ad,* 'in the cottage belonging to me,' etc. Some of the MSS. omit the word.

2. 'I have a great fancy for this unmanageable (child).' *Durlalita, i.e., durlabham īpsitaṁ yasya* [Ś.], 'difficult to be coaxed or pleased,' 'wayward,' 'naughty.' Kāṭavema reads *durlasitāya* and interprets by *dhūrtāya,* 'roguish,' 'mischievous.' The causal sense of the root *lal* is 'to coax,' though *dur-lālita* might then be expected. The primitive idea is certainly that of 'sporting,' 'toying,' 'taking pleasure,' as in the root *las.* So in Vikramorvaśīya, Act II, the king complains that his eye-sight has become *durlalitam, i.e.,* 'difficult to be pleased,' 'fastidious' by looking on Urvaśī, and that the beauties of Nature have no longer any charms for him; *upavana-latāsu cakṣur na badhnāti dhṛtiṁ tad-aṅganāloka-durlalitam.* The Scholiast there explains the word by *dur-āgrastam.* In the Sāhit.-darp., p. 193, line 1, the following is cited from the Mahābh. : *Dhik dhik sūta kiṁ kṛtavān asi vatsasya me prakṛti-durlalitasya,* where *durlalita* is explained by *durvilasita.*

अङ्काश्रयप्रणयिनस् तनयान् वहन्तो
धन्यास् तदङ्गरजसा मलिनीभवन्ति[1] ।। 181 ।।

तापसी : होदु। ण मं अअं गणेदि (पार्श्वर्वम् अवलोकयति)

तापसी : भवतु। न माम् अयं गणयति (पार्श्वम् अवलोकयति)

को एत्थ इसिकुमाराणं (राजानम् अवलोक्य) भद्दमुह। एहि दाव।

कोऽत्र ऋषिकुमाराणां (राजानम् अवलोक्य) भद्रमुख।[2] एहि तावत्।

मोएहि इमिणा दुम्मोअहत्थग्गाहेण डिम्भलीलाए बाहीअमाणं

मोचय अनेन दुर्मोचयहस्तग्राहेण डिम्भलीलया बाध्यमानं

बालमिइन्दअं।

बालमृगेन्द्रकम्।[3]

1. 'Happy (those parents who), carrying (their) little-sons fondly-soliciting-a-refuge-in-their-lap, having-buds-of-teeth-just-[scarcely, slightly] visible by their innocent [causeless, without reason] smiles, while-attempting-charming-prattle-in-indistinct-accents, are soiled by the dust of their (infantine) limbs!' *Ālakṣya* : *ā* is here the prefix of diminution : *see* p. 225, note 1. *Praṇayinaḥ* = *prārthakāḥ* : Ś., Ch. *Malinī;* the Bengālī have *paruṣī.* This is the verse with which Chézy is enraptured : '... strophe incomparable, que tout père, on plutōt toute mère, ne pourra lire sans sentir battre son coeur, tant le poète a suny rendre, avec les nuances les plus délicates, l'expression vivante de l'amour maternel.'

2. 'O gentle sir,' *lit.*, 'O thou with auspicious countenance.' According to the Sāhit.-darp. [p. 179, line 16] *bhadra-mukha* and *saumya* are the titles used by the inferior characters in addressing the king's son : *saumya bhadra-mukhetyevam adhamaistu kumārakaḥ.* They do not seem to be so restricted, as in the 5th. Act the Bengālī MSS. make Gautamī address the king himself as *bhadra-mukha;* and and Kāṭavema extends the application of both terms to any *mānya,* honorable person : *Bhadra-mukheti mānyasyāmantraṇe yathoktaṁ saumya bhadra-mukhetyevaṁ mānyo rājñaḥ suto vā.*

1. 'Release the young lion being tormented in childish play by this (boy) the-grasp-of-whose-hand-is-difficult to unloose.' Some MSS. have *maindam* or *maindaam* for *mṛgendram* : the Mackenzie, *miindam.*

Verse 181. Vasanta-tilakā (variety of Śakkarī). *See* Verses 8, 27, 31, 43, 46, 64, 74, 80, 82, 83, 91, 93, 94, 95, 100, 104, 105, 108, 123, 124, 144, 148, 152, 157, 168, 170.

राजा : (उपगम्य। सस्मितम्) अयि भो महर्षिपुत्र।

एवम् आश्रमविरुद्धवृत्तिना
संयमः किमिति जन्मनस् त्वया।
सत्त्वसंश्रयसुखोऽपि दूष्यते
कृष्णसर्पशिशुनेव चन्दनम्[1] ।। 182 ।।

तापसी : भद्दमुह। ण हु अअं इसिकुमारओ।

तापसी : भद्रमुख। न खलु अयम् ऋषिकुमारः।

राजा : आकारसदृशं चेष्टितम् एवास्य कथयति।[2] स्थानप्रत्ययात् तु वयम् एवंतर्किणः (यथाभ्यर्थितम् अनुतिष्ठन् बालस्पर्शम् उपलभ्य। आत्मगतम्)

अनेन कस्यापि कुलाङ्कुरेण
स्पृष्टस्य गात्रेषु सुखं ममैवम्।

1. 'How is it that by thee, whose behaviour is opposed to (the peaceful character of) a hermitage, (thy) father's humanity [forbearance], that delights-in-the-protection-of-the-animals is thus outraged; like the sandal-tree by the young of the black serpent?' *Āśrama-viruddha* : compare p. 38, 1. 8. *Saṁyamaḥ = śamaḥ* : K., 'a vow to forbear hurting animals.' *Kim iti = kimartham* : K. : *iti* is frequently thus joined with *kim* : compare p. 71, 1. 1. *Janmanas = janmano hetoḥ* : K. So *prabhava = janma-hetu* : p. 83, line 2, note 1; otherwise I should translate 'from thy birth.' The Bengālī MSS. have *janmadas* and *saṁyamī* agreeing with it. *Sukho* : the Mackenzie and Kāṭavema have *guṇ [=dharmaḥ* : K.] *Candanam* : as to the sandal, see p. 172, note 4. This celebrated tree seems to have paid dearly for the fragrance of its wood : 'the root is infested by serpents; the blossoms by bees; the branches by monkeys; the summits by bears. In short, there is not a part of the sandal-tree which is not occupied by the vilest impurities :' Hitop., verse 162, ed. Johnson.

2. 'His behaviour (which is) conformable to his mien says as much [bespeaks it, betokens it].' *Kathayati* : compare p. 221, line 2.

Verse 182. *Rathoddhatā* (variety of Triṣṭubh) containing eleven syllables to the half-line, each half-line alike.

—◡—◡◡◡—◡—◡—||

कां निर्वृतिं चेतसि तस्य कुर्याद्

यस्यायम् अङ्गात् कृतिनः प्ररूढः[1] ।। 183 ।।

तापसी : (उभौ णिर्वर्ण्य) अच्छरिअं अच्छरिअं।

तापसी : (उभौ निर्वर्ण्य) आश्चर्यम् आश्चर्यम्।

राजा : आर्ये। किमिव।

तापसी : इमस्स बालअरूबस्स देबि संवादिणी आकिदित्ति विम्हाबिदन्हि। अपरिइदस्सबि दे अप्पडिलोमो संवृत्तोत्ति।

तापसी : अस्य बालकरूपस्य तेऽपि संवादिनी आकृतिरिति[2] विस्मापितास्मि। अपरिचितस्यापि तेऽप्रतिलोमः संवृत्त इति।

राजा : (बालम् उपलालयन्[3])। न चेन् मुनिकुमारोऽयम्। अथ कोऽस्य व्यपदेशः।

तापसी : पुरुवंसो।

तापसी : पुरुवंशः।

राजा : (आत्मगतम्) कथम् एकान्वयो मम। अतः खलु मदनुकारिणम् एनम् अत्रभवती मन्यते। अस्त्येतत् पौरवाणाम् अन्त्यं कुलव्रतम्।

भवनेषु रसाधिकेषु पूर्वं

क्षितिरक्षार्थम् उशन्ति ये निवासम्।

1. Such (being) the-thrill-of-delight in the limbs of me touched by this scion of the family of some one (unknown to me); what bliss must he cause in the heart of that happy-man from whose body [loins] he sprang!' Hindū poets are fond of alluding to the thrilling effect of the touch of a child on the limbs of its parent, and *vice versā*. Compare the parallel passages in the 5th Act of the Vikramorvaśīya, and the following from the Mahābh. : *Putrasparśāt sukhataraḥ sparśo loke na vidyate. Aṅgāt* : some MSS., including my own, have *aṅkāt*, 'from whose loins.' *Kṛtinaḥ = bhāgyavataḥ*, 'fortunate.' *Kṛtī* is properly 'one who has accomplished the desire of his heart.'

2. 'The speaking-resemblance of form;' 'la ressemblance parlante :' Chézy.

3. *Upalālayan*, 'fondling :' see p. 284, note 2. *Vyapadeśaḥ*, 'family :' *see* page 201, note 3.

Verse 183. *Upajāti* or *Ākhyānakī* (variety of *Triṣṭubh*). *See* Verse 41, 107, 121, 126, 142, 156, 158, 166, 169.

नियतैकयतिव्रतानि पश्चात्
तरुमूलानि गृहीभवन्ति तेषाम्[1] ।। 184 ।।

(प्रकाशं) न पुनर् आत्मगत्या मानुषाणाम् एष विषयः।[2]

तापसी : जह भद्दमुहो भणादि। अच्छरासम्बन्धेण इमस्स जणणी

तापसी : यथा भद्रमुखो भणति। अप्सरःसम्बन्धेन[3] अस्य जननी

एत्थ देवगुरुणो तबोवणे पसूदा।

अत्र देवगुरोस्[3] तपोवने प्रसूता।

राजा : (अपवार्य) हन्त द्वितीयम् इदम् आशाजननं (प्रकाशं) अथ सा तत्र भवती किमाख्यस्य राजर्षेः पत्नी।

तापसी : को तस्स धम्मदारपरिच्चाइणो णाम सङ्कीतिदुं चिन्तिस्सदि।

तापसी : कस् तस्य धर्मदारपरित्यागिनो नाम सङ्कीर्तितुं चिन्तयिष्यति।

1. 'This (custom of retiring to a hermitage) is the last family-observance of the descendants of Puru. (They) who first of all for the sake of protecting the earth choose a residence in palaces abounding-in-all-the-pleasures-of-sense, to them [of them] the roots of trees where the one religious vow of ascetics [*i.e.*, control of the passions, mortification] is rigidly maintained, become a dwelling-place.' *Rasādhikeṣu* : the Bengālī MSS. have *sudhāsiteṣu*, 'white with stucco or chunam.' *Uśanti* [3d pers. pl. pres. of *vaś*] = *icchanti* : Ś. = *vāñchanti* : K. *Taru-mūlāni* : so Manu enjoins that the hermit is to be *vijitendriyo dharāśayo vṛkṣa-mūla-niketanaḥ*, 'his passions kept in subjection, sleeping on the bare ground, dwelling at the roots of trees :' vi, 26. It seems to have been a constant practice in ancient India for kings when they had reigned sufficiently long, to retire from the charge of government and betake themselves to penitential exercises. They first associated the *Yuva-rāja* or heir-apparent with themselves, and then left him in quiet possession of the throne.

2. 'But this (sacred) place is not (accessible) to mortals by their own means [condition].' *Viṣayaḥ=pradeśaḥ* : Schol., Chézy. The Mackenzie MS. has *katham* for *na.*

3. 'In consequence of her relationship to a nymph.' *Deva-guros* = *Kaśyapasya.*

Verse 184. *Aupacchandasika. See* Verses 77, 78.

राजा : (स्वगतम्) इयं खलु कथा माम् एव लक्षीकरोति। यदि तावद् अस्य शिशोर् मातरं नामतः पृच्छेयं (विचिन्त्य) अथवा। अन्यायः परदारपृच्छव्यापारः।[1]

तापसी : (प्रविश्य मृन्मयूरहस्ता) सव्वदमण।। सउन्दलावण्णं पेक्ख।

तापसी : (प्रविश्य मृन्मयूरहस्ता) सर्वदमन। शकुन्तलावण्यं[2] प्रेक्षस्व।

बालः : (सदृष्टिक्षेपं) कहिं वा मे अम्बा।

बालः : (सदृष्टिक्षेपम्) कुत्र वा मे अम्बा।[3]

उभे : णामसारिस्सेण वञ्चिदो माउवच्छलो।

उभे : नामसादृश्येन वञ्चितो मातृवत्सलः।

द्वितीया : वच्छ। इमस्स मित्तिआमोरअम्स रम्मत्तणं देक्खत्ति भणि-

द्वितीया : वत्स। अस्य मृत्तिकामयूरकस्य रम्यत्वं पश्येति भणितो-

दोसि।

ऽसि।

राजा : (आत्मगतम्) किं वा शकुन्तलेत्यस्य मातुर् आख्या। सन्ति पुनर् नामधेयसादृश्यानि। अपि मृगतृष्णिकेव नाममात्रप्रस्तावो मे विषादाय कल्पते।[4]

1. So reads the Mackenzie MS. The others *tarhy anāryaḥ para-dāravyavahāraḥ.*

2. *Śakunta = pakṣin,* 'a bird.' By joining it with *lāvaṇyam,* the hermitess unconsciously pronounces Śakuntalā. *Śakuntasya pakṣiṇo lāvaṇyam. Śakunta-lāvaṇyaṁ śleṣeṇa śakuntalā-śabdaḥ uktaḥ* : Schol. Chézy.

3. For *ambā* (the reading of the Mackenzie MS., supported by K.) some have *ajjū* for Sanskrt *ajjukā*, and again, subsequently *ajjuā* for *ajjukā,* where Kāṭavema has *ajjaā* for *āryakā* or *āryā.* I have everywhere followed Kāṭavema in rejecting *ajjukā,* as, according to Amara [I, 1, 7, 11] and Sāhit-darp. [p. 179 at end], this word, in theatrical language, is applied only to a *veśyā* or harlot.

4. 'Perhaps the mention of a mere name, like the mirage-of-the-desert, is destined to (cause) me bitter-disappointment.' *Mṛga-tṛṣṇikā* : see p. 246, note 1 at end. *Nāma-mātra-prastāvo* may mean 'the occasion of a mere name,' but the verb *pra-stu* has the sense of 'mentioning,' 'declaring.' *Kalpate,* 'is sufficient,' or simply 'becomes a cause of;' compare p. 188, l. 8, p. 256, 1. 3.

बालः : अज्जए। रोअदि मे एसो भद्दमोरओ (इति क्रीडनकम्

बालः : आर्यके। रोचते मे एष भद्रमयूरकः[1] (इति क्रीडनकम्

आदत्ते)।

आदत्ते)।

प्रथमा : (विलोक्य। सोद्वेगं) अम्हहे। रक्खाकरण्डअं से मणिबन्धे

प्रथमा : (विलोक्य। सोद्वेगम्) अहो। रक्षाकरण्डकम्[2] अस्य मनिबन्धे

ण दीसदि।

न दृश्यते।

राजा : अलम् अलम् आवेगेन। नन्विदम् अस्य सिंहशावविमर्दात् परिभ्रष्टम्। (इत्यादातुम् इच्छति)

उभेः मा खु मा खु। एदं अविलम्बिअ कहं गहिदं णेण।।

उभे : मा खलु मा खलु। एतद् अविलम्ब्य कथं गृहीतम् अनेन (इति विस्मयाद् उरोनिहितहस्ते परस्परम् अवलोकयतः।।

राजा : किमर्थं प्रतिषिद्धाः स्मः।

प्रथमा : सुणादु महाराओ। एसा अबराजिदा णाम ओसही इमस्स

प्रथमा : श्रृणोतु महाराजः। एषा अपराजिता[3] नाम औषधिर् अस्य

1. A peacock, whether living or in the form of a toy, seems to have been a favourite play-thing. So the boy in the fifth Act of the Vikramorvaśī : *yaḥ suptavān madaṅke taṁ me jāta-kalāpaṁ preṣaya śikhinam.* For *ārye* the Beṅgālī have *anṭike. Anṭikā=bhaginī jyeṣṭhā=dhātrī* : Ś.

2. 'The amulet,' 'the talisman,' *lit.*, the guardian casket, the magical casket. One sense, however, of *karaṇḍaka* is 'a kind of plant,' or 'herb:' Compare the next note. It was probably a kind of locket, containing some herb with talismanic properties, worn round the waist, to serve as an amulet. *Karaṇḍaka* certainly usually signifies 'a little box,' but it may possibly be the name for the herb itself. Kāṭavema explains it by *rakṣā-ghuṭikā* [? *guṭikā*], 'a magical ball.' Some of the Beṅgālī have *rakṣā-kāṇḍo;* Śaṅkara and Candra-ś., *rakṣā-gaṇḍo* and *rakṣā-gaṇḍako.*

3. 'This herb, called *aparājitā* [unconquered, invincible], was given by his reverence Kaśyapa to this child, on the occasion of the natal (ceremony).' As to the name *aparājitā*, compare p. 261, note 3.

जादकम्मसमए भअवदा मारीएण दिणा। एदं किल मादापिदरो अप्पाणं
जातकर्मसमये भगवता मारीचेन दत्ता। एतां किल मातापितराव् आत्मानं
च वज्जिअ अबरो भूमिपडिदं ण गेण्हादि।
च वर्जयित्वा अपरो भूमिपतितां न गृह्णाति।

राजा : अथ[1] गृह्णाति।

प्रथमा : तदो तं सप्पो भविअ दंसइ।

प्रथमा : ततस् तं सर्पो भूत्वा दशति।

राजा : भवतीभ्यां कदाचिद् अस्याः प्रत्यक्षीकृता विक्रिया।

उभे : अणेअसो।

उभे : अनेकशः।

राजा :(सहर्षम्। आत्मगतम्) कथम् इव सम्पूर्णमपि मे मनोरथं नाभिनन्दामि। (इति बालं परिष्वजते)

द्वितीया : सुव्वदे। एहि। इमं वुत्तन्तं णिअमव्वाबुडाए सउन्दलाए
द्वितीया : सुव्रते। एहि। इमं वृत्तानतं नियमव्यापृतायै शकुन्तलायै
निवेदेम्ह (इति निष्क्रान्ते)।
निवेदयावः (इति निष्क्रान्ते)।

बालः : मुञ्च मं। जाव अम्बाए सआमं गमिस्सं।

बालः : मुञ्च माम्। यावद् अम्बायाः सकाशं गमिष्यामि।

राजा : पुत्रक। मया सहैव मातरम् अभिनन्दिष्यसि।

बालः : ममक्खु तादो दुस्सन्दो। ण तुमं।

बालः : मम खलु तातो दुष्यन्तः। न त्वम्।

राजा : (सस्मितम्) एष विवाद एव प्रत्याययति।[2]

The *jāta-karma* is the fourth of the twelve Saṁskāras, or purificatory rites described in Manu [ii, 27, etc.], and the first after the child's birth : compare p. 254, note 1; p. 195, note 6. It was performed by giving the child honey and clarified butter out of a golden spoon, before separating the nevel-string.

1. *Atha* must here be equivalent to *yadhi tu*, 'supposing now.'

2. 'Even this contradiction convinces me.' *Pratyāyayati*, 'causes me to believe,' 'me inducit ad credendum:' compare page 225, line 12.

[ततः प्रविशत्येकवेणीधरा[1] शकुन्तला]

शकुन्तला : विआरकालेबि पकिदित्थं सव्वदमणस्स ओसहिं सुणिअ

शकुन्तला : विकारकालेऽपि[2] प्रकृतिस्थां सर्व्वदमनस्य औषधिं श्रुत्वा

ण मे आसा आसि अत्तणो भाअहेएसु। अहवा जह माणुमदीए

न मे आशा आसीद् आत्मनो भागधेयेषु।[3] अथवा यथा सानुमत्या

आचक्खिदं। तह सम्भावीअदि एदं।

आचष्टम्।[4] तथा सम्भाव्यते एतत्।

राजा : (शकुन्तलां विलोक्य) अये। सेयम् अत्रभवती शकुन्तला। यैषा

वसने परिधूसरे वसाना
नियमक्षाममुखी धृतैकवेणिः।
अतिनिष्करुणस्य शुद्धशीला
मम दीर्घं विरहव्रतं बिभर्ति[5] ।। 185 ।।

1. Comapre Megh., verse 90 [*sārayanti eka-veṇīṁ kareṇa*], and verse 98 [*abalā-veṇi-mokṣotsukāni*]. The Hindū women collect their hair into a single long braid, as a sign of mourning, when their husbands are dead, or absent for a long period.

2. 'Even at the time of metamorphose,' *i.e.*, even on an occasion when it ought to have changed its form. As to *prakṛti*, 'the natural form or state,' as opposed to *vikāra*, compare p. 72, line 2. *Auṣadhi* : see p. 290, note 3.

3. 'I had no hope in my own destiny,' 'I had no trust in my fortunes.'

4. Compare page 257, line 2 and p. 258, line 2.

5. 'She who, wearing a pair of dark-grey vestments, having a countenance emaciated by penitential-exercises, bearing (on her head) a single braid of hair, chaste [pure] in her behaviour, undergoes a long vow of separation from me, excessively unmerciful.' *Vasane*, acc. du. neut. : *see* p. 158, note 1, and compare *vāsasī* in Mṛcchakaṭika, Act 4. It seems that men's clothes, as well as women's, consisted of two pieces : compare in Bhaṭṭi, iii, 20, *manorame vastre,* which, in one commentary, is rendered by *manoramaṁ vastra-dvayam*, and in the other, by *ceto-hāriṇī vastre.*

Verse 185. Aupachchhandasika. *See* verses 77, 78, 184.

शकुन्तला : (पश्चात्तापविवर्णं राजानं दृष्ट्वा) एक्खु अज्जउत्तो

शकुन्तला : (पश्चात्तापविवर्णं राजानं दृष्ट्वा) न खलु आर्य्यपुत्र

विअ। तदो को एसो दाणिं किदरक्खामङ्गलं दारअं मे गत्तसंसग्गेण

इव। ततः क एष इदानीं कतरक्षामङ्गलं[1] दारकं मे गात्रसंसर्गेण

दूसेदि।

दूषयति।

बालः : (मातरम् उपेत्य) अम्ब। को एसो पुरिसो मं पुत्तेत्ति

बालः : (मातरम् उपेत्य) अम्ब।[2] क एष पुरुषो मां पुत्रेति

आलिङ्गदि।

आलिङ्गति।

राजा : प्रिये। क्रौर्यमपि मे त्वयि प्रयुक्तम् अनुकूलपरिणामं संवृत्तं। यद् अहम् इदानीं त्वया प्रत्यभिज्ञातम् आत्मानं पश्यामि।

शकुन्तला : (आत्मगतं) हिअअ। समस्सस समस्सस। परिच्चत्तमच्छरेण

शकुन्तला : (आत्मगतम्) हृदय। समाश्वसिहि समाश्वसिहि। परित्यक्तमत्सरेण

अणुअम्पिदम्हि देव्वेण। अज्जउत्तोक्खु एसो।

अनुकम्पितास्मि दैवेन। आर्यपुत्रः खलु एषः।

Pari-dhūsare : as the preposition *ā* is employed diminutively, so the prepositions *pari* and *sam* give force and intensity, much as (*sym*) and (*sym*) in Greek, and *per* and *con* in Latin. *Pari* is even more intensitive than *sam* : thus, *samāpti*, 'completion,' *pari-samāpti*, 'entire completion;' *sampūrṇa*, 'very full,' *paripūrṇa*, 'completely filled;' *saṁ-śuṣka*, 'dried up,' *pari-śuṣka*, 'quite dried up; *āpāṇḍu*, 'palish,' *pari-pāṇḍu*, 'very pale;' *pari-śrānta*, 'completely wearied, etc., etc. *Dhṛtaika-veṇi* : see p. 292, note 2. Śaṅkara and Candraśekhara quote the following from Bharata : *amalāsvavadhāraṇam* [*? amalā avadhāraṇam* : Ś.] *alakānāṁ ca kalpanam anulepana-saṁskāraṁ na kuryāt pathikāṅganā* ['a woman whose husband is absent on a journey :' compare p. 227, note 1]; *pāṇḍu-chāyā kṛśa-tanur veṇī-yuta-śiroruhā lambālakā dīnaveśā vibhūṣaṇa-vivarjitā.*

1. 'Furnished with a lucky talisman,' 'protected by an auspicious amulet.' As to *ārya-putra* in the preceding line, *see* p. 194, note 1.

2. The feminine *ambā* makes its vocative *amba*, by special rule.

राजा : प्रिये!

स्मृतिभिन्नमोहतमसो दिष्ट्या प्रमुखे स्थितासि मे सुमुखि।
उपरागान्ते शशिनः समुपगता रोहिणी योगम्[1] ।। 186 ।।

शकुन्तला : जेदु जेदु अज्जउत्तो (इत्यर्द्धोक्ते वाष्पकण्ठी विरमति)।

शकुनतला : जयतु जयतु आर्यपुत्रः (इत्यर्द्धोक्ते वाष्पकण्ठी[2] विरमति)।

राजा : सुन्दरि।

वाष्पेण प्रतिषिद्धेऽपि जयशब्दे जितं मया।
यत् ते दृष्टम् असंस्कारं पाटलोष्ठपुटं मुखम्[3] ।। 187 ।।

1. 'By-the-kindness-of-fortune, O lovely-faced-one, thou standest (once again) before me, the darkness of whose delusion is dispelled by recollection. At the end of the eclipse, Rohiṇī has been (again) brought to an union with the moon.' *Diṣṭyā* is generally an exclamation equivalent to 'Hail!' 'good luck!' corresponding to Shakspere's 'Now fair befall thee!' I have preferred to regard it here as an adverbial instrum. case, 'by the kindness of destiny,' 'fortunately,' 'happily.' *Uparāga;* the following is the Hindū notion of eclipses :—A certain demon, which had the tail of a dragon, was decapitated by Viṣṇu at the churning of the ocean; but, as he had previously tasted of the amrit or nectar reproduced at the time, he was thereby rendered immortal, and his head and tail, retaining their separate existence, were transferred to the stellar sphere. There head was called Rāhu and became the cause of eclipses, by endeavouring, at various times, to swallow the sun and moon. *Rohiṇī* : as to the love of the moon for Rohiṇī, the fourth lunar constellation, see p. 112, note 2.

2. Lit., 'Having tears in her throat,' *i.e.*, 'having her voice choked with tears.' *Vāṣpa* is not the tear itself, but the lachrymal moisture [see p. 167, note 1 in middle] which may find its way into the throat and impede the utterance.

3. 'Though the (utterance-of) the word 'victory' be obstructed

---

Verse 186. *Āryā* or *Gāthā*. *See* Verse 2.

⏑⏑— | ⏑—⏑ | ⏑⏑— || —— | ⏑⏑— | ⏑—⏑ | —⏑⏑ | ⏑
⏑⏑— | —— | ⏑⏑— || ⏑⏑⏑⏑ | —— | ⏑ | —— | —

Verse 187. *Śloka* or *Anuṣṭubh*. *See* Verses 5, 6, 11, 12, 26, 47, 50, 51, 53, 73, 76, 84, 87, 125, 127, 146, 154, 155, 160, 164, 173, 177, 178, 179.

बालः : अम्ब। को एसो।

बालः : अम्ब। क एषः।

शकुन्तला : वच्छ। दे भाअहेआइं पुच्छेहि।

शकुन्तला : वत्स। ते भागधेयानि पृच्छ।

राजा : (शकुन्तलायाः पादयोः प्रणिपत्य[1])।

सुतनु हृदयात् प्रत्यादेशव्यलीकम् अपैतु ते
किमपि मनसः सम्मोहो मे तदा बलवान् अभूत्।
प्रबलतमसाम् एवम्प्रायाः शुभेषु हि वृत्तयः।
स्रजमपि शिरस्यन्धः क्षिप्तां धुनोत्यहिशङ्कया[2] ।। 188 ।।

by (thy) weeping, victory-has-been-gained by me, since thy unadorned countenance, having-the-surface [skin] -of-its-lips-pale-red, has been seen (by me).' *Jaya-śabda,* the word 'Victory!' *i.e., jayatu* or *vijayī-bhava* was the regular form of saluting kings : compare p. 65, note 3. *Asaṁskāram,* so reads the Taylor MS.; the others have *asaṁskāra,* which violates the usual caesura. If the latter be retained, translate 'the skin of whose lips is pale red from the absence of colouring or paint.' There is no doubt that unpainted lips were a sign of mourning, but this is sufficiently implied in *pāṭaloṣṭha,* and it is a question whether *saṁskāra* can ever mean 'paint.' Some of the Beṅgālī, and amongst them the old MS. [Bodleian, 233], supported by Śaṅkara and Candraśekhara, read *asaṁskārāl lolālakam idaṁ mukha,* 'this countenance, having its curls hanging loosely from want of dressing.' *Oṣṭha-puṭa,* 'the covering of the lip;' so *akṣi-puta,* 'the skin covering the eye,' 'the eye-lid.' The student is reminded that in a compound, *oṣṭha* optionally causes the elision of a preceding *a.* The Mackenzie MS. has *pāṭaloṣṭhaṁ mukham priye.*

1. Śaṅkara quotes the following from Bharata : *Kākubhiḥ praṇipātaiś ca bhāgya-nindādibhis tathā, evaṁ kṛte ca narīnāṁ puruṣo'ti-priyo bhavet.*

2. 'O fair one! let the unpleasant-feeling [unpleasantness] of (my) repudiation (of thee) depart from thy heart. Somehow-or-other at the time the infatuation of my mind was strong. For such, for the most part, is the behaviour of those over-whom-(the quality of)-darkness-has-the-mastery, on happy (auspicious)-occasions. A

Verse 188. *Hariṇi* (variety of *Atyaṣṭi*). *See* Verse 66, 99.

शकुन्तला : उट्ठेदु अज्जउत्तो। णूणं मे सुअरिअप्पडिबन्धअं पुराकिदं
शकुन्तला : उत्तिष्ठतु आर्यपुत्रः। नूनं मे सुचरितप्रतिबन्धकं पुराकृतं
तेसु दिअहेसु परिणाममुहं आसि। जेण साणुक्कोसोबि अज्जउत्तो मइ
तेषु दिवसेषु परिणाममुखम् आसीत्। येन सानुक्रोशोऽपि आर्यपुत्रो मयि
विरसो संवुत्तो (राजोत्तिष्ठति) अह कहं अज्जउत्तेण सुमरिदो
विरसः संवृत्तः[1] (राजोत्तिष्ठति) अथ कथम् आर्यपुत्रेण स्मृतो
दुक्खभाई अअं जणो।
दुःखभागी अयं जनः।

राजा : उद्धृतविषादशल्यः[2] कथयिष्यामि।

blind man shakes off even the garland thrown on his head, suspecting it to be [with the suspicion of its being] a snake.' *Vyalīkam* = *apriyam*, K. = *vipriyam*, Ch. *Apaitu* : some of the Beṅgālī MSS. have *upaitu*, which is unintelligible. *Kimapi, i.e., anirvacanīya-rūpaṁ yathā syāt*, 'in a manner not to be explained :' Ś. *Tadā* = *pratyādeśa-kāle*, 'at the time of repudiation.' *Prabala-tamasām, prabalam ajñānaṁ yeṣaṁ te tathoktāḥ* : K. According to the Hindū philosophy there were three qualities or properties incident to the state of humanity, *viz.* : 1. *Sattva*, 'excellence' or 'goodness' [quiescence], whence proceed truth, knowledge, purity, etc. 2. *Rajas*, 'passion,' or 'foulness' [activity], which produces lust, pride, falsehood, etc., and is the cause of pain. 3. *Tamas*, 'darkness' [inertia], whence proceed ignorance, infatuation, delusion, mental blindness, etc. *Śubheṣu* = *sat-karmasu*, 'in auspicious matters :' Ś. *Vṛttayaḥ* = *vyavahārāḥ* : Ś. *Dhunoti* = *nirasyati* : K. *Srajam* : *see* p. 267, note 2.

1. 'Assuredly my (evil deeds), committed in a former (birth), opposed to virtuous conduct, were in those days drawing towards (their appointed evil) issue, (seeing) that my husband, although of-a-compassionate-nature, became unfeeling towards me.' *Purā-kṛtam, i.e., janmāntara-karma*, Ś. : *see* p. 183, note 3 at end. *Pariṇāma-mukham [pariṇatābhimukham* : K.], 'about to issue in their appointed fruit, in their matured result,' 'ripe for an evil result.' *Pariṇāma* is 'the last stage of anything,' 'the stage of ripeness or maturity,' 'the final result :' *mukha* like *unmukha* [*lit.*, 'looking towards'] has here the sense of 'tending towards,' 'being about,' 'being on the point.'

2. Compare p. 267, 1. 8; and *uddharen no hṛdaya-śalyam* in Vikram., Act 1.

मोहान् मया सुतनु पूर्वम् उपेक्षितस् ते
यो वाष्पविन्दुर् अधरं परिबाधमानः।
तं तावद् आकुटिलपक्ष्मविलग्नम् अद्य
वाष्पं प्रमृज्य विगतानुशयो भवेयम्[1] ।। 189 ।।

[इति यथोक्तम् अनुतिष्ठति]

शकुन्तला : (नाममुद्रां दृष्ट्वा) अज्जउत्त। एदं तं अङ्गुलीअअं।

शकुन्तला : (नाममुद्रां दृष्ट्वा) आर्यपुत्र। एतत् तद् अङ्गुलीयकम्।

राजा : अस्माद् अङ्गुलीयोपलम्भात् खलु स्मृतिर् उपलब्धा।

शकुन्तला : विसमं किदं णेण। जं तदा अज्जउत्तस्स पच्चाअण-

शकुन्तला : विषमं कृतम् अनेन। यत् तद् आर्यपुत्रस्य प्रत्यायन[2]-

काले दुल्लहं आसि।

काले दुर्लभम् आसीत्।

राजा : तेन ह्युतुसमवायचिह्नं प्रतिपद्यतां लता कुसुमम्।[3]

1. 'O graceful lady! I should in a manner be freed from (my) remorse by wiping off that moisture now clinging to thy slightly curved eye-lashes, which formerly (in the form of) a tear-drop corroding thy lip, was unnoticed [overlooked] by me through mental-delusion.' *Pūrvam, i.e., pratyādeśavelym. Paribdhamāna = pīḍayan* : Ś. *Ākuṭila* : compare ātāmra, p. 225, l. 5, and p. 292, note 2. *Vigatānuśayo = apagata-paśācāt-tāpo.* For *vāṣpam* in the fourth line, some of the Beṅgālī have *kāne,* unsupported by any of the Devanāgarī MSS. The repetition of *vāṣpa* seems at first unnecessary, but not if it be borne in mind that *vāṣpa* is, appropriately, the moisture in the eye, and *vāṣpa-vindu,* the tear-drop when it has left the eye : *see* p. 167, note 1 in middle.

2. A noun formed from the causal verb explained in p. 297, note 2.

3. 'Therefore, let the creeper receive again (its) flower, as a pledge [mark, token] of its inseparable-union with the (spring) season,' *i.e.,* 'Receive thou back this ring, as the beautiful twining plant receives again its blossom, in token of its reunion with the

---

Verse 189. *Vasanta-tilakā* (variety of *Śakkarī*). *See* Verses 8, 27, 31, 43, 46, 64, 74, 80, 82, 83, 91, 93, 94, 95, 100, 104, 105, 108, 123, 124, 144, 148, 152, 157, 168, 170, 181.

शकुन्तला : ण मे विस्ससामि। अज्जउत्तो एव्व णं धारेदु।

शकुन्तला : न अस्मै विश्वसामि। आर्यपुत्र एव एनद् धारयतु।

[ततः प्रविशति मातलिः]

मातलिः : दिष्ट्या।[1] धर्मपत्नीसमागमेन पुत्रमुखदर्शनेन चायुष्मान् वर्धते।

राजा : अभूत् सम्पादितस्वादुफलो मे मनोरथः। मातले। न खलु विदितोऽयम् आखण्डलेन[2] वृत्तान्तः स्यात्।

मातलिः : (सस्मितम्) किम् ईश्वराणां परोक्षम्। एत्वायुष्मान्। भगवान् मारीचस् ते दर्शनं वितरति।[3]

राजा : शकुन्तले। अवलम्ब्यतां पुत्रः। त्वां पुरस्कृत्य भगवन्तं द्रष्टुम् इच्छामि।

शकुन्तला : हिरिआमि अज्जउत्तेण सह गुरुसमीबं गन्तुं।

शकुन्तला : जिह्रेमि आर्य्यपुत्रेण सह गुरुसमीपं गन्तुम्।

राजा : अप्याचरितव्यम् अभ्युदयकालेषु।[4] एह्येहि।

[सर्वे परिक्रामन्ति]

[ततः प्रविशत्यदित्या सार्द्धम् आसनस्थो मारीचः]

मारीचः (राजानम् अवलोक्य) दाक्षायणि।

पुत्रस्य ते रणशिरस्ययम् अग्रयायी
दुष्यन्त इत्यभिहितो भुवनस्य भर्ता।

spring.' *Tena hi,* with the sense of 'therefore,' occurs very frequently in dramatic composition : compare p. 81, 1. 2, p. 83, 1. 2, and p. 84, 1. 9. *Ṛtu* : *see* p. 225, note 1 at end. *Samavāya,* 'inseparable or intimate connexion.' The Beṅgālī MSS. have *ṛtu-samāgamāśaṁsi,* and Śaṅkara *ṛtu-saṅgama-sūcakam.*

1. *Diṣṭyā, see* p. 294, note 1. As to *putra-mukha,* etc., see p. 219, note 2.

2. *Ākhaṇḍala* is one of a class of epithets [such as *puran-dara, bala-bhit, giribhid,* etc.] applied to Indra, as breaking cities, mountains, etc., into fragments with his thunderbolt : see p. 86, note 1.

3. 'Allows thee a sight (of him),' *i.e.,* 'Graciously permits thee to be presented to him,' 'vouchsafes thee an audience.'

4. 'But on joyful [festive] occasions the (usual) practise must be observed.' The Mackenzie MS. has *gantavyam* for *ācaritavyam.*

चापेन यस्य विनिवर्तितकर्म जातं

तत् कोटिमत् कुलिशम् आभरणं मघोनः[1] ।। 190 ।।

अदितिः : सम्भावणीआणुभावा से आकिदी।

अदितिः : सम्भावनीयानुभावा अस्य आकृतिः।[2]

मातलिः : आयुष्मन्। एतौ पुत्रप्रीतिपिशुनेन चक्षुषा[3] दिवौकसां पितराव् आयुष्मन्तम् अवलोकयतः। ताव् उपसर्प।

राजा : मातले। एतौ–

प्राहुर् द्वादशधास्थितस्य मुनयो यत् तेजसः कारणं

भर्तारं भुवनत्रयस्य सुषुवे यद् यज्ञभागेश्वरम्।

यस्मिन्न् आत्मभुवः परोऽपि पुरुषश् चक्रे भवायास्पदं

द्वन्द्वं दक्षमरीचिसम्भवम् इदं तत् स्रष्टुर् एकान्तरम्[4] ।। 191 ।।

1. 'O Dākṣāyiṇī [*i.e.*, Aditi : see p. 279, note 3], this is he that marches foremost at the head of thy son's [Indra's] battles, the so-called 'Duṣyanta,' the lord [protector] of the earth, through whose bow that edged thunderbolt of Indra, having rested from its work, has become (a mere) ornament.' *Raṇa-śirasi* : compare p. 263, line 13, and p. 86, note 2. *Koṭimat = sāgram = tīkṣṇam. Kuliśam = vajram. Maghavan*, 'Indra,' may change *va* to *u* before the accus. pl. and other vowel terminations.

2. 'His dignity may be inferred from his form,' *lit.*, 'his form has its dignity inferrible.'

3. 'With an eye that betrays [betokens] affection for (thee as for) as son.' *Piśuna* : compare p. 273, line 6.

4. 'This is that pair [Aditi and Kaśyapa], the offspring of Dakṣa and Marīci, one remove from the Creator [Brahmā], which (said pair) sages call the cause [origin, author, maker] of he solar-light subsisting in twelve forms [having a twelve-fold subsistence], which (pair) begot the ruler of the three worlds, the lord of the (Gods who are the) sharers of (every) sacrifice, (and) in which (pair) Nārāyaṇa (or Viṣṇu), he (who was) even superior to the Self-existent [Brahmā],

Verse 190. *Vasanta-tilakā* 9variety of *Śakkarī*). *See* Verses 8, 27, 31, 43, 46, 64, 74, 80, 82, 83, 91, 93, 94, 95, 100, 104, 105, 108, 123, 124, 144, 148, 152, 157, 168, 170, 181, 189.

Verse 191. *Śārdūla-vikrīḍita* (variety of *Atidhṛti*). *See* Verses 14, 30, 36, 39, 50, 63, 79, 85, 86, 89, 97, 98, 111, 137, 138, 149, 172, 175, 176.

मातलिः : अथ किम्–

chose [made] the site for (his) birth.' *Dvādaśadhā* : there are twelve Ādityas or forms of the sun, which represent him in the several months, or, as some say, attend upon his car : see p. 275, note 1. They are the children of Aditi and Kaśyapa, and the gods Viṣṇu and Indra are reckoned among them. The other ten, according to the Viṣṇu-purāṇa [p. 234], are Dhātṛ, Aryamat, Mitra, Varuṇa, Vivaswat, Pūṣan, Parjanya, Aṁśu, Bhaga, and Tvaṣṭṛ; but the names of the Ādityas vary in the other Purāṇas, *Tejasaḥ, i.e., sūryātmakasya*, 'consisting of the sun :' K. : = *sūryasya* : Ś. : = *ādityasya* : Schol. Chézy. *Bhuvana-trayasya, i.e., svarga-martya-pātālasya* : Ś. [see p. 308, note 3]. *Yajña-bhāgeśvaram* may simply mean 'the lord of a share of (every) sacrifice;' it seems, however, likely that *yajña-bhāga* is here synonymous with *kratu-bhuj*, 'a god,' though *yajña-bhāj* would be the more usual form. *Ātma-bhuvaḥ* [abl. case from *ātmabhū*] = *svayambhuvaḥ = brahmaṇaḥ* : K., Ch. *Paro = śreṣṭho. Puruṣa = Viṣṇu* : K. : = *Nārāyaṇa* : Ś., Ch. *Bhavāya = janmane* : K. = *avatārāya* : Ś. *Āspadam = pratiṣṭhām = sthitim* : K., Ś. *Upendrāvatārasya kāraṇam uktam bhavati* : K. *Dvandvam = mithunam = strī-puṁsayor yugalam. Sraṣṭur = Brahmaṇaḥ* : K., Ś. *Ekāntaram = ekāntaritam* : Ś. *Ekaḥ puruṣaḥ antaraṁ vyavadhānaṁ yasya tat tathoktam. Brahmaṇo Marīciḥ, Marīceḥ Kaśyapaḥ, Brahmaṇo Dakṣaḥ, Dakṣād Aditir iti ekāntaram* : K. *Ekaḥ puruṣo antaram antardhāḥam yasya tad dwandwam* : Chézy. As Kaśyapa and Aditi were the grand-children of Brahmā, they were only removed from him by Marīci and Dakṣa, their parents and his children : see p. 275, note 1. Viṣṇu, as Nārāyaṇa, or the supreme spirit, [*puruṣa*] moved over the waters before the creation of the world, and from his navel came the lotus from which Brahmā sprang. As Viṣṇu, or the Preserver, he became incarnate in various forms, and chose Kaśyapa and Aditi, from whom all human beings were descended, as his medium of incarnation or place of birth, especially in the *Avatāra* in which he was called 'Upendra,' (or *Indrānuja, Indrāvaraja*) 'Indra's younger brother' [according to some identified with Kṛṣṇa], and in his Vāmana, or Dwarf-Avatāra : see p. 271, note 1. *Puruṣa* is properly 'that which sleeps or abides in the body' [*puri śete*]. The worshippers of Viṣṇu identify him with Nārāyaṇa and with Brahmā, and name him Mahā-puruṣa, Puruṣottama, *i.e.*, 'the supreme spirit,' thus exalting him above

राजा : (प्रणिपत्य) उभाभ्यामपि[1] वासवानुयोज्यो दुष्यन्तः प्रणमति।

मारीचः : वत्स। चिरं जीव। पृथिवीं पालय।

अदितिः : वच्छ। अप्पडिरहो होहि।

अदितिः : वत्स। अप्रतिरथो[2] भव।

शकुन्तला : दारअसहिदा वो पादवन्दणं करेमि।

शकुन्तला : दारकसहिता वां पादवन्दनं करोमि।

मारीचः : वत्से।

आखण्डलसमो भर्ता जयन्तप्रतिमः सुतः।
आशीर् अन्या न ते योगया पौलोम्या सदृशी भव[3] ।। 192 ।।

अदितिः : जादे। भत्तुणो बहुमदा होहि। अवस्सं दीहाऊ वच्छओ
अदितिः : जाते। भर्तुर् बहुमता भव। अवश्यं दीर्घायुर् वत्स

उहअकुलणन्दणो होदु। उबविसह।
उभयकुलनन्दनो भवतु। उपविशत।

[सर्वे प्रजापतिम्[4] अभित उपविशन्ति]

मारीचः : (एकैकं निर्दिशन्)

दिष्ट्या शकुन्तला साध्वी सदपत्यम् इदं भवान्।
श्रद्धा वित्तं विधिश् चेति त्रितयं तत् समागतम्[5] ।। 193 ।।

Brahmā, the Creator. Kālidāsa seems by this verse to include himself among the Vaiṣṇavas.

1. *Ubhābhyām* [dat. dual.], *i.e., Aditi-Mārīcābhyām* : Ś. *Vāsavānuyojyo = Indrājñā-kārī*, 'Indra's servanat :' Ś. The Beṅgālī MSS. have *vāsavaniyojyo* : compare p. 268, line 4.

2. 'An invincible hero :' see p. 174, line 12, note 2 in middle.

3. '(Thy) husband (being) like Indra, thy son resembling Jayanta [Indra's son], no other blessing (would be) suitable to thee : mayst thou be like Paulomī! :' *see* p. 267, note 2 at end. As to *Ākhaṇḍala*, *see* p. 298, note 2.

4. As to the title Prajāpati, see p. 275, note 1.

5. 'All hail! the virtuous Śakuntalā, (her) noble offspring, your highness (Duṣyanta)! Piety [faith], Fortune [wealth], Action : this

---

Verse 192. *Śloka* or *Anuṣṭubh. See* Verses 5, 6, 11, 12, 26, 47, 50, 51, 53, 73, 76, 84, 87, 125, 127, 146, 154, 155, 160, 164, 173, 177, 178, 179, 187.

Verse 193. *Śloka* or *Anuṣṭubh. See* preceding verse.

राजा : भगवन्। प्राग् अभिप्रेतसिद्धिः। पश्चाद् दर्शनम्। अतोऽपूर्वः खलु वोऽनुग्रहः।[1] कुतः।

उदेति पूर्वं कुसुमं ततः फलं
घनोदयः प्राक् तदनन्तरं पयः।
निमित्तनैमित्तिकयोर् अयं क्रमस्
तव प्रसादस्य पुरस् तु सम्पदः[2] ।। 194 ।।

trio is here combined.' *Diṣṭyā* : see p. 294, note 1. *Sad, i.e., ubhaya-kula-guṇa-sampannam. Śraddhā,* being feminine, of course represents Śakuntalā; *Vittam,* being neuter, her offspring [*apatyam*], *viz.,* Sarvadamana or Bharata; and *Vidhi,* being masculine, Duṣyanta. *Vidhi,* according to Candraśekhara, is *veda-bodhitācaraṇam,* 'putting in practice the precepts of the Vedas;' it may, perhaps, imply power as exhibited in action. A parallel passage occurs in Ragh., ii, 16 : *Babhau sā tena śraddheva sākṣād vidhinopapannā,* which Stenzler renders 'She appeared [shone forth] like Faith visibly manifested, accompanied by action [works].'

1. 'First (came) the accomplishment of my desires; afterwards, the sight (of thee). Hence thy favour (towards me) has indeed been unprecedented.' Śaṅkara gives the following interpretation : *Śakuntalā-prāpakaṁ bhavaddarśanaṁ bhaviṣyati iti evaṁ mamābhipretam āsīt, tāvat prabhāvāt darśanapūrvaṁ nirvyūḍham. Tathā ca naimittikānantaram nimittotpattir iti anugrahasy- āpūrvatvaṁ iti bhāvaḥ :* 'My desire was that the sight of thee might lead to my recovery of Śakuntalā. But (my meeting her) was arranged through (thy) divine power, before my presentation to thee. Thus, after the effect was the appearance of the cause. The meaning is, that the favour (of my seeing thee and receiving thy blessing) did not precede (the attainment of my desire), and hence that the favour was unprecedented, as the accomplishment of my wishes ought naturally to have resulted from thy blessing.' There seems to be a double meaning in *apūrvaḥ.*

2. 'First appears the blossom, then the fruit; first the rising of clouds, afterwards the rain. This (is) the regular-course of cause and effect; but the success-of-my-wishes (came) before thy favour.'

Verse 194. *Vaṁśasthavila* (variety of *Jagati.*) *See* Verses 18, 22, 23, 67, 81, 114, 117, 119, 145, 150, 161, 174, 180.

मातलिः : एवं विधातारः प्रसीदन्ति।[1]

राजा : भगवन् इमाम् आज्ञाकरीं वो गान्धर्वेण[2] विवाहविधिनोपयम्य कस्यचित् कालस्य[3] बन्धुभिर् आनीतां स्मृतिशैथिल्यात् प्रत्यादिशन्न् अपराद्धोऽस्मि तत्रभवतो युष्मत्सगोत्रस्यस कण्वस्य।[4] पश्चाद् अङ्गुलीयकदर्शनाद् ऊढपूर्वां तद्दुहितरम् अवगतोऽहं। तच्चित्रम् इव मे प्रतिभाति।

यथा गजो नेति समक्षरूपे
तस्मिन्न अतिक्रामति संशयः स्यात्।
पदानि दृष्ट्वा तु भवेत् प्रतीतिस्
तथाविधो मे मनसो विकारः[5] ।। 195 ।।

Naimittika, 'that which is connected with the *nimitta* or is dependant on it,' 'the effect.' *Puras = prathamatas* : Ś. *Sampadaḥ* [nom. pl.] = *abhīṣṭa-siddhiḥ* : Ś. It is clearly meant to be synonymous with *abhipreta-siddhiḥ* in the previous clause.

1. 'Thus (it is that) the creator of-all-beings perform favours.' *Vidhātṛ* must here be equivalent to Prajāpati : see p. 275, note 1.

2. See page 126, note 3, and page 132, line 4.

3. *Kasyacit kālasya, i.e., kasmiṁścit kāle* : Ch.

4. Called Kāśyapa as being of the race of Kaśyapa : see p. 22, note 4.

5. 'As if one were to say, "(that) is not an elephant," its form being before one's eyes, and doubt were to arise (in one's mind) on its walking past, but conviction were to take place after seeing its footsteps; of such a kind has been the change of my mind,' *i.e.,* My mind has passed through similar transitions. Thus, as Kāṭavema observes, when Duṣyanta first saw Śakuntalā, he repudiated her [*see* p. 197, l. 7, and p. 198, l. 1]; when she passed out of his presence, he began to relent and doubt [see the last verse of Act V, p. 215]; and, when he saw the ring, he was convinced she was his wife. *Neti* : *see* p. 138, note 2 in middle. *Samakṣa-rūpe, i.e., samakṣa-vidyamānarūpe* : Ch. *Padāni = pada-cihnāni* : Ch. *Vikāraḥ = svarūpānyathā-bhāvaḥ* : Ś. May not *saṁśayaḥ* govern both lines ? thus:

Verse 195. *Upajāti* or Ākhyānakī (variety of Triṣṭubh). *See* Verses 41, 107, 121, 126, 142, 156, 158, 166, 169, 183.

मारीचः : वत्स। अलम् आत्मापराधशङ्कया।[1] सम्मोहोऽपि त्वय्यनुपपन्नः। श्रूयताम्।

राजा : अवहितोऽस्मि–

मारीचः : यदैवाप्सरस्तीर्थावतरणात्[2] प्रत्यक्षवैक्लव्यां शकुन्तलाम् आदाय मेनका दाक्षायणीम् उपगता। तदैव ध्यानाद् अवगतोऽस्मि। दुर्वाससः शापाद् इयं तपस्विनी सहधर्मचारिणी त्वया प्रत्यादिष्य नान्यथेति। स चायम् अङ्गुलीयकदर्शनावसानः।[3]

राजा : (सोच्छ्वासम्) एष वचनीयान्[4] मुक्तोऽस्मि।

शकुन्तला : (स्वगतं) दिट्ठिआ। अकारणपच्चादेसी ण अज्जउत्तो।

शकुन्तला : (स्वगतम्) दिष्ट्या। अकारणप्रत्यादेशी न आर्यपुत्रः। न खलु शप्तं[5] आत्मानं स्मरामि। अथवा प्राप्तो मया स हि शापो विरहशून्यहृदयया[6] न विदितः। यतः सखीभ्यां सन्दिष्टास्मि। भर्तुर् अङ्गुलीयक

ण हु सत्तं अत्ताणं सुमरेमि। अहवा पत्तो मए स हि साबो विरहसुणहिअआए ण विदिदो। जदो महीहिं सन्दिट्ठनिह। भत्तुणो अङ्गुलीअअं दंसइदव्वंत्ति।

दर्शयितव्यमिति।

'As if there were a doubt that that is not an elephant, while he is marching along, his form obvious to the eye.'

1. The Mackenzie MS. and my own have *aparādha;* the others, *apacāra.*

2. 'After [in consequence of] her descent to Apsaras-tīrtha :' see p. 266, note 1, and p. 212, 1. 1, According to Śaṅkara, *Apsaras-tīrtha = sacītīrtha : see* p. 202, l, 7. Menakā was Śakuntalā's mother : *see* p. 44, 1, 11.

3. 'That this thy poor faithful [lawful] wife was repudiated in consequence of the curse of Durvāsas, and on no other account, and that this same (curse) would terminate on the sight of the ring.' *Durvāsas : see* p. 135, note 2. *Tapasvinī = anukampyā* : Ś. [compare p. 246, 1. 4.] *Saha-dharma-cāriṇī* = pativratā : Ś.

4. *Vacanīyān, i.e., sādhvī-nirākaraṇa-rūpāpavādāt. Vacanīyam* = *vācyam* : p. 195, line 9.

5. The Colebrooke and Mackenzie MSS. and my own have *sattam* or *satam* for *śatam,* supported by Śaṅkara. The Taylor has *saccam* for *satyam,* supported by Kāṭavema and the Beṅgālī,

6. Compare page 135, line 12, note 2.

मारीचः : वत्से। चरितार्थासि।[1] सहधर्मचारिणं प्रति न त्वया मन्युः कार्यः। पश्य।

शापाद् असि प्रतिहता स्मृतिरोधरूक्षे
भर्तर्यपेततमसि प्रभुता तवैव।
छाया न मूर्छति मलोपहतप्रसादे
शुद्धे तु दर्पणतले सुलभावकाशा[2] ।। 196 ।।

राजा : भगवन्। अत्र[3] खलु मे वंशप्रतिष्ठा (इति बालं हस्तेन गृह्णाति)।

मारीचः : तथा भाविनम्[4] एनं चक्रवर्तिनम् अवगच्छतु भवान्। पश्य।

रथेनानुत्खातस्तिमितगतिना तीर्णजलधिः
पुरा सप्तद्वीपां जयति वसुधाम् अप्रतिरथः।।

1. 'Thou hast gained thy object.' *Caritārthā* = *labdhārthā* = kṛ*tārthā*. The Mackenzie has *viditārthā*.

2. 'Thou wast repulsed in consequence of the curse, (thy) husband being harsh [cruel] through the obstruction of (his) memory; (but now) indeed, on (the heart of) him freed from darkness, thy influence-is-supreme. (Even as) an image has no effect on the surface of a mirror whose brightness is tarnished with dirt, but on a clean-one easily makes impression [gains admission].' *Smṛti-rodha*, the Mackenzie has *smṛti-doṣa*. *Apeta-tamasi* : compare p. 294, note 3. *Prabhutā* : Kātavema refers to verse 73, p. 123. *Chāyā = pratvimbam*. *Mūrchati = vyāpnoti* : K. = *sphurati* : Ś. see p. 198, note 2. *Malopahata-prasāde = malāpagata-prasannatve* : Ś. = *mālinyena naṣṭā prasannatā* : K. *Sulabhāvakāśā = sukhena labhyaḥ praveśaḥ yasyāḥ = prāpta vasthitiḥ* : Ś. [compare p. 47, line 1.] Saṅkara observes that *darpaṇa-tale* answers to *bhartari; malopahata* to *smṛti-rodha; chāyā* to *prabhutā;* and, we may add, *śuddhe* to *apeta-tamasi.*

3. That is, *asyāṁ Śakuntalāyām, kuloddhāraka-putrotpādakatvena,* 'in this Śakuntalā, because she has given birth to a son, the upholder of my family?' K. : compare p. 256, line 2, and p. 123, line 4.

4. *Tena prakāreṇa kuloddhārakatvena bhaviṣyantam* : K. *Cakravartinam = sārva-bhaumam*, 'a monarch of the whole earth :' K. see p. 16, lines 1 and 2, note 1.

Verse 196. *Vasanta-tilakā* (variety of *Śakkarī*). *See* Verses 8, 27, 31, 43, 46, 64, 74, 80, 82, 83, 91, 93, 94, 95, 100, 104, 105, 108, 123, 124, 144, 148, 152, 157, 168, 170, 181, 189.

इहायं सत्त्वानां प्रसभदमनात् सर्वदमनः
पुनर् यास्यत्याख्यां भरत इति लोकस्य भरणात्[1] ।। 197 ।।

राजा : भगवता कृतसंस्कारे सर्वम् अस्मिन् वयम् आशास्महे।[2]

1. 'Previously (as) an-invincible-warrior, having crossed the ocean in a chariot whose motion is not (made) unsteady by uneven-ground, he will subjugate the earth, consisting of seven islands. Here, from his forcible taming of the animals, he (is called) Sarva-damana; but (then) he will acquire the appellation Bharata, from his support of the world.' *Rathena* : *see* p. 9, line 1. *Anutkhāta*, etc. [*nimnonnata-pradeśasyābhāvād anutkhātam* : K.] : so reads the Mackenzie MS., supported by Kāṭavema; the others, *anudghāta* : compare p. 10, l. 6, note 3. *Stimita* = *aniṣkampa* : K. = *Aprati-bandhārtha-durgamanena* : Ś. 'By this epithet it is indicated that the chariot would have the power of going in the air' [*tena viśeṣaṇena rathasya ākāśagāmitvam sūcitam*] : K. *Sapta-dvīpām* : according to the mythical geography of the Hindūs, the earth consisted of seven islands, or rather insular continents, surrounded by seven seas. That inhabited by men was called Jambudvīpa, and was in the centre, having in the middle of it he sacred mountain Meru or Sumeru, a kind of Mount Olympus, inhabited by the gods. About Jambu flowed the sea of salt-water [*lavaṇa*], which extends to the second *Dvīpa*, called *Plakṣa*, which is in its turn surrounded by a sea of sugar-cane-juice [*ikṣu*]. And so with the five other *Dvīpas, viz.*, *Śālmali, Kuśa, Krauñca, Śāka*, and *Puṣkara*, which are severally surrounded by the seas of wine [*surā*], clarified butter [*sarpis*], curds [*dadhi*], milk [*dugdha*], and fresh-water [*jala*]: Vish.-pur., p. 166. *Aprati-ratha* = *atulya-ratha* = *mahāratha* : Ś. *see* p. 174, note 3 in middle. *Iha* = *asmin āśrame* : K. *sattvānām* = *prāṇināṁ siṁhādīnām* : Ś. = *śarabha-siṁhādinām* : K. *Prasabha-damanāt* = *balātkāreṇa mardanāt*. The name Bharata is derived from the root *bhṛ* [fero] 'to support.' Many Indian princes were so named, but the most celebrated was this son of Duṣyanta and Śakuntalā, who so extended his empire that from him the whole of India was called Bharatavarṣa or Bhārata-varṣa; and whose descendants, the sons of Dhṛtarāṣṭra and Pāṇḍu, by their quarrels, formed the subject of the great epic poem called Mahābhārata : *see* p. 15, note 2.

2. 'We invoke all blessings on him for whom the prescribed-

Verse 197. *Śikhariṇī* (variety of *Atyaṣṭi*). *See* verses, 9, 24, 44, 62, 112, 141.

अदितिः : भअवं। इमाए दुहिदुमणोरहसम्पत्तीए कणोबि दाव

अदितिः : भगवान्। अस्या दुहितृमनोरथसम्पत्ते कण्वोऽपि तावत्

सुदवित्थारो करीअदु। दुहिदुवच्छला मेणआ इह एव्व मं परिचरन्ती चिट्ठइ।

श्रुतविस्तारः क्रियतां।[1] दुहितृवत्सला मेनका इह एव मां परिचरन्ती तिष्ठति।[2]

शकुन्तला : (आत्मगतं) मणोरहोक्खु मे भणिदो भअवदीए।

शकुन्तला : (आत्मगतं) मनोरथः खलु मे भणितो भगवत्या।

मारीचः : तपःप्रभावात् प्रत्यक्षं सर्वम् एव तत्रभवतः।

राजा : अतः खलु ममानतिक्रुद्धो मुनिः।

मारीचः : तथाप्यसौ प्रियम् अस्माभिः प्रष्टव्यः। कः कोऽत्र[3] भोः।

शिष्यः : (प्रविश्य) भगवन्। अयम् अस्मि।

मारीचः : गालव। इदानीम् एव विहायसा गत्वा मम वचनात् तत्रभवते कण्वाय प्रियम् आवेदय। यथा पुत्रवती शकुन्तला तच्छापनिवृत्तौ स्मृतिमता दुष्यन्तेन प्रतिगृहीतेति।

शिष्यः : यद् आज्ञापयति भगवान् (इति निष्क्रान्तः)

मारीचः : वत्स। त्वमपि स्वापत्यदारसहितः[4] सख्युर् आखण्डलस्य रथम् आरुह्य ते राजधानीं प्रतिष्ठस्व।

राजा : यद् आज्ञापयति भगवान्।

rites were performed by your holiness,' or 'we have high hopes and expectations of him,' etc. As to *kṛta-saṁskāre, see* p. 253, 254, and p. 196, note 1.

1. 'Let Kaṇva also be made acquainted with all the circumstances,' etc. Śaṅkara has *jñāta-vistaraḥ;* the Beṅgālī MSS., *vijñātārathaḥ.*

2. 'Here, and in the insertion of *me* in the next line, I have followed the Mackenzie MS. and my own, as I have never hesitated to do, when supported by Kāṭavema.

3. 'Notwithstanding, he must be questioned by us about (this) joyous-event. Ho ! there !' *Śiṣyāṇāṁ madhye ka atra tiṣṭhaṭi iti arthaḥ,* 'Which among my pupils is in waiting here ? such is the meaning of *Kaḥ,* etc.' : Ś. Compare p. 68, l. 10; p. 258, l. 9.

4. Here I have followed the Colebrooke MS. The others have *sāptya-dāra-sahitaḥ;* the Beṅgālī, *sāpatya-dāraḥ.*

मारीचः : अपि च।

तव भवतु विडौजाः प्राज्यवृष्टिः प्रजासु
त्वमपि विततयज्ञः स्वर्गिणः प्रीणयालम्।
युगशतपरिवर्तान् एवम् अन्योन्यकृत्यैर्
नयतम् उभयलोकानुग्रहश्लाघनीयैः[1] ।। 198 ।।

राजा : भगवन्। यथाशक्ति श्रेयसे[2] यतिष्ये।

मारीचः : वत्स। किं ते भूयः प्रियम् उपहरामि।

राजा : अतः परमपि प्रियम् अस्ति। यद् इह भगवान् प्रियं कर्तुम् इच्छति तर्हीदम् अस्तु भरतवाक्यम्।[3]

1. 'May Indra be bountiful of (his) rain towards thy subjects. Do thou also, abundantly-dispensing [distributing, diffusing] sacrifices, gratify [satisfy] the gods [inhabitants of heaven] to the full. Thus pass (both of you) periods [revolutions] of hundreds of ages with with reciprocal friendly acts, laudable on account of the favours (thus conferred) on both worlds : 'That is, You by sacrificing, and Indra by showers, confer benefits on the inhabitants of Swarga and the earth respectively. The two worlds are of course Heaven and Earth, not including the third world Pātāla : see p. 271, note 1. *Viḍaujas* or *Viḍojas* in one of the class of Indra's names, explained in p. 298, note 2. *Prājya-vṛṣṭiḥ=pracura-varṣaṇah. Vitata-yajñaḥ=vistṛta-yāgaḥ* : K. *Svargiṇaḥ=devān* : Ś. *Prīṇaya alam - alam bhāvaya* : K. - *atyarthena santoṣaya* : Ś. *Yuga-śata-parivartān=yugānāṁ śatāni teṣāṁ parivartanāni.*

2. Kāṭavema has *śreyasi* and interprets by *dharme*. Śaṅkara has the same and explains by *praśasta-kṛtye*.

3. 'Is there any favour still greater than this ? As (however) on this occasion his holiness desires to confer a favour, then let this saying of Bharata be (fulfilled).' *Atah param*, i.e., *adhikam. Atra praśnārthe kākur anusandheyā* : see p. 259, note 4. The Bharata here intended must not be confounded with the young prince. He was a holy sage, the director or manager of the gods' dramas, and inventor of theatrical representations in general. He wrote a work containing precepts and rules relating to every branch of dramatic writing,

---

Verse 198. *Mālinī* or *Māninī* (variety of *Ati-Śakkarī*). *See* Verses 10, 19, 20, 38, 55, 109, 110, 120, 171.

प्रवर्ततां प्रकृतिहिताय पार्थिवः।
सरस्वती श्रुतिमहतां महीयताम्।[1]

which appears to have been lost, but is constantly parted by the Commentators. He seems to have superintended the exhibition of the drama called *Lakṣmī-svayaṁvara* [composed by Sarasvatī : see p. 28, note 1 at end] in Indra's heaven. *See* Vikram., Act 3, and middle of Act 2, *Muninā bharatena yaḥ prayogo bhavatiṣu aṣṭa-rasāśrayo nibaddhaḥ,* etc. It was not unusual to close the plays by quoting one of Bharata's verses : compare the conclusion of the Ratnāvalī. The Scholiast supposes that there is here an intentional ambiguity as to whether this verse is spoken in the name of the young prince or of the sage.

1. 'Let the king exert himself for the welfare of his subjects. Let Sarasvatī be honoured among (those who are) mighty in the scriptures [lovers of literature]. Moreover, may the purple-god [Śiva] who-is-self-existent, (and) whose-Energy-is-every-where-diffused, put an end to my future birth [deliver my soul from passing into another state of being].' *Pravartatām = prayatatām. Sarasvatī [= Bhāratī :* K.] is the wife of the god Brahmā. She is the goddess of speech and eloquence, patroness of the arts and sciences, and inventress of the Sanskṛt language. *Sarasvatī* signifies 'flowing,' and is also applied to a river. *Śruti-mahatām,* etc. : some have *śruti-mahatī mahīyasām* : K. *śrutamahatām.* According to the latter, *śruta = śāstra, mahatām = śreṣṭhānām.* I see no reason why *mahatām* should not be the gen. c. plur. of the present part. regularly formed from *maḥ,* 'to honour.' *Śruti-mahatām* might then mean 'lovers of literature.' *Mahīyatām = pūjyatām* : K. *Nīla-lohitāḥ,* 'blue and red,' *i.e.,* according to Kāṭavema, *vāma-bhāge nīlaḥ, dakṣiṇa-bhāge lohitaḥ,* 'on the left side blue, on the right side red.' Śiva is usually represented as borne on a bull, his colour, as well as that of the animal he rides, being white, to denote the purity of Justice over which he presides. In his destroying capacity, he is characterised by the quality *tamas* [see page 295, note 2] and named Rudra, Kāla, etc., when his colour is said to be purple or black. 'In the beginning of the Kalpa, as Brahmā purposed to create a son, a youth of purple

---

Verse 199. *Ruchirā* or *Prajbhāvatī* (variety of *Ati-Jagatī*) containing thirteen syllables to the half-line, each half-line being alike.

ममापि च क्षपयतु नीललोहितः
पुनर्भवं परिगतशक्तिर् आत्मभूः ।। 199 ।।

[इति निष्क्रान्ताः सर्वे]

[सप्तमोऽङ्कः]

[समाप्तम् इदम् अभिज्ञानशाकुन्तलं नाम नाटकम्]

[शुभं भूयात्]

complexion [blue and red, *nīla lohita*] appeared, crying and running about [*ru, dru,* whence Rudra]:' Viṣ.-Pur., p. 58. Some refer this name to the colour of his throat : see p. 253, note 1. *Parigata-śaktih; prāptiḥ śaktiḥ Pārvatī yena sa tathoktaḥ*. Hence, *Śakti* = *Pārvatī*, Śiva's wife. The wives of the deities were supposed to perosnify their energy or active power. *Ātma-bhū,* although properly a name of Brahmā, is applied equally to Viṣṇu and Śiva by those who give the preference to these deities. Exemption from further transmigration and absorption into the divine soul was the *summum bonum* of the Hindū philosophy : compare p. 182, note 3 at end. Kālidāsa indulges the religious predilections of his fellow-townsmen by beginning and ending the play with a prayer to Śiva who had a large temple in Ujjayinī, the city of King Vikramāditya, and abode of the poet. Both actors and spectators would probably repeat the prayer after the speaker and appropriate it to themselves.

APPENDICES

Appendix - I
Selected Fragments

अकृताऽर्थेऽपि मनसिजे रतिमुभयप्रार्थना कुरुते।

अतिस्नेहः पापशङ्की

अनतिक्रमणीयानि श्रेयांसि।

अनार्यः परदारव्यवहारः।

अनियन्त्रणानुयोगस्तपस्विजनो नाम।

अनिर्वर्णनीयं परकलत्रम्।

अर्थो हि कन्या परकीय एव।

अवसरोपसर्पणीया राजानः।

अविश्रमोऽयं लोकतन्त्राधिकारः।

अहो कामी स्वतां पश्यति।

अहो चेष्टप्रतिरूपिका कामि (जन) मनोवृत्तिः।

अहो विघ्नवत्यः प्रार्थितार्थसिद्धयः।

अहो सर्वास्ववस्थासु रमणीयत्वमाकृतिविशेषाणाम्।

आपन्नस्य विषयनिवासिनो जनस्यार्तिहरेण राजा भवितव्यम्।

इष्टप्रवासजनितान्यबलाजनस्य दुःखानि नूनमतिमात्रसुदुःसहानि।

उत्सर्पिणी खलु महतां प्रार्थना।

उत्सवप्रियः खलु मनुष्यइः।

उपपन्ना हि दारेषु प्रभुता सर्वतोमुखी।

ओदकान्त स्निग्धो जनोऽनुगन्तव्यः।

क इदानीं शरीरनिर्वापयित्रीं शारदीं ज्योत्सनां पटान्तेन वारयति।

क इदानीं सहकारमन्तरेणातिमुक्तलतां पल्लवितां सहते।

कदाऽपि सत्पुरुषाः शोकवास्तव्य न भवन्ति।

कष्टं खल्वनपत्यता।

किमत्र चित्रं यदि विशाखे शशाङ्कलेखामनुवर्तेते।

किमिव हि मधुराणां मण्डनं नाकृतीनाम्।

को नामोष्णोदकेन नवमालिकां सिञ्चति।

कोऽन्यो हुतवहाद्दग्धुं प्रभवति।

गण्डस्योपरि पिटकः (पिण्डकः) संवृत्तः।

गुर्वपि विरहदुःखमाशाबन्धः साहयति।

छाया न मूर्छति मलोपहतप्रसादे शुद्धे तु दर्पणतले सुलभावकाशा।

न खलु धीमतां कश्चिदविषयो नाम।

न प्रभातरलं ज्योतिरुदेति वसुधातलात्।

पूर्वावधीरितं श्रेयो दुःखं हि परिवर्तते।

प्रवातेऽपि निष्कम्पा गिरयः।

बलवदपि शिक्षितानामात्मन्यप्रत्ययं चेतः।

बहुवल्लभाः राजानः।

भवितव्यता खलु बलवती।

भवितव्यानां द्वाराणि भवन्ति सर्वत्र।

मलिनमपि हिमांशोर्लक्ष्म लक्ष्मीं तनोति।

रन्ध्रोपनिपातिनोऽनर्थाः।

राजरक्षितव्यानि तपोवनानि नाम।

राज्ञां तु चरितार्थता दुखोतरैव।

लभेत वा प्रार्थयिता न वा श्रियं श्रिया दुरापः कथमीप्सितो भवेत्।

यशिनां हि परपरिग्रहसंश्लेषपराङ्मुखी वृत्तिः।

विकारं खलु परमार्थतोऽज्ञात्वाऽनारम्भः प्रतीकारस्य।

विनीतवेषेण प्रवेष्टव्यानि तपोवनानि नाम।

विवक्षितं ह्यनुक्तमनुतापं जनयति।

सतां हि संदेहपदेषु वस्तुषु प्रमाणमन्तःकरणप्रवृत्तयः

सरसिजमनुविद्धं शैवलेनापि रम्यम्।

सर्वः कान्तमात्मीयं पश्यति।

सर्वः प्रार्थितमर्थमधिगम्य सुखी संपद्यते जन्तुः।

सर्वः सगन्धेषु विश्वसिति।

सागरमुज्झित्वा कुत्रवा महानद्यवतरति।

स्निग्धजनसंविभक्तं हि दुःखं सह्यवेदनं भवति।

स्रजमपि शिरस्यन्धः क्षिप्तां धुनोत्यहिशङ्कया।

स्वाधीनकुशलाः सिद्धिमन्तः।

Appendix - II
Verse Fragments

Verse No.

अतः परीक्ष्य कर्तव्यं विशेषात् सङ्गतं रहः।
अज्ञातहृदयेष्वेवं वैरीभवति सौहृदम्।। 125

आलक्ष्यदन्तमुकुलान् अनिमित्तहासैर्
अव्यक्तवर्णरमणीयवचःप्रवृत्तीन्।
अङ्काश्रयप्रणयिनस् तनयान् वहन्तो
धन्यास् तदङ्गरजसा मलिनीभवन्ति।। 181

औत्सुक्यमात्रम् अवसादयति प्रतिष्ठा
क्लिश्नाति लब्धपरिपालनवृत्तिर् एव।
नातिश्रमापनयनाय न च श्रमाय
राज्यं स्वहस्तधृतदण्डम् इवातपत्रम्।। 108

ज्वलति चलितेन्धनोऽग्निर् विप्रकृतः पन्नगः फणं कुरुते।
प्रायः स्वं महिमानं क्षोभात् प्रतिपद्यते हि जनः।। 163

भवन्ति नम्रास् तरवः फलागमैर् नवाम्बुभिर् दूरविलम्बिनो घनाः।
अनुद्धताः सत्पुरुषाः समृद्धिभिः स्वभाव एवैष परोपकारिणाम्।। 114

भानुः सकृद्युक्ततुरङ्ग एव रात्रिन्दिवं गन्धवहः प्रयाति।
शेषः सदैवाहितभूमिभारः षष्ठांशवृत्तेर् अपि धर्म एषः।। 106

मेदश्छेदकृशोदरं लघु भवत्युत्थानयोग्यं वपुः
सत्त्वानामपि लक्ष्यते विकृतिमच् चित्तं भयक्रोधयोः।
उत्कर्षः स च धन्विनां यद् इषवः सिध्यन्ति लक्ष्ये चले।
मिथ्यैव व्यसनं वदन्ति मृगयाम् ईदृग्विनोदः कुतः।। 39

रम्याणि वीक्ष्य मधुरांश्च निशम्य शब्दान्
पर्युत्सुकीभवति यत् सुखितोऽपि जन्तुः।
तच् चेतसा स्मरति नूनम् अबोधपूर्वं
भावस्थिराणि जननान्तरसौहृदानि।। 104

शमप्रधानेषु तपोधनेषु गूढं हि दाहात्मकम् अस्ति तेजः।
स्पर्शानुकूला इव सूर्यकान्तास् तद् अन्यतेजोभिभवाद् वमन्ति।। 41

शुश्रूषस्व गुरून् कुरु प्रियसखीवृत्तिं सपत्नीजने
भर्तुर् विप्रकृतापि रोषणतया मास्म प्रतीपं गमः।
भूयिष्ठं भव दक्षिणा परिजने भाग्येष्वनुत्सेकिनी
यान्त्येवं गृहिणीपदं युवतयो वामाः कुलस्याधयः।। 98

सतीमपि ज्ञातिकुलैकसंश्रयां जनोऽन्यथा भर्तृमतीं विशङ्कते।
अतः समीपे परिणेतुर् इष्यते तदप्रियापि प्रमदा स्वबन्धुभिः।। 119

सहजं किल यद् विनिन्दितं न खलु तत् कर्म्म विवर्जनीयम्।
पशुमारणकर्म्मदारुणो अनुकम्पामृदुर् एव श्रोत्रियः।। 133

सिध्यन्ति कर्मसु महत्स्वपि यन् नियोज्याः
सम्भावनागुणम् अवेहि तम् ईश्वराणाम्।
किं वाभविष्यद् अरुणस् तमसां विभेत्ता
तं चेत् सहस्रकिरणो धुरि नाकरिष्यत्।। 168

स्त्रीणाम् अशिक्षितपटुत्वम् अमानुषीषु
सन्दृश्यते किमुत याः प्रतिबोधवत्यः।
प्राग् अन्तरिक्षगमनात् स्वम् अपत्यजातम्
अन्यैर् द्विजैः परभृताः खलु पोषयन्ति।। 123

Appendix - III
Verse Index

Verse	Verse No.	Verse	Verse No.
अक्लिष्टबालतरु	152	अयमरविवरेभ्य:	171
अत: परीक्ष्य कर्तव्यं	125	अर्थो हि कन्या परकीय	102
अद्यापि नूनं हर	56	अर्धपीतस्तनं मातु:	178
अधर: किसलयराग:	21	असंशयं क्षत्रपरिग्रह	22
अध्याक्रान्ता वसति	48	अस्भात्पर बत यथा	157
अनवरतधनुर्ज्या	38	अस्मान्साधु विचिन्त्य	97
अनाघ्रातं पुष्पं	44	अहन्यहन्यात्मन	158
अनिशमपि मकर	57	अहिणवमहुलोलुपो	103
अनुकारिणि पूर्वेषां	50	आखण्डलसमो भर्ता	192
अनुमतगमना शकुन्तला	90	आचार इत्यवहितेन	105
अनुयास्यन्मुनितनयां	29	आजन्मन: शाठ्य	126
अनेन कस्यापि कुला	183	आतम्भरहरिअपण्डुर	134
अन्तर्गतप्रार्थन	166	आ परितोषाद्विदुषां	2
अन्तर्हिते शशिनि सैव	83	आलक्ष्यदन्तमुकुला	181
अपरिक्षतकोमलस्य	77	इत: प्रत्यादेशात्स्वजन	141
अभिजनवतो भर्तु:	99	इदं किलाव्याजमनो	18
अभिमुखे मयि सैहृत	45	इदमनन्यपरायण	72
अभ्यक्तमिव स्नात:	113	इदमशिशिरै	66
अभ्युन्नता पुरस्तात्	61	इदमुपनतमेवं	120
अमी वेदी परिता:	88	इदमुपहितसूक्ष्म	19
अयं स ते तिष्ठति	67	ईसीसिचुम्बिआइं	4

Verse	Verse No.	Verse	Verse No.
उग्गलिअदब्भकवला	92	क्षामक्षामकपोल	63
उत्पक्ष्मणोर्नयनयो	95	क्षोभं केनचिदिन्दु	85
उत्सृज्य कुसुमशयनं	75	गच्छति पुर: शरीरं	34
उदेति पूर्वं कुसुमं	194	गान्धर्वेण विवाहेन	76
उन्नमितै कभ्रुलत	68	गाहन्तां महिषा निपान	40
उपोढशब्दा न रथाङ्ग	174	ग्रीवाभङ्गाभिरामं	7
एकैकमत्र दिवसे	144	चलापाङ्गां दृष्टि	24
एवमाश्रमविरुद्ध	182	चित्रे निवेश्य परिकल्पित	43
एष त्वामभिनव	159	चूतानां चिरनिर्गता	136
एषा कुसुमनिषण्णा	151	जन्म यस्य पुरोवंशे	12
एसा वि पिएण	96	जाने तपसो वीर्य	54
औत्सुक्यमात्रमव	108	ज्वलति चलितेन्धनो	163
क: पौरवे वसुमतीं	25	णावेक्खिओ गुरुअणो	118
कथं नु तं बन्धुर	145	तत्साधुकृतसंधानं	11
का कथा बाणसंधाने	53	तदेषा भवत: कान्ता	127
कामं प्रत्यादिष्टां	132	तपति तनुगात्रि	70
कामं प्रिया न सुलभा	35	तव कुसुमशरत्वं	55
कार्या सैकतलीन	149	तव भवतु बिडौजा:	198
का स्विदवगुण्ठनवती	115	तव सुचरितमङ्गुलीय	143
किं शीतलै:	74	तवास्मि गीतरागेण	5
किं तावत् व्रतिना	111	तस्या: पुष्पमयी	
कुतो धर्मक्रियाविघ्न:	116	तीव्राघातप्रतिहत	33
कुमुदान्येव शशाङ्क:	129	तुंसि मए चूदङ्कुर दिण्णो	135
कुल्याम्मोभि: पवन	15	तुज्झ ण आणे	69
कुतं न कर्णापित	150	तुरगखुरहतस्तथा	32
कृर्ता: शरव्यं हरिणा	161	त्रिस्त्रोतर्स वहति यो	170
कृताभिमर्शामनु	121	त्वन्मति: केवला	164
कृत्यायोभिन्नदेशत्वा	51	त्वमर्हतां प्राग्रसर	117
कृष्णसारे ददच्चक्षु:	6	दर्भाङ्कुरेण चरण:	46
क्व वयं क्व परोक्ष	52	दिष्ट्या शकुन्तला	193

Verse	Verse No.	Verse	Verse No.
दुष्येन्तेनाहितं तेजो	84	मुक्तेषु रश्मिषु निरायत	8
न खलु न खलु	10	मुनिसुताप्रणयस्मृति	140
न नमयितुमधिज्य	37	मुहूरङ्गुलिसंवृता	78
नियमयसि विमार्ग	110	मूढः स्यामहमेषा वा	130
नीवाराः शुकगर्भ	14	मेदश्छेदकृशोदर	39
नैतच्चित्रं यदयमुदधि	49	मोहान्मया सुतनु	189
परिग्रहबहुत्वेऽपि	73	यतो यतः षट्चरणो	23
पातुं न प्रथमं	89	यथा गजो नेति	195
पुत्रस्य ते रणशिर	190	यदालोके सूक्ष्मं वज्रति	9
पृष्य जनेन सम दुःख	64	यदि यथा वदति	128
प्रजाः प्रजाः स्वा इव	107	यदुतिष्ठति वर्णेभ्यो	47
प्रजागरात्खिलीभूतः	154	यद्यत्साधु न चित्रे	146
प्रत्यादिष्टविशेष	138	ययातेरिव शर्मिष्ठा	87
प्रथमं सारङ्गाक्ष्या	139	यस्य त्वया व्रणविरोपण	94
प्रथमोपकृतं मरु	165	यात्येकतोऽस्तशिखरं	82
प्रलोभ्यवस्तुप्रणय	180	या सृष्टिः स्रष्टुराद्या	1
प्रवर्तता प्रकृतिहिताय	199	यास्यत्यद्य शकुन्तलेति	86
प्राणानामनिलेन	176	येन येन वियुज्यन्ते	155
प्राहूर्द्वादशधा स्थितस्य	191	यो हनिष्यति बध्यं त्वां	160
वाष्पेण प्रतिषिद्वेऽपि	187	रथेनानुद्धातस्तिमित	197
भवनेषु रसाधिकेषु	184	रम्यं द्वेष्टि यथा पुरा	137
भवन्ति नम्रास्तरवः	114	रम्याणि वीक्ष्य मधुरांश्च	104
भव हृदय साभिलाषं	28	रम्यान्तरः कमलिनी	91
भानुः सकृद्युक्ततुरङ्ग	106	रम्यास्तपोधनानां	13
भूत्वा चिराय चतुरन्त	100	वाल्मीकाग्रनिमग्न	175
मनोरथाय नाशंसे	177	वसने परिधूसरे	185
मय्येव विस्मरण	124	वाचं न मिश्रयति	31
महतस्तेजसो बीजं	179	विचिन्तयन्ती यमनन्य	81
महाभागः कामं	112	विच्छित्तिशेषैः सुरसुन्दरीणां	169
मानुषीषु कथं वा	26	वृथैव संकल्पशतै	58

Verse	Verse No.
वैखानसं किमनया	27
व्यपदेशमाविलयितुं	122
शक्यमरविन्दसुरभिः	60
समप्रधानेषु तपोधनेषु	41
शममेष्यति मम शोकः	101
शहजे किल जे विणि	133
शान्तमिदमाश्रमपदं	16
शापादसि प्रतिहता	196
शुद्धान्तदुर्लभमिदं	17
शूश्रूषस्व गुरून्कुरु	98
शैलानामवरोहतीव	172
संरोपितेऽप्यात्मनि	156
सख्युस्ते स किल	162
संकल्पितं प्रथममेव	93
सतीमपि ज्ञातिकुलैक	119
संदष्टकुसुमशयना	71
संमीलन्ति न तावत्	59
सरसिजमनुविद्धं	20
साक्षात्प्रियामुपगता	148
सा निन्दन्ती स्वानि	171
सायतने सवनकर्मणि	80
सिध्यन्ति कर्मसु	168
सुतनु हृदयात्प्रत्या	188
सुभगैसलिलावगाहाः	3
सुरयुवतिसंभवं किल	42
स्तनन्यस्तोशीरं	62
स्त्रीणामशिक्षितपटुत्व	123
स्निग्धं वीक्षितमन्यतो	36
स्मर एव तापहेतु	65
स्मृतिभिन्नमोह	186
स्त्रस्तांसावतिमात्र	30
स्वप्नो नु माया नु	142
स्वसुखनिरभिलाषः	109
स्वायम्भुवान्मरीचेर्यः	173
स्विन्नाङ्गुलिविनिवेशो	147

Appendix - IV
General Index

Actions 49, 183
Active 64
Agni 148
Altar 142
Anger 135
Animals 73
Apsarās 31, 86
Arrow 94, 95
Art 261
Ascetics 280
Aśoka-tree 279
Auspicious 225
Auspicious ablution 152
Auspicious countenance 285
Auspicious flowers 149
Aśvattha 146

Bad omen 191
Beautiful figure 79
Birthday-gifts 151
Body 63, 90, 106, 117, 184
Brahmā 2, 7, 23, 36, 79, 195
Brahmacārī 94
Brāhmaṇas 2, 8, 16, 30, 35, 40, 44, 50, 83, 88, 146, 147, 148

Cakravāka 168, 169
Castes 215, 216
Celestial beings 261
Celestial nymph 77
Ceremony 111
Character 73
Chariot 13, 56, 269
Cherry-tree 279
Cocoanut tree 149
Colours 269, 309
Creation 1, 79, 153
Creator 1, 79
Creatures 71, 177
Creepers 102, 108, 112, 131, 163, 164, 276, 277
Cuckoo 160, 161
Cupid 100, 101, 205, 234
Curse 135

Daityas 263
Darbha-grass 142, 162
Darbha-water 129
Daśaratha 15
Deer 73
Deities 45, 134, 154, 161
Deity 157
Demons 35, 86, 94, 275
Desires 64, 119, 120, 187, 267
Destiny 80
Destruction 72, 74, 98
Devotion 35, 40, 137, 170, 190
Dharma 126

Dialogue 97
Digit of the moon 77
Divine power 79
Dānavas 263
Drama 63
Dramatic language 59, 89
Duṣyanta 8, 11, 31, 39, 48, 51, 57, 89, 111, 113, 134, 144, 148, 150, 169, 269
Durgā 219
Duty of kings 88

Elephants 70, 124, 125, 150, 185, 262
Emancipation 104
Energy 74
Enjoyment 64, 129
Evil spirits 35
Eye-lashes 130

Festival 224
Fig-tree 154
Fire 36, 74, 131, 159
Fisherman 213, 215
Flowers 25, 26, 57, 63, 80, 83, 94, 99, 112, 115, 120, 125, 137, 143, 219, 222, 235
Flower-arrows 99
Fortunes 116, 150, 153, 211
Friendship 206
Fruit 149, 256
Functions 72

Gaṅgā 150
Ganges 270, 277
Garlands 149, 154
Gift 151
God of justice 189
God of Love 224
Goddess 79, 148, 238
Goddess of beauty 189
Gods 20, 86, 91, 176, 263, 275, 306
God's canopy 185
Golden ornaments 153
Good deeds 81
Grass 20, 57, 83, 205
Great sacrifices 177, 257
Guru 50, 171

Haṁsa 262
Happiness 152, 183, 225
Heaven 95, 146, 268, 269, 271, 272, 308
Hermitage 42, 74, 75, 76, 85, 87, 91, 94, 153
Hermits 19, 84, 92, 102, 156
Hindū mythology 44
Hindū poetry 251
Hindū poets 230, 287
Hindū woman 156
Hindūs 74, 146, 270
Homage 275
Horses 141, 185
Hospitality 57
Human being 45
Hymns 158

Incarnate 56
India 28
Indra 12, 20, 36, 86, 87, 91, 182, 270, 280, 299
Instrument 74

Jewels 84, 115
Joys 38, 109
Justice 40

Kṣatriya 30, 31
Kṣatriya woman 33
Kalpa 309
Kalpa-tree 278
Kingdom 67
Kāma 100
Knowledge 32, 96, 155
Kuśa-grass 82, 94, 111, 129, 166, 179

Language 36, 203
Legend 23
Liberation 182
Limbs 125
Lions 72
Lord 1
Lotus 25, 26, 53, 95, 130, 181, 209, 278
Lotus-feet 25
Lotus-fibres 106, 120, 131, 248
Lotus-flower 53
Lotus-leaves 95
Love 65, 105, 112, 115, 143, 205, 245
Love-letter 131
Love's shafts 122

Mahābhārata 15, 68
Mahādeva 2
Mango-tree 28, 163
Mantra 176
Manu 28, 30, 35, 36, 40, 49, 72, 84, 94, 141, 147, 151, 176, 177, 194, 196, 207, 277
Marks of greatness 283
Marriage 16, 31, 126, 132, 170, 179
Medicinal plants 140
Medicine 149
Memory 135
Mental act 50
Mental faculty 224
Messenger 109
Mind 78, 79, 87, 135, 183, 231
Moon 1, 17, 25, 113, 141, 142, 224, 248, 294
Moonlight 117
Mortal body 91
Mountains 95, 140, 142, 172, 273

Nectar 22, 127

Object 55, 81, 120, 130, 135, 146, 158
Object of worship 224
Oblation 101, 158
Ocean 100, 112, 123
Offerings 151
Omen 154
Organs 272
Organs of perception 272
Ornaments 76, 111, 123, 152, 153, 155, 160, 247

Painting 155
Palace 122
Passion 74
Penances 45, 56, 137, 275, 278
Pictures 79, 80, 139, 251
Plant 67, 125
Pleasure 59, 84
Pleasure-ground 245
Power 67, 126, 198, 259
Practice of austerities 42
Practice of bodily mortification 43

Prajāpatis 23, 36
Prakṛti 72
Preceptor 94
Priests 1, 60, 95, 210
Prince 60, 91
Profession 31

Qualities 184

Rays of the moon 99
Religion 49
Religious ceremony 40
Religious mendicant 156
Religious rites 40, 194
Religious students 94, 150
Ṛgveda 12, 158, 159
Rites 36, 94, 196
Rivers 67, 92, 112, 128
Rākṣasas 89
Rāmacandra 15
Rāmāyaṇa 15

Sacred fire 96, 147, 179
Sacred grass 149
Sacred grove 40
Sacrifices 9, 19, 88, 91, 94, 95, 136, 146, 177, 216
Sacrificial 147, 277
Sacrificial grass 19
Sacrificial hearth 96
Sacrificial purposes 103
Saint 39
Śakuntalā 4, 11, 28, 42, 44, 45, 47, 48, 49, 50, 51, 62, 76, 78, 83, 96, 103, 109, 112, 113, 123, 134, 144, 148, 152, 169
Śaṅkara 2, 4, 6, 17, 18, 20, 25, 33, 37, 38, 41, 42, 47, 48, 49, 53, 66, 67, 70, 73, 78, 84, 91, 95, 117, 119, 143, 169
Sandal-tree 172, 286
Scripture 217
Sign of happiness 225
Sky 146
Solar race 91
Sorrows 109, 141
Space 37
Speech 199, 241
Spirits 71, 178
Śūdras 32
Sun 1, 12, 36, 75, 77, 78, 140, 141, 269, 270, 294
Sun's rays 75
Supreme Spirit 42
Śiva 1, 2, 9, 100, 219, 253, 268, 310

Tīrtha 212
Throne 93
Tree 60, 78, 153, 249
Trees 102, 192, 267
Truth 207

Union with the moon 294
Universal 59
Universe 194

Vedas 32, 42, 83, 146, 159
Viṣṇu 9, 310
Vipra 217
Virtuous acts 81
Vows 101
Vyāsa 15

Waters 111, 159, 185
Water of life 150

Water-pots 94
Weapon 89
Women 49, 63, 78, 130, 149, 151, 197, 204
Worlds 197, 299, 308
Worshipper 124
Worshippers 159, 300

Yama 220